THE
Frozen
REPUBLIC

THE
Frozen
REPUBLIC

How the
Constitution
Is Paralyzing
Democracy

DANIEL LAZARE

Harcourt Brace & Company

New York San Diego London

Requests for permission to make copies of any part of the
work should be mailed to:
Permissions, Harcourt Brace & Company,
6277 Sea Harbor Drive, Orlando, Florida 32887-6777.

The epigraph to chapter seven is from *Death of a Salesman* by
Arthur Miller. Copyright 1949, renewed © 1977 by Arthur
Miller. Used by permission of Viking Penguin, a division of
Penguin Books USA Inc.

Library of Congress Cataloging-in-Publication Data
Lazare, Daniel.
The frozen republic: how the Constitution is paralyzing
democracy/Daniel Lazare.—1st ed.
    p.   cm.
Includes bibliographical references and index.
ISBN 0-15-100085-9
1. United States—Politics and government. 2. United
States—Constitutional history. I. Title.
JK31.L39 1996
342.73'02—dc20   95-22354
[347.3022]

Printed in the United States of America

First edition

A B C D E

To my parents, for teaching me that nothing is more fun than a good intellectual argument: *De omnibus dubitandum.*

CONTENTS

Acknowledgments

A number of people contributed to this project in various ways. Lucia Stern offered philosophical guidance on the subject of the relationship between a founding text and a society that grows up around it. Jim Chapin helped out on the history and was also kind enough to read a portion of the manuscript. Doug Henwood supplied ample portions of political wit and insight. I'd also like to extend my sincerest appreciation to: Alane Mason, the Harcourt Brace editor who pulled this project onboard; Walter Bode, who worked diligently in getting it in shape for publication; and my wife, Andrea, who not only provided invaluable editorial assistance but also put up with my incessant mutterings about amending clauses and separation of powers. But I am perhaps most grateful to my agent, Diane Cleaver, who was tireless in her search for a publisher willing to take on a book as quixotic as this one. A woman who enjoyed life to the utmost and was surrounded by innumerable friends, Diane died suddenly in April 1995 at age 53. She will be missed.

Introduction

AMERICA IS A RELIGIOUS SOCIETY caught up in a painful contradiction. On one hand, its politics rest on faith in the Founding Fathers—a group of planters, merchants, and political thinkers who gathered in a stuffy tavern in Philadelphia in 1787—and the document they produced during the course of that summer, the Constitution. These are the be-all and end-all of the American system, the alpha and the omega. On the other hand, the faith isn't working. Problems are mushrooming, conflicts are multiplying, and society seems increasingly out of control. As a result, Americans find themselves in the curious position of celebrating the Constitution and Founders, who comprise America's base, yet cursing the system of politics they gave birth to. The more the roof leaks and the beams sag, the more fervent the odes to the original architects and builders seem to grow.

This is curious but not unprecedented. In one form or another, Americans have been simultaneously praising the Constitution and cursing the government since virtually the moment George Washington took office. What is different, however, is the degree. Constitution worship has never been more fervent, while dissatisfaction with constitutional politics has never been greater. Yet rather than attempting to work through the contradiction—rather than wondering, for instance, whether the fact that the house is falling down doesn't reflect poorly on those who set it up—the general tendency over the last two decades or so has been to blame anyone and everyone except the Founders. If the original conception is pure and perfect—and it is an article of faith in America's civic religion that it is—then the fault must lie with the subsequent generations who allowed it to be trampled in the dust. We have betrayed the legacy by permitting politicians, the media, special interests, minorities, etc., to have their way. Therefore, our duty as loyal subjects of the Constitution is to pick it up, dust it off, and somehow restore it to its original purity.

This is the way religious societies think—when confronted with the problems of the modern world, their first instinct is to retreat to some long-lost Eden, where everything was good and clean and honest. This book, however, is here to say it ain't necessarily so, that Eden was never what it was cracked up to be, and that the Founders were never as far-seeing and all-wise as their followers allege. The problem with American politics, it argues, is not that they are the flawed expression of a perfect plan, but that they are the all too faithful expression of a flawed Constitution. Where the document devised in Philadelphia in 1787 neatly fit the needs of American society at the time, it proved woefully inadequate to the needs of American society in subsequent decades. In 1861, the constitutional system fairly disintegrated under the pressure of seventy years or so of pent-up change, unleashing one of the worst military conflicts of the entire nineteenth century. For approximately the next three-quarters of a century, it proved to be a political straitjacket, in which even the mildest social reform was prohibited on the grounds that it would interfere with the minority rights of bankers and industrialists; then, following a brief golden age after World War II, it has resulted in crippling gridlock and paralysis. The Constitution has performed this way not despite the Founders, but because of them. They created a system in which the three branches of government were suspended in almost perfect equipoise so that a move by one element in any one direction would be almost immediately offset by a countermove by one or both of the others in the opposite direction. The result was a counterdemocratic system dedicated to the virtues of staying put in the face of rising popular pressure. The more the system refused to budge, the more the constitutional sages praised its essential immobility.

The problem with the Constitution lies not with any single clause or paragraph, but rather with the concepts of balance and immutability, indeed with the very idea of a holy, all-powerful Constitution. James Madison, who did more in Philadelphia than anyone else to shepherd the Constitution through to completion, saw the document as an anchor in a flyaway world. An anchor, however, is precisely what is holding American society back. There are times when society needs to fly away and leave the past behind—to cast off old assumptions, to adopt new theories, to forge new frameworks of politics and government. This is precisely what the Madisonian Constitution was designed to prevent and something it has succeeded all too well in doing. As a result, U.S. society is laboring under what is at best an eighteenth-century mode of government as it prepares to enter the twenty-first century.

America must cast off the constraints. At the same time, it has never seemed more unequal to the task. Society has never been more fragmented, politics have never been narrower or more shortsighted, while the extended constitutional priesthood—judges, eminent professors of constitutional law, op-ed columnists, and so forth—has never been more dogmatic. Even as they try to choke each other to death, liberals and conservatives have never been more united in their devotion to the secular religion that supposedly holds society together but is in fact tearing it apart. They are like Catholic and Protestant theologians of the sixteenth and seventeenth centuries, each one claiming to be more faithful to the Word than the other. The outlook for reform seems grim as a consequence, which only makes it all the more *necessary*. What Americans need is less faith and more thought, less willingness to put their trust in a bygone political order and a greater realization that they, the living, are the only ones capable of maneuvering society through the storm. Instead of beginning with the Constitution as the essential building block, they should realize that there are no givens in this world and that all assumptions, beginning with the most basic, must constantly be examined and tested.

This must seem very strange to readers who have been trained from childhood to think of the Constitution as America's rock and foundation, without which it would disintegrate into an unthinking mob. Yet constitutional faith is a form of thoughtlessness, since it means relying on the thought of others rather than on one's own. The alternative is to emancipate oneself from the past, to wake up to the realization that two centuries of struggling and fighting have not been for naught and that we know a few things the Founders didn't as a consequence. Rather than continually deferring to their judgment, it means understanding that we are fully competent to make our way through the modern world on our own. This is not to say we should ignore Madison, Jefferson, et al., merely that there is no reason we should feel bound by their precepts.

In a sense, America has to fight what Jonathan Swift called "The Battle of the Books," a half-forgotten intellectual war that erupted in the 1690s between those who argued that ancient authorities were superior because they were ancient and those who contended that, thanks to progress and advancement, modern scholars knew more than ancient ones could ever have imagined and that there was no reason therefore to bow to their example. The argument raged for half a century, and if the ancients were not completely toppled in the end, at least they were dented. Latter-day Americans have got to take up arms as well against the eighteenth-century *philosophes* who wrote The

Federalist Papers and created the Constitution and have been post-humously lording it over the United States ever since.

The alternative is continuing breakdown and decay. Government in America doesn't work because it's not supposed to work. In their infinite wisdom, the Founders created a deliberately unresponsive system in order to narrow the governmental options and force us to seek alternative routes. Politics were dangerous; therefore, politics had to be limited and constrained. But America cannot expect to survive much longer with a government that is inefficient and none too democratic by design. It is impossible to forge ahead in the late twentieth century using governmental machinery dating from the late eighteenth. Urban conditions can only worsen, race relations can only grow more poisonous, while the middle class can only grow more alienated and embittered. Politics will grow more irrational and self-defeating, while the price of the good life—that is, a nice home, good schools, a quiet street in a safe neighborhood—can only continue its upward climb beyond the reach of all but the most affluent. Rush Limbaugh, Howard Stern, and other demagogues of the airwaves will continue to make out like bandits, while the millions of people who listen to them will only grow angrier and more depressed. Eventually, every other society caught up in such a bind has snapped. Sooner or later, the United States will as well. The stays have already begun to fray.

Societies can regenerate, though. For those who know their English history (as all educated Americans did once upon a time), the example that springs immediately to mind is Britain in the early nineteenth century. After a quarter-century of intermittent warfare against revolutionary France, the British found themselves in a predicament not altogether different from that of the United States at the end of its half-century-long crusade against the Soviet Union. The government was over its head in debt, the political structure fairly creaked with age, and, even by modern standards, the political classes were amazingly stupid and corrupt. Rather than marching forward into the brave new world of the nineteenth century, the ruling class showed every sign of retreating into the tired old world of the eighteenth century, in which backwoods country squires slept with the hounds, and judges in horsehair wigs sentenced half-grown pickpockets to the gibbet. (British politicians of the early nineteenth century believed in the morally salutary effects of capital punishment even more fervently than American politicians do today.) The ruling class was committed to the idea that the key to Britain's strength lay in its "Ancient Constitution," as the country's bundle of moss-backed political institutions and traditions was known. Britain had defeated Napoleon by sticking to the Ancient Constitution and, by jingo, it would defeat whatever the postwar era had to offer by doing so as well.

But then the unexpected occurred—the immovable moved. The reformers grew louder and more insistent, the middle classes pricked up their ears and began to listen, and beginning in 1832, the country embarked on a program of deep-seated constitutional reform. The squirearchy retreated, while a new kind of politics gained a toehold, a kind of politics that was progressive, utilitarian, and broader based. Over the next few decades, Britain went from having the worst government in Europe to having the cleanest, the most efficient, and the most responsive. Rather than collapsing, something that most radicals (including Jefferson) thought was likely at any moment, the country gained a new burst of life and went on to conquer the globe.

Regeneration was inseparable from reconstitution. In order to pick itself up by the bootstraps, British society had to overthrow the old idea of an Ancient Constitution that was unknowable, unapproachable, miraculous, and unmoving, the political equivalent of the laws that Moses had brought down from the mountaintop. The parallels with modern-day America could not be more obvious. The United States is also saddled with an ancient Constitution, the oldest in the world by now, and one equally far removed from the needs of late-twentieth-century society. It also has the worst form of politics in the advanced industrial world (a belt extending from Western Europe across North America to Japan, New Zealand, and Australia), the most inefficient government, and the oiliest, most self-serving politicians. Since 1994, Congress has been in the grips of Republican zealots eager to return to the days of *Ozzie and Harriet* and Dwight D. Eisenhower. Police are more brutal than in any comparable country, prisons are filled to overflowing, and social policies in general grow harsher and more punitive with every passing year. Yet in no country is the range of accepted political debate more narrow. A prominent Anglo-American journalist named E. L. Godkin once remarked that the United States has

> far outstripped the rest of the world in what are called "constitutional lawyers." Our judges and commentators have acquired the widest celebrity as skilled and shrewd expounders of the organic law. Their application of its provisions to the complex phenomena of our social and political conditions have been marvels of ingenuity and erudition. But the examination and elucidation of the principles on which governments ought to rest, one of the highest and most interesting pursuits in which the human understanding can engage, has generally been neglected. . . . Political speculation has been regarded as an occupation fit only for French or German "reds" or for boy debaters.[1]

Godkin wrote these words at the height of the Civil War. For a time, it appeared amid the passionate disorder of the 1860s that the country might actually follow his advice and embark on a program of thoroughgoing constitutional reform. But then the Radical Republicans faltered in the latter part of the decade and lost their grip, political energy began to recede, and the country returned to its prewar somnolence.

If they are to emerge from their latest paralysis, Americans will have to resume the job they failed to finish in the 1860s. Rather than mindlessly cursing government and politicians, they will have to get to the bottom of the American predicament and figure out why politics in this country have grown so abysmal. Instead of rallying to this or that favorite son, they will have to figure out why even the best candidates wind up being defeated by the system they have vowed to change. Rather than relying on the Founding Fathers for answers, it means looking to themselves—to their own intelligence, their own analytical powers, their own creative abilities.

This book is an attempt to get that process rolling. On a personal note, I should add that when I embarked on this project, I assumed the task would be relatively straightforward. I would show how the Constitution works—or, rather, fails to work—and how much more easily other governments go about tackling the mundane task of running a modern society. A lightbulb would then go on over everybody's heads, and people would immediately set about making the necessary changes. I quickly wised up. For one thing, as I soon discovered, plenty of people had already written such books, yet ultimately the results had been like firing a peashooter at a battleship. A few changes were made around the edges, but the system as a whole had steamed on regardless.

Moreover, the underlying principle of checks and balances was much subtler than I had imagined. As every schoolchild knows, the Founders had wanted a Constitution that would serve the people as "a safeguard against the tyranny of their own passions."[2] As Supreme Court Justice Louis Brandeis put it in *Myers v. U.S.* (1926), "The doctrine of the separation of powers was adopted . . . not to promote efficiency but to preclude the exercise of arbitrary power"—which, put another way, meant that inefficiency was the price Americans had to pay for freedom and democracy. But there was a catch here. How was one to *evaluate* a system that was inefficient by design? What output criteria could one develop? If it was performing well, that is, efficiently, then it was performing in a way that was dangerous and threatening. If it was performing poorly, that is, *in*efficiently, then it was performing well. Bad was good and good was bad—a conundrum designed to stop even the most ardent reformer in his tracks.

Essentially, Madison and his colleagues in Philadelphia had created a puzzle palace in which logic was turned on its head. Or, rather, they had employed a different kind of logic, a pre-industrial version that would prove incomprehensible to citizens of the industrial era. Rather than a simple, straightforward analysis, therefore, this book is arranged chronologically in an attempt to show why ideas like separation of powers and limited government acquired such a powerful hold on people in the eighteenth century and why they proved so difficult to dislodge—even though they were so obviously unsuited to the problems of the nineteenth and twentieth centuries. The basic theme is not only that the Constitution is out of date but that by imposing an unchangeable political structure on a generation that has never had an opportunity to vote on the system as a whole, it amounts to a terrible dictatorship by the past over the present. Americans are prisoners, in effect, of one of the most subtle yet powerful systems of restraint in history, one in which it is possible to curse the president, hurl obscenities at Congress, and all but parade naked down Broadway, yet virtually impossible to alter the political structure in any fundamental way. They live in a system not only of limited government, but of limited democracy, which is why politics of late have become so suffocating and destructive. It is like a prison with no guards and no walls, yet from which no one ever escapes.

The answer is not less democracy—which is what term limits, a balanced-budget amendment, and other checks on legislative power represent—but more. Rather than checks and balances, the American people need to cast off constitutional restraints imposed more than two centuries ago and use their power *as a whole* to rebuild society as they see fit. This is not an invitation to lawlessness, but, quite the contrary, a call for the democratic majority to begin refashioning society along more rational and modern lines. Rather than less freedom, it is a plea for more, beginning with the freedom of the popular majority to modify its political circumstances in whatever way it sees fit. Rather than submitting to an immutable Constitution, Americans should cast off their chains and rethink their society from the ground up. They have nothing to lose—except one of the most unresponsive political systems this side of the former Soviet Union.

1

CONCEPTION

THE ANTIDOTE to the notion of the Constitution as the embodiment of timeless wisdom is to understand it as the very timely and time-bound product of a specific era. If the past is a foreign country, then the Constitution is a document in a foreign language, one which has to be seen in historical context before it can be deciphered and rendered intelligible to the modern reader.

In the 1960s, a Harvard professor of government named Samuel P. Huntington drew attention in academic circles with his thesis of America as a Tudor polity.[1] Building on the work of earlier scholars such as Charles McIlwain and E. S. Corwin, Huntington argued that the U.S. Constitution was not so much a product of the eighteenth century as a codification of certain principles of government that had reached their fullest flowering some two centuries earlier under the Tudors, the English royal family that gave us the monumental personalities of Henry VIII and Elizabeth I. Huntington's thesis was simple. Although commonly thought of as royal despots par excellence, the Tudors actually practiced a kind of politics that in certain respects was decentralized and pluralist. Unlike France, where power was concentrated in the throne, power in England was balanced among a broad array of governing institutions—the monarchy, the two houses of Parliament, and the church, plus a host of lesser bodies such as the great municipal corporations, the Inns of Court (which served as guardians of the common law), and others. Rather than being locked into a fixed structure, the various constituent elements buzzed around one another like bees around a hive. Each was sovereign in its own special sphere, each felt itself the heir to ancient rights and privileges that were sacred and immutable, and each was highly jealous of interference by competing institutions, up to and including the Crown. The Ancient Constitution, as it was called, was the web that held it all together, an intricate network of traditions and obligations that was supposedly the basis of English liberty. Unlike the later American version, this Ancient Constitution was never written down. Nonetheless, all politically conscious Englishmen believed in it and were convinced that it was the key to England's greatness.[2]

The Tudors were famous for their ruthlessness and brutality, yet were oddly respectful when it came to those other bodies' ranks and constitutional privileges. When Henry VII, who founded the dynasty in 1485, stepped into the political void created by the War of the Roses, he came as close to being elected by Parliament as any monarch until George I, the first of the Hanover line, in 1714.[3] Henry clashed with Parliament repeatedly, but did not try to curtail its power. As the Spanish ambassador reported, Henry "would like to govern England in the French [i.e., absolutist] fashion but he cannot."[4] His otherwise ruthless son, Henry VIII, kept within constitutional bounds as well, at least after a fashion. Famous for casting off wives and executing Sir Thomas More, he also encouraged Parliament, particularly the increasingly dynamic House of Commons, to take on more and more power and responsibility as the business of the state began to grow. Between 1533 and 1539, it is estimated that Parliament had more legislative business on its plate than at any time until the 1830s.[5] In 1536 alone, it oversaw the liquidation of some three hundred Roman Catholic monasteries, the unification of England and Wales, the creation of new law courts, the confiscation of certain business monopolies, plus some sixty-odd minor bits of legislation covering everything from repairing the banks of the river Thames to regulating the price of meat.[6] While some of this legislation was initiated by the Crown, much of it came from members of Parliament (or MPs, as they are known) or from favor seekers and lobbyists. Observed the historian Penry Williams:

> The politics of the pressure-group were highly developed in Tudor England. Towns like London and York knew how to organize the procedures of Parliament and whom to lobby. Trading guilds and companies maneuvered to have their industry organized to their own advantage. . . . To most of the people who used Parliament in this way—and probably to most of its members—it was a complex political organism which, handled carefully, might produce something to their advantage.[7]

What was fascinating for Huntington was the curious resemblance all this bore to the system that would later spring up in the United States. Power was dispersed and decentralized, government was limited by custom and tradition, and an immutable constitution was what held it all in place. As another scholar, the English historian J. P. Kenyon, put it, few people thought "that constitutional relationships, which they believed had existed time out of mind, might change." Instead, they believed that "the structure of politics and society was governed by laws as immutable as those which controlled the revolution of the sun and stars around the earth"[8]—which, apart from certain changes in cosmology, was pretty much how Americans would come to see their constitutional relationships in the nineteenth and twentieth centuries. Law was a source of comfort and stability. Men were corrupt, but the law, by virtue of its permanence and immutability, was supposed to be pure and above the fray. At the same time, corruption was not without its comforts as well. Because the power structure was porous and inefficient, it was filled with nooks and crannies in which everyone could find a niche, from influence peddlers in and around Parliament to the ordinary man in the street.

But it was under Elizabeth I, who took over in 1558, following five years of bloody strife under her half-sister, Mary I, that this proto-American system reached its apex. Elizabeth, the last of the Tudors, was as strong-willed as anyone else in her family, yet she had to do business with a Parliament that was increasingly strong-willed as well. As a result, she was forced to "work" Parliament in a way that was much closer to that of a U.S. president like Lyndon Johnson than to a modern British monarch or prime minister. She dispensed favors and patronage, set up guidelines forbidding members of Parliament to discuss certain matters while "graciously" permitting them to discuss others, summoned and received parliamentary delegations, and, when need be, descended magnificently upon Parliament in her coach or open chariot to address them through the Lord Keeper.[9] When leaders of Parliament urged her to marry in order to settle the succession issue, she dawdled and delayed, yet refrained from issuing a direct no. The same happened when Puritan MPs tried to push her to take up arms in behalf of the Protestant cause on the Continent: she again dragged her feet rather than issue an outright refusal. She could be tough and overbearing. "Liberty of speech," she had one of her emissaries remind Parliament at one point, meant freedom "to say Yea or Nay to Bills" and not "to speak . . . of all causes . . . and to frame a form of religion or a State of government as idle brains shall seem fitting." Yet she knew when to give ground and humble herself. In 1601, with Parliament at the point of revolt over her habit of handing out lucrative business monopolies to royal favorites, she issued a rare royal apology. "Though God hath raised me high," she offered, "yet this I count the glory of my crown, that I have reigned with your loves. . . . [T]hough you have had, and may have, many mightier and wiser princes sitting in this seat, yet you never had, nor shall have, any that will love you better."

Thus, the Elizabethan system was based on continuing tension between the executive branch (i.e., the monarch) and the legislative (i.e., Parliament), with the other institutions hovering nearby. The resemblance to modern American practice does not stop there, though. Unlike the modern British Parliament, with its all-powerful House of Commons and essentially ceremonial House of Lords, the Elizabethan period was a golden age of bicameralism. The two houses were equally matched in terms of political clout, and since they were often at loggerheads, conference committees sprang up between them to iron out differences, just as they would later spring up between the House and Senate in the United States. Originally employed only sporadically, these committees became standard operating procedure as of the 1570s. Within each house, another committee system arose to shape and refine individual pieces of legislation. By the 1560s and 1570s, the practice of referring bills to committee had become standard as well. Since the committees were often where the most serious business was transacted, they were where what we would now call special interests flocked, for example, those West Country members interested in voyages of discovery who filled the parliamentary committee that authorized Sir Walter Raleigh to set up a colony in America, the ill-fated Roanoke Island adventure, in the 1580s.[10]

These were all techniques that American legislators, both in the Colonial assemblies and in the later U.S. Congress, would embrace, develop, and carry to astonishing extremes. Where twentieth-century Members of Parliament tend to be concerned with national policy rather than local politics, Elizabethan MPs were much more parochial, much more concerned with serving the interests of their constituents—which also makes them closer to modern American congressmen as well. The Elizabethan Parliament was also dominated by lawyers, which is to be expected when politics takes place under an immutable system of law, just as the U.S. Congress has been dominated by lawyers from its inception. In 1593, the number of members of the House of Commons who had been educated in the law stood at forty-three percent, whereas in 1994, some four centuries later, the comparable figure in the U.S. House and Senate stood at . . . forty-three percent.[11] Just as Elizabeth relied on her royal veto to keep fractious members of Parliament in line, chief executives in the United States came to rely on the presidential veto as well.

Thus, twentieth-century America wound up being more Elizabethan than the Elizabethans. But what is curious about this development is that England itself subsequently reversed course and headed off in a very different direction. As the House of Commons rose in power during the seventeenth and eighteenth centuries, bicameralism receded and its earlier rival, the House of Lords, became a shadow of its former self. Conference committees between the two houses became increasingly infrequent before disappearing altogether in the 1830s. With power increasingly concentrated in the hands of the prime minister and the cabinet, the swarm of legislative committees within the House of Commons faded away even more rapidly. After 1707, the royal veto fell into disuse. Where in theory the monarch could say no to Parliament whenever he or she wished, in practice the throne always played along. The intense localism so characteristic of Tudor politics also declined, and the once-powerful legal profession steadily lost its grip. From the high-water mark of the late sixteenth and early seventeenth centuries, the number of MPs educated in the law steadily declined to a level in the early 1990s of just fourteen percent, roughly the same level as the German Bundestag and the Canadian House of Commons.[12] By the eighteenth century, even an MP chosen by a handful of voters in some obscure country hamlet was assumed to owe primary loyalty to the kingdom as a whole. Rather than local, all politics in Britain were quickly turning national.

Moreover, with the House of Commons fast becoming the only game in town, a development that became especially marked after 1721, British politics, at least institutionally speaking, were growing *less* pluralistic as well. The overwhelming power of Parliament, particularly that of the lower house, was by the eighteenth century the marvel of Europe. Where Westminster had once buzzed with lobbyists, old-fashioned influence peddling by the mid-1800s was clearly on the wane. Corruption, which in the eighteenth century had been flagrant and wide open, was in retreat. Where once the British power structure had been as open and drafty as a medieval castle, it was now increasingly lean, efficient, and tightly sealed. The American system, by comparison, remained as porous as ever and a lobbyist's delight.

With so much in common, why did England and America veer off in opposite directions? The crucial link, as Huntington and others have explained it, was the Puritans, those doughty religious reformers who began packing up and leaving England by the thousands precisely as the old Tudor ideas of decentralized government were losing their grip and radical new theories were threatening to take their place.

The flight of the Puritans was the anguished response of a middle-class group of merchants and tradesmen who had enjoyed growing power and influence during Elizabeth's forty-five-year reign only to suffer a devastating reversal of fortunes under her successors. Elizabeth had never been the militant religious crusader, the English "Deborah," the Puritans had been hoping for. She had not cleaned up the church at home or energetically intervened in the defense of Protestant interests abroad. She was often impatient and high-handed in her dealings with Parliament. Yet she was also a pragmatist who was willing to bow to the reality of Parliament's growing political clout, whereas her successors, members of the Stuart family in Scotland, were not. James I, who succeeded her to the throne in 1603, rejected the notion, part and parcel of the theory of the Ancient Constitution, that the king was under the law as much as his subjects. Whereas the thirteenth-century English legal authority Henry de Bracton had written that "law makes the king," James had asserted five years earlier in his *Trew Law of Free Monarchies* that kings "were the authors and makers of laws" rather than the other way around. He disliked

Puritanism, arguing that it "agreeth as well with a monarch as God and the devil," and he believed that if laymen were given the right to criticize their bishops, "then Jack and Tom and Will and Dick shall meet and at their pleasure censure me and my Council and all our proceedings"—a situation, needless to say, he was determined to prevent. Conditions under his son, Charles I, who succeeded to the throne in 1625, grew even worse. Charles tried to abolish Parliament altogether, asserted his right to levy and collect customs duties unilaterally, and stepped up the repression of religious and political dissidents under the reign of the infamous Archbishop Laud. In 1630, a Scottish pamphleteer had his ears cut off for denouncing the power of the Anglican bishops. In 1633, a fiery Puritan lawyer named William Prynne had his ears cropped for slandering the king and queen. Four years later, when Prynne was again prosecuted for offenses against the Crown along with two other Puritans, supporters turned out by the thousands to strew flowers in their path and demonstrate support.

The results for the Puritans were deeply shocking, roughly comparable to the effects of McCarthyism in the 1950s on those unrepentant liberals who still longed for the glory days of the New Deal. Memories of Elizabeth blossomed into something like a cult. The old queen's indecisiveness, her shilly-shallying, and her abrupt handling of Parliament were forgotten. Instead, what people remembered was her toughness and spirit, her patriotism, and of course her smashing triumph over the Spanish (i.e., Catholic) Armada in 1588, a victory that James and Charles, with their pro-Catholic policies, had done so much to undermine. The upshot, as the English Marxist historian Christopher Hill put it, was a growing "legend of an Elizabethan golden age, in which Parliament and crown worked in harmony, in which the church was resolutely protestant, in which bishops were subordinated to the secular power, and protestant sea-dogs brought gold and glory back from the Spanish main."[13]

The cult had a constitutional dimension as well since Elizabeth was by now synonymous with religious freedom, pluralistic government, and obeisance to the Ancient Constitution. Under Elizabeth, the ancient law had been obeyed, and England had been strong. Now, under the Stuarts, the law was being trampled, and England was weak. MPs had been arrested for speaking their mind, royal expenditures were out of control, and a war against Catholic France in 1627 had ended in failure and humiliation under the leadership of an incompetent royal favorite, the Duke of Buckingham. The way to put England back on track was to restore the law to all its ancient glory.

It is Huntington's thesis that the Puritans took this neo-Elizabethan ideology and transported it to the New World, along with their Bibles and other worldly possessions, during the mass flight of the 1620s. Once arrived in Massachusetts, they set about building their "shining city upon a hill" according to principles they had learned from their fathers or their clergymen or that they remembered from their youth. In contrast to England under the Stuarts, government was to be limited and balanced. The laws that held society in place, derived as they were from the Bible, were to be made solid and eternal. Instead of an autocracy issuing orders from the top down, power would flow from the bottom up. Each star in the political firmament—the individual, the community, and later the states—would only grudgingly cede power to those higher up, making sure to hedge it about with all manner of restrictions and conditions. Decades before John Locke made it the basis of his social philosophy, the colonists tended to think of society as resting on a contract between the rulers and the ruled. The stronger and more inflexible the contract, the greater the constraints on those in power and the greater the sense of security on the part of those below.

The curious thing about the great Puritan migration is that it was so brief. By the late 1630s, it was essentially over. Indeed, as the struggle between Parliament and the Crown began to heat up at home, the tide began to reverse.[14] The Massachusetts Bay Colony continued to prosper and expand (due in no small measure to the colonists' amazingly high birthrate), but the colonists were cut off from the titanic, two-sided revolution that was beginning to take shape on the other side of the Atlantic, a revolution not only against the king—which culminated in Charles I's beheading in January 1649—but a revolution within the Puritan cause as well, resulting in the overthrow of many of their own most cherished beliefs.

The old image of the Puritans as grim, pinch-nosed spoilsports—the sort of people who "hated bear-baiting, not because it gave pain to the bear, but because it gave pleasure to the spectators," as Macaulay put it—has undergone much revision in recent decades thanks to the efforts of the great historian Christopher Hill and others. In this more sympathetic view, the Puritans are seen as a diverse, quarrelsome movement of lawyers, parliamentarians, preachers, and revolutionary mystics roughly grouped around a set of beliefs that, by modern standards, were an ungainly blend of the reactionary and progressive. Groups like the Levellers—who comprised the movement's left wing and whose "agitators" ranged like Bolshevik commissars through the ranks of Oliver Cromwell's New Model Army during the English Civil War of the 1640s—could be remarkably democratic. "The poorest he that is in England has a life to live as the greatest he, and therefore . . . every man that is to live under a government ought first by his own consent to put himself under that government," Colonel Rainborough, one of their leaders, declared in 1647, some 130 years before Thomas Jefferson gave vent to similar sentiments in the Declaration of Independence. At the same time that they marched confidently into the future, however, their eyes were fixed resolutely on the past—on the age of Elizabeth, on the supposedly golden age of the Anglo-Saxons before the arrival of the "Norman yoke" in 1066, and, of course, on the Garden of Eden before the Fall, a topic that was the special province of John Milton, Cromwell's secretary for foreign correspondence and the Puritan movement's foremost literary light. Elizabeth, Alfred the Great (so-called because he had fought off a Danish invasion in the ninth century), and King Arthur were their patriotic heroes, William the Conqueror and now the Stuarts their special villains.

The Stuarts were more complex ideologically than the Puritan image of corrupt, Jesuit-loving, Francophilic tyrants as well. On one hand, there could be no doubt as to their autocratic tendencies. In attempting to govern without Parliament between 1629 and 1640, Charles I was clearly following in the footsteps of Louis XIII, who had governed without the French Estates General since 1615, not to mention numerous other Continental absolutists who were busily suppressing representative institutions in the seventeenth century from Portugal to Hungary.[15] On the other hand, the Stuarts were also modernizers, members of a new breed of monarchs who wished to clear away the feudal underbrush in order to standardize, rationalize, and update the political structure. Rather than the cornerstone of English liberties, the Stuarts saw the Ancient Constitution as a legal briar patch consisting of outdated rights, duties, and feudal obligations. It had to be trimmed, pruned, and even hacked into shape. Where the Puritans hewed to a concept of the law as fixed and eternal, the Stuart view that the law had to be subservient to the political needs of the day was actually more modern. The Puritans responded with shock and disapproval. "No man ought to be wiser than the law," replied Sir Edward Coke, the leading legal authority of the day.[16] The cropped-eared William Prynne was characteristically thunderous: "the Principal Liberties, Customs, Laws" of the kingdom, he declared, particularly those in the *"great Charters,"* are "FUNDAMENTAL, PERPETUAL, AND UNALTERABLE."[17] Law had an existence apart from man, whose job was merely to interpret the law and see that it was applied.

All of which was decidedly messy from a twentieth-century point of view. Instead of progressive democrats versus royal reactionaries, the kind of neat alignment we have come to expect these days, the democrats were in some respects the traditionalists while the royalists were in some respects the rationalists and modernizers. Things began sorting themselves out in the 1640s when Parliament and the Crown came to blows, Cromwell's Ironsides prevailed on the battlefield, and the famous Puritan-dominated Long Parliament found itself running the entire government. Although nominally committed to the

Elizabethan ideal of balanced government, the House of Commons, by 1649, had executed the king, abolished the House of Lords, divided the country up into military districts, and imposed a dictatorship more stringent than anything under Charles I, albeit for different purposes. Although also committed to the ancient constitutional ideal that Parliament's job was not to make new law but to discover and interpret old law, the Long Parliament found itself doing things that were clearly novel. Under Cromwell, observed Christopher Hill,

> the Long Parliament kept Sir Simonds D'Ewes as its tame antiquarian, sending him off to the archives in the Tower every now and then to "search for precedents" which would justify what the House wanted to do. The sad day came when Sir Simonds reported that he could find no precedent. That did not stop the House from acting as it wished, but it helped men to overcome the "stop in the mind" and evolve a theory of sovereignty which countered that of the Divine Right of Kings.[18]

In May 1642, refusing a demand to surrender the town of Hull to the king's forces, both houses of Parliament declared in a joint resolution:

> As for "the duty and modesty of former times, from which we are said to have varied," . . . if we made any precedents in this parliament, we have made them . . . upon the same or better grounds of reason and law than those . . . which our predecessors first made any for us. And as some precedents ought not to be rules for us to follow, so none can be limits to bound our proceedings, which may and must vary according to the different conditions of times.[19]

This was indeed a revolutionary moment, one in which Parliament declared that it was now free to pick and choose which precedents were binding and which were not. Its scope was now unlimited; it could do anything it felt was necessary to see itself through the current crisis. Despite its hatred for Stuart-style absolutism, Parliament was moving toward a not dissimilar view that placed the law under government rather than over it.

Yet that other branch of the Puritan family, in Massachusetts Bay, remained devoted to law that was solid and unalterable. Precisely because the New Englanders had the field to themselves and had no kings to do battle with, the atmosphere remained both highly democratic and highly conservative. They did not debate Parliament's right to abrogate the most fundamental features of the constitution in order to prevail against the king. Quite the contrary, as historian David Hackett Fischer observed, reform in Massachusetts was still regarded

> mainly as a process of recovery and preservation. Reformation meant going backward rather than forward, on the assumption that error was novel and truth was ancient. . . . The Protestant Reformation meant a reversion to primitive Christianity. In politics, reform was a return to the ancient constitution.[20]

Instead of dragging themselves out of the muck and mire, the Puritans saw life as a struggle to recover lost innocence, to return to the glorious paradise before the Fall.

The Puritans were only one part of American culture, however, and Americans in general were only one outpost in an English-speaking ideological world bounded roughly by London and Edinburgh on the east and Boston and Barbados on the west. Although it took weeks to sail from one end of this expanse to the other, it was to a high degree united. Thanks to an academic revolution mounted since the 1960s by such historians as J. G. A. Pocock, Bernard Bailyn, Jack P. Greene, John M. Murrin, and Joyce Appleby, we have a much better understanding of what this transatlantic political culture was about. By the latter part of the seventeenth century, it was divided along two poles known at various times as Whigs and Tories and as Court and Country. The two were not synonymous, just as liberal and conservative in twentieth-century America are not quite synonymous with

Democratic and Republican. The first—Whigs and Tories—referred to the opposing sides in the ongoing battle between Parliament and the throne, a struggle that did not end in the 1640s but resumed in somewhat different guise in the 1660s and 1670s when the Cromwellian republic was overthrown and the monarchy restored. The Whigs, broadly speaking, stood for parliamentary authority and the rising bourgeoisie, those merchants and bankers who were pressing for a more modern form of government, while the Tories stood for royal prerogatives and drew their support from the more conservative sections of the aristocracy as well as a major portion of the tradition-bound, backwoods gentry.

The terms Court and Country are more obscure, yet in some ways more relevant to subsequent American development. The Court, obviously, stood for the throne, although the term meant something different politically before and after England's second revolution of 1688–89 (the so-called Glorious Revolution) and a third quasi revolution in 1714. Before 1688, the throne connoted a king ruling in proud opposition to a Whig-dominated Parliament. After 1688, when yet another overweening Stuart, King James II, had been sent packing and his son-in-law, William of Orange, had been brought in to take his place, the Court referred to the royal family ruling in a somewhat uneasy alliance with Whiggish parliamentarians. And after 1714, when the Whigs imported a German aristocrat who did not speak a word of English to rule over Britain as King George I, the Court referred mostly to the coterie of parliamentary Whigs who now ran Britain essentially on their own.

The Country referred to all those who were on the outs during this rocky period, namely, the Whigs prior to 1688, various Whig factions in the extremely unsettled period between 1689 and 1714, and, after the period of 1714–21, to those dissident members of the ruling party who called themselves Old or True Whigs, as well as to the Tories who were aghast at the unbridled corruption and centralization of power that had grown up under George I. The term *Country* thus had a threefold connotation. It stood for the interests of the country as a whole, as opposed to those of the courtiers and financiers who were misappropriating the national wealth for their own purposes; for rural interests, as opposed to urban; and for the counties (i.e., shires or provinces), as opposed to the government and the financial center in the City of London. According to historian Lawrence Stone:

> The Country is firstly an ideal. It is that vision of rustic arcadia that goes back to the Roman classics and which fell on the highly receptive ears of the newly educated gentlemen of England who had studied Virgil's Georgics at Oxford or Cambridge. It was a vision of environmental superiority over the City: the Country was peaceful and clean, a place of grass and trees and birds, the city was ugly and dirty and noisy, a place of clattering carts and coaches, coal dust and smog, and piles of human excrement. It was also a vision of moral superiority over the Court; the Country was virtuous, the Court wicked; the Country was thrifty, the Court extravagant; the Country was honest, the Court corrupt; the Country was chaste and heterosexual, the Court promiscuous and homosexual; the Country was sober, the Court drunken; the Country was nationalist, the Court xenophile; the Country was healthy, the Court diseased; the Country was outspoken, the Court sycophantic; the Country was the defender of the old ways and old liberties, the Court the promoter of administrative novelties and new tyrannical practices; the Country was solidly Protestant, even Puritan, the Court was deeply tainted by Popish leanings.[21]

The Country party, one might add, was also the minority party in England, where all the forces were on the side of urbanization and centralization and where the idea of running a modern European power according to some sixteenth- or seventeenth-century Elizabethan blueprint struck most people, at least those in power, as more than a little daft. In America, though, the Country was in the clear majority. Its ideas of balanced government (which by the mid-eighteenth century was understood to refer to the need to rein in Parliament and augment the powers of the Crown) and fidelity to the Ancient Constitution fit in perfectly with American beliefs about ancient liberties, decentralization, and rural self-sufficiency. As unrealistic as the Country's program seemed in England, it seemed quite the opposite in a lightly settled country far removed from any foreign threat (other than the French in Canada, who were no longer a factor after 1760) and which therefore could afford to make do with only the most minimal government.

The same balled-up confusion of progressive and reactionary elements that existed among the Puritans and Royalists of the seventeenth century pertained to the Court and Country partisans of the eighteenth as well. The Country, while more democratic in some respects, was also more reactionary; while the Court—stuffed to the gills with contracts and payoffs though its members might be—was, not unlike the Stuarts of a century earlier, more forward-looking and innovative. Sir Robert Walpole, the Whig back-bencher who had emerged from obscurity to take charge of British finances after the South Sea Bubble disaster of 1721, was clearly forging a new form of government, one in which power was increasingly concentrated in an executive committee of the House of Commons known as the cabinet, with himself as "prime" minister (a title that was originally meant as a term of derision). Where Lord Bolingbroke, the leading Country ideologue of the day, campaigned to have power restored to the king and for a complete separation of executive and legislative authority, Walpole campaigned for an ever closer merger of the two, in which power was increasingly monopolized by leading legislators operating at the behest of the throne.

On the other side of the Atlantic, Country ideology helped nurture that proud and prickly independence that was fast defining the Anglo-American personality. As Pocock and others have noted, Country ideology, with its fear and loathing of modernity, was imbued with the sense of tragedy and pessimism that comes from fighting a lost cause. It saw the world as eternally poised between law and public virtue on one hand and tyranny on the other, with the advantage of late clearly going to the latter. Where the Court saw corruption as a necessary evil that allowed the wheels of government to turn more smoothly, the Country saw it as a disease that brought with it oppression and moral collapse. Power from the Country point of view was endlessly problematic, something that was necessary yet dangerous. For coffeehouse radicals and pamphleteers like John Trenchard and Thomas Gordon, authors of the immensely influential "Cato's Letters," power was "like fire; it warms, scorches, or destroys according as it is watched, provoked, or increased."[22] Yet, under Walpole, power and centralization were clearly out of control, while freedom was everywhere in retreat.

The Country feared modernization, progress, and particularly the strange new world of high finance, with its accounting tricks, speculative manias, and huge destructive crashes. In some respects, its critique of the new eighteenth-century money economy was almost Marxist. As Pocock observed: "Their language was humanist, their enemy was modernity, and their posture had something of the sixteenth century about it and something of the twentieth."[23] Country stalwarts were horrified at the way new money was tearing away at old social bonds. Yet rather than rushing to embrace the socialist millennium, needless to say, the Country's response was to retreat into an idealized version of the feudal past in which a lord looked out for his servants, and honor and loyalty meant more than money in the bank.

Bolingbroke, who is all but forgotten today but was considered essential reading by John Adams and Thomas Jefferson, was the crucial intellectual figure in this period.[24] A Tory under Queen Anne (who had succeeded to the throne after the death of William of Orange in 1702), Bolingbroke engaged in some clumsy, last-minute machinations in an attempt to prevent the accession of George I in 1714 and then, fearing for his life, panicked and fled to France, where followers of the ousted James II were living in exile under the protection of Louis XIV. A few years later, he paid a huge bribe and slunk back home, whereupon he took his revenge on the Court Whigs for the humiliation he had suffered by taking over leadership of the Country opposition. Beginning in 1726, he edited the *Craftsman*, a weekly newspaper which served as the rallying point for anti-Walpole forces. Bolingbroke's ideas were an amalgam of the feudal, the authoritarian, and what might now be described as the protofascist. He had little sense of democracy and saw himself as a lonely man of virtue standing firm against the mob. Ironically for a politician who was first and foremost a partisan ideologue, he regarded the very idea of party as inherently corrupt, an idea that would prove immensely influential in Philadelphia in 1787. "The spirit of liberty and the spirit of faction are not only different," he declared, "but repugnant and incompatible: so that the life of either is the death of the other."[25] His most famous essay, "The Idea of the Patriot King," was a strange, almost mystical meditation on the notion of a powerful new monarch who would rein in Parliament and rule directly over people, "espous[ing] no party, but . . . govern[ing] like the common father of his people . . . where the head and all the members are united by one common interest, and animated by one common spirit."[26] The idea of the king as father of his people would prove highly important in the creation of the American presidency.

No less central to the Court-Country split—and to the U.S. Constitution that would take shape a few decades later—was the issue of sovereignty, a legal concept kicking around since the sixteenth century. Sovereignty was simply the principle that in a modern society, some individual or institution had to be the boss and take responsibility for whatever the government might do. Sir William Blackstone would later define it in his *Commentaries on the Laws of England* as "supreme, irresistible, absolute, uncontrolled authority," in other words, authority that was over the law rather than under it. Royal absolutism as defined by James I was one form of sovereignty, while the doctrine that began taking shape in 1642 that Parliament had the power to do whatever was necessary to prevail against the king was another. Parliament *made* law, in other words, rather than merely obeying it. Its word *was* the law, rather than an interpretation. After 1688, the supreme authority became something known as the "king-in-parliament," meaning the two branches acting in concert, but the underlying legal principle was the same. As Jean-Louis DeLolme, an eighteenth-century French constitutional theorist, put it, the only restraints on Britain's Parliament were those imposed by nature. Parliament could, he said, "do anything except make a man a woman or a woman a man."

For Bolingbroke and the rest of the Country forces, this was all profoundly heretical. They argued that neither the king, Parliament, nor anyone else should have the final say in the political sphere, but rather that the law should reign supreme. If human institutions could make or unmake law at will, then the Ancient Constitution—"that noble fabric, the pride of Britain, the envy of her neighbors, raised by the labor of so many centuries, repaired at the expense of so many millions, and cemented by such a profusion of blood," as Bolingbroke put it[27]—would be lost. Since power would no longer be distributed among an array of competing institutions according to a time-honored formula, but would be concentrated in a single branch, balanced government would be lost as well.[28] Instead of being restricted by custom, practice, and law, people would be free to do whatever they wanted. Society could move in whatever direction it wished, whereas Bolingbroke argued that the only proper direction for society to move was toward the past—"to draw it back," as he put it, "on every favorable occasion, to the first good principles on which it was founded."[29]

This was the Country's great gift to the New World. Bolingbroke's rejection of human sovereignty and his neomedieval concept of law as something over and above society, which society was eternally required to obey, became the cornerstone of the American theory of government. Henry Adams, that brooding turn-of-the-century thinker, observed that the new republic defined itself by its rejection of the very idea of political sovereignty:

Supreme, irresistible authority must exist somewhere in every government—[this] was the European belief. . . . America, on the other hand, asserted that the principle was not true; that no such supreme power need exist in a government; that in the American government none such should be allowed to exist, because absolute power in any form was inconsistent with freedom, and that the new government should start from the idea that the public liberties depended upon denying uncontrollable authority in the political system in its part or its whole.[30]

Yet this rejection of sovereignty led to an unfortunate paradox. If final authority did not rest with the national government, then with whom did it rest—the individual states, the community, or even the individual? If final authority rested with the law, what was to be done if the law was unclear, inapplicable, or dysfunctional? If no one was empowered to step in and fix the Constitution when it was broken, if no one was to serve as master of the machinery because that would imply a concept of political sovereignty the Americans had rejected, then government could become crippled and paralyzed. Of course, Bolingbroke or one of his cothinkers would reply that such a scenario was impossible because the law was so perfect it could never fall into disrepair. Yet with the world changing so rapidly, who could possibly say?

The American Revolution was where the conflict between Court and Country at last came to a head. It was both a national conflict and a civil war within the far-flung English-speaking world. The French and Indian War of 1756–63 (known as the Seven Years' War in Britain), which the two sides viewed through opposite ideological lenses, proved to be the turning point. The colonists were intensely proud of their role as scouts and volunteer militiamen, while the British authorities were outraged that colonial legislatures had taken advantage of the emergency to wrest new concessions from royal governors and that American merchants had continued to trade with the enemy as if it were the most natural thing in the world.[31] Lord Loudown, commander in chief of the British forces in North America, complained to his superiors in London that "every impediment" the colonists could possibly invent "is thrown our way." Colonial legislatures "assumed to themselves, what they call Rights and Privileges, totally unknown to the Mother Country. . . ."[32] The problem, as the Court saw it in London, was plain as day. Anglo-American relations had been left in an undisturbed "natural" state for far too long and were due for an overhaul. Now that the war with the French was over, the Court was determined to see that it took place.

The British were plainly correct: government in America *was* overdue for reform. Yet there was no way that the Court could undertake such an overhaul without arousing the deepest fears of their opponents. The problem was the Ancient Constitution, which both sides claimed to be loyal to, but which both now interpreted in starkly different ways. For the Court, the Ancient Constitution meant the age-old authority of the king-in-parliament to do whatever was necessary to advance the interests of the realm. For America's Country stalwarts, the Ancient Constitution meant the right of various parts of the realm to continue exercising ancient liberties as they had always done in the past. Where the Court saw the emerging British empire as a hierarchical arrangement in which some people gave the orders and others carried them out, the Americans (who still saw themselves as Britons) viewed it as a voluntary federation in which the London authorities would agree to respect American prerogatives in return for the Americans agreeing to respect those of London. The theory of virtual representation, by which every MP was said to represent the empire as a whole, may have made perfect sense to Court Whigs in London, but it struck Americans as perfect lunacy. As absurd as it was to imagine an MP from some half-deserted English country hamlet speaking in behalf of a late-sprouting industrial center like Manchester, which was unrepresented in Parliament, it was doubly and triply absurd to imagine him speaking in behalf of a Bostonian or a frontiersman in western Pennsylvania. By the same token, the slogan of "no taxation without representation," which struck Americans as eminently sensible, seemed in the eyes of the Court to be a recipe for anarchy and fragmentation in which every country bumpkin and buckskin-clad colonial would agree to recognize London's authority only to the degree he was represented in Parliament. As far as London was concerned, it would be impossible to run a far-flung empire on such a basis.

In effect, Britons and Americans spoke different political languages. The more they grappled for a solution, the angrier and more uncomprehending each side became. Americans were shocked when the British said they would require them to support a standing army. In the Court's view, it was the least the colonists could do to reduce the cost of a military presence from which they derived immense benefit. Yet, in Country eyes, a standing army was synonymous with jack-booted military dictatorship. The colonists were also shocked when Parliament approved the Quebec Act in 1774, which restricted Anglo-Americans to a position east of the Appalachians and awarded the entire Ohio Valley to the French Canadians. For the Court, it was a way of appeasing the restive Quebecois. Yet the Country, which had long believed in westward expansion as the alternative to endless military imbroglios on the European continent, was astonished that London was now ceding the western territories to French Papists.[33] The Stamp Act was explosive because it represented the first effort at imposing an internal tax, a prerogative the colonists had always regarded as theirs alone to exercise. From the Court's point of view, sovereignty meant nothing if not the right to impose taxes anywhere the king-in-parliament might wish. Yet from the Country point of view, the fact that such a tax was unprecedented meant that it amounted to a usurpation of ancient constitutional rights.

Both sides were absurd, the Americans for believing they could carry forward the practices of the past indefinitely into the future and the Court party for failing to understand that local interests in the colonies would have to be accommodated. When the Americans complained they were being shut out of decision making in London, they were seriously advised to hire lobbyists to work the corridors of power just as other interested parties did. Everyone else got their way by pulling strings, so why not the Americans? At one point it was even suggested that wealthy Americans might retire to England, buy up some of the many "rotten boroughs" that were openly for sale throughout the countryside, and send a few handpicked representatives to Parliament to represent their interests.[34] That was what wealthy West Indian planters had done, with the result that by 1770 they controlled a score of seats in Parliament and had turned themselves into a formidable "West India interest."[35] Yet the American economy was too advanced for ideas like these to work. Its interests were too diverse to be represented by a few lobbyists and handpicked MPs. Rather than a society of wealthy nabobs, it was a country of farmers, tradesmen, and small- to midsize merchants, none of whom had the means to buy up a rotten borough or an English country estate and few of whom had any desire to move to a place where even the wealthiest among them would be made to feel like a poor country cousin. The thirteen colonies accounted for roughly a fourth of the population of the British empire by the 1770s, yet the powers that be in Westminster were unable to find room for any of them at the table.

Moreover, the Americans were correct in their belief that whatever solution the Court was likely to hit upon to the problem of how to put the empire on a sounder footing, it would almost certainly be at the colonists' expense. Indeed, political power was already receding from the hands of the Americans. Although the royal veto had died out in Britain, royal governors were vetoing local legislation in the New World with growing abandon. Whereas five out of the seven mainland colonies in British North America had elected their governors as of the mid-seventeenth century, only two out of the thirteen were still doing so as of the mid-eighteenth.[36] While Parliament was still porous and corruptible, the reins of government were being visibly tightened out on the periphery. As a result, royal governors who had once been willing to wheel and deal with colonists on more or less equal terms now refused to act without instructions from Westminster, where American influence was nil. Finally, American manufactured goods were beginning to invade British markets, setting off alarm bells from one end of the country to the other. The British authorities wanted raw materials from their colonies, not finished goods. They wanted an economic relationship between the center and the periphery that was complementary rather than competitive, which was yet another reason why the Americans would have to be brought to heel.

Viewing such developments through the prism of Country ideology, Americans thought the meaning was all too clear. In the aftermath of the French and Indian War, power was being centralized and rationalized under an all-powerful Parliament. Tyranny and political modernization were advancing hand in hand, while freedom was in retreat, just as Bolingbroke and his cothinkers had said it would be. As the Declaration of Independence put it, in tones ringing with Country outrage:

> The history of the present King of Great Britain is a history of repeated injuries and usurpations, all having in direct object the establishment of an absolute tyranny. . . . He has dissolved Representative Houses repeatedly, for opposing with manly firmness his invasions on the rights of the people. . . . He has erected a multitude of new offices, and sent hither swarms of officers to harass our people, and eat out their substance. . . . [He has] tak[en] away our charters, abolish[ed] our most valuable laws, and alter[ed] fundamentally the forms of our governments.

The Court was corrupt, tyrannous, and, what was pretty much the same thing, innovative. George III was fundamentally altering the form of government, imposing change on a backward-looking people who believed that change could only be for the worse. Thus, the patriots took up arms not to move society forward, but to restore it to its pristine purity. For Americans, liberty was something that had existed in the distant past but was now retreating before the onrush of modernity. In order to be reestablished, the clock had to be turned back, not ahead. As Bolingbroke had written, as soon as "the orders and forms of the constitution are restored to their primitive integrity," the laws will "become what they are intended to be, real barriers against arbitrary power, not blinds nor masks under which tyranny may be concealed."[37] Once the Ancient Constitution was put back on its throne, liberty would again prevail.

The American Revolution represented the triumph of a school of thought that was already antique by the standards of the eighteenth century. It was the only such triumph that the school would see. In Britain, Country ideology would soon go the way of the stagecoach and the powdered wig. In America, however, it gained a new lease on life by virtue of a refurbished Ancient Constitution, which, unlike the original, would be written down for all to see and would therefore become all the more immovable as a consequence.

2

BIRTH

THE CONSTITUTIONAL CONVENTION, which gathered in Philadelphia eleven years after the Declaration of Independence, consisted of a roomful of Country gentlemen faced with the most unlikely of prospects: the formation of a Country government. Given the party's deep suspicion of political power, the idea was almost a contradiction in terms. Yet power was now unavoidable. Rather than resolving the contradictions inherent in Country ideology, the revolution had exacerbated them. Intensely jealous of their own rights and privileges, the newly liberated colonies had banded together in the loosest of voluntary confederations. Congress, the body that sat at the head of this association, lacked the power to tax, to preserve order among the states, or even to pay its own troops. This was as it should be according to Country ideology, yet the results were plainly disastrous. Mutineers had chased Congress out of Philadelphia and sent it wandering from Trenton to Princeton and Annapolis before finally settling down in New York. New York and New Hampshire were engaging in saber rattling over ownership of nominally independent Vermont, while Vermont was contemplating a hookup with British-controlled Canada. Congress's appeal for support in suppressing Shay's Rebellion, a major revolt by indebted farmers in western Massachusetts in 1786, had ended in embarrassment. Not only had the states refused to contribute funds, but Massachusetts had refused even to allow federal troops already within its borders to take the field. The economy was in ruins—current estimates put the economic decline between 1775 and 1790 at as much as forty to fifty percent, equal to or greater than the Great Depression of the 1930s[1]—while a swarm of self-serving politicians was wreaking havoc at the local level. "The vile State governments are sources of pollution which will contaminate the American name for ages," Henry Knox advised Rufus King, a member of the Massachusetts delegation. "Smite them, smite them in the name of God and the people."[2] James Madison, a veteran of four dispiriting years in the Virginia state assembly, wrote that state politicians were "carrying localism to an absurdity,"[3] and Alexander Hamilton would later write that the United States had reached "almost the last stage of national humiliation."[4] The revolution had been fought in the name of liberty, yet now it appeared that liberty would have to be rolled back in the name of order. The people would not stand for it, yet the people would also not stand for the alternative, which was anarchy and decay.

The Philadelphia delegates, who represented the American economic and social elite, betrayed all the agony of men caught on the horns of an acute dilemma. Elbridge Gerry, a delegate from Massachusetts, despaired that the people of his state "have at this time the wildest ideas of government in the world," yet he was plainly terrified of supporting any changes that might rouse them to anger.[5] Edmund Randolph, another delegate, stated that the convention delegates were of one mind that the real problem lay in "the turbulence and follies of democracy."⁶ Yet popular passions were too powerful to oppose. As John Dickinson of Delaware put it, a limited monarchy might normally be considered "one of the best governments in the world," but under current conditions it was plainly "out of the question." "The spirit of the times," he went on, "the state of our affairs, forbade the experiment."⁷ As the eighteenth century saw it, democracy was synonymous with disorder and chaos. Therefore, the problem that presented itself in Philadelphia was how to persuade a people ablaze with the spirit of liberty to relinquish a degree of democracy in order to promote unity and order.

The convention contained one extreme centralizer—Hamilton— but otherwise consisted of people from the broad, establishmentarian middle who believed that a way had to be found to strengthen the federation while somehow preserving the rights and privileges of the individual states. Madison was typical in this regard, a cautious, deliberate Virginian who had only slowly come around to the view that the Articles of Confederation were unreformable and had to be completely scrapped. Once the convention got under way, he took the lead in soothing over disputes and preventing either hotheaded Southerners or recalcitrant Northerners from walking out. Eventually, under Madison's guidance, an answer began to take shape, an elaborate framework of government in which the various elements—legislative, executive, and judicial power; the state governments and the new federal entity; even liberty and authority themselves—would all be balanced in a state of perpetual tension. No single element would be predominant; rather, each one would check the power of the rest and see to it that no one overstepped its bounds.

This was an old Country idea. As Trenchard and Gordon had written in "Cato's Letters,"

> Power and sovereignty . . . in free countries . . . [must be] so qualified, and so divided into different channels, and committed to the discretion of so many different men, with different

interests and views, that the majority of them could seldom or never find their account in betraying their trust in fundamental instances. Their emulation, envy, fear, or interest . . . [must make] them spies or checks upon one another.[8]

Or as Madison would characterize it, a bit more succinctly, in The Federalist Papers: "Ambition must be made to counteract ambition."[9] Since the wielders of power would forever be envious, fearful, and "interested" (an eighteenth-century term that translates as selfish and corrupt), their envy and self-interest had to be pitted against one another so that they canceled each other out—just as they had in Elizabethan England.

As the broad outlines of the new government became apparent, the Philadelphia delegates set to work haggling over the details. An elderly Benjamin Franklin, the convention's *éminence grise*, described the process as "sawing boards to make them fit," a phrase that neatly summed up the convention's practical, workmanlike approach. As compromise was piled on top of compromise and differences split and resplit, the hallowed Country doctrine that legislative, executive, and judicial powers should be kept firmly separate underwent a revision. Since making each branch supreme in its own separate sphere threatened to lay the groundwork for the sort of confrontations between branches that had repeatedly shaken the English system, it was decided that powers should be separate but also somehow overlap. The solution the convention came up with was to further mix and match responsibilities and powers so that no one branch wound up being wholly legislative, executive, or judicial. The chief executive was given a limited veto over legislation (ARTICLE I, SECTION 7), which would thrust him deeply into the affairs of Congress. The Senate was given a blanket veto over presidential appointments (ART. II, SEC. 2), which would thrust it deeply into the affairs of the executive. Thanks to the doctrine of judicial review, which the Founders regarded as implicit in the new Constitution, the Supreme Court would meanwhile be thrust deeply into the affairs of the other two branches. Each branch would be separate, yet each would have a hand in each other's pocket as well.

If separation of powers was compromised, checks and balances were thus reinforced. In other respects, the convention hewed closer to traditional Country formulas. The old Country goal of purifying Parliament by forbidding royal "placemen," or appointees, from serving as MPs was achieved with a clause in the new Constitution stipulating that "no person holding any office under the United States [i.e., in the executive branch], shall be a member of either House during his continuance in office" (Art. I, Sec. 6). Although two-year terms for members of the House of Representatives fell short of the Country's long-standing demand for yearly parliamentary elections ("where annual elections end," the old slogan had it, "tyranny begins"), they were close enough to satisfy all but the most extreme Country stalwarts. Country fears of foreign military adventures were allayed by a plank stipulating that only Congress would have the power to declare war (Art. I, Sec. 8), a requirement that in subsequent years, of course, would prove all too easy to circumvent. And in response to Country fears about political sovereignty in general, the document specified (or, rather, *appeared* to specify, since it would later be argued to the contrary) that the granting of powers to the new federal government would be strictly limited—a concept the Bill of Rights would later underscore by specifying that "powers not delegated to the United States . . . are reserved to the States respectively, or to the people." Ultimately, all power would flow from the people, although only one ruling institution would be popularly elected. But it would be divided up and filtered through a half-dozen or more institutions in order to create a structure that was balanced and stable.

The Constitution was thus a mix of democratic and "republican" elements, which in eighteenth-century parlance meant a fixed, legal structure in which power was distributed among a broad array of forces. Two questions, however, proved nearly insoluble. One was the issue of states' rights. If the thirteen states had been created equal, the convention's job would have been easier, but that was obviously not the case. The states ranged from tiny specks like Rhode Island and Delaware to massive trans-Appalachian empires like Virginia and New York. As a result, the states, particularly the small ones, were jealous not only of the new federal government that was taking shape but of each other. The remedy the framers of the Constitution came up with, as every student of the era knows, was to split the legislature in two in what was formally the British fashion, giving each state equal representation in the upper chamber while apportioning seats on the basis of population in the lower. Legislative power, which was deemed to be the most dangerous of the three forces, would thus be divided and checked against itself, while each state, large or small, would acquire something approaching an equal stake in the new arrangement.

Slavery was a good deal trickier. Under the Articles of Confederation, the issue had smoldered on the back burner. But now that the states were coming together to form a tighter unit, it quickly moved to the fore. On May 30, just four days into the convention, Hamilton, a member of the New York delegation, moved "that the rights of suffrage in the national Legislature ought to be proportioned to the number of free inhabitants."[10] This was explosive because it meant that the Southern states, in which whites were in some cases an outright minority, would be overwhelmed by the burgeoning population of the nonslave North. The temperature inside the tavern where the delegates met promptly rose. Southern delegates would not allow Southern interests to be outvoted by Northerners with whom they felt little in common, while Northerners could hardly be expected to stand by while their voting power was diluted. When Southerners argued that slaves should be counted for the purposes of apportioning seats in Congress even though, as property, they could not be allowed to vote, the irrepressible Elbridge Gerry shot back that if that was to be the case, he wanted Northern horses and cattle to be counted as well.[11] Eventually, the delegates settled on a three-pronged solution. First, the principle of equal state representation in the Senate, which would give the five major slaveholding states a near veto over legislation and an absolute veto over constitutional amendments, was elevated from a promise to an all but ironclad guarantee. This was done with the addition of a few judiciously chosen words to Article V, the amending clause, which stipulated that "no State, without its consent, shall be deprived of its equal suffrage in the Senate." As long as Virginia insisted on the same two votes in the upper chamber as Massachusetts, in other words, it would have them.

Second, even though slaves could not vote, the convention decided that they would be counted as three-fifths of a person for purposes of congressional apportionment (ART. I, SEC. 2), a decision that would eventually give the slave states some twenty-five additional seats in the House and twenty-five extra votes in the electoral college. Finally, each state would be given the right to choose its own "times, places, and manner" for holding Congressional elections (ART. I, SEC. 4) and to determine who could and could not vote (ART. I, SEC. 2), which meant that pro-slave politicians in the South would gain an enormously useful tool for controlling politics in their own bailiwicks.

The combination was enough to render slavery all but impregnable. Slave owners would exercise disproportionate influence in Congress, in the executive branch, and, because the Senate would have veto power over presidential appointments of judges, in the judiciary as well. They would wield an iron veto over constitutional amendments, and they would have the means to see that their home bases were secure as well. Additional protections in the form of a clause requiring the return of runaway slaves (ART. IV, SEC. 2) and an absolute ban on interference with the slave trade until the year 1808 (ART. I, SEC. 9, and ART. V) were merely the icing on the cake. As Charles Cotesworth Pinckney, a delegate from South Carolina, reported to his state legislature:

> We have a security that the general government can never emancipate them, for no such authority is granted, and it is admitted, in all hands, that the general government has no powers but what are expressly granted by the Constitution, and that all rights not expressed were reserved by the several states.[12]

Eventually, of course, it would be this limitation on federal power that would cause the entire constitutional apparatus to collapse during the Civil War. But for the moment, the Constitution seemed to be the perfect compromise, an agreement which left the great majority of delegates feeling that they had come away from the convention with more than they had given up. Indeed, the Constitution not only reflected the spirit of compromise, but entrenched it for generations to come. By splitting government up into so many pieces, the document created in Philadelphia ensured that no one component would be able to get its way without the cooperation of the others. Rather than sharpening disputes, the new constitutional machinery did the opposite—it fairly forced politicians to smooth them over, to seek common ground, to wheel and deal so that differences might be bridged. The new system of government would muddy the waters in order to preserve the peace.

This spirit of compromise and deal making is so intrinsic to American politics that Americans have long forgotten that there is any other way. Yet even in the 1780s it was far from universal. Two years after Philadelphia, the *abbé* Sieyès, leader of the new French National Assembly, helped beat back a proposal by certain *Américainistes* for a bicameral legislature and a system of separation of powers and checks and balances. Sieyes objected to separation of powers for precisely the same reason that the Philadelphia delegates supported it. He *didn't* want a legislative process characterized by compromise and behind-the-scenes deal making. Rather, he wanted an all-powerful, unicameral National Assembly in which debate would be both public and concentrated. Rather than a system that glossed over differences, he wanted one in which differences would be clarified so that debate would be principled and sharp. As the historian R. R. Palmer noted, Sieyès "took a sour satisfaction in preferring principles to common sense."[13] During the Reign of Terror that took hold in France a few years later, the *Américainistes*, who by this point had gone into exile, no doubt felt vindicated. By eschewing compromise, Sieyes had cleared the deck for confrontation of a particularly horrendous sort.

Yet, had he been alive in the 1860s, Sieyès would have been able to take a certain grim satisfaction from a civil war far bloodier than anything that occurred during the French Revolution. By dulling and diffusing debate, he would have no doubt pointed out, the American system did not resolve differences but merely buried them in such a way as to allow them to fester and grow. Rather than preventing confrontation over the slavery issue, the system only delayed the debate, thereby guaranteeing that the showdown would be all the more terrible when it finally arrived.

A few months after the close of the Philadelphia convention, Madison laid out the thinking behind the new constitutional structure in exquisite detail. In *Federalist* No. 10, probably the most important of the eighty-five Federalist Papers that he and Hamilton dashed off during the ratification battle in New York, he addressed himself to the old conundrum of majority rule versus minority rights, private corruption versus public virtue, and passion versus intellect, all of which, according to the eighteenth-century Anglo-American view, were closely related. When a corrupt and selfish minority tried to bend society to its will, Madison wrote, there was no problem. Since the majority held power, as it did to a degree in the proposed new American system, it would have the ability to stop a corrupt minority in its tracks. But what would happen, Madison asked, if "an interested and overbearing *majority*" tried to bend society to its will? In a system based on strict majority rule, there would be nothing to get in its way. Assuming they had the votes—which they unquestionably did in eighteenth-century America—hard-pressed farmers would be able to ram through schemes that Madison regarded as lunacy, plans to flood the economy with worthless "paper money," for instance, "for an abolition of debts, for an equal division of property, or for any other improper or wicked project"—yet they would be unstoppable.[14] But, he went on, the "mixed" system devised in Philadelphia offered a way out. Given the ever present threat of conflict between rich and poor, every state boundary, every division in the proposed new federal structure, would serve as a fire wall preventing popular passions in one part of society from spreading to another. The multiplicity of such fire walls would serve to isolate such outbreaks until good sense could be restored:

> The influence of factious leaders may kindle a flame within their particular States but will be unable to spread a general conflagration through the other States. A religious sect may degenerate into a political faction in a part of the Confederacy; but the variety of sects dispersed over the entire face of it must secure the national councils against any danger from that source.[15]

There was safety in complexity, in other words, just as there had been in sixteenth-century England. Rather than focusing energy, the new system would disperse, muffle, and absorb it.

Two centuries later, it's child's play to pick such logic apart. The chief difficulty lay with the phrase "interested and overbearing majority." For an essentially backward-looking intellectual like Madison, it was hard to think of a majority that would *not* be interested and overbearing, that is, passionate, volatile, and in need of external constraints. Yet such attitudes were already in a state of flux and in the coming decades would undergo a complete reversal. As a later generation of democratic theorists would make clear, the notion of an "interested" majority, in other words, one that was narrow and selfish, was a contradiction in terms since the majority's interests were synonymous with those of the public at large. Thanks to the principle of majority rule, the majority *was* the public. Its interests *were* the public's interests. It could not be overbearing because if the majority was truly sovereign in a democratic society, its power was infinite and there would be no bounds for it to overstep. Thus, for these democratic theorists, such as Jeremy Bentham and James Mill, there was no need for a remedy to the problem of an interested and overbearing majority for the simple reason that an interested and overbearing majority cannot exist.

Ironically for someone so concerned with the need to promote public virtue, Madison had very little concept of what we now call the public interest. He saw society instead as a collection of atomized private interests contending for control. Elsewhere in *Federalist* No. 10, he wrote that in weighing disputes between "a landed interest, a manufacturing interest, [or] a mercantile interest," the legislative branch would have to make "judicial determinations, not indeed concerning the rights of single persons, but concerning the rights of large bodies of citizens."[16] Yet fashioning a public policy entailed more than just picking and choosing among a multitude of private interests. It meant discerning a public interest that would cleanly bisect the interests of private groups in order to benefit society as a whole. After all, disputes between landed and manufacturing interests involved not just farmers, plantation owners, and America's growing artisan class. Rather, they affected numerous other groups as well—city dwellers, for example, who were likely to benefit from a pro-manufacturing policy that would no doubt stimulate urban growth; public-education enthusiasts who realized that industrialization would lead to demands for a better educated workforce; and so on.

Identifying, promoting, and developing this public interest was a way of uniting society and keeping special interests at bay. Yet Madison's strategy was exactly the opposite—to *retard* the development of a public interest and to encourage private interests to proliferate. In the interests of stability, he was creating a political system based on fragmentation, in which thousands of different lobbying groups, everyone from beekeepers to mohair growers, would thrust and grapple for control of the various organs of government. His fear of interested and overbearing majorities drove him to create a system in which a stable, coherent majority would be all but impossible to achieve.

But if Madison mistrusted majority rule, what sort of rule did he favor? The answer was not entirely clear. The Constitution itself seemed confused as to who, ultimately, was to be in charge. The Preamble, for instance, in some of the most famous lines ever written, stated quite unambiguously:

We the People of the United States, in order to form a more perfect Union, establish justice, insure domestic tranquility, provide for the common defense, promote the general welfare, and secure the blessings of liberty to ourselves and our posterity, do ordain and establish this Constitution for the United States of America.

Not the individual states but the people were all-powerful. They were simultaneously canceling one constitution, the disastrous Articles of Confederation, and ordaining another to take its place. As numerous commentators have pointed out, the proposed new Constitution was technically illegal since Article VII, which declared that it would be considered ratified when approved by nine states, was plainly in violation of Article XIII of the Articles of Confederation, which was still the law of the land and which declared that any constitutional change must be approved by all thirteen. Yet such legal fine points were irrelevant. The people were sovereign, as the Preamble seemed to attest. They could therefore make and unmake law as they saw fit.

But by the time the Constitution got around to the amending clause some four thousand words later, the tune had changed. Rather than being all-powerful, it now appeared that the people were severely constrained in modifying the very Constitution they had supposedly established and ordained. Article V, the amending clause, stipulated that any amendment to the Constitution would have to be approved by two-thirds of both houses of Congress plus a simple majority in three-fourths of the states. Even the work of a constitutional convention had to be approved by three-fourths of the states as well. Rather than a simple majority of fifty percent plus one, constitutional change had to be approved, depending how it was computed, by a supermajority of sixty-seven percent, seventy-five percent, or perhaps even more.

Had the barriers to amending the Constitution been lower, the elaborate checks and balances would have been meaningless since the people would have been able to cast them aside anytime they wished. Had they been higher, the system would have been so rigid that it might very well have cracked. Instead, the framers strove for yet another of those delicate balances, in this case a balancing point somewhere midway between "extreme facility, which would render the Constitution too mutable; and that extreme difficulty, which might perpetuate its discovered faults," as Madison described it in The Federalist Papers.[17] Its purpose was to provide just the right combination of strength and flexibility to keep the structure from tumbling in a heap.

The amending clause, which was adopted in Philadelphia with very little debate, amounted to a recognition on the part of the Founders that change of some sort was inevitable. At the same time, the clause represented an effort to slow down change and subject it to permanent regulation. In addition, Article V contained two clauses that actually went further. One, which is now only of historical interest, was a twenty-year ban on any amendment interfering with the slave trade, a flat prohibition from which there was absolutely no appeal. In early 1790, a group of Quakers petitioned Congress to conduct an "impartial inquiry" into "whether . . . it be not in reality within your power to exercise justice and mercy, which, if adhered to, we cannot doubt must produce the abolition of the slave trade."[18] Yet even if every last American had voted to end the trade, Congress would theoretically have been powerless to stop it—or so the Constitution said.

The second exception was the equal suffrage clause, the stipulation that, notwithstanding the tortuous amending process already described, "no state, without its consent, shall be deprived of its equal suffrage in the Senate." While twelve states might agree that it was absurd that Rhode Island would have the same two votes in the Senate as Virginia even though it had less than a tenth its population at the time the Constitution was promulgated, Rhode Islanders had the power to turn their back on the rest of the Republic and just say no. It would continue to enjoy equal representation in perpetuity if that was what it desired. With this one clause, so uncontroversial that it was adopted without formal debate,[19] the convention went beyond trying to slow down change to preventing it altogether. Come what may, this group of men who gathered in Philadelphia in 1787 in effect said, state equality in the upper chamber would be, for all intents and purposes, perpetual.

While the Preamble suggested that the people were sovereign, Article V suggested the contrary. The people were severely hampered from deviating from the plan laid down in Philadelphia. Their power was boundless, yet bounded. As the creators of the Constitution, they were over the law, yet under it. This was the central contradiction in what the Philadelphia delegates had wrought in 1787, one that would bedevil the American Republic, as we shall see, for the next two hundred years.

Hamilton, who had joined Madison in organizing the Philadelphia convention, was the odd man out in this emerging constitutional consensus. Born in Saint Kitts in the Virgin Islands, he moved to Saint Croix as a child and grew up at a time when the island was still nominally under Danish control. Thus, of the half dozen most important Founders (the others being Franklin, Washington, Jefferson, Madison, and John Adams), he was the only foreigner, not only in terms of America but in terms of the British Empire as well.[20] Perhaps this explains why he did not fit very neatly into the Anglo-American Court-Country ideological continuum. On one hand, he had turned into a raging patriot upon moving to New York in his midteens (the Country regarded patriotism as its special province), dashing off incendiary pamphlets and enlisting in the Continental Army at the first opportunity in 1776. On the other hand, he seems to have been comparatively uninfected by hoary old Country myths about ancient liberties and separation of powers. Rather than limited government, he believed in a strong state and a strong army. Instead of Country-style pastoralism, he believed in urbanization and building up an industrial economy much like the one just getting under way in Britain. In contrast to the rather cautious Madison, he was also more radical in his thinking. Madison spent much of the 1780s arguing that the Articles of Confederation needed only a bit of patching up to make them work. Hamilton, a classic young man in a hurry, concluded early on that the structure was unsound and had to be totally rebuilt. As General Washington's right-hand man during much of the Revolutionary War, he knew all too well the futility of trying to weld together thirteen jealous baronies into anything approaching a unified war machine. He collaborated closely with Madison in laying the groundwork for the Philadelphia convention, yet grew impatient once the gathering got under way and soon bailed out for New York. Although a lawyer by training, Hamilton found the atmosphere of legal pettifoggery stifling. "The prevailing apprehension among thinking men is that the Convention, from a fear of shocking the popular opinion, will not go far enough," he wrote Washington, who implored him to return.[21] He wanted to move fast, yet the convention insisted on moving along at a slow walk.

Hamilton's behavior in Philadelphia has earned him the opprobrium of generations of historians, for all the wrong reasons. Three weeks into the convention, he delivered a four-hour speech in which he advanced a theory of government as different from anything the convention had been considering as the Articles of Confederation had been from British parliamentary government. Instead of a federation, he urged the convention to move toward a tightly unified state consisting of a democratic assembly, a lifetime senate, and a lifetime president with both an absolute veto over both national legislation and absolute power to appoint governors of the individual states. Instead of limited powers, he called for a central government that would be sovereign in the fullest sense of the term, one whose unqualified writ would extend to the farthest reaches of the realm. Rather than an equal partner with the states, which is more or less how the other delegates saw the federal government, he wanted a national authority that would be clearly superior, with power to override state legislation whenever it wished. According to Madison's notes of the convention proceedings, the other delegates listened to the speech in silence, although whether it was shocked or bemused silence is impossible to determine.[22] After adjourning, they never mentioned it again. Many concluded, no doubt, that they had a would-be Caesar on their hands, one who was either offering himself up for the role of all-powerful president-for-life or angling to become the power behind the throne. Historians have mostly agreed.

Yet Hamilton's proposal was not what it seemed. It was no less democratic than what the convention was heading toward and possibly more so. Where the Constitution would leave it up to the states to decide who could vote in congressional elections, Hamilton's plan specified that the proposed national assembly would be elected "by the people," which meant it would be up to the national authorities to determine who could vote and who could not. The difference was crucial because it meant that voting regulations would have to be uniform from one end of the country to the other. If free blacks were permitted to vote in some states (as they were in much of the North), they would have to be in all—an idea with stunning implications for Southern slave owners. Under Hamilton's plan, Senate seats would also be apportioned according to population rather than by state—equal state representation, he declared, "shocks too much the ideas of justice and every human feeling"[23]—which was fairer and more egalitarian, while state power in general would have been pared to a minimum.

Hamilton's proposals could conceivably have led to a dictatorship, as subsequent historians assumed, yet this was exceedingly unlikely in a society as liberal as the United States. Rather, the results would likely have been much closer to France under de Gaulle. As an honor-bound country gentleman with a horror of partisan politics, Washington, virtually the unanimous choice for head of state, would undoubtedly have preferred to preside over the country from afar and remain above the fray. Day-to-day governance would very likely have passed to the legislative branch. Hamilton might have thrown a monkey wrench into the works had he decided to set up shop in the executive branch as Washington's all-purpose aide-de-camp. But if he chose the legislative route instead by running for the national assembly, he would very likely have emerged as an American prime minister, a new Walpole, only one that was far more principled and intellectual than the original version. In the event of a conflict between the two branches, there also would be little doubt as to the outcome. In an age of growing popular democracy, an assembly freshly endorsed by the people in national elections would have had an inestimable advantage over a chief executive elected years earlier for life. His popular mandate would be musty and aged, while theirs would be recent and strong. However unlimited the president's power on paper, it seems likely that eventually he would have had to defer to the people's representatives, much as the House of Lords and the Crown in Britain had been deferring to the House of Commons since the early eighteenth century.

Hamilton was still a man of the eighteenth century. Nonetheless, he was clearly moving toward a kind of popular politics that would be national in scope and highly focused. This was the kind of popular politics that would begin taking shape in France after 1789 but would remain worlds apart from the American version for decades to come. By resolving the issue of sovereignty at the outset, at least in terms of the national government as a whole, his plan would have cut short two centuries of tedious debate over federal prerogatives versus states' rights. Rather than encouraging a form of politics that was dithering and indecisive, borne aloft on great billows of empty rhetoric, the unitary republic he was proposing would have encouraged a different kind of politics, one that was sharp and crisp by virtue of being organized around a single chamber. Instead of muddying the waters, it would have encouraged debate that was strong and concentrated.

There would also have been no question about the ability of such a system to deal vigorously with the slavery issue. Since the central government would be omnipotent as far as all things political were concerned, it would have been able to sweep away any and all constitutional impediments with a wave of its hand. In a national assembly of the type Hamilton was describing, Northern whites would have enjoyed a three-to-two edge over Southern whites, while Southerners who actually owned slaves would have been in an even more extreme minority. Since it would have added to their electoral strength, Northern whites would have had an incentive to see that free blacks were given the vote rather than to disenfranchise them, which was the pattern throughout the North in the 1820s and 1830s.[24] Racism would hardly have vanished overnight. Yet the nonslave majority would not have found itself frustrated at every turn by a slaveholding minority that enjoyed special protection under an ironclad Constitution.

Hamilton represents a lost constitutional opportunity in U.S. history, an alternate route of political development that seemed to open up in the Federalist era but was soon squeezed shut by Jefferson's overwhelming victory in the elections of 1800. Probably the best thing written about Hamilton and the Constitution is to be found in R. R. Palmer's magisterial *Age of the Democratic Revolution*, a two-volume study published 1959–64, which—very unusual for an American work of history—went to great lengths to place the Revolution and the Constitution in a broader, more global context. At a time when liberal historians were celebrating Madison and Jefferson as champions of the common man and excoriating Hamilton as a capitalist authoritarian, Palmer argued that Hamilton, despite his hostility toward the French Revolution, was actually more of a forward-looking revolutionary, more of a Jacobin, than either he or his opponents realized. Hamilton, he wrote,

> was more impatient of the compromises on which the federal constitution rested, he wanted to make over the country, and he would have liked, if he could, to abolish the states (especially Virginia) and replace them with small *departements* created by a national government, as in the French and other revolutionary republics in Europe. Jefferson . . . spoke for

a kind of liberty and equality that had long existed in America . . . a liberty that meant freedom from government, and an equality of the kind that obtained among yeoman farmers—a way of life that had been threatened by British policy before 1775, and was threatened by Hamiltonian policy after 1790.[25]

What made this difficult for later generations to comprehend, Palmer continued, is that in America at the time, just as in the British world generally, the usual political categories were jumbled and confused. In France, rural landowners after 1789 were generally conservative and counterrevolutionary. Yet the large-scale landowning element in the United States, the Southern plantation owners, were second to none in cheering on the new French tricolor. In France, tradesmen and small merchants, known collectively as the *sans-culottes*, were the backbone of the revolution. In America, the same urban elements tended for various economic and political reasons to be pro-British and anti-French. Left was Right, and Right was Left, to use a couple of terms that only came into popular usage with the French Revolution.

While Jefferson, the American ambassador to France in the late 1780s, was typical of his fellow Virginians in his ardor for all things French, Palmer pointed out that his views at the time of the French Revolution were actually closer to those of the conservative opposition, those dreamy aristocrats who believed that the answer to the crisis of the monarchy was to return to a decentralized feudal never-never land where clerics, nobles, and peasants lived in rural harmony. Hamilton, similarly, was much closer to those restless young modernizers who were inspired by the events in Paris to try to turn Europe upside down. If not actually a fan of *liberté, égalité,* and *fraternité,* he shared in the revolutionaries' desire to sweep away all the old forms of government and usher in the new. As Palmer pointed out, the great conflict between the Northern Hamiltonians and Southern Jeffersonians had its parallel in several European countries in the 1780s and

1790s—in Switzerland, for instance, where a conflict was beginning to take shape between the conservative southern cantons, for whom freedom meant a return to time-honored Alpine ways, and French-style radicals in the northern cities, who were eager to modernize and centralize; and in Holland and Belgium, where provincial tradition-alists and urban democrats were also at each others' throats. The difference lay in the outcome. Where the modernizers were able to prevail in countries touched by the French Revolution, at least until the defeat of Napoleon in 1815, in America, thanks to the Jeffersonian "Revolution of 1800," they were quickly overthrown.

Jefferson may have been more democratic in some respects, but his idea of democracy was essentially reactionary—rural, arcadian, premodern. Urban radicalism filled him with disgust. As he declared in 1783:

> Those who labor in the earth are the chosen people of God, if ever he had a chosen people, whose breasts he has made his peculiar deposit for substantial and genuine virtue. . . . The mobs of great cities add just so much to the support of pure government, as sores do to the strength of the human body.[26]

Hamilton, by the same token, was less democratic but more at home in this new urban culture. City folk, he argued in his famous "Report on Manufactures," written in late 1791, were the real seeds of a new America. Where subsistence farmers were content to sit back and watch the corn grow thanks to cheap land and a favorable climate, the urban population was as busy as ants, constantly working, schem-ing, and planning. City dwellers opened businesses, sought out new markets, and developed new modes of production. Unlike the anti-social, anti-intellectual subsistence farmers celebrated by the Jeffer-sonians, they were intellectually restless and open to new ideas.

Hamilton was much closer to the Jacobins in relation to another issue—race. Like the French revolutionaries who freed the slaves in Haiti and other French colonies, Hamilton detested slavery and helped form one of the first antislavery societies in New York. He argued that returning runaway slaves to their owners was as *"odious and immoral* a thing as can be conceived" and during the Revolutionary War had urged the formation of an all-black battalion in which slaves would earn their freedom by fighting for independence. "I have not the least doubt that the negros [sic] will make very excellent soldiers," he wrote, "for their natural faculties are probably as good as ours."[27] Jefferson, by contrast, insisted on the right of Southerners to take their slaves with them as they settled the western frontier and in his later years even opposed the Missouri Compromise, which barred slavery in the northern territories.

The issues behind the Hamilton-Jefferson split were economic and philosophical. Hamilton favored a flexible constitution and a strong state, while the Jeffersonians favored a rigid constitution and a weak state. Hamilton favored intensive development and was cool to western expansion, while the Jeffersonians favored extensive development across the entire continent. As the historian John Murrin observed:

> Hamilton . . . hoped that America by 1900 would be a dramatically different place from what it was in 1800. Jefferson, by contrast, wanted the economy of the United States in 1900 to look pretty much the same as it did in 1800, except that it would accommodate vastly more people over a much greater space.[28]

Hamilton was also in favor of consolidating public debt under the control of the central government, both as a means of asserting national power over the states and of creating a framework for large-scale capitalist development. He led the charge for a national bank and, as he indicated in his "Report on Manufactures," believed passionately in what Americans now call industrial policy and the French call *dirigisme,* a policy of using government grants, tariffs, and tax policy to shape and encourage industrial growth. Jefferson and Madison opposed a national bank for the same reason that Country politicians had opposed formation of the Bank of England back in

1694—out of sheer terror over the capitalist economic forces such projects would unleash.

The Hamilton-Jefferson rift began midway through Washington's first term as a typical American debate over the meaning of a legal text, in this case the interstate commerce clause in Article I. In a remarkable anticipation of New Deal arguments, Hamilton contended that by giving Congress power to regulate commerce between the states, the Constitution, in effect, had given it power to regulate commerce *within* them as well. "What regulation of commerce," he asked, "does not extend to the internal commerce of every state?"[29] In an equally astonishing feat of legal legerdemain, he also argued that the sweeping goals set forth in the Preamble, in combination with the clause in Article I giving Congress the right to do everything "necessary and proper" to fulfill its powers under the Constitution, added up to a sweeping grant of power for the legislative branch to do whatever it wanted, wherever it wanted, to ensure domestic tranquility, promote the general welfare, and the like. "Necessary," he argued, meant "needful, requisite, incidental, useful, or conducive to"—anything, in other words, that was convenient or opportune.

> If the end be clearly comprehended within any of the specified powers, and if the measure have an obvious relation to that end, and is not forbidden by any particular provision of the Constitution, it may safely be deemed to come within the compass of the national authority.[30]

Thus, even though the Philadelphia convention had turned its back on Hamilton's plea for an unlimited national government, he now argued that that was what the convention had wound up creating after all. This was sovereignty through the back door and was all but designed to drive Country stalwarts into a frenzy.

Madison and Jefferson were not long in responding. In early 1791, Madison, who had been elected to the House from Virginia, took to the floor to denounce Hamilton's proposal for a national bank as unconstitutional. Jefferson, a member of the cabinet, followed up with a lengthy memo to the president taking issue with Hamilton's interpretation of "necessary and proper." If "necessary" meant all the things Hamilton said it did, he wrote, then there was no measure "which ingenuity may not torture into a *convenience, in some way or other.* . . ." Whatever the federal government wanted to do, it could. Limited government would cease to exist. Moreover, if Congress indeed had the "power to do whatever would be good for the United States," then considering that members "would be the sole judge of the good or evil, it would be also a power to do whatever evil they pleased."[31] Congress would be the judge of its own actions and would be subject to no checks and balances other than its own. As Madison had argued in the Federalist Papers: "The accumulation of all powers, legislative, executive, and judiciary, in the same hands, whether of one, a few, or many, and whether hereditary, self-appointed, or elective, may be justly pronounced the very definition of tyranny."[32] Yet this was precisely what Hamilton was proposing.

The constitutional battle raged throughout the decade. Where Hamilton pushed for an ever stronger national government, Jefferson and Madison fought back tooth and nail. In 1796, Hamilton's Federalists narrowly held on to the presidency despite a strong challenge from Jefferson and Madison's new Republican Party (soon to be renamed the Democrats). By 1798, the two sides seemed to be on the verge of civil war. The Federalists had rammed the Alien and Sedition Acts through Congress, which aimed to nip Republicanism in the bud, while Madison and Jefferson, anticipating Southern arguments of the 1830s and later, had responded by convincing state legislators in Virginia and Kentucky to approve resolutions arguing that the Constitution was nothing more than an interstate compact that would be dissolved if the federal government continued to overstep its bounds. Worries over an impending conflict with Napoleon added fuel to the fire. The Federalist-controlled Congress authorized Hamilton to begin building up a national army to counter reputed French plans for an invasion of Virginia, where Bonaparte would undoubtedly find numerous friends and *collaborateurs* among disaffected Republican planters. Rather than fearing such an invasion, Hamilton welcomed the prospect as an opportunity to crush the Southern planters once and for all and to break up the giant state of Virginia "into more manageable jurisdictions."[33] A constitutional amendment allowing Congress to subdivide the states, he said, would be "indispensable to securing the government and . . . the union."[34] Hamilton immediately set about "Federalizing" the new army, weeding out officers suspected of Republican sympathies.[35] Sweeping Federalist victories in the 1798 congressional elections strengthened his hand. As Palmer observed, Hamilton was by now "the nearest thing the United States ever produced to a Bonaparte."[36] As a boy, he had once confided in a friend that what he wanted most was a war to get him out of Saint Croix; now he was clearly wishing for one again to get rid of Jefferson's Republicans.[37] As his friend Gouverneur Morris remarked:

> He well knew that his favorite form [of government] was inadmissable, unless as the result of civil war; and I suspect that his belief in that which he called an approaching crisis arose from a conviction that the kind of government most suitable, in his opinion, to this extensive country, could be established in no other way.[38]

Yet Hamilton had seriously overreached. His political judgment, uncannily accurate during the early part of the decade, had begun failing him toward the end. President John Adams negotiated a peace treaty with the French behind his back, which averted the threat (or promise) of an invasion and left him high and dry as the head of an army for which there was no longer any use. Voters were shocked to see the Alien and Sedition Acts used to put Republican journalists in jail and were even more put off when the federal government used unnecessarily brutal means in quashing a revolt among German-speaking farmers in eastern Pennsylvania in 1799. The Federalists were beginning to look like arrogant bullies. The elections in 1800 resulted in a sweeping Republican victory that all but finished the Federalists off as a national electoral force.

The election also finished off the idea of a sovereign national government. Hamilton was trying to take a Country Constitution in a direction it did not want to go—that is, toward a form of government that would be strong, flexible, and utilitarian. The Federalists, or at least their Madisonian wing, had created the Constitution, but now that Madison and Jefferson had broken away, the document worked to the Hamiltonians' disadvantage. The three-fifths clause, to begin with the most obvious, artificially boosted the clout of Southern planters, who had largely gone over to the Jeffersonian side. But the very *logic* of checks and balances worked against them as well. If the federal government's authority was essentially unlimited, as Hamilton claimed, then those parts of the Constitution that painstakingly outlined the powers of each branch were little more than window dressing. This was something the mass of Americans would not accept. The Constitution was fresh and new, a body of abstruse judicial commentary had not yet grown up around it, so any deviation from a strict reading of the text was bound to seem suspect. Moreover, the Federalists' descent into authoritarianism seemed to confirm everything the Country opposition had said about the relationship between law and power. Law existed to restrain power. Freedom was impossible without a strong and strict constitution to rein in government. From a Country perspective, it was a very short step from Hamilton's loose interpretation of the "necessary and proper" clause at the beginning of the decade to the Federalist abuses at the end. More than a dozen years earlier, Hamilton had argued in *Federalist* No. 1 that "vigor of government is essential to the security of liberty."[39] Now it seemed that strong, vigorous government was a threat to liberty.

Although finished as an organized political force, the Federalists were not completely extinguished ideologically. Henceforth, elements of the Hamiltonian program began to seep back into American politics. John Marshall, a Virginia Federalist whom John Adams had appointed chief justice in the waning days of his presidency, turned the Supreme Court into a Federalist redoubt, using it to rein in states' rights and to prevent local politicians from interfering with the sanctity of business contracts, an important step in the Hamiltonian program of turning the entire country into a single, unobstructed free-trade zone. John C. Calhoun, an economic nationalist before becoming a bitter states' rights advocate, began pushing after the War of 1812 for a neo-Hamiltonian program of high tariffs to protect nascent American industries and for federally sponsored roads and canals to knit the country closer together. As he told one of Hamilton's sons, Hamilton's ideas on economic development were "the only true policy for the country."[40] Moreover, as the economic pace picked up, the very idea of America as a small-scale agrarian democracy seemed more and more antique. Rather, the rhythms of American life were becoming more urban, more industrial, more Hamiltonian. As a Baltimore editor exulted in 1815:

> Everywhere the sound of the axe is heard opening the forest to the sun, and claiming for agriculture the range of the buffalo. Our cities grow and towns rise up as by magic. . . . The busy hum of ten thousand wheels fills our seaports, and the sound of the spindle and the loom succeeds the yell of the savage or the screech of the night owl in the later wilderness of the interior.[41]

This was the future that Hamilton welcomed and that Jefferson had dreaded, although subsequent Republicans found it easier to embrace.

Nonetheless, despite such changes, the basic constitutional framework remained essentially Jeffersonian. Cities were expanding, industry was taking root, yet limited government was still seen as the key to the preservation of liberty. Even when those limits were bent so that Congress could charter a second national bank founded in 1816 or embark on a program of internal improvements, they were always lurking in the background, ready to reimpose their will at a moment's notice. In 1791, at the start of the Jeffersonian-Hamiltonian rift, Jefferson had maintained that the federal government lacked proper authority to incorporate a national agricultural society, much less a national bank.[42] In 1800, he went a step further by arguing that the federal mandate extended to little more than foreign affairs:

The true theory of our Constitution is . . . that the states are independent as to everything within themselves, & united as to everything respecting foreign nations. Let the general government be reduced to foreign concerns only, and let our affairs be disentangled from those of all other nations, except as to commerce, which the merchants will manage the better, the more they are left free to manage for themselves, and our general government may be reduced to a very simple organization, & a very inexpensive one; a few plain duties to be performed by a few servants.[43]

Subsequently, Jefferson did everything in his power to see to it that this sort of constitutional minimalism was enforced. In 1805, he informed his treasury secretary, Albert Gallatin, that federal funds could be spent on canals, roads, education, and other internal improvements only if a constitutional amendment was approved authorizing such expenditures—something which, as he knew, was exceedingly unlikely.[44] In 1817, Madison vetoed a canal- and road-building measure on the grounds that it allowed Congress to insinuate itself deeply into local affairs and thereby threatened states' rights— not coincidentally the same reason cited by Country gentlemen in opposing a national highway program in England a century earlier.[45] In 1822, President James Monroe, the third member of the so-called Virginia Dynasty, vetoed on constitutional grounds a bill authorizing tolls to be charged on the National Highway to generate revenue for repairs. Charging tolls represented an extension of federal power that was too dangerous to be allowed. In 1819, Chief Justice John Marshall had tried to reverse the ideological pendulum by declaring in *Mc-Culloch v. Maryland* that "though limited in its powers," the federal government was "supreme within its sphere of action." This was a partial return to Hamilton's necessary-and-proper thesis. Yet the fact remained that the "sphere of action" was being defined ever more narrowly. If the federal government was supreme, it was supreme over an exceedingly small realm.

This period was the golden age of constitutional immutability. Where Federalists had seen the Constitution as a framework of government, Jeffersonians tended to see it as a *contract*, static and immutable, between the people, the states, and the federal authorities. The document was the closest thing to a sovereign power in the United States, since its powers were superior to those of the people or their government. For more than sixty years after passage of the Twelfth Amendment, a purely technical modification providing for the separate election of president and vice president, no further constitutional changes were approved. The very idea seemed faintly heretical. Any attempt to alter the terms of the agreement of 1787–88 would throw the entire contract into question. In 1815, representatives of five New England states met in Hartford, Connecticut, to demand abolition of the three-fifths clause, which, as New York governor De Witt Clinton would later put it, subjected the burgeoning cities of the North "to the domineering aristocracy of Virginia."[46] Yet it was too late. The North was locked in. As Hamilton had foreseen, only a civil war could set it free.

3

BREAKTHROUGH
IN BRITAIN

THE TRAGEDY of Alexander Hamilton is that he was never quite able to escape the clutches of the eighteenth century. He had a long list of things he wanted government to accomplish, yet the only kind of government that eighteenth-century ideology allowed for was either strong and authoritarian or weak, democratic, and decentralized. Hamilton chose vigor over weakness, which is why his authoritarianism became more and more pronounced the harder he tried to make the system do his bidding. Ultimately, his strategy failed. The rising democratic temper of the times refused to permit an authoritarian solution to the problem of government. In the end, it was left to a quirky young Londoner named Jeremy Bentham to show how government could be vigorous, effective, *and* democratic. Bentham, a lawyer who hated law and refused to practice, spent more than thirty years working his way through the problem. When at last he succeeded, he triggered a revolution that, while less dramatic than the one in France, was hardly less sweeping in its consequences.

Britain also entered a constitutional deep freeze during this period when the French Revolution shook the British establishment as few other events had before. The late unpleasantness in America had been something of a family quarrel about the nature of the Ancient Constitution. But the events in France were something very different, a social explosion of volcanic proportions that was practically on England's doorstep. It was a revolt against law, monarchy, and all else that the British elite held sacred. The Gordon Riots of 1780, two weeks of arson and violence that had set much of London ablaze, were a reminder that the British ruling class was sitting atop its own urban tinderbox. One spark from Paris and the entire structure could go off.

The result was a quarter century of repression, a long, dark winter of political despair from the point of view of political reformers that was comparable in certain respects to McCarthyism in the United States after World War II or the great Red scare after World War I. The right of habeas corpus was suspended, and reform organizations were broken up and their leaders prosecuted for treason. Britain's unwritten but nonetheless potent constitution was frozen in place for more than a generation. The Whig leader and essayist Edmund Burke had been a liberal during the American crisis but underwent a metamorphosis after 1789 and emerged as a deep, almost mystical reactionary. The British constitution, he wrote, was not merely a convenient or effective form of government but a timeless bond "between those who are living, those who are dead, and those who are to be born."[1] Consequently, citizens were powerless to alter the essential political framework because, as "temporary possessors and life-renters," they merely held the nation in trust for the other two groups.[2] In 1793, a Scottish judge thundered as he sentenced a British radical to fourteen years' exile in Australia: "The British constitution is the best there ever was since the creation of the world and it is not possible to make it better."³ Since change could only be for the worse, change was strictly forbidden. Britain's emergence as leader of the anti-Napoleonic coalition caused the freeze to deepen even further, so that by Waterloo it seemed as if the very idea of constitutional reform had been banished from the landscape. Britons could say anything they wanted as long as they did not question the political structure. They were free because their constitution was timeless and unbending.

Nowadays, it is tempting to dismiss this sort of unthinking resistance to change as blind stupidity. That it *was*, but it had been vindicated by years of experience. In 1790, Burke had predicted that those "petulant, assuming, short-sighted coxcombs of philosophy" who had taken charge of the French Revolution would lead the country to ruin,⁴ and, in the eyes of the British establishment, that was exactly what had happened. Where the French had opened themselves up to newfangled notions about popular sovereignty and the rights of man, the British had stopped up their ears and emerged victorious. The British, Burke wrote, were like "thousands of great cattle . . . [who] chew the cud and are silent" while grasshoppers buzzed at their feet.

> Thanks to our sullen resistance to innovation, thanks to the cold sluggishness of our natural character, we still bear the stamp of our forefathers. We have not . . . lost the generosity and dignity of thinking of the fourteenth century; nor as yet have we subtilized ourselves into savages. We are not the converts of Rousseau; we are not the disciples of Voltaire; Helvétius has made no progress amongst us. Atheists are not our preachers; madmen are not our lawgivers.⁵

Normally, it would not be very flattering to compare a people to a herd of cattle. Yet ignorance was strength, as far as propagandists like Burke were concerned, and slavery to ancient ways was freedom.

Moreover, such ideas were *constitutional*, which is to say they were part and parcel of the very idea of an Ancient Constitution. The important thing about the Ancient Constitution was that it was *not* something that individuals had created in order to improve English government, but an institution that had existed since time immemorial, hovering above English society like a cloud. "Magna Charta is such a fellow that he will have no sovereign," Sir Edward Coke, the leading legal authority of the late sixteenth and early seventeenth centuries, had declared, meaning that the law was superior to any earthly power. In his *Commentaries on the Laws of England,* written in the 1760s, Sir William Blackstone had taken Coke's theory that "no man ought to be wiser than the law" and given it an ingenious spin. Whereas individually the king, the House of Lords, or the House of Commons might be mistaken on some point or other, he explained, together "they jointly impel the machine of government in a direction different from what either, acting by itself, would have done . . . a direction which constitutes the true line of liberty and happiness of the country."[6] Each of the components might be wrong, in other words, yet the judgment of the whole was always right.

Ideas like these existed for one purpose only: to preserve the status quo. Flogging sailors half to death and hanging preadolescent pickpockets might *seem* bad in isolation, yet, according to panegyrists like Blackstone and Burke, these acts were part of a coherent whole that was unquestionably great. The late eighteenth century was also the heyday of a system of wide-open, semiofficial corruption in which royal sinecures and seats in Parliament were bought and sold like bushels of wheat. This too was part of British greatness. The political structure was festooned with quaintly named titles and sinecures—Groom of the Bedchamber, Master of the Jewel Office, Clerk of the Venison Warrants, Master of the Hamper, and so on—that existed only to serve the greed of the wealthy and the ambitious.[7] One political operator of the day had snared a half-dozen lucrative posts for himself, none of which required him to perform a single duty beyond traveling to the royal mint once a week to down a free dinner.[8] Yet "Old Corruption," as it was fondly called, was "right" because it was the grease that allowed the wheels of government to turn. It was essential to the Court party's concept of the English constitution and was therefore not to be disturbed.

Jeremy Bentham, the Londoner who did so much to overturn such assumptions, never quite got the message, however. Like Hamilton, Bentham was educated in the law. But that is where any resemblance between the two men ceased. Hamilton was charming, dapper, and a ladies' man; Bentham was shy, peculiar, and a lifelong bachelor. Where Hamilton saw action during the Revolutionary War and, after 1789, created an entire federal government nearly from scratch, Bentham never got near a uniform, never fired a gun, and never held office. And though Hamilton had little formal schooling, Bentham was, if anything, overeducated. Born into a comfortable middle-class family in 1748, he was a child prodigy who was studying Latin by age three and had entered Oxford by age twelve. He was unhappy at Oxford, an intellectual backwater at the time geared mainly to turning out Anglican clergy and providing idle young aristocrats with a gloss of culture. Yet he was equally unhappy at the Inns of Court, the medieval law school in the City of London. In 1769, he was called to the bar, as the British say, but chose never to practice. He resolved instead to make his living with his pen. Thereafter, he spent nearly his entire adult life behind a desk covering thousands of pages with minutely detailed plans for model governments, prisons, and the like, some seventy thousand sheets of manuscript in all, which his faithful young disciples then hacked into shape and published.

A Fragment on Government, a slim volume that Bentham published in 1776, marked his debut. 1776, of course, was a very big year, one that saw the appearance of Edward Gibbon's *Decline and Fall of the Roman Empire*, Adam Smith's *Wealth of Nations*, as well as Jefferson's Declaration of Independence. Yet *A Fragment*, in its own curious way, was the most revolutionary of the lot. An extended attack on Blackstone's best-selling *Commentaries on the Laws of England*, which had proved a publishing sensation when it appeared the previous decade, it was Bentham's effort to demolish the age-old notion of the law as a mysterious and unapproachable corpus of wisdom and learning. This was the view embraced by Blackstone and every other legal authority of the day, yet, from Bentham's point of view, it was sheer humbug. As he knew from his legal studies, British law was neither wise nor profound. Rather, it was filled with parliamentary statutes and hair-splitting judicial decisions that had piled up over the centuries, a tangle of technicalities and convoluted procedures whose only purpose, as far as Bentham could tell, was to waste time and allow barristers to wring more fees out of their clients. It had survived so long in this condition only because people like Blackstone promoted an attitude of semi-religious veneration and awe rather than scrutiny, skepticism, and analysis.

A Fragment was Bentham's effort to knock Blackstone off his pedestal and show how all this talk of mystery and profundity promoted "a spirit of obsequious *quietism*" that made reform all but impossible.[9] It was also an effort to make himself rich and famous by publicly demolishing a best-selling author. But the book was a flop. Part of the problem was his writing style, which was quirky, repetitive, and close to unreadable. But another shortcoming was his ideas, which were so novel as to be barely comprehensible to the bulk of the reading public. A few influential individuals managed to wade through his prose, but otherwise one of the most radical books of its time went largely unread for more than a generation.

Stung and confused, Bentham withdrew into a kind of internal exile. He retreated to the privacy of his study, where he spent the next several years writing for "the desk drawer," as Soviet intellectuals would put it in the 1970s. He traveled to Russia, where his younger brother had gotten a job as a technical adviser to Catherine the Great, turned out another book, *The Principles of Morals and Legislation*, in 1789, and then invested more than a decade in trying to interest Parliament in a new type of prison, the "Panopticon," designed in such a manner as to allow a single warden to monitor the activities of hundreds of prisoners at a time. Parliament was unpersuaded as to the merits of the idea, whereupon Bentham found himself out in the cold once again.

The ice began to crack in 1802 when a French admirer brought out an edition of his work that brought him growing attention on the Continent. In 1808, an energetic young Scotsman named James Mill (father of John Stuart Mill) sought him out after reading some of his works and helped put him in touch with a group of talented young politicians and would-be reformers. By the teens and twenties, when the establishment's hold on power was visibly loosening, Bentham was becoming famous. He was "the hermit of Queen Square Place," a thoroughgoing English eccentric who surrounded himself with handsome young acolytes, turned away visitors at the door, dined on vegetables and springwater, and employed a jokey, schoolboyish vocabulary in which an after-dinner stroll became a "postprandial circumgyration." Aaron Burr, who was able to gain admission into the great man's presence, praised his "inexhaustible goodness," although others found him at this point to be vain, childish, and cranky.[10]

Yet Bentham was the seminal figure of his age, the political thinker who did most to bridge the gap between the classical age of the eighteenth century, in which balance and symmetry were all, and the nineteenth-century age of progress, with its great emphasis on dynamic change and forward motion. Large sectors of the reading public viewed him and his fellow utilitarians with horror as mad radicals out to strip away tradition and religion in the name of progress and reform. According to Macaulay, no one was more unpopular.[11] Yet no one proved more influential. More than a century after his death, Bertrand Russell pronounced his influence "astonishingly great." John Maynard Keynes, who fully shared in the Bloomsbury group's disdain of utilitarianism, described him as "the worm which has been gnawing at the insides of modern civilization and is responsible for its present moral decay."[12] Although most historians dismissed Bentham's Panopticon as a quixotic venture that was doomed to failure, the French philosopher Michel Foucault described the proposal as a kind of founding document for an industrial age based on mass production, mass observation, and mass control.[13]

Bentham's career was a tribute to the wonders of the *idée fixe*. He began with a notion that had been buzzing around for years in the works of the Italian legal theorist Cesare Beccaria, the French philosopher Claude Helvétius, and even Benjamin Franklin—the notion, as Bentham put it, that "it is the greatest happiness of the greatest number that is the measure of right and wrong."[14] Yet if the idea was unoriginal, Bentham's genius was to use it as an all-purpose yardstick for measuring whether laws and institutions were performing up to par. If an institution was contributing to the greatest happiness, it would be allowed to stay. If it was not, out it would have to go, no matter how ancient, august, or tradition-laden it might be. Allowing it to linger a moment more than necessary meant reducing the sum of human happiness, which was illogical. Bentham's "hedonic calculus" was ruthless and unsparing. It was not *a* consideration, but *the* consideration in judging the worth of human institutions from ancient times to the present.

This was rationalism, but rationalism of a very different sort from that practiced by either the American Founders or the French *philosophes* who had made the term famous. Bentham's method was to break each problem down into its component parts, isolate the source of confusion, and then take prompt action to remove it. He was tireless in ferreting out contradictions and inconsistencies. The Declaration of Independence, for instance, struck him as "a hodge-podge of confusion and absurdity in which the theory to be proved is all along taken for granted."[15] Rather than holding certain truths to be self-evident, he believed that Jefferson should have taken the time to demonstrate why all men should be considered equal and what a newly independent America would do to advance the cause of human equality. He was equally hard on the French Declaration of the Rights of Man and the Citizen on the grounds that rights were not inherent in the individual, but something that individuals created en masse through government.[16] Although he lavishly praised the Federalist Papers, it is difficult to believe that he actually made his way through Madison and Hamilton's mass of contradictions without throwing them on the fire.[17]

Bentham started out his career as a democrat but later veered right in response to the French Revolution. Not unlike Hamilton, he became something of an authoritarian reformer, someone who was forever trying to catch the ear of a despot like Catherine the Great or some other well-placed person whom he could win over to his point of view. "I was . . . a great reformist," he later explained, "but never suspected that the people in power were against reform. I supposed that they only wanted to know what was good in order to embrace it."[18] The hookup with James Mill sent him leftward again to the point where he eventually emerged among the most uncompromising of English radicals. Rather than looking for friends in high places, he now believed there was a conspiracy among the wealthy and well-born to prevent reform at the expense of the people.

The idea of popular democracy allowed Bentham to solve the chief problem facing his theoretical system, which was how to compute where the greatest good for the greatest number might actually lie. In his predemocratic phase, the answer had been rather vague. Either it was up to the social engineer or the enlightened political leader to determine, or in the case of basic reforms involving public hygiene and education, the answer was so obvious as to be beyond dispute. After his democratic conversion, the answer became easier. It was up to the greatest number themselves to determine what constituted the greatest good.

To today's readers, a breakthrough of this sort may seem less than earthshaking. Yet it allowed Bentham to toss out the entire body of eighteenth-century political science as understood by Madison, Hamilton, Blackstone, and Burke. Where the eighteenth-century thinkers regarded democracy as inherently emotional and disorderly, Bentham conceived of a new kind of democracy that would be intellectual and analytical. Guided by the principle of the greatest good for the greatest number, the people would learn to abjure emotionalism just as they had learned to abjure medieval superstition. Since the people would measure all aspects of governmental performance—serving as judge, jury, and Lord High Executioner all at once—there was also no reason to fragment the people and divide them against themselves. Quite the contrary, the majority should be in a position to determine its interest in as clear and unencumbered a fashion as possible. The only checks and balances that made sense to Bentham and his followers were those exerted by the voters through frequent elections. "The efficient cause of constitutional liberty," he wrote as early as 1790, ". . . is not the division of power among the different classes of men entrusted with it but the dependence immediate or mediate of all of them on the body of the people."[19] "Balance! balance!" he wrote on another occasion. "Know ye not, that in a machine of any kind, when forces balance each other, the machine is at a stand? . . . Know ye not . . . that, in the case of the body *natural,* so in the case of the body *politic,* when motion ceases, the body dies?"[20] Instead of the Madisonian concept of government as a restraint on human passions, he wanted government that was quick and responsive to human needs.

Since the people were all-powerful, Bentham also believed that any government they created must be all-powerful as well. The only limits were those that the people imposed themselves, which, in their omnipotence, they could do away with anytime they wished. In perhaps the most fundamental break with eighteenth-century ideology of all, Bentham married the concept of democracy with the idea of political progress. Previously, people had thought of democracy either in terms of the Greek city-states or sturdy Anglo-Saxon yeomen battling to defend their ancient liberties against the Norman invaders. In Bentham's hands, democratic reform was redefined so that it meant moving forward to something different and better, not returning to a long-lost golden age. Bentham reviled the Court Whigs, but, as J. G. A. Pocock has pointed out, he was even more distant from the Country opposition.[21] He rejected Country-style technological pessimism and instead anticipated the kind of sunny, optimistic liberalism of the later nineteenth century, in which it was believed that no problem was so intractable that it could not be solved with the application of a bit of science, reason, and practical know-how.

Bentham honed his skills during the long post-1789 ice age by seizing on various constitutional myths and ripping them to shreds.

The greater the shibboleth, the more enthusiastic the demolition. Subservience to legal and constitutional precedent, he wrote in his highly amusing *Book of Fallacies*, meant that "the aggregate body of the living would remain for ever in subjection to an inexorable tyranny, exercised, as it were, by the aggregate body of the dead."[22] Constitution worship was equally mindless. "Rally round the constitution," he observed sarcastically,

> . . . that is, rally round waste, rally round depredation, rally round oppression, rally round corruption, rally round election terrorism, rally round imposture—imposture on the hustings, imposture in the Honorable House, imposture in every judiciary.[23]

Bentham also favored voting rights for women—how else to obtain the greatest good of the greatest number if half of humankind was disenfranchised?—and, more astonishingly, legalization of prostitution and homosexuality. Noting that the law of the day described homosexuality as an "offense against the safety of individuals," he wondered, "How a voluntary act of this sort by two individuals can be said to have anything to do with the safety of them or any other individual whatever is somewhat difficult to be conceived."[24]

The Benthamites were precisely the sort of cold-fish "sophisters, oeconomists, and calculaters" who, according to Burke, were to be the death of Europe.[25] Yet as British politics began to thaw after 1815, the Benthamites proved far more effective in pushing for reform than more passionate sorts with seemingly more popular appeal. The fiery journalist William Cobbett was typical in this regard, a cranky kind of Tory populist who opposed popular education, damned James Watt for inventing the steam engine and starting the industrial revolution, and was not above an occasional display of anti-Semitism.[26] "We want *great alteration*, but we want *nothing new*," he declared. "Alteration, modification to suit the times and circumstances; but the great principles ought to be and must be the same, or else confusion will follow."[27] Bentham had nothing like Cobbett's immense popular following, yet he had the advantage of knowing far better where politics were heading. As the historian Elie Halevy observed:

> Radicalism . . . was reviving, but it was under a new form. It was no longer Cobbett's agrarian Radicalism, at once reactionary and revolutionary. . . . Nor was it the Radicalism of Byron, pessimistic, romantic, and aristocratic. . . . It was the Radicalism—respectable, middle-class, prosaic, and calculating—of Bentham and his followers.[28]

Bentham was rational, optimistic, and pro-industrial. His forte was the abuse right in front of one's nose, the wrong that everyone else somehow overlooked, the myth that no one questioned. For John Stuart Mill, Bentham was "the great subversive . . . the great questioner of things established."

> It is by the influence of modes of thought with which his writings inoculated a considerable number of thinking men, that the yoke of authority has been broken, and innumerable opinions, formerly received on tradition as incontestable, are put on their defense and required to give an account of themselves. Who, before Bentham, . . . dared to speak disrespectfully, in express terms, of the British Constitution, or the English Law?[29]

Of course, just as it is child's play nowadays to pick apart Madison's writings in the Federalist Papers, it is child's play to make mincemeat out of a good deal of Bentham as well. Bentham believed that popular democracy would usher in a system based on reason and logic, and hence he could never have understood how mass politics might also lead to mass hysteria and demagogy. He had no sense of the limitations of the nation-state, of capital versus labor, or of the awesome political issues that would arise in an era of mass democracy. As Marx pointed out, he was almost completely devoid of historical consciousness.[30] According to Bentham's black-and-white view, the course of human events was divided in two parts, an age of ignorance followed by an age of reason and science, which he was helping to usher in. All had been darkness, but soon all would be light. Rather than studying the past, the thing to do was to forget it as quickly as possible, to cast it off, so that society could advance as rapidly as possible. Bentham was a logician of the most relentless, single-minded sort imaginable, one who came along at a time when the British system had never been messier, more illogical, or more in need of a clean sweep.

Utilitarianism came into its own in the years following Waterloo. The final victory over Napoleon had a paradoxical effect on British politics. Not unlike the United States after the Cold War, Britain emerged from the struggle as the world's sole remaining superpower. Yet as the only country in Europe that had been spared Napoleon's political reforms, it also emerged with the most backward and archaic form of government. The "Peterloo Massacre" of 1819, in which drunken cavalrymen slashed their way through a dense throng of sixty thousand people attending an outdoor meeting in Manchester on parliamentary reform, was a critical event in Britain's political development. Eleven people were killed, some six hundred were wounded, yet the real loser was the government, whose hopeless stupidity was put on display for all to see. As Shelley put it, it was now clear that Britain was controlled by men "who neither see nor feel nor know, but leech-like to their fainting country cling. . . ."

Bentham and his followers started a utilitarian journal, the *Westminster Review*, and proceeded to churn out an endless series of books and articles criticizing all aspects of government policy, from public health to England's centuries-old system of poor relief. They had a special knack for zeroing in on the establishment's weak points, those seventeenth- and eighteenth-century relics that were regarded as sacred and unalterable merely as a consequence of their extreme age. The more the utilitarians hacked away, the more the establishment's defenses began to crumble. Finally, shortly after Bentham's death in 1832, came the great breakthrough: Parliament's passage of an epic Reform Bill that placed the voting system on a somewhat more equitable footing and started British politics on a long march to modernization.

How did the utilitarians do it? From a modern U.S. perspective, the difficult thing to understand is that they did not *do* anything at all, at least not in the American sense. They did not form political action committees to raise funds, lobby Congress, or cut deals on Capitol Hill. Instead, they wrote, published, and debated, rallying the manufacturers, the middle classes, and even a portion of the working class to their point of view. Although the Reform Bill represented a fundamental constitutional change, they did not have to shepherd it through two legislative houses plus dozens of state legislators or whatever the British equivalent might be. The Court party had done them the inestimable favor of concentrating political power in a single house, thus leaving them with only one peak to scale. The voting system was still wildly unrepresentative, yet the buildup in public pressure was impossible to resist. Because the mechanisms of government were unencumbered by formal checks, balances, or limits on the power of Parliament, change proved surprisingly fluid.

It's difficult to exaggerate the impact of the 1832 Reform Bill. At first glance, the bill seemed fairly modest. The landed aristocracy still held on to a disproportionate share of the seats in Parliament, while better than ninety percent of the population still lacked the vote. A stiff property qualification remained in effect, voting districts were riddled with anomalies, and the much-abused Irish were still grossly underrepresented. Burkean ancestor worship was down but was far from out. Yet there was no doubt that something had changed. The immovable had moved. The ribald, rollicking world of the eighteenth century was beginning to give ground to the prim, proper, middle-class politics of the nineteenth century.

What any of this had to do with the United States was nothing—which is precisely the point. Bentham's movement, which did not really get rolling until after 1808, came too late to benefit the infant American Republic, where politics had already frozen along very different lines. In his later years, Bentham turned into an American fellow traveler of the most enthusiastic sort. He lavishly praised the U.S. system to all who would listen. The American economy was growing by leaps and bounds, public works were forging ahead, and the federal budget was consistently in the black—all the result, Bentham declared, of "matchless good government," that is, government that was cheap, innovative, efficient, and honest.[31] As he wrote in 1809 (with his own eccentric method of punctuation):

> There you have—not merely democratic ascendancy—but democracy—pure democracy, and nothing else. There you have—not democracy, but a whole cluster of democracies: there, all is democracy; all is regularity, tranquility, prosperity, security: continual security . . . no aristocracy, no monarchy; all that dross evaporated.[32]

This was simplistic, but not altogether inaccurate. The U.S. economy *was* burgeoning, its government *was* economical, if only because it was so minuscule, and officials' salaries, by British standards, were downright measly. In the early 1790s, for instance, Hamilton's salary as secretary of the treasury had added up to barely a fifth of the four thousand pounds a year Edmund Burke earned as paymaster of the forces.[33] There were also no hordes of the poor as there were in London, no legions of government spies and political police as on the Continent. By the 1820s and 1830s, nearly all white males had the vote, property owners and factory hands alike, at a time when only a tiny minority had it in Britain and an even tinier fraction in France or Germany.

In 1811, Bentham wrote to President Madison offering to help draw up a comprehensive new U.S. legal code. It was five years before Madison condescended to reply, and then only in the form of a polite refusal from one of his aides. Bentham followed up with a similar proposal to several of the individual state governments, also to no avail.[34] In 1830, he sent a letter to President Andrew Jackson modestly urging him to abolish the Senate; "my researches," he informed him, "have led me to reckon the whole of your Senate—not merely the whole expense thrown away, but the whole authority, much worse than useless."[35]

There is no record of a response. Assuming he read it, however, there is no doubt that Jackson got a good chuckle. The same Jeremy Bentham who praised American government so lavishly apparently did not understand that not only did the president lack power to abolish the Senate, he lacked power even to introduce a constitutional amendment to that effect in Congress. The Constitution gave that responsibility solely to Congress or to a convention of the states. This was a marvelous demonstration of the foolishness of foreign "experts." Yet the joke was really on the United States. The British parliamentary system that Bentham was helping to rejuvenate would soon become a model for democratic reformers throughout the world; despite the lingering influence of kings, generalissimos, and various autocrats, the institution of the prime minister and his cabinet, answerable to a majority in the legislature, would become standard, at least nominally, from one end of the Continent to the other. America's form of government, by contrast, was so impenetrable that, as Bentham's letter indicated, even its greatest admirers were unable to fathom its intricacies. Its constitutional structure had become frozen in a way that was difficult for outsiders to grasp. Though Bentham believed that America had turned its back on tradition, the truth was more complex. In creating a Constitution along neo-Elizabethan, Country lines, America had, in a sense, refurbished the past, codified it, and invested it with new authority. As a result, it was far more resistant to change than the British system that Americans had rejected a half century or so earlier.

Indeed, America was beginning to pose a serious problem for British liberals by this point in much the same way that Stalinist Russia would pose a serious theoretical problem for leftists in the 1930s. The new American Republic was highly democratic in terms of the right to vote, yet its politics were crude and lowbrow, just as conservatives had predicted democratic politics would be. The puffed-up American loudly singing the praises of his country and Constitution was becoming a common caricature. In 1832, Frances Trollope, mother of the novelist Anthony Trollope, published *Domestic Manners of the*

Americans, an account of her three-year stay in the United States, which caused a sensation when it appeared in London during the debate over parliamentary reform. Tories were delighted with her acid-edged portraits of bumptious American republicans. Yet while Trollope's portrait was one-sided and unfair, which was what one might expect of a snobbish middle-class Englishwoman stranded amid tobacco-chewing frontiersmen, it was not far off the mark either. America's treatment of the Indians, she wrote, was hypocritical in the extreme: "You will see them one hour lecturing their mob on the indefeasible rights of man and the next driving from their homes the children of the soil, whom they have bound themselves to protect by the most solemn treaties."[36] The level of debate in Congress, she went on, could not have been lower:

> If I mistake not, every debate I listened to . . . was upon one and the same subject, namely the entire independence of each individual state. . . . I speak solely of the very singular effect of seeing man after man start eagerly to his feet, to declare that the greatest injury, the basest injustice, the most obnoxious tyranny that could be practiced against the state of which he was a member, would be a vote of a few million dollars for the purpose of making their roads or canals; or for drainage; or, in short, for any purpose of improvement whatsoever.[37]

Although British reformers were quick to dismiss *Domestic Manners of the Americans*, Charles Dickens, a liberal, came up with similar findings when he made the trek a decade later. Congress, he found, was controlled by "desperate adventurers," politics had been subjected to "the meanest perversion . . . ever wrought," and corruption flourished. Political principles were entirely absent. "They who in other countries would, from their intelligence and station, most aspire to make the laws," he declared, "do here recoil the farthest from that degradation."[38]

Although Trollope and Dickens had no real way of knowing, the nature of American politics flowed directly from the nature of

America's updated version of the Ancient Constitution. The neo-Elizabethan obsession with local representation encouraged congressmen to be limited and parochial in the extreme. Devoted to the Country-Jeffersonian notion that that government was best which governed least, they competed with one another to see who could denounce every federal initiative more vociferously. American government was at war with itself. Politicians postured and prated in public, then retreated behind closed doors to attend to the serious work of hammering out compromises among the various sections and factions. It was the friends of the new American Republic, not its enemies, who found the results most dispiriting.

And then, of course, there was slavery. In Britain, the slavery issue had provided the new middle-class forces with their first great victory after passage of the Reform Bill. Slavery, of course, had never been more than minuscule in England itself. Over the course of about a century, planters had imported some fourteen thousand slaves into the mother country from the West Indies, a practice that came to a halt in 1772 when an English court declared slavery unconstitutional. But vast numbers of slaves continued to be held in British possessions from the Bahamas to Barbados under conditions that, in many respects, were even worse than in the United States. In 1831, a slave named Nat Turner threw much of the American South into turmoil when he led a group of slaves in a bloody rampage through Southampton County, Virginia, which claimed the lives of some fifty whites. Yet as historian James Walvin has pointed out, such events were hardly more than "a flicker on the Richter scale" compared to the epic uprisings that had periodically shaken the giant British outpost of Jamaica since the mid-1600s.[39]

Given the region's bloody history, one might expect that emancipation, when it finally arrived, would have been protracted and difficult. Yet the opposite proved the case. In Britain, a mass antislavery campaign began gathering steam in the 1820s as petitions bearing millions of signatures began pouring into Parliament. Churches passed antislavery resolutions by the thousands, while printing presses churned out antislavery tracts and pamphlets in immense volumes. The outpouring was unprecedented, both in the number of people caught up in the campaign and the depth of the feeling that was aroused. As long as they held on to Parliament, the Tories refused to listen. But with the passage of the Reform Bill, Parliament found it impossible to say no to a movement that was both massive and middle class. In 1833, accordingly, it passed an act emancipating slaves over a four-year period and setting aside twenty million pounds to compensate their owners. Compensation is something that no doubt grates on modern sensibilities; after all, if anyone deserved compensation, it was a slave population that had been robbed of the value of its labor for nearly two centuries. Yet the consequences in the Caribbean sugar fields were nonetheless impressive. As newly liberated slaves began demanding wages to do what they had previously done for free, money began to circulate. Stagnant backwater economies sprang to life, and towns began to bustle and expand. In Antigua, imports rose as blacks began demanding better food and clothing. According to a visitor in 1841, villages were "rising up in every direction," with new homes being built of superior materials like stone and shingle. Productivity rose, planters reported, for the simple reason that workers performed better when they were paid than when they were not.[40] In Barbados, an English traveler reported a few years after emancipation that the ex-slave who offered him "wine, porter, and fresh meat" when he knocked at a country cabin lived better than agricultural laborers back home.[41]

Even more astonishing from an American perspective was the fact that there was no backsliding, no rebirth of racist terrorism, no Ku Klux Klan. Once free, the ex-slaves stayed free without having to worry about night riders forcing them into some new form of servitude. The new Parliament's authority was as unchallengeable as the old, although it now answered to a broader, more progressive, more middle-class electorate. Once it was persuaded to act, it did so with dispatch. For the utilitarians, the results were a triumph. A goal had been set and a plan drawn up, one that was carried out to the letter.

The slavery question had been tackled in a calm, logical, systematic manner that was coming to be seen as quintessentially British.

For American abolitionists, who came from essentially the same ranks of churchgoers and middle-class reformers, the results were a shock. The British government was supposed to be stuffy, aristocratic, and out of touch, yet it had responded with more alacrity than the supposedly more democratic U.S. Congress. When American abolitionists tried to emulate British tactics, they ran into a solid wall of hostility. In the South, postal officials censored their material from the mails, while Northern officials made no effort to interfere with a growing wave of mob violence. Antiabolitionists went on a three-day rampage against blacks in New York City, dragged William Lloyd Garrison by a halter through the streets of Boston, demolished an abolitionist newspaper office in Cincinnati and an abolitionist meeting hall in Philadelphia, and killed abolitionist editor Elijah Lovejoy in Alton, Illinois—all in the 1830s. In 1836, the Southern-dominated House of Representatives passed an infamous "gag resolution" automatically tabling any and all antislavery petitions that might come its way. John Quincy Adams, elected to Congress after a term as president, denounced the measure as "a direct violation of the Constitution of the United States, of the rules of the House, and the rights of my constituents," but slaveholding members shouted him down. In 1842, Dickens pointed out that slaves were paraded past the Capitol "like cattle, linked to each other by iron fetters," yet Congress refused to intervene. Freedom, he noted, had undergone a strange permutation in American hands. Rather than the freedom of the individual, the term now referred to the freedom of some individuals to keep others in chains:

There are many kinds of hunters engaged in the Pursuit of Happiness, and they go variously armed. It is the Inalienable Right of some of them to take the field after their Happiness, equipped with cart and cart-whip, stocks and iron collar, and to shout . . . (always in praise of Liberty) to the music of clanking chains and bloody stripes.[42]

This was the great political puzzle of the age. Britain had responded swiftly to a growing clamor among its citizens, while America, the most democratic country in the world, had stuffed up its ears. Any number of explanations offered themselves. For the British, slavery was faraway; therefore, they could afford to be moral and upright in grappling with its consequences. Britain's limited franchise tended to amplify the voices of the middle class at the expense of the far larger working class, which did not go to church for the most part and may have been less susceptible to moral appeals about the evils of slavery. In the United States, by contrast, where virtually all white males had the vote by the 1830s, politicians were quick to respond to white workingmen who viewed not just slavery but black people generally as an economic threat.

Explanations like these are useful, but they leave out the most important factor of all, which was *constitutional*. Despite John Quincy Adams's complaint about the gag rule, the Constitution not only protected slavery, but virtually enshrined it. The various pro-slave provisions—the three-fifths clause, equal state representation in the Senate, the fugitive slave clause, and so on—were all but set in stone. It would be decades at least before the antislavery forces would be able to muster the overwhelming majorities needed to remove such impediments under the amending rules established in 1787. As electoral victories by antislavery candidates in the 1840s and 1850s would demonstrate, a growing portion of the voting public wanted the issue resolved, yet the Constitution, although allegedly created in the name of the people, stood in the way.

In a sense, the British and American systems were moving in opposite directions in the first half of the nineteenth century. Britain was democratizing only slowly at the base, but loosening up dramatically at the top. Under the influence of Bentham and his utilitarians, the country had adopted, at least in principle, the idea of a malleable, adaptable constitution, in which the state was considered to be in a constant process of self-adjustment and self-reinvention. Americans, meanwhile, were doing the opposite—that is, democratizing rapidly at the base (at least as far as the white male population was concerned), while stiffening up at the top. Congress was sovereign over nothing, not over itself, not over the Constitution, and not over the country at large, where various states' rights advocates were at war with the very idea of federal authority. Where Britain had opted for constitutional flexibility, America had opted for extreme constitutional rigidity. Where Britain had emerged from the age of faith as far as the constitution was concerned, America had plunged back in. The result, at least as far as the slavery question went, was a growing sense of stalemate and paralysis.

4

BREAKDOWN IN AMERICA

THE CONCEPT OF SOVEREIGNTY underwent a metamorphosis in the great transformation from the pre-industrial to the industrial era. In the 1760s, Blackstone's definition of sovereignty as "supreme, irresistible, absolute, uncontrolled authority" meant, in essence, the power of the House of Commons in tandem with the king and lords to control every last aspect of society throughout the empire. Given that an estimated six thousand or so landowners and economic magnates effectively controlled the Commons thanks to the skewed "rotten borough" voting system, Blackstone's characterization amounted to a formula for an oligarchical dictatorship of the most undisguised sort.[1] But with the rise of political democracy during and after the French Revolution, Blackstone's doctrine underwent a revision. Sovereignty was now to be understood as the supreme power of the *people* to order every last aspect of their political environment, to debate an issue through to completion, to formulate a plan of action, and then to see that it was carried out to the jot. The people were supreme not only over their representatives, but over the government as a whole, over the constitution, and even over themselves. They could force Parliament to reverse course on slavery, as happened in 1833. They could adopt new voting laws, rein in the power of the House of Lords, and otherwise fiddle with what had once been seen as an unchangeable power structure. Since the people were supreme over the constitution, they were also supreme over the law. They were the masters; the legal structure, the state, and the rest of the political apparatus were the servants.[2] But as different as this was from the eighteenth-century theory of sovereignty, one thing remained the same: the fundamental understanding that some sort of well-defined final authority was necessary to a well-functioning society. Even Bentham, whose entire career amounted to a running feud with Blackstone, would not have thought to disagree.

Yet the United States remained curiously resistant. Although far and away the most democratic country in the world in some respects, in terms of sovereignty the United States was still in the days of Good Queen Bess, back in a time when no one—neither Parliament, the monarchy, nor the people—was fully in charge and relations between various ruling institutions were competitive rather than hierarchical. The White House was jealous of Congress, Congress was jealous of the White House, the states were jealous of the federal government, and so on ad infinitum. When one unit of government stuck its chest out and asserted its rights, others invariably followed suit. Thus, while the election of Andrew Jackson in 1828—the first president with anything like a mass following—reinvigorated the executive branch, it reinvigorated Congress and the state governments as well. The result, as Frances Trollope noted, was a veritable orgy of populist chest-thumping as one section of government tried to outdo the other. The states' rights movement reached a crescendo in 1832 when South

Carolina proclaimed its right to unilaterally "nullify" a tariff imposed by Congress. Andrew Jackson forced South Carolina to back down and preserved the Union with a bit of saber rattling, but the crisis was a sign of things to come. Given the numerous and overlapping lines of authority in the American system and the competitive power structure, more such conflicts were inevitable.

"We the People," the Preamble seemed to suggest, were sovereign, yet there was much they could not do. They were powerless to change the Constitution except through the complicated procedure outlined in Article V. They were almost completely powerless to change the outrageously undemocratic provision guaranteeing each state two votes in the Senate regardless of population. They could not rein in the power of the states without Southern firebrands threatening to bolt the Republic. Indeed, given the widespread perception in the antebellum period that the Constitution was so perfect as to render any further amendments unnecessary, there was precious little about the overall political structure that they could alter. The Benthamite notion that the people should periodically revamp government from top to bottom to make it more efficient was utterly alien. Rather than remodeling government, virtually all elements in America saw their mission as *fulfilling* a sacred legacy dating from 1787.

An antebellum writer has given us a picture of what this nonhierarchical pre–Civil War political system was like:

The President has one postmaster in every little village; but the inhabitants of that village choose their own selectmen, their own assessors of taxes, their own school-committee, their own overseers of the poor, their own surveyors of highways, and the incumbents of half a dozen other little offices corresponding to those which, in bureaucratic governments, are filled by appointment of the sovereign. In all these posts, which are really important public trusts, the villagers are trained to the management of affairs, and acquire a comprehensiveness of view, a practical administrative talent, and a knowledge of business which are, or ought to be, among the chief objects of every system of education. And this training is very general; for owing to our republican liking for rotation in office, the incumbents of these humble posts are changed every year or two, till every decent man in the place has had his turn.[3]

Although supposedly the first among equals, the president was plainly outnumbered. Real influence lay with the hordes of state and local politicians, whose ears were close to the ground and who rubbed shoulders with the citizens daily in innumerable Main Streets and village squares. Yet rather than promoting "a comprehensiveness of view," this system actually promoted the opposite—a narrowing of politics. Since no one individual or institution was in charge of American society, no one caused it to move. Either the system moved of its own accord, through some mysterious internal dynamic, or it did not move at all. Progress was something that occurred in the economic or personal sphere, but not in the political. There, thanks to the matchless Constitution, stasis reigned.

Without quite realizing it, the Americans had created one of the most immovable political structures this side of the as-yet-hermetically sealed kingdoms of Korea and Japan. Theodore Lowi, a maverick political scientist at Cornell, has argued that, properly speaking, the United States did not have a government prior to the Civil War but rather a central agency operating under a limited grant of authority from the states. The federal government (perhaps "entity" would be a better word) could impose tariffs, manage and dispose of public lands, supervise patents and coinage, and dole out subsidies. But the real business of government—business, property, and criminal law, family law, public health and education, and the like—was almost entirely in the hands of the states.[4] Under such conditions, the only way a national politician could get along was by assiduously cultivating the support of those below by doling out patronage or voting for pork-barrel subsidies. The last thing he would want to do would be to

address the many problems pressing in on American society in anything like a principled, logical fashion.

And, of course, no problem was more terrifying than slavery, an
issue that leaped to the fore with the battle over the Missouri Compromise in 1820 and then again in the 1830s following the Nat Turner
rebellion in Virginia and emancipation of the slaves in the British
West Indies. Slavery was the quadruple whammy of American politics,
a problem that was at once intractable, intolerable, growing worse with
every passing year, and constitutionally insoluble to boot. The combination was enough to drive American society to the brink of a collective nervous breakdown. The Founders had expected slavery to
wither away of its own accord and therefore had made no provision
in case it did not. Yet thanks to the power loom and the cotton gin,
cotton production—and the slave system on which it rested—was
booming. Northerners, whether moderates or outright abolitionists,
were left powerless. By 1820, white Southerners accounted for less
than thirty percent of the national population, while by 1860 they
accounted for only a fourth. Yet the Constitution gave the pro-slavery
forces virtually a stranglehold on national policy. Thanks to the three-
fifths clause and the principle of equal state representation in the
Senate, they exercised disproportionate influence over both houses of
Congress, over the electoral college, and over judicial appointments
as well. As long as they controlled more than a third of the House or
Senate and more than a fourth of the states, the pro-slavery forces
wielded an absolute veto over constitutional amendments. The Constitution's various pro-slavery provisions were all but impregnable.
The North had the numbers, yet the South had a set of legal guarantees that were both ironclad and perpetual.

It was an impossible situation that was only resolved when the
dam finally burst in 1860. The South lost control of both houses of
Congress for the first time since the Federalist era, and John C. Breck-
inridge of Kentucky, the only outright pro-slavery presidential candidate in a field of four, finished up in a humiliating third place behind
Lincoln and Stephen A. Douglas. Legally, nothing had changed. The
pro-slavery forces still controlled enough seats in Congress and

enough state governments to ward off constitutional change for the foreseeable future. Politically, though, the "slavocracy" had been swamped by the sheer weight of numbers pressing down from the North.

This was not only a new factor in American politics, but a new theory of government, one which differed as much from Madison's theory of a checked and balanced power of the majority as the Constitution had differed from the Articles of Confederation. As no less an authority than John C. Calhoun put it a few weeks before his death in 1850, the character of the American Republic was changing. It was growing

> from a Federal Republic, as it originally came from the hands
> of its framers, . . . into a great national consolidated Democ-
> racy . . . as absolute as that of the Autocrat of Russia, and as
> despotic in its tendency as any absolute Government that ever
> existed.[5]

Or as the abolitionist Moncure Conway declared shortly after the surrender of Fort Sumter: "The revolution is on our side, and as soon as the nation feels that, and acts upon it, the strength of the South is gone. . . . WE ARE THE REVOLUTIONISTS."[6] What Conway called "the nation" was the people acting not through their states and representatives, but coming together in a way that quite superseded the old channels and boundaries. Calhoun regarded the principle of unbounded majority rule as contrary to the Madisonian system of checks and balances and therefore illegal. Technically speaking, it was. But in fact it was supralegal. The people were the new lawmaking, law-breaking authority. Or, rather, considering the role of "we the People" in canceling the Articles of Confederation and inspiring a new constitution to take its place, they were the old authority brought back to life.

The journey from a system of checks and balances to "government of the people, by the people, for the people"—Lincoln's shorthand definition of popular sovereignty—was long and tortuous. As historian

Arthur Bestor noted in an influential essay in the mid-1960s, the Constitution imposed "a barrier" in terms of the slavery issue "that was both insuperable and respected." As a result, Northern moderates were forced to embark on "a strategy so indirect as to appear on the surface almost timid and equivocal."[7] This was the strategy of containment, which Northerners adopted on the heels of the Mexican-American War. If not abolished, at least slavery would not be allowed to spread beyond the southeast quadrant. Yet even this policy came with a Catch-22. Even as it compelled such a strategy, the Constitution all but doomed it to failure. Its pro-slavery provisions were so impregnable that the South was able to use them to turn tables on the North. For a brief period in the 1850s, it appeared that it was the free states that had been bottled up and contained in the northeast quadrant, while the slave owners solidified their grip on national power. It was this startling reversal that forced Northerners to examine their most basic political assumptions and embark on an ideological journey that would eventually lead to the Emancipation Proclamation and the Gettysburg Address.

The process began in 1846 when a Pennsylvania congressman named David Wilmot introduced a resolution in the House to bar slavery from the vast southwestern territories newly conquered from the Mexican republic. Wilmot's reasoning was simple. Since Mexico had not permitted slavery in those parts before, there was no reason to permit it now. Protecting slavery where it currently existed was one thing, extending it quite another. This was something the Constitution did not mandate and which the majority of Americans clearly opposed. Therefore, Congress was within its rights to see that it did not occur.

The Wilmot Proviso, as it was called, was explosive in a way that not even the Missouri Compromise had been a quarter century earlier. The reason would have been instantly apparent to anyone at the time on Capitol Hill. While the Missouri Compromise had closed off the northern territories to slavery, it had also strengthened the idea of North-South parity. With the nation divided horizontally into two roughly equal portions, the slave and nonslave sections would be able to march together in tandem as the Republic advanced to the west. Now, however, Wilmot was proposing to put an end to parity by bottling up slavery in the Southeast. The long-term implications were unmistakable. As population expanded and new states were admitted to the Union, it would be only a matter of time before Southern representation in the House and Senate slipped below the one-third-plus level needed to ward off constitutional change. The delicate balance between Northern and Southern interests would be eliminated, and slavery's days would be numbered. The Southern way of life, based as it was on black slavery, would be destroyed.

The South responded with a counterthrust worthy of a Robert E. Lee. John C. Calhoun, the dean of Southern constitutionalists, stepped forward with a theory developed some years earlier arguing that not only did the federal government lack the constitutional authority to prohibit slavery in the newly acquired Southwest, it lacked authority to prohibit it in *any* of the territories. Not only was the Wilmot Proviso unconstitutional, but the Missouri Compromise was as well. If Calhoun's thesis had been patently unreasonable, the North would have happily laughed it off. Unfortunately, it was not. The Constitution was exceedingly unclear about the nature and extent of Congress's authority over the territories. Although Article IV stated that Congress "shall have power to dispose of and make all needful rules and regulations respecting the Territory or other property belonging to the United States," it was also clear that, in so doing, Congress could not abrogate the fundamental constitutional rights accorded to other citizens of the United States. One of those rights, Calhoun argued, was the right of each resident to determine if his state should permit or prohibit slavery. As the caretaker of state interests, the federal government was required to ensure that territorial residents would have a right to make the same choice once their territories were incorporated into states as well. Hence, until such a decision was made, Southerners had as much right to bring their property into the western territories as Northern settlers had to bring along their mules and plows.

Whether or not Calhoun's reading of the Constitution was "correct" (whatever that word might mean in this context), he had the better part of the constitutional apparatus on his side. The result was the painstaking Compromise of 1850, which admitted California as a free state, opened up the rest of the Southwest to slavery, and, as a further nod to the slavocracy, imposed a tough new fugitive slave act preventing accused runaways from filing habeas corpus petitions in Northern courts when apprehended for return to the South. Southern bounty hunters thus acquired carte blanche to snatch blacks off Northern streets and return them to slavery. "I will not obey it, by God!" raged Ralph Waldo Emerson, never known for his abolitionist zeal. Yet Northerners were caught in a legal bind when it came to habeas corpus just as they had been in respect to territorial slavery. Article IV stated quite plainly that any "person held to service or labour in one State, under the laws thereof, escaping into another, . . . shall be delivered up on claim of the party to whom such service or labour may be due." It also declared that each state shall give "full faith and credit . . . to the public acts, records, and judicial proceedings of every other State," which presumably included slave laws. To allow accused runaways to apply for hearings before Northern juries that were invariably hostile to slavery amounted to an abrogation of Southern property rights. As the slave owners saw it, Northern states were encouraging slaves to flee by promising them full political rights once they made it across the Mason-Dixon line. Slavery would not be secure unless Southern property rights were recognized throughout the Union.

On July 4, 1854, the abolitionist William Lloyd Garrison held up a copy of the Constitution before an antislavery audience in Framingham, Massachusetts, proclaimed it "a covenant with death, an agreement with hell," and set it afire. The speech was the most dramatic single moment in Garrison's long and dramatic career, but politically it was a dead end. The Constitution was unfair, clearly, but it was also what held the Union together. Dissolving it meant dissolving the Union and allowing the South to go its own way. The problem for the North was how to dissolve slavery, or at least rein it in, while preserving and strengthening national ties. Rather than going its own way, the North had to figure out a way to prevent the South from going *its* own way while simultaneously resolving the slavery issue once and for all.

Nowadays, it is difficult to appreciate just how painful the Northern predicament was during this period. Much of the reason has to do with a liberal historical tradition that has long painted Lincoln as the great preserver and protector of the constitutional order, while painting Southerners as rebels and usurpers. This is history as written by the victors, however, when in fact the situation was a good deal more complex. The South was far from unjustified in claiming the mantle of constitutional legitimacy. Its concept of the United States as a voluntary union was much closer to the views expressed by Madison and Jefferson in the famous Kentucky and Virginia Resolutions of 1798, while Lincoln's concept of a perpetual union actually paralleled those of the discredited Alexander Hamilton. Jefferson had described the Constitution as an interstate compact whose meaning was fixed and permanent, whereas Lincoln seemed to believe that the terms were open to reinterpretation. In a very real sense, it was Lincoln who was the usurper of the Constitution as it had taken shape under Jefferson and Madison, and the South that was struggling to uphold it.

The two great constitutional controversies of the immediate prewar period, the *Dred Scott* decision and the secession issue itself, illustrate what kind of constitutional handicap the North was laboring under as the country careered toward civil war.

Dred Scott

This seminal event is still nettlesome for constitutional scholars. For conservatives, it is troubling because it shows strict constructionism used to ends that all sides now agree were disastrous. For modern liberals, it is disturbing because it shows elected officials roughly shoving the high court aside because of a decision they didn't like and

substituting their own judgment instead. Rather than passively accepting the Supreme Court's verdict, the voters mutinied and elected
a Republican slate committed to its overthrow. As Lincoln declared
in his inaugural address in 1861: "If the policy of the government
upon vital questions concerning the whole people is to be irrevocably
fixed by decisions of the Supreme Court, . . . the people will have
ceased to be their own rulers, having to that extent practically resigned
the government into the hands of that eminent tribunal." Given the
circumstances, it was difficult to imagine how Lincoln could have said
otherwise. Yet when Edwin Meese, attorney general under Ronald
Reagan, advanced the same thesis in 1986, arguing that the elected
branches had as much say over what was constitutional and what was
not as the Supreme Court, liberals were aghast.[8]

How to resolve the discrepancy? The usual response among modern constitutionalists has been to characterize *Dred Scott* as sui generis,
a decision so wide-ranging and awful as to justify the elected branches
taking extraordinary action in seeing that it was overturned. Laurence
Tribe described it as "wholly gratuitous" in his widely used textbook,
American Constitutional Law,[9] while, at the other end of the spectrum,
Robert Bork described it as "the worst [Supreme Court decision] in
our history until the twentieth century provided rivals for that title."[10]
But these are ex post facto judgments, rendered under very different
conditions than those pertaining in the 1850s. Under the pre–Civil
War Constitution, a case could be made that *Dred Scott* was something
very different, "a plausible, coherent, and even ingenious" effort (to
quote one of the few modern legal scholars willing to consider it in
historical context) to adapt constitutional law to what seemed to be
the needs of the day.[11] The real problem with *Dred Scott* was not
that it was unreasonable, but that it represented a reasonable interpretation of an unreasonable, illiberal Constitution—something that
modern constitutionalists, needless to say, cannot bring themselves to
admit.

Dred Scott, of course, was a slave transported by his master from
Missouri to the free state of Illinois, then to an unorganized territory

north of the old Missouri Compromise line, where slavery had long been forbidden, and finally back to Missouri where his journey had begun. Following his return, he sued for freedom, first in state court and then in federal, on the grounds that having once set foot in free territory, he was free forevermore. Slavery opponents argued that the central issue in *Dred Scott* was the right of Northern states to abolish slavery within their borders and the right of the federal government to abolish it in the territories, while slaveholders regarded the whole affair as an intolerable assault on Southern property rights. If each state was to give "full faith and credit . . . to the public acts, records, and judicial proceedings of every other State," as the Constitution declared in Article IV, then it had to be recognized that a Southerner's right to a slave was the same as a Northerner's right to a book, a home, or a farm animal. If a cow wandering into a neighboring yard should be returned, why not a slave crossing into a neighboring territory or state? If an errant slave did not have to be returned, were Southerners somehow justified in "liberating" Northern property that somehow had crossed over into their jurisdiction?

For abolitionists, questions like these were repellent because slavery was repellent. The legal system, which viewed slavery as normal and legitimate, was not so sure. As Chief Justice Roger B. Taney subsequently ruled, an important principle was at stake involving the Fifth Amendment guarantee that no person shall "be deprived of life, liberty, or property, without due process of law." When Dred Scott's owner had transported his slave across state lines, he had been given no warning that he was forfeiting up his property, no hearing, and no right of appeal, all hallmarks of due process. Since the 1830s, state and federal courts had been steadily expanding the meaning of due process so as to rule out a host of state laws that arbitrarily robbed citizens of their property or businesses. This was "one of the outstanding judicial achievements of the . . . century," as one constitutional historian has noted.[12] If Dred Scott's backers were correct, however, one sort of property was now to be considered exempt. In seeking freedom for Dred Scott, as Southerners saw it, they were proposing to confiscate a U.S. citizen's property without so much as a nod to due process.

In retrospect, it is difficult to see how the Supreme Court could have allowed anything so peremptory. As Taney put it in *Dred Scott:*

> An Act of Congress which deprives a citizen of the United States of his liberty or property merely because he came himself or brought his property onto a particular territory of the United States and who had committed no offense against the laws could hardly be dignified with the name of due process of law.[13]

If this was not correct, then state officials would be free to appropriate other types of property as well, a formula for interstate anarchy even worse than the one that already existed.

In declaring the Missouri Compromise of 1820 to have been unconstitutional—which struck at Dred Scott's claim that he was free by virtue of his crossing over into the northern territories—the chief justice had essentially adopted John C. Calhoun's argument that the federal government's role in the territories was limited to that of care-taker until such time as they were ready to be carved up into states. Only then, Taney asserted, would the residents decide whether they were to be pro-slavery or free. Yet where "free soil" advocates argued that allowing Southerners to bring their property into unincorporated territories gave them an economic advantage over Northern settlers, who could not possibly compete with slave labor—that "neutrality," in other words, was implicitly pro-slavery—Taney did not shy away from the consequences. He was convinced, as one modern legal scholar noted, that "if a choice must inevitably be made between giving preference to the system of free labor or slave labor, then slavery must prevail because of its specially protected status under the Constitution."[14]

This is deeply shocking to modern sensibilities, but it was not shocking to antebellum moderates who believed that Southern interests had to be accommodated if the Union was to be preserved. This in turn meant abiding by the agreement of 1787 and seeing to it that slave owners' minority rights were preserved despite overwhelming popular pressure from the North. Taney's myriad of modern-day critics have also accused him of hubris and arrogance in overturning a seventy-year-old precedent in declaring that Congress could not bar slavery from the territories. Yet this is unfair as well. While Congress had barred slavery from the old northwest territory as far back as 1787, much had changed in the ensuing decades, which is why Taney felt justified in reopening the issue.

What's more, Congress *wanted* him to reopen it. The legislative branch had become so tangled up over the issue of territorial slavery that the most prominent leaders were agreed that the judiciary was the only branch capable of sorting things out. As Henry Clay declared in the Senate in 1850, the only wise course was "to leave the question of slavery or no slavery [in the territories] to be settled by the only competent authority that can definitely settle it forever, the authority of the Supreme Court."[15] Abraham Lincoln seconded the motion when he declared in 1856 that "the Supreme Court of the United States is the tribunal to decide such questions, and we will submit to its decisions"—although afterward, when the decision proved not to his liking, he changed his tune.[16] Indeed, since all sides were looking to the Court for an answer, the real shock would have been if Taney had not faced up to the territorial slavery issue but had ducked it as well. The results "would have been inconsistent with the tradition of judicial power and with the Court's assigned role as final arbiter of constitutional questions," as one historian put it.[17]

Of course, the most notorious part of *Dred Scott* is the section that declares that even free blacks could not be considered U.S. citizens and consequently had "no rights which the white man was bound to respect." Taney was wrong in arguing that the Founders had believed that blacks were racially inferior and that they could not possibly have been referring to blacks when they declared "that all men are created equal [and] that they are endowed by their Creator with certain unalienable rights." In fact, the historical record was not nearly as clear as Taney made out: opinion among the Founders ran the gamut from the racially egalitarian to the outrightly racist. Yet although Taney's history was faulty, there was no doubt that opinion was changing and that he was expressing the dominant opinion of the day. Attitudes had hardened not only in the South after the 1830s, but also in the North, where black voters had been widely disenfranchised and pseudobiological theories of black inferiority were gaining influence. As Alexis de Tocqueville observed in 1835, "the prejudice of race appears to be stronger in the states that have abolished slavery than in those where it still exists."[18]

Congress, for its part, certainly behaved as if blacks had no rights worthy of respect. It had excluded free blacks from the Navy and Marine Corps as early as 1798; prohibited them from voting or engaging in certain businesses in the District of Columbia; refused to interfere with the slave trade in the capital, even though it was the one part of the country where Congress's power in this regard was unchallenged; and had promulgated a slave code in the capital no less brutal than those in the South.[19] Even that old Federalist war horse, Chief Justice John Marshall, had concurred as far back as 1834 that blacks were ineligible for U.S. citizenship.[20] So, in a sense, did the Radical Republicans after the war when they rammed through the Fourteenth Amendment, the opening line of which declared that "all persons born or naturalized in the United States, and subject to the jurisdiction thereof, are citizens of the United States and of the State wherein they reside." If Taney's interpretation of the Constitution had been wrong, there would have been no need to change the Constitution's language. The fact that the Republicans *did* change it was a tacit admission that, strictly speaking, perhaps he had been right after all.

As constitutional historian Bernard Schwartz has argued:

Negro citizenship [at the time of *Dred Scott*] was a legal euphemism. The current of judicial decision was relegating the free Negro to a subordinate status, regardless of whether he was clothed with the formal title of citizen. Actually, a third class of free residents in this country was being created in the law: there were now citizens, free Negroes, and aliens. In this sense, the Dred Scott decision was . . . only confirming the pre–Civil War trend of court decisions on the subject.[21]

None of which is to say that *Dred Scott* was anything other than morally reprehensible. Yet what all but the most radical abolitionists could not bring themselves to admit was that morality and the Constitution were sharply diverging. In a bizarre way, *Dred Scott* represented a last-ditch effort to keep the Union together by assuring slaveholders that the judiciary would see to it that their constitutional interests were protected. Yet the effort was doomed. As Lincoln declared a year after Taney's ruling, "this government cannot endure permanently half slave and half free," which was another way of saying that the North could not bear to live under a Constitution that was explicitly pro-slavery. Rather than criticizing the Constitution, though, Northerners found it much more convenient to criticize the Court. Just as error in the Middle Ages had to be the fault of the king's ministers and never of the king, error in the United States had to be the fault of the Constitution's interpreters and never of the Constitution itself.

Secession

For decades, Lincoln's argument that secession was unconstitutional because the Union had preceded and given rise to the states has been taken as dogma. As he explained in his first inaugural address, he and his fellow Republicans were committed to the proposition that the United States had never been a conditional or temporary alliance, but had been perpetual from the start. The historical record, he argued, was clear:

The Union is much older than the Constitution. It was formed in fact, by the Articles of Association in 1774. It was matured and continued by the Declaration of Independence in 1776. It was further matured and the faith of all the then thirteen States expressly plighted and engaged that it should be perpetual, by the Articles of Confederation of 1778. And finally, in 1787, one of the declared objects for ordaining and establishing the Constitution, was "to form a more perfect union."[22]

In other words, the Republic *preceded* the individual states, which only came into existence after the nation launched its collective struggle for independence. Since the states had never enjoyed independent status, they were in no position to claim what had never been theirs to begin with.

Yet there were problems with Lincoln's argument, serious problems. For starters, there was the little matter of Texas, which had enjoyed a brief existence as a sovereign, independent republic prior to joining the Union in 1845 and therefore, according to Lincoln's line of reasoning, was in a better position to demand a return to its previous status. Yet Lincoln still refused to let it go. The situation concerning the other Confederate states, particularly those that were part of the original thirteen colonies, was not much better. While the record was clear that, as Lincoln argued, some kind of national union had preceded the Constitution and even the Declaration of Independence, a *perpetual* union in which the states were without sovereignty was another matter. As historian Kenneth Stampp noted in a 1978 essay, the kind of union that most people had in mind during the Revolution and immediately after was a voluntary, conditional association. True, the Articles of Confederation, adopted in 1781, had referred to the union as "perpetual." Yet the Articles had lasted a scant seven years before being overturned by a constitution that made no such pronouncement. Thereafter, said Stampp,

> the most common perception of the Union was as an experiment whose future was uncertain at best. . . . Not many were inclined to challenge John Randolph when he declared in 1814 that the Union was "the means of securing the safety, liberty,

and welfare of the confederacy, and not itself an end to which these should be sacrificed."[23]

Lincoln also overstated matters concerning the closely related issue of continuity—whether the union that began to take shape as early as 1774 was the same union in 1787–88, after the states had been formed. Unfortunately for the legal case the Republicans were trying to put together, the evidence was clearly on the side of discontinuity. The Constitution was not an extension of the Articles of Confederation but a fresh start. Article VII, which declared that the Constitution would go into effect when approved by nine of the thirteen states, was, as we have seen, a clear violation of the Articles of Confederation, which required unanimous approval. Thus, the Constitution amounted to a break with the existing legal structure, a point the Founders themselves freely conceded. Madison expressed hope that supporters of the proposed new Constitution would see "a speedy triumph over the obstacles to re-union" during the ratification battle in 1788, while Philadelphia delegate Charles Cotesworth Pinckney, appearing before the South Carolina state legislature, brought with him the news that not only did the new Constitution safeguard slavery, but that "the old Confederation . . . was virtually dissolved."[24] Even as they ratified the new Constitution, state after state emphasized that they were doing so voluntarily, without surrendering an ounce of their existing sovereignty. Virginia's resolution on ratification affirmed "that the powers granted under the Constitution being derived from the People of the United States may be resumed by them whensoever the same shall be perverted to their injury or oppression." Seven states ratified only on condition that the Constitution be changed to recognize, in the words of the Massachusetts resolution, "that all Powers not expressly delegated . . . are reserved to the several States, to be by them exercised"[25]—language subsequently incorporated into the Constitution via the Tenth Amendment. John Dickinson, the Philadelphia delegate from Delaware, assured his state that the new arrangement would be "a confederacy of republics . . . in which the sovereignty of each state was equally represented,"[26] and Madison assured New Yorkers in *Federalist* No. 39 that "each State, in ratifying the Constitution, is considered as a sovereign body independent of all others, and only to be bound by its own voluntary act."[27]

Even the phrase "to form a more perfect Union," which appears in the Preamble, was far more ambiguous than Lincoln was willing to grant. Lincoln interpreted it to mean that the Constitution had been created to render the existing union more perfect than it already was. Yet it might just as easily mean that the Constitution was establishing a *new* union to replace the one that had just broken down. Most damning of all was the fact that while an early draft of the Constitution had specified that "the Union shall be perpetual," the phrase had been dropped prior to adoption of a final document. No record exists as to why, although Stampp speculated that

> the Philadelphia delegates, who endowed the federal government with substantial power, thought such language too risky. Perhaps they also found it slightly embarrassing to declare their intention to build a new perpetual Union on the wreckage of the old.[28]

To be sure, there was a countervailing, Hamiltonian tradition holding that the nation was indeed sovereign over the states. But it was far less firmly established. In 1821, for instance, Chief Justice Marshall asserted in *Cohens v. Virginia* that the states were "members of one great empire—for some purposes sovereign, for some purposes subordinate."[29] During the nullification crisis of 1832, Andrew Jackson insisted that the United States is

> a *government*, not a league. . . . It is a Government in which all the people are represented, which operates directly on the people individually, not upon the States. . . . How, then, can that State be said to be sovereign and independent whose citizens owe obedience to laws not made by it?[30]

Unquestionably, such views were gaining ground as newspapers, roads, and canals knit the various regions closer together and contributed to a growing sense of nationalism. But they were still far from predominant. Jackson based his own argument in behalf of national supremacy on the obedience owed by state residents to federal law. If the people were bound to obey, he reasoned, then the states were bound to obey as well. Yet most people still preferred to think of the United States not as a society based on obedience and command, but as one based on free will and consent. The states were part of the Union because they wanted to be, not because they had to be.

Finally, whether or not a majority of Americans were coming around to Jackson's point of view was irrelevant as far as Southern strict constructionists were concerned. What mattered was not what people chose to believe now, amid growing tension over the slavery issue, but what people understood back in 1787–88, when the Constitution was drafted and ratified. The Constitution was not a leaf to be blown hither and yon by every gust of public opinion. Rather, it was an agreement between sovereign powers. Once the agreement was entered into, the terms could not be changed or the meaning altered without the consent of all parties. Anything less was a breach of contract, in which case the ties that bound the Union would be dissolved and the parties released from the agreement. Secession, in this view, was a constitutional response to the unconstitutional assertion of federal power.

Of course, the pro-secessionist argument was not entirely free of murkiness as well. Whether or not the states retained their former sovereignty, clearly they had given *something* up, some element of self-determination, in ratifying the Constitution and joining the Union. When Lincoln argued in his first inaugural address that "it is safe to assert that no government proper ever had a provision in its organic law for its own termination,"[31] he obviously had a point. A government in which a minority was free to leave whenever it wanted was no government at all, merely a temporary agreement between independent parties, each with veto power over the decisions of the whole. No such federation could survive longer than a month. The Confederate revolt was an extreme Country reaction against the very idea of central government, no matter how weak.

Yet in the end it was the South that had the better of the legal argument. The fact that the Constitution itself did not squarely address the secession issue was clearly to its advantage. However absurd it might be that the states should be free to bolt the Union at will, it was clear the states were free to do whatever the Constitution did not explicitly forbid, a point underscored by the Tenth Amendment in the Bill of Rights. The result was an escape clause that no one was able to close. The real problem was not so much what the Constitution said as the absence of any mechanism for clarifying or updating the rather vague pronouncements handed down by the Founders. The Constitution's silence concerning the right to secede amounted to a tacit "yes" that the South could go where it pleased.

Thus, Lincoln headed into the Civil War on the shakiest possible legal ground. His party had taken office on a vow to overturn a legitimate (albeit morally disastrous) Supreme Court ruling, to deny the Southern states their right to withdraw from what had long been perceived as a voluntary federation, and to employ military force in an unprecedented fashion to hold the Union together. But force alone would not do the trick. Lincoln and the Republicans needed a legal rationale with which to oppose Southern strict constructionism.

Eventually, they were able to piece one together out of the Declaration of Independence and the Preamble to the Constitution. "We the People" and "all men are created equal" were more than just a couple of famous entries in the mid-nineteenth-century political phrase book. Rather, at a time when only one European nation (France) was even a republic, they amounted to a universally recognized American creed. The problem, however, was how to give these words the force of law. The Declaration was not a statute, not a resolution of Congress, and not a part of the Constitution; its legal standing, hence, was nil. Where Hamilton had tried to use the Preamble as a hook on which to hang his theory of federal sovereignty, the Jeffersonians had long regarded it as a mere rhetorical flourish. The response of the newly created Republican Party in the 1850s, however, was to raise both to the level of a formal statement of purpose, the legal foundation on which all else rested. Since both items posited a very different relationship between the people and their government, the results added up to a legal revolution. Where Article V stated that the people's ability to change the Constitution was limited and constrained, the Preamble implied that the people's power over the Constitution was infinite and *un*constrained. They could rip up old constitutions and make new ones as they wished in order to advance the goals of establishing justice, ensuring domestic tranquility, and so forth. The Declaration's language was, if anything, even more sweeping. "Whenever any form of government becomes destructive," it stated, ". . . it is the right of the people to alter or to abolish it, and to institute new government"—not the right of two-thirds of both houses of Congress plus three-fourths of the states, but the right of the people as a whole. Moreover, the "we the People" of the Preamble did not refer to the people acting in their separate capacities as Virginians, New Yorkers, or Rhode Islanders, but rather to "we the People of the United States." The people were sovereign as a national unit and therefore superior to any component part.

This became the chief justification of the war to preserve the Union—the right of the people to determine their destiny as whole and to rein in any dissident minorities that might wish to break away. Whereas government was limited under the terms set forth in the Constitution, the power of the people that stood behind it was unlimited. Instead of a sonorous introduction, the Preamble contained the real substance of the Constitution, the only words that counted, while all else that followed was mere postscript.

Equally important, however, was not *what* this new order amounted to, but *how* it was implemented. The core of the Republican national platform of 1860 was a resolution declaring, in rather cumbersome legal language, that

the maintenance of the principles promulgated in the Declaration of Independence and embodied in the Federal

Constitution, "That all men are created equal; that they are endowed by their Creator with certain inalienable rights; that among these are life, liberty and the pursuit of happiness; that, to secure these rights, governments are instituted among men, deriving their just powers from the consent of the governed," is essential to the preservation of our Republican institutions; and that the Federal Constitution, the Rights of the States, and the Union of the States, must and shall be preserved.[32]

On one level, this was sheer balderdash. The Constitution clearly did not embody the sentiments that all men were created equal. If it did, it would not have hedged slavery about with so many protective devices. Yet, on another level, it made perfect sense. In asserting that the Constitution embodied equal rights when it obviously did not, the party was declaring, in effect, that it would *force* the document to incorporate such sentiments. Regardless of what the Constitution said, the Republicans were determined to squeeze it into whatever shape necessary to preserve the Union. Equally important, moreover, was who would do the squeezing. The answer was not Congress and the states according to the prescription set forth in Article V, but the voters to whom the resolution was clearly addressed. Without changing so much as a comma, the people would impose new meaning on the Constitution so that the values set forth in the Declaration became part of the official text.

5

FORWARD TO THE PAST

TO ANYONE WHO KNOWS British history, the parallels between
the events of the mid-nineteenth century and the mid-seventeenth are
inescapable. In one case, middle-class Puritans organized themselves
into a military force and after years of seesaw battle under generals of
dubious loyalty, found a leader in Oliver Cromwell and routed the
Royalist forces. In the other, middle-class Northerners organized
themselves into a military force, and after even worse military re-
versals, found a leader in Ulysses S. Grant and scattered the neo-
aristocratic South. In the first instance, Puritans fought for the right
of the individual conscience against the religious dictates of bishops
and king, while, in the second, their descendants, prolific breeders
who had spread from New England across upstate New York and the

Midwest, fought for the rights of the slave against the dictates of the slave owner. It was after the war, however, that the two events really converged. The bitter conflict between a Republican-controlled Congress and a Democratic president almost exactly paralleled the struggle between a Puritan-controlled Parliament and the Crown. The issues were identical: whether authority would rest with an unelected chief executive (Andrew Johnson having acceded to the throne only on the death of his boss) or with an elected legislature. So was a good deal of the rhetoric. In both cases, the chief executive claimed to be better able to speak for the people as a whole than a rump legislature representing only a portion of the electorate. Both heads of state, whether Andrew Johnson or King Charles I, claimed to be defending separation of powers against a lawless legislative mob, while the opposing forces insisted that they were the only ones capable of defending the revolutionary gains of the past few years and preventing the onset of one-man rule.

Both experiments ended up similarly as well. Nine years after Charles's execution for treason in January 1649, Cromwell died. Two years later, his revolutionary republic collapsed, whereupon England found itself back under a monarchy much like the old. Following Andrew Johnson's impeachment and acquittal, Radical Republican rule in America collapsed as well and a revamped version of the *ancien régime* also took its place. The slavery issue had been resolved, as had the question of secession. But much else remained unchanged. Blacks found themselves thrust back into a new kind of servitude, states' rights were once again on the ascendant, and the Constitution returned to its semiparalyzed prewar state. Between 1870 and 1913, no new amendments were approved, just as during the long drought from 1804 to the Civil War. Social tensions were becoming explosive, yet once again the Constitution was considered to have reached a pinnacle of perfection in which no further improvement was either possible or necessary.

The Civil War thus turned out to be the bloodiest path possible from constitutional stagnation to constitutional stagnation. The question of how this came about is one of the chief riddles of U.S. history. Historians who have tried to get to the bottom of why Reconstruction failed to change American society have zeroed in on racism, the disenchantment with politics caused by widespread corruption, the rise of a conservative capitalist class up North, and so forth. All are important, yet none speaks to the question of *why* such forces proved triumphant. The reason is the sacrosanct nature of the Constitution as the great untouchable, which prevents historians from examining how the structure of the American state served to inhibit democracy, scatter the energy of reformers, and allow civil rights to ebb. In fact, the role of the Constitution was crucial. The conservative structure of American politics served as an inertial guidance mechanism to ensure that once the late unpleasantness was concluded, American society would return to something very much like its prewar state.

The process by which American society wound up circling back on itself between 1860 and 1868 was long and complicated. Initially, a return to constitutional stasis seemed like the most distant of possibilities. Rather, all things constitutional seemed to be up for grabs. Just as Milton had reported in the midst of the English Civil War that the country was filled with people "disputing, reasoning, reading, inventing, discoursing, even to a rarity and admiration, things not before discoursed or written of,"[1] the journalist E. L. Godkin reported a little over two centuries later that "the spell has been broken by the war; criticism has been let loose even upon the Constitution of the United States."[2] William H. Seward, Lincoln's secretary of state, reported a feeling akin to constitutional vertigo. As the members of Lincoln's cabinet issued emergency orders during the panicky first weeks of the war, they did so, he later told an acquaintance, knowing that they were taking steps that if unsuccessful "might have brought them all to the scaffold."[3] "Let us save the country," Seward advised on another occasion, "and then cast ourselves upon the judgment of the people, if we have in any case, acted without legal authority."[4] Legal authority, in other words, was up in the air. Rather than the Supreme Court, still under the control of the discredited Roger Taney, the only constitutional authority was the people themselves. They would decide what was legal or not, although, to the discomfort of officials like Seward, the people would not make their views known until after the fact. Until then, the cabinet was on its own.

This was what it must have been like to have been part of the Directory during the French Revolution, when it was all its members could do to hold on for dear life. For Lincoln, the ideological journey was particularly tortuous. The sixteenth president did not belong to the Republican Party's radical wing, but to its more conservative, cautious center. As a young man in Illinois, he had once declared, "Every American, every lover of liberty, every well-wisher to his posterity . . . [must] swear by the blood of the Revolution, never to violate in the least particular, the laws of the country; and never to tolerate their violation by others."[5] He was cool to the abolitionists and kept them at arm's length in the 1850s and, during the 1860 campaign, tried to paint the approaching conflict as one between those who were loyal to the Constitution and those who would violate it. In December 1861, he told Congress that he was determined that the conflict not degenerate into "a violent and remorseless revolutionary struggle,"[6] and as late as August 1862 he was informing Horace Greeley that his goal was to "save the Union . . . the shortest way under the Constitution," adding: "If I could save the Union without freeing *any* slave, I would do it."[7]

Yet rhetoric was one thing, actions quite another. Despite his legal scruples, Lincoln ordered a blockade of Southern ports in the first crucial weeks following Fort Sumter, saw to it that federal funds reached pro-Union forces in the border states, issued a call for volunteers, and federalized some seventy-five thousand state militia, all, as he freely acknowledged, without formal authorization of Congress and "without any foundation of law."[8] In order to put a halt to secession fever in the all-important border state of Maryland, he had his generals occupy Baltimore, suspend habeas corpus, and threaten to arrest any state legislator who voted to leave the Union. After repeatedly protesting to Congress that he lacked constitutional authority to free the slaves without a formal amendment, in September 1862 he announced that he had discovered the authority after all to declare a proclamation of emancipation, effective the following January. Although radical members of his party criticized the proclamation for bypassing the border states and freeing slaves only in the Confederacy—Lincoln, it was said, had left slavery intact where he had the power to end it and had ended it where it was beyond his reach—there was no doubt that the proclamation had radicalized the war. Rather than preserving the Union, the North was now fighting to change it. "For one, I don't care a rag for 'the Union as it was,' " declared Albion Tourgee, an abolitionist turned Union soldier, referring to an old Republican slogan. "I want to fight for the Union better than it was."[9] Formerly in the minority, people like Tourgee now expressed the majority view.

Lincoln resorted to various methods to somehow align strict constitutionalism with radical change. One analogy he favored, for example, was the medical. "By general law," he wrote in 1864, "life *and* limb must be protected; yet often a limb must be amputated to save a life; but a life is never wisely given to save a limb." As he confessed on another occasion:

> I felt that measures, otherwise unconstitutional, might become lawful by becoming indispensable to the preservation of the institution, therefore the preservation of the nation. . . . I could not feel that, to the best of my ability, I had even tried to preserve the Constitution if, to save slavery, or any minor matter, I should permit the wreck of government, country, and Constitution all together.[10]

In order to save the Constitution as a whole, he had to be willing to break certain parts—in effect the same rationale advanced by Cromwell and the Long Parliament to justify the extraordinary measures taken in support of the revolutionary English Commonwealth in the 1640s and 1650s.

Although it's unknown whether he ever used the phrase, what Lincoln had discovered was actually the principle of *raison d'état*, the old notion that survival of the state, which Lincoln equated with survival of the people, took precedence over all rights, privileges, or laws that may have existed under it. In early 1862, William Whiting, the top legal official in the War Department, issued an opinion stating that the government's power to ensure its own continuation was unqualified and absolute. Echoing Alexander Hamilton's arguments concerning the "necessary and proper" clause in the early 1790s, he wrote that the Preamble's injunction to "promote the general welfare" amounted to a blanket authorization for the federal government to carry out any and all emergency measures necessary to carry it through the current crisis. Although slavery had seemed to be securely embedded in the Constitution before the war, he added, the current emergency had at last provided Congress or the president with the tools to excise it. The government could cite its duty to ensure domestic tranquility, to suppress domestic insurrection (set forth in ART. I, SEC. 8), to maintain a republican form of government for the states (ART. IV, SEC. 4), and so on—all of which could conceivably provide the powers that be with a rationale with which to bypass the cumbersome old constitutional machinery and institute change by fiat.[11] *Raison d'état*, the war-powers doctrine, became the all-purpose justification for doing whatever it took to secure victory both on the battlefield and off.

Yet *raison d'état* was more than just a shortcut; because its justification could be found in the Constitution, particularly the Preamble and the "necessary and proper" clause, it became a tool for turning the Constitution inside out. Rather than merely permitting Lincoln to shuck off the old Madisonian constraints, it compelled him to. Ordinary folks could be excused for believing that when the First Amendment declared that "Congress shall make no law . . . abridging the freedom of speech, or of the press," that was what it meant. Yet through the miracle of *raison d'état*, it was now discovered that those words actually meant the opposite, that when national survival was at stake, the president, with backing from Congress, was *required* to make laws abridging free speech or a free press. Anything less would be dereliction of duty and therefore unconstitutional. Consequently, despite thousands of political arrests, the suppression of hundreds of newspapers, and even the closing of unfriendly churches, Lincoln told a supporter in 1863 that his chief worry was that future generations would criticize him "for having made too few arrests rather than too many."[12] Too few arrests meant a failure to take responsibility, whereas too many merely reflected a certain excess of zeal that under the circumstances was all too excusable.

Of course, *raison d'état* could also serve as a justification for dictatorship. If survival of the state was the overriding factor, then the president, as head of state, could conceivably use it to suppress democracy and ride roughshod over the legislative branch. The real question, the one that had escaped Hamilton but had preoccupied Bentham and his colleague James Mill, was not only how to make government strong, but how to make it strong *and* democratic. Or, as Lincoln put it in July 1861, the issue was whether government "must, . . . of necessity, be too strong for the liberties of its own people, or too weak to maintain its own existence."[13] The question was a particularly sensitive one for Congress, which saw itself as the popular, democratic branch and could never forget how, in other countries, strong men had arisen during periods of turmoil to establish one-man rule. With his remarkable sense of modesty and restraint, Lincoln seemed to be the last person for the role of an American Caesar. Yet there was no shortage of other candidates waiting in the wings. "If the factious abolition leaders do not speedily draw in their horse," warned the anti-Republican *New York Herald* in late 1861, "they may find in General McClellan such a tartar as the Long Parliament found in Cromwell or the Council of Five Hundred found in Napoleon Bonaparte."[14] Following the disaster at Fredericksburg, in which more than twelve thousand Union troops were slaughtered when General Ambrose Burnside ordered a pointless frontal assault on Lee's forces in Virginia in December 1862, Union general Joseph Lee Hooker seemed to be setting himself up for such a role as well. Indeed, Lincoln himself acknowledged the rumors about Hooker's ambitions when he placed him in charge of the Army of the Potomac. "I have heard, in such a way as to believe it, of your recently saying that both the army and the government needed a dictator," he wrote. But "only those generals who gain successes can set up dictators. What I now ask of you is military success, and I will risk the dictatorship."[15] Fortunately or not, Hooker proved inept as a battlefield commander as well, and the threat of dictatorship was removed.

It was Congress, however, that turned out to be the crucial ideological battleground of the Civil War period. Despite the prevailing atmosphere of "constitutionolatry" before the war, the old parliamentary traditions of the eighteenth century still lingered. During the war, however, they blossomed. Under the Republicans, a new kind of party that was more tightly organized and ideologically coherent than anything Americans had been used to, Congress emerged as a surprisingly disciplined and militant body. Rather than compromisers and deal makers, it was now dominated by moral crusaders who believed that temporizing could only lead to defeat. The most powerful figure was Thaddeus Stevens, the Radical Republican representative from Pennsylvania, who would not have been out of place in Cromwell's Long Parliament. Stevens saw the war in terms that were as much social as military; his tone was often apocalyptic and revolutionary. In mid-1862, for instance, he said of the slaveholders:

> I would seize every foot of land, and every dollar of their property as our armies go along, put it to the uses of the war, to the pay of our debts. I would plant the South with a military colony if I could not make them submit otherwise. I would sell their land to the soldiers of independence; I would send those soldiers there with arms in their hands to occupy the heritage of traitors, and build up there a land of free men and of freedom, which, fifty years hence, would swarm with its hundreds of millions without a slave upon its soil.[16]

Stevens was openly contemptuous of constitutional constraints— he once called the Constitution "a worthless bit of old parchment"[17]

—and, in contrast to the old theory of checks and balances, argued that Congress was in fact superior to the other two branches. The president executed the laws, he argued, but Congress made the laws for the president to carry out. Or, as Benjamin F. Wade, the Radical Republican senator from Ohio, explained, "It is for Congress to lay down the rules and regulations by which the executive shall be governed in conducting the war."[18] The president was commander in chief of the armed forces, but Congress was commander in chief of the nation.

As Congress quickly moved to outflank the executive, the old rivalry between the two turned into something more serious. In July 1861, the House passed a resolution condemning "slave-catching" Union generals who had adopted a policy of returning runaway slaves to their owners. Although Lincoln argued that the Constitution's fugitive slave clause in Article IV must be observed if the Union was to uphold the mantle of constitutional legitimacy, the House was clearly running out of patience with such constitutional niceties. In August 1861, the House and Senate both passed a bill calling on the president to issue an emancipation proclamation immediately. Dissatisfied with the conduct of the war, the two houses took the dramatic step in December 1861 of forming a joint Committee on the Conduct of the War, dominated by the Radical Republicans, to monitor military progress, interrogate officers, and assess strategy. Although the White House regarded the committee as pesky interlopers who did nothing but spread confusion and dissension in the ranks, Congress insisted on the right to exercise its separate authority.

The committee was a dramatic step by a legislative body that had previously been content to act through the executive branch, not around it. Clearly, the Republican-controlled Congress was pushing war policy in a more radical direction, much as the Puritan-controlled Parliament had pushed for an ever more radical military policy in the mid-1640s. Just as Parliament was suspicious of aristocratic officers who continually made excuses for doing badly in the field, Congress was suspicious of West Pointers (the military academy had been a Southern stronghold before the war) who made excuses for their own military performance. Yet in seeking to transform the war, Congress was transforming itself as well. The military conflict had cut the legislative branch loose from its constitutional moorings and was forcing it to carve out a new role for itself. Members were aware not only of what Parliament had done during the English Civil War but of all that had followed. Parliament was the part that had swallowed the whole, an institution that had gone from being a branch of the government to the entire show. It was an example, many Radical Republicans believed, to be emulated.

Thus, following the Fredericksburg debacle, congressional Republicans sent a delegation to the White House to demand a cabinet shake-up. It was an unprecedented invasion of executive turf, and although Lincoln stood his ground and refused, both sides were conscious of a Rubicon having been crossed. "It was whispered," one historian noted, "that the Jacobin machine had served Lincoln with an ultimatum—he must get rid of . . . the conservatives in the Cabinet . . . [or] the army or the radicals would push through Congress a vote of want of confidence in the administration."[19] William Pitt Fessenden, one of the more moderate Republicans in the Senate, observed: "The story of the last few days will mark a new point in history, for it has witnessed a new proceeding—one probably unknown to the government of the country."[20]

The gap between Congress and the presidency was widening. The next two years, though, proved to be something of an anticlimax. On January 1, 1863, Lincoln's Emancipation Proclamation went into effect, thereby muting a good deal of the criticism out of Congress. A few months later came the triumphs at Vicksburg and Gettysburg. The string of victories that followed seemed to vindicate the Radical Republican proposition that the war could only be won if transformed into a soul-stirring moral crusade. If tension was abating between the White House and Capitol Hill, it was because Congress was at last getting its way. The executive was swinging around to the legislature's point of view, not the other way around.

Harmony was not long-lasting, however. In mid-1864, Lincoln

vetoed a bill aimed at toughening up Reconstruction policy in newly conquered portions of the South, whereupon the authors, "Bluff Ben" Wade of Ohio and Representative Henry Winter Davis of Maryland, issued a hotly worded manifesto accusing the president of "dictatorial usurpation." It was once more unto the breach, although Lincoln was able yet again to smooth things over by signaling to Congress that he would soon come up with a Reconstruction policy more to its liking. The radicals were "utterly lawless—the unhandiest devils to deal with," he confided, but their faces were "set Zionwards."[21] Hence, he would have find a way to work with them. Earlier, Lincoln had not protested when a newly organized white government in Union-controlled Louisiana had introduced a "black code" aimed at restoring slavery in everything but name. But now that revolutionary changes were sweeping the South, silent acquiescence in the discredited methods of the past was no longer possible. In January 1865, General Sherman carved out a strip of four hundred thousand acres in coastal Georgia and South Carolina for the exclusive settlement of some forty thousand ex-slaves. In March, ex-slaves erupted in "grand jubilee" in newly liberated Charleston; a few weeks later, they did the same when Grant moved into Richmond. During a walking tour of the city the following day, Lincoln was visibly embarrassed as one ex-slave after another fell at his feet hailing him as the "Messiah." As one black man told his former owner, "All is equal. . . . All the land belongs to the Yankees now and they gwine divide it out among de colored people." On April 11, two days after Appomattox, Lincoln delivered his last speech, in which he indicated some limited support for black suffrage and declared that a more fully developed Reconstruction policy would soon follow.[22]

The assassination came three days later and, with it, a vast shift in the political firmament. Within months, the conflict that had been simmering between the two branches broke out in open warfare. There are any number of reasons why it erupted when it did and not sooner. The war itself was the most obvious. As long as the bullets were flying, the legislature and executive had an incentive to cooperate and keep disagreements within bounds. Lincoln, with his remarkable rhetorical powers and deft political touch, was another factor: he was determined to keep things under control and succeeded. The fact that he and the congressional leadership came from the same party was important as well. The GOP functioned during the war as a well-oiled political machine to coordinate policy, to drum up support at all levels of government, and to dampen disputes within the government. It was a conspiracy, in a sense, to *transcend* separation of powers, one that performed triumphantly.

Finally, there was the Constitution itself. During the war, the document had, in a sense, been considered suspended for the duration. Under the war-powers doctrine, the government's powers were so sweeping as to place the old doctrine of checks and balances in virtual abeyance. But with the peace, some kind of sorting out was inevitable. Americans had to decide what was left of the Constitution and what was not, a reckoning bound to raise the level of conflict in Washington as certain institutions gained in power and others lost. Just as in 1861, Congress was faced with problems that the Founders could never have anticipated and that, inadvertently, they had helped create. The most nettlesome concerned the status of the newly conquered Confederate states. If Lincoln had been correct in arguing in 1861 that secession was unconstitutional, then, in a sense, it had never occurred. Now that the war was over, the doctrine implied that the rebel states were free to resume their old places in the constitutional order. During the war, Congress had refused to seat representatives of Louisiana's newly reconstructed state government on the grounds that they were Confederate wolves in Unionist clothing. Yet, now that the Confederate states were back in the fold, white Southerners had marked their return by voting a host of leading ex-Confederates back into Congress—four Confederate generals, five colonels, several members of the now-defunct Confederate Congress, even former Confederate Vice President Alexander H. Stephens—all of whom expected to be seated now that the conflict was behind them.[23] It was as if German voters had elected a solid slate of top Nazis immediately after World War II. What was Congress to do?

Even worse was the bizarre constitutional situation that had arisen when slavery was abolished while black voting rights were still up in the air. Where Southern blacks had previously counted as three-fifths of a person for purposes of apportioning seats in Congress, as free citizens they now counted as five-fifths, which meant that the ex-Confederate states stood to gain as many as twenty seats in the House and the electoral college over their already inflated prewar total. Since the ex-slaves were still by and large disenfranchised, that additional political clout would be exercised by white ex-Confederates. If the old three-fifths clause was "a bounty on slave holding," as William Lloyd Garrison had once put it, then the new five-fifths arrangement was an even more potent incentive for Southern white racists to deprive blacks of access to the ballot box for as long as possible. Every ex-slave who did not vote was an extra vote for whites who did. For Radical Republicans, the consequences were worse than immoral; they were suicidal. If allowed to stand, Northern "Copperhead" Democrats would be able to join forces with unrepentant ex-Confederates in the South to form a majority. The people who fought the war would once more be out in the wilderness. All hope of reform would be lost.

Clearly, the Republicans would have to act quickly, yet once again the Constitution stood in the way. Under the old Constitution, voting rights in congressional elections were a state prerogative, which meant that if the federal government was going to guarantee ex-slaves access to the ballot box, the Constitution would have to be changed. Yet while the Republicans commanded a majority in terms of the popular vote, particularly after the GOP's sweeping election victory in 1866, the party did not command the supermajority needed to force through a constitutional amendment. Assuming they were readmitted into the fold, the eleven ex-Confederate states would still be able to stop constitutional change in its tracks.

One way out of the bind would have been for Congress simply to have seized the amending power for its own, rewritten the

Constitution, and dared anyone to say otherwise. It had the power, the popular support, and had just come through a war in which all the old verities had gone up in smoke. As one legal scholar recently suggested, it could have formed itself into a second constitutional convention and drafted a new document beginning with the words: "We the People of the United States, in order to form a more perfect Union after the terrible ordeal of Civil War, do ordain this Constitution . . ."[24] Other countries had done the same under similar circumstances, so why not the United States?

Unfortunately, the old Constitution's spell was still too strong for any but the most determined radicals to embark on such a revolutionary course. Instead, the Republicans opted for something more moderate. Rather than a new constitution, they decided to use novel means to modify the old one both to stay in power and to bring meaningful reconstruction to the South. This was a new stage in the constitutional struggle, one which actually began during the final months of the war when the Thirteenth Amendment to abolish slavery, the first amendment in more than sixty years, began wending its way through Congress. On January 31, 1865, after it had already passed the Senate, the House gave it the necessary two-thirds approval and prepared to send it on to the states as required under Article V.

But then a curious question presented itself: which states? The two dozen that had remained loyal to the Union or the eleven that had not? It was absurd, of course, to give the Confederate states a say in reforming a republic they had sought to destroy, yet that was what the Constitution seemed to require. Thaddeus Stevens argued that the reconquered Confederate states should be excluded from the vote "until they are duly admitted to the family of States by the law-making power of their conqueror," yet other members shrank from doing something so obvious.[25] Instead, Congress persuaded eight Southern states where temporary minority governments had been set up under military tutelage to vote yes on the amendment; then, a short time later, it withdrew recognition from these same puppet governments and turned them out of power. The solution was perhaps not as clean as Stevens would have liked. Yet it was evidence all the same of Congress's willingness to bend the rules to get the job done.

Southerners who complained that the results made a mockery of constitutional procedure were undoubtedly correct. Yet the results were a variation on the old schoolyard conundrum about a tree falling in a forest. If the Constitution is violated yet either no one cares or no one is in a position to do anything about it, did the violation really occur? Obviously, slavery had to be expunged from the Constitution. Whether or not it was done according to the strict letter of the law was irrelevant—it simply had to be done. Yet in doing what was necessary, there was no doubt that Congress was substituting its own authority for that of the Founders. While ostensibly abiding by the terms of Article V, it was, in fact, manipulating the state role in such a way as to underscore the reality that Congress was the only show in town. Congress used similar techniques a few years later in ramming through the epic Fourteenth Amendment, which for the first time provided the federal government with authority to intervene directly in the states in defense of individual civil rights. Congress, or rather the rump representing the North, approved the amendment, forwarded it to the Northern states for approval, and then informed the Southern states still suffering under military governments that they would have to approve the amendment as a condition of readmission as full-fledged members of the Union. One by one, the Southern states complied. When two Northern states, Ohio and New Jersey, changed their minds and rescinded their ratification votes, Congress ignored them and pressed ahead. When Southerners attacked the amendment as a "force bill" that was being shoved down their throats in a way that made a mockery of proper legal procedure, it ignored them as well. Congress alone would decide what was valid procedure and what was not.[26]

The more Congress gathered up the constitutional reins, the more unavoidable a showdown with the executive branch became. Initially, Andrew Johnson had seemed to be cut from the same cloth as his predecessor. Both were from the upper South, Lincoln from Kentucky originally and Johnson from Tennessee. Both were poor boys who had made good, Lincoln as a lawyer, Johnson, an illiterate tailor who had to be taught to read by his wife, as a politician. Both were implacably opposed to the slaveholding plantocracy, with Johnson, if anything, the more militant of the two in his hatred. As a champion of poor white Tennesseans, he had distinguished himself before the war by thundering against the big slave owners as a "pampered, bloated, corrupted aristocracy." As military governor of Tennessee, he had impressed even the Radical Republicans with his ruthlessness in putting down pro-Confederate elements. "Treason must be made odious, and traitors must be punished and impoverished," he had declared.[27] "Whenever you hear a man prating about the Constitution," he remarked on another occasion, "spot him as a traitor."[28]

Yet Johnson was a more complex figure than congressional leaders realized. A pro-war Democrat rather than a Republican, he had been a strict constructionist before the war, even to the point of once opposing a congressional appropriation to pave Washington's muddy streets. While he despised large-scale slave owners, he despised neo-Hamiltonian Republicans even more fervently. Like many poor Southern whites, he also turned out to be deeply racist. As late as 1865, he was still defending the virtues of slavery and, according to his private secretary, was incensed that black troops were still occupying his native state. In early 1868, he was even heard expressing annoyance at the presence of black laborers on the White House grounds. According to a report in the *New York World*, he burst into a rage following a meeting with the black abolitionist Frederick Douglass. "I know that damned Douglass," he reportedly said; "he's just like any nigger, and he would sooner cut a white man's throat than not."[29]

Constitutionally, Johnson's position was essentially the same as that of Charles I confronting the Long Parliament. Just as the Parliament in the 1640s represented only the reforming, anti-Royalist side of English society, Congress in the 1860s only represented the portion of American society that had remained true to the Union. As a result,

Johnson fell into the Stuartlike role of arguing that since the legislature was unequipped to represent the nation as a whole, only the executive branch was so qualified. "As eleven States are not at this time represented in either branch of Congress," he declared in vetoing the Freedmen's Bureau Bill in February 1866, "it would seem to be his [i.e., the president's] duty, in all proper occasions, to present their just claims to Congress."[30] In effect, Johnson was arguing in favor of executive supremacy, a form of limited one-man rule until the Union was restored to its former shape and size. From Congress's perspective, this was intolerable. Johnson was clearly trying to shut it out of power, yet its options were limited. The confrontation escalated several months later when the president vetoed the 1866 Civil Rights Act on the grounds that it violated states' rights. Congress had no right to act, he said, when the states most affected were not permitted to participate in the debate. Johnson also condemned black suffrage as "ill-timed, uncalled for, and calculated to do much harm."[31] Yet black suffrage was vital to the Reconstruction effort. With the Democratic ranks newly replenished with the addition of white voters in the South, the GOP needed the black vote in order to solidify its grip on power.

Indeed, the GOP was obliged to move quickly in order to preserve what power it had. Thanks to the disarray in Washington, the situation in the South was spinning out of control. In May 1866, a collision in Memphis between a horse-drawn hack driven by a black and one driven by a white led to a ferocious white rampage in which at least forty-six blacks were killed, five black women were raped, and hundreds of black homes, churches, and schools were pillaged and torched.[32] In July, whites engaged in a similar orgy of violence in New Orleans, killing some thirty-seven blacks and three whites who had gathered to take part in a convention called to draw up a more progressive state constitution. Johnson openly sided with the white mob and suppressed a report by a Northern general on the scene who accused local police of complicity in the violence so "unnecessary and atrocious as to compel one to say it was murder."[33] When a white bystander upbraided a member of the mob carrying a weapon still covered with fresh blood and bits of hair, the man replied: "Oh hell! Haven't you seen the papers? Johnson is with us."[34]

Obviously, Radical Republicans could not stand idly by and watch as their best-laid plans were rent asunder. As November 1866 approached, both sides took to the campaign trail hoping to turn the upcoming congressional elections into a referendum on Reconstruction. Touring the Midwest, Johnson wrapped himself in the mantle of constitutional legitimacy. "For myself, I want no better constitutional league as that formed by Washington and his compeers," he proclaimed. Expressing contempt for Radical Republicans, he lambasted "a body called, or which assumes to be, the Congress of the United States, while in fact it is a Congress of only a part of the States."[35] The Republicans, for their part, appealed to patriotism, memories of the war, and fears that former rebels were beginning to regroup. Although most party members tiptoed gingerly around the race issue, Thaddeus Stevens, the Republican leader of the House, faced up to it with admirable frankness. Responding to cries of "down with the nigger party, we're for the white man's party," he declared:

> A deep-seated prejudice against races has disfigured the human mind for ages. . . . This doctrine [of equal rights] may be unpopular with besotted ignorance. But popular or unpopular, I shall stand by it until I am relieved of the unprofitable labors of the earth.[36]

The results were astonishing. So great was the Republican landslide that even if the Southern states had returned a solidly Democratic contingent (something they were not allowed to do), the GOP would still have had a commanding majority in Congress. As it was, they had more than enough to override a presidential veto. Congress convened early the following year in what might be described as a mood of high Cromwellianism. Where Cromwell had divided England up into eleven military districts, each governed by a major general with wide-ranging powers, the newly radicalized Congress divided the South into five districts, each ruled by a military governor under the overall direction of General Grant. The military authorities banned veterans' organizations and other groups deemed threatening to the new order, fired thousands of local officials and half a dozen governors, and purged state legislatures of pro-Confederate elements as well. A twenty-thousand-strong army of occupation, aided by a black militia, enforced order. Military courts took jurisdiction over cases involving violence against blacks in which civilian courts had shown themselves incapable of dealing fairly. Political rights were withdrawn from thousands of Confederates who had been granted executive clemency by the president, and all told some one hundred thousand white voters were stricken from the rolls. So many ex-slaves were signed up that black voters outnumbered whites in five states and fell just shy of a majority in two others.[37] Whether it was antiracism or political expediency that drove the Republicans, there is no doubt that an interracial, interregional partnership was being forged. The Republicans needed the ex-slaves to maintain their majority in Congress, while the ex-slaves needed the Republicans to help maintain their freedom. Meanwhile, the once bottom-up structure of American politics was reversed. Instead of following local trends, Congress was dictating change from above while local officials snapped to attention.

For all his rhetorical fierceness, Thaddeus Stevens, by now the most powerful man in Washington, stressed that his goal was to transform the South rather than punish it:

> I have never desired bloody punishments to any extent, even for the sake of example. But there are punishments quite as appalling, and longer remembered, than death. They are more advisable, because they would reach a greater number. Strip a proud nobility of their bloated estates; reduce them to a level with plain republicans; send them forth to labor, and teach their children to enter the workshops or handle the plow, and you will thus humble the proud traitors. Teach his posterity to respect labor and eschew treason. Conspiracies are bred among the rich and the vain, the ambitious aristocrats.[38]

With the formation of a Joint Committee on Reconstruction along the lines of the old Committee on the Conduct of the War,

Congress was well on its way to taking over the entire government. The isolation of the president was nearly complete. Charles Nordhoff, editor of the *New York Evening Post*, visited Johnson in late February 1867 and found him "much excited" and certain that "the people of the South . . . were to be trodden under foot 'to protect niggers.' "[39] In March, Congress passed the Tenure of Office Act, which forbade Johnson to remove officeholders without Senate approval. Since the upper house was required to advise and consent on appointments, Congress figured it should advise and consent on dismissals as well. In August, Johnson threw down the gauntlet by suspending Secretary of War Edwin Stanton, a close ally of the radicals; the Senate countermanded the suspension as soon as it reconvened. Johnson could have then pursued the matter in the courts, but instead sounded out General Philip Sheridan about a strange scheme to assemble a special body of troops near Washington outside the normal chain of command, answerable only to Sheridan and himself. It was an invitation to a military coup d'état, which Sheridan wisely refused.[40] A few months later, Johnson began encouraging white Southerners to resist the radical Reconstruction program handed down by Congress and replaced several military governors in the South with more conservative officers.[41] On February 21, 1868, he dismissed Stanton outright. A week later, the House voted to impeach.

The impeachment trial was the great climax of the American Civil War just as Charles I's trial was the great climax of the English. In both cases, the legislative leadership could be accused of cynicism in that it claimed to be acting under the law and in defense of the constitution, when quite plainly it was acting against both. Yet in both instances, it had no choice. As long as Charles was around to rally the Royalists, the danger of renewed warfare was ever present; as long as Andrew Johnson was in office to rally the ex-Confederates and cripple government policy, Reconstruction would be hobbled in the South. "Didn't I tell you?" said Stevens when word reached Capitol Hill of Stanton's dismissal. "What good did moderation do you? If you don't kill the snake, it will kill you."[42] Yet where the English republicans had gone ahead and found the king guilty despite opposition from the English legal establishment and fears and misgivings on their own side, their American counterparts soon became bogged down.

One reason had to do with the role of the upper and lower houses. When the House of Lords balked at putting Charles on trial in 1649, the Commons had simply shoved the Lords out of the way and proceeded on its own. For that very reason, the Founders had seen to it in America that the process would be reversed. The House would indict, while the more conservative Senate would conduct the actual trial. From a Radical Republican point of view, the prospects were not promising. The Senate was more vacillating and less determined than the House and less disciplined as well. It had a higher proportion of noisy blowhards. Yet Thaddeus Stevens and his colleagues in the House could only watch in frustration as Senate Republicans lived up to expectations and made a complete hash of the prosecution.

The impeachment trial was not only a power struggle between the executive and legislative branches, but a struggle over the shape of American government. If Johnson prevailed, it would be multipolar and heterogeneous, with Congress free to draft one Reconstruction policy for the South and the president free to impose quite another. If Congress prevailed, it would be unipolar and homogeneous: the legislative branch would set policy and see to it that it carried it out every step of the way. Obstruction by the executive branch would not be tolerated. *Harper's Weekly*, which was hostile to the radicals but not imperceptive, observed that if Johnson was convicted, "it is plain that impeachment of the Executive will become an ordinary party measure, and the independence of the Executive contemplated by the Constitution being thus destroyed, the balance of the whole system comes to an end."[43] On the other side of the spectrum, the radical *New York Tribune* urged that impeachment be understood not as "a mode of punishment, but a means of security and of avoiding political maladministration."[44] The even more radical *Boston Commonwealth* called on the Republicans to not only toss out Johnson but to abolish the presidency outright, while the *Anti-Slavery Standard* went it one further by calling on House Republicans to abolish "the three remaining oligarchies"—the presidency, the Senate, and the Supreme Court.[45] Stevens himself emphasized the superiority of the British parliamentary system and, despite constitutional language stipulating that a president can only be removed for "treason, bribery, or other high crimes and misdemeanors," urged that Johnson be removed for political betrayal rather than any supposed criminal or quasi-criminal offenses.[46]

British liberals, viewing the events in America through parliamentary lenses, were also on the congressional side. *Blackwood's Edinburgh Magazine* declared that "the sooner the cumbrous and costly office [of the presidency] is abolished the better for the public peace."[47] Walter Bagehot, the famous commentator and journalist who was editor at the time of the *Economist* in London, also favored Congress, but was dismayed by the legalism of American politics in general, the tendency of politicians of all stripes to enter into Talmudic disputes about the Founders as if words written in the late eighteenth century somehow held the key to problems that had arisen in the mid-nineteenth. "Mr. Johnson," he wrote, "makes a mere fetish idol of the Constitution. He . . . altogether conducts himself as if the Constitution had not been made for Americans but rather Americans for the Constitution." While the radicals "realised that the Constitution has, for a certain purpose at least, broken down . . . even they have not been able to realise that they need to create something wholly unprovided for at the time of the formation of the Constitution."[48] The Republicans had to create new forms of government to deal with new problems. This was the language of modern utilitarianism, reflecting as it did the notion that while people should learn from experience, they should not allow themselves to be encumbered by the past in dealing with situations that were essentially new. On the question of how to reconstruct the South, Bagehot remarked:

> President and radicals alike seem to be sheerly unable to recognize that, to a certain extent, they had no law and precedent

to go upon,—that they had to begin again, without the help of any documentary and legal basis from which to start. The documentary superstition was strong in both alike.[49]

Congress was clearly trying to find a way out of the constitutional tangle by getting rid of an obstructionist president. Unfortunately for the cause of constitutional flexibility, it failed—the impeachment trial proved to be a catastrophe. Chief Justice Salmon P. Chase imposed strict legal procedure, which meant that the Republicans were forced to stick closely to the criminal complaint against Johnson despite its obvious weakness. Benjamin Butler, the Republican senator who served as chief prosecutor, was an embarrassment, alternating between trivial legalism and absurd exaggeration. In his opening remarks, he all but accused Johnson of taking part in the assassination conspiracy against Lincoln. "By murder most foul," he declared, "he succeeded to the presidency, and is an elect of an assassin to that high office."[50] Yet it is a tribute to Republican discipline that when the final vote came, an overwhelming majority voted to convict—although still one vote short of the two-thirds margin required by the Constitution.

Johnson's acquittal was a triumph for the law and a defeat for democracy. As a glamorous young senator named John F. Kennedy wrote in the mid-1950s, the senators voting for acquittal had taken a "stand against legislative mob rule"[51]—which is to say they had resisted the terrible temptation to follow Britain down the parliamentary path. If the Senate had voted the other way, it would have indeed been a legal travesty, much as it had been a legal travesty when Parliament convicted Charles I. Yet the break with the past would have been all the more decisive as a consequence. By violating the law, Congress would have shown that the law was subordinate to popular sovereignty.

Instead, the very opposite proved to be the case—the Constitution emerged unbroken while popular sovereignty was dashed against the rocks. The power of the Radical Republican machine was broken, and Reconstruction in the South began rapidly to unwind. "Now that you are strengthened in your position," a white admirer of Johnson wrote from Memphis, "your friends will expect universal amnesty. We'll fully expect it of you, if it can be made to relieve us of this miserable Negro rule under which we groan in despair. . . ." The Republican Party's scattered network of Southern supporters sent back alarming reports about a rising tide of racial violence. "Our condition . . . is a perilous one," a black Georgian reported following the acquittal; "colored men have been thrown out of employment and driven from their homes. . . . I myself had to be guarded at night by colored men and finally had to leave the country on account of the threats against my life." In Mississippi, A. L. Alcorn, the state's Reconstruction-era governor, warned that violence toward freedmen was becoming so pervasive as to make slavery seem good by comparison: "Better a thousand times for the negro that the government should return him to the custody of his original owner where he would have a master to look after his well being, than that his neck should be placed under the heel of a society vindictive towards him because he is free."[52]

The effects of Republican demoralization can be seen in the Fifteenth Amendment, which declared that "the right of citizens of the United States to vote shall not be denied or abridged . . . on account of race, color, or previous condition of servitude." Written in the wake of Johnson's acquittal, the amendment did nothing to strike down literacy tests or property requirements, which could be used to prevent poor people in general from voting, white as well as black. As a consequence, not only did it prove a dead letter as far as Southern blacks were concerned, but by failing to help poor whites it failed to provide a means by which the two groups might come to see that their interests were intertwined.

Sensing its weakness, the Supreme Court, which had generally laid low during the war, resumed the offensive. The *ex parte Milligan* decision in 1866, which voided military arrests except in areas where civilian government had hopelessly broken down due to insurrection, roused Radical Republicans to such a fury that the justices had quickly backed off. For the radicals, military courts were the only places where blacks could get justice in the South, and they were therefore not about to see them curtailed.[53] Seven years later, however, the Court's decision in a series of suits brought by private butchers in New Orleans, known as the *Slaughterhouse* cases, left the new Fourteenth Amendment all but gutted. The suits argued that an initiative to establish a state monopoly in the butcher's trade violated rights guaranteed by the new amendment, yet the Court ruled that the rights in question were limited to a pitiful few—the right to gain access to ports and navigable waterways, to travel to the seat of government, to run for federal office, and so on. *U.S. v. Cruikshank* (1876) was an even more devastating blow. Overturning the conviction of three whites who had taken part in the infamous Colfax Massacre, the single bloodiest instance of terror in the entire postwar period, the Court ruled that the federal government was empowered to move against civil rights violations only by states and not by individuals. While state officials were enjoined from wreaking violence on blacks, they were free to watch while private citizens did the same.[54] Thus was born the image of the Southern sheriff who sees no evil and hears no evil as neo-Confederates go on a terror spree against newly freed blacks.

The return of old-style constitutional balance also led to an unprecedented explosion of political corruption up North. One reason was the inefficient, balkanized political structure, with its countless nooks and crannies for crooked politicians to hide in. Another was the general political paralysis, which led to defeatism, despair, and a mood of anything goes. Not unlike American wheat or steel production, the United States' output of political corruption would soon astonish the world.

"Their ignorance is awful, and it is not tempered and restrained as the ignorance of the corresponding class is in Europe by contact with foreign nations." Thus spoke E. L. Godkin, the English-born editor of the *Nation*, concerning members of Congress in 1874. This was the same E. L. Godkin who a decade earlier had waxed so hopeful and enthusiastic about American prospects.[55] The various forces at work in post–Civil War America—corruption, political paralysis, ignorance—came to a head in the 1876 presidential election between Democrat Samuel J. Tilden, governor of New York, and Republican Rutherford B. Hayes of Ohio. While Tilden squeaked through with a narrow victory in terms of the popular vote, Republican-controlled state election boards invalidated enough returns from violence-torn portions of South Carolina, Florida, and Louisiana to give Hayes a one-vote lead in the electoral college. Both parties were guilty of chicanery, the Republicans by fiddling with the vote totals and the Democrats by using violence to keep large numbers of Southern black voters away from the polls. Yet when the election was turned over to the House, the only result was that chicanery rose to a new level. Ultimately, a handful of leading Republicans and Democrats met in a Washington hotel in late February 1877 to hammer out a deal. The details are still unknown, but they apparently involved a trade-off in which Hayes would become president, a Democrat would become postmaster general (thereby giving the party control of the biggest patronage mill in town), while whatever remained of Reconstruction would be dismantled. "To think that Hayes could go back on us when we had to wade through blood to help place him where he is now," exclaimed one black Southerner.[56] Years later, a number of the architects of the Compromise of 1877 gathered at an elite Washington dinner party to swap stories. "What would the people of this country think," exclaimed President Grover Cleveland, among those present, "if the roof could be lifted from this house and they could hear these men?" Replied one of the participants: "If anyone repeats what I have said, I will denounce him as a liar."[57] The American people were once more in the dark about the workings of their own government.

This was the golden age of the backroom deal and the smoke-filled room. The disputed 1876 election had led to some rash talk among Southern hotheads about refighting the battles of the Civil War if Tilden was denied victory, yet in the end neither side was in the mood for renewed bloodletting.[58] Still, the threat of renewed violence was sufficiently frightening that for a generation after, as one historian put it, "politicians preferred to deal with superficialities, for they feared that any attempt to deal with the cankers eating at the vitals of the nation would cause another civil war."[59] For both the Republicans and Democrats, the advantage lay in preservation of the status quo.[60] Henceforth, said C. Vann Woodward,

> there were no serious infringements of the basic agreements of 1877—those regarding intervention by force, respect for state rights, and renunciation of Federal responsibility for the protection of the Negro. In 1883 the Supreme Court pronounced the Civil Rights Act unconstitutional. The decision constituted a sort of validation of the Compromise of 1877. . . . "The calm with which the country receives the news shows how completely the extravagant expectations . . . of the war have dried out," observed the *New York Evening Post.*[61]

Ironically, the Republicans, anxious to see that the Thirteenth, Fourteenth, and Fifteenth Amendments were fully enforced, emerged as the new party of constitutional literalism during this period. In 1876, the GOP party platform asserted that "all parts of the Constitution are sacred and must be sacredly obeyed—the parts that are new no less than the parts that are old."[62] So frozen and formalist did constitutional interpretation become that Oliver Wendell Holmes was moved to cry out in 1881 that public policy concerns and "the felt necessities of the time . . . had always been the creative force in the growth of the common law," rather than the "sterile logic" that was being increasingly applied.[63] With slavery removed as an irritant between North and South, strict constructionism was once more in force.

6

CONSTITUTIONAL ORTHODOXY RESTORED

PERHAPS THE MOST perceptive constitutional thinker of the 1860s was a gentleman farmer of pronounced conservative views named Sidney George Fisher. Fisher, who lived outside Philadelphia and came from an old shipping family, had married into wealth and thereafter looked down on anyone who had not had the good sense to do the same. He held no political office or military commission during the war—the closest he ever got to fighting was arguing with his Copperhead relatives—although he regularly contributed articles to the *Philadelphia North American* and the *North American Review*.[1] In 1862, he assembled his ideas on the fundamental problems facing the American political system in a volume entitled *The Trial of the Constitution*. The book was well received and influential, but as the political temper began to change toward the end of the decade, it gradually fell from view. By the time a new generation of constitutional critics came to the fore in the 1880s—most prominent of which would be a rising young academic star named Woodrow Wilson—it was all but forgotten.

This is unfortunate because Fisher's book contained some of the most penetrating constitutional commentary in the history of the Republic. Educated in the law, Fisher trained his highly analytical mind on what he saw as the chief problem posed by the war: how a country with vast natural resources, an educated population, a high degree of democracy, and an almost complete lack of external enemies had wound up so spectacularly on the rocks. "There can be no doubt that the vast majority of the people preferred peace and Union," he wrote.[2] Yet what they had gotten was disunion and war. If the job of democratic government was to give the people what they wanted, how was it that Americans had wound up with the opposite? Something had obviously gone wrong, Fisher decided, casting about for an answer.

He found it in the endlessly interesting, endlessly problematic Article V. The amending clause, he wrote, was supposed to be a way of changing the law whenever the law had irrevocably broken down. Yet "the safety valve did not work, and the boiler has burst."[3] The reason was clear: Article V set an impossibly high standard for compliance that neither side could meet. Throughout all the years of struggle prior to the war,

> neither party could get control of the key, so carefully was it guarded. Neither North or South could have secured a vote of two-thirds of Congress or of three-fourths of the States, to propose an amendment to the Constitution or to call a convention for that purpose. Nor could such a convention have made a settlement of the question at issue [i.e., slavery], that would have been ratified by three-fourths of the State Legislatures. . . .[4]

The result was a deadlock that continued as long as the established rules prevailed. But where the Founders thought they were imposing stability on a fractious nation, Fisher argued that constitutional rigidity of this sort had resulted in the opposite, namely, an overflow of passions that he preferred to see contained. As a conservative democrat, he believed that the Founders' mistake was in trying to bottle up the will of the majority. "A fixed, unchangeable Government, for a changeable, advancing people," he wrote, "is impossible. . . ."[5] Any attempt at denying popular sovereignty could only backfire by driving the people to desperate extremes.

Yet now that the worst had occurred, Fisher was elated. Previously, there had seemed to be no way out from America's political dilemma. The Constitution had been a closed circle, "a finality," he wrote, something "to be interpreted only by itself, and to be altered only in the manner appointed by itself."[6] But the war had put an end to such nonsense by dissolving the old Constitution, at least for the moment, and setting the people free. "The people see the Government overstep what have generally been considered its constitutional limits every day, and they rejoice," Fisher wrote. "Who but a madman," he went on, "would now propose recourse to the cumbrous forms of amendment appointed by the Constitution?"[7] The old methods were either too slow, too ineffectual, or they were so unsuited to the current crisis that they no longer made sense.

But what was to take their place? Here was where Fisher's conservative mind turned most revolutionary. The genie of popular sovereignty was out of the bottle, he said, and there was no putting it back. "The people rule. The country is theirs and they govern it. The Constitution is theirs, and they can and will mould and modify it to suit their wishes." Fisher's advice was to break free of the box. He called on Congress to seize constitution-making authority and to amend the Constitution on its own through a simple majority vote. It should present the nation with a fait accompli and then dare anyone to say anything to the contrary. Obviously, no one could. Due to the wartime power vacuum, there was no one capable of mounting a challenge. The Supreme Court was discredited and in retreat, while the president would not dare go against the popular will. None of the remaining pro-Union states would dare oppose the popular will either. Said Fisher:

The alleged legal restraint on the power of Congress cannot be enforced, and therefore there is no restraint on it. The whole power of the people, within the sphere of the General Government, does and must, in the nature of things, reside in Congress, and the security of the people consists in their control over Congress by the ballot-box.[8]

In effect, he was calling for a democratic coup d'état in which Congress, particularly the more popular House, would transform itself into a constitutional convention-cum-revolutionary assembly. Americans, Fisher went on, must show that they are masters of the Constitution, not servants. "The Constitution belongs to the people—to the people of 1862, not to those of 1787," he declared. "It must and will be modified to suit the wishes of the former, by their representatives in Congress, just as the English Constitution has been modified by Parliament, or it will be destroyed."[9] Popular sovereignty was the only force capable of preventing secession, resolving the slavery issue, and putting the Union back together again on a sounder footing.

Conceivably, if Congress had taken Fisher's advice and had rammed through such changes in the heat of the war, it might have succeeded. But the Republicans wanted to have things both ways. They wanted to be able to say they were fighting to preserve the Constitution, while at the same time extricating themselves from its more onerous provisions. The result was a series of halfway measures that, however radical by American standards, were never quite radical enough. The impeachment crisis, an attempt to overthrow checks and balances *through* the Constitution rather than counter to it, was their Waterloo. The country once again fell under the tyranny of the Ancient Constitution.

The six decades or so from the end of Reconstruction to the New Deal were, with one or two interruptions, an era of renewed constitutional orthodoxy. Where previously the Constitution had protected the minority rights of Southern slaveholders, it now protected the minority rights of Northern capitalists. For all its flaws, the United

States in the first half of the nineteenth century had still been in the forefront of democracy, a place where political speech was, for the most part, free and vigorous, and working people (white, male working people, that is) had the vote. But now that began to change. Where voting rolls expanded in much of northern Europe to take in more and more of the working class, in America they began to contract. In the South, blacks were disenfranchised by the thousands, while Northern state legislatures, dominated by rural interests, adopted discriminatory registration laws aimed at paring the ranks of urban voters.[10] What with lynchings (which peaked at 230 a year in 1892[11]) and the often hysterical assaults on socialists and other dissidents, American civil liberties no longer looked so attractive. While Bismarck's Germany experimented with unemployment insurance and public pension laws, federal judges in the United States repeatedly struck down even child labor laws as unconstitutional. American democracy had run into a wall, and once again it was the immutable, antimajoritarian Constitution that was the focus of popular ire.

Arthur Hadley, president of Yale at a time when it was a straightforward training school for the American ruling class, summed up the orthodox view of the immutable Constitution in 1908:

> The fundamental division of powers in the Constitution of the United States is between voters on the one hand and property owners on the other, the forces of democracy on one side . . . [and] the forces of property on the other side, with the judiciary as arbiter between them; the Constitution itself not only forbidding the legislature and executive to tread upon the rights of property, but compelling the judiciary to define and uphold those rights in a manner provided by the Constitution itself.[12]

American society was still divided between the forces of democracy and certain specially protected minorities—slaveholders before the Civil War, Northern capitalists after. Despite government of, by, and for the people, the power of the people was as limited after 1868 as it had been before 1861. In 1887, Grover Cleveland vetoed a farm relief bill in terms strikingly similar to those used by Franklin Pierce in vetoing the construction of a federally funded insane asylum some three decades earlier. Where Pierce had said he could not "find any authority in the Constitution for making the federal government the great almoner of public charity," Grover Cleveland declared that "the lesson should constantly be enforced that though the people support the Government, the Government should not support the people."[13] A few years later, Supreme Court Justice S. F. Miller sought to clear up a popular misunderstanding about American democracy by explaining that "in the true sense in which that term is properly used, . . . [the United States] is about as far from it as any other which we are aware."[14] William Howard Taft, president from 1909–13 and later chief justice of the Supreme Court, summed up half a century of arrested political development when he declared that America is "really the most conservative country in the world"—a condition that he was determined to see continue as long as possible.[15]

The triumph of the most forbidding type of constitutional orthodoxy, however, did not mean the cessation of constitutional debate. Quite the contrary, the worse conditions became, the more fervent the debate grew. Perhaps the most important critic to come along in the decades following the Civil War was a brilliant political science student who signed his name W. Thomas Wilson—only later would he drop the middle name and go by the first: Woodrow. Like Sidney George Fisher (whose work he seems never to have read), Wilson was a conservative modernizer. Unlike Fisher, he did not live in a revolutionary period in which ancient shibboleths were tumbling right and left, but in a period of political stagnation in which old taboos had never seemed more potent. Thus, where Fisher was concerned with carrying the political revolution of 1860–61 through to completion, Wilson faced the very different problem of how to breathe life into a system that was all but comatose. His focus was on the more technical problem of how to make the machinery more efficient and responsive.

Ultimately, as a result, Wilson and Fisher arrived at opposite solutions. Where Fisher wanted Congress to take power in the interest of popular sovereignty, Wilson believed that a revitalized presidency provided the way out. Only the chief executive could rise above the pettiness and parochialism that were endemic in American politics. Only the president could triumph over bossism. What was remarkable about Wilson, of course, is that, following stints as president of Princeton University and governor of New Jersey, he found himself catapulted into the White House, where he got an opportunity to put his theories into practice.

Wilson got into the business of constitutional criticism early. During his senior year at Princeton, he wrote a paper on the American political system that he was later able to spin off as an article for the prestigious *International Review* in 1879—quite a coup for a budding twenty-three-year-old political scientist. Unlike other pundits of the day, Wilson did not focus on scandals or corruption in explaining where American politics had gone wrong, but on the more demanding question of structure. America's problem, he wrote, was that it was saddled with a kind of nongovernment government. Where other countries took it for granted that government existed to get things done, Americans took it for granted that the government existed to make sure that as little change occurred as possible. Checks and balances, which the Founders had created to prevent government from becoming too big or oppressive, mainly ensured that the different branches were constantly operating at cross-purposes. Congress itself was fragmented among some forty-seven committees, in which the most important legislative business took place behind closed doors. "Almost *absolute* power," he declared, "has fallen into the hands of men whose irresponsibility prevents the regulation of their conduct by the people from whom they derive their authority."[16] If something went wrong amid all this institutionalized fragmentation, as it all too often did, the opportunities for buck passing were endless. Congress could blame the president, the president could blame Congress, both could blame the Supreme Court, and so on and so forth. The political parties, which during the Civil War had helped overcome the contradictions inherent in the American system and inject a modicum of coherence, were by now useless. "Eight words," Wilson wrote, "contain the sum of the present degradation of our political parties: *No leaders, no principles; no principles, no parties.*"[17] Amid all this wheeling and dealing, political accountability had fallen to near zero.

As scathing a critique as the *International Review* piece was, it was only a warm-up for a much more ambitious work, *Congressional Government*, which Wilson published in 1885 at the ripe old age of twenty-nine. The book, which went through numerous reprintings and became something of a classic of American political science, made Wilson, by now an instructor at Bryn Mawr, an academic star. *Congressional Government* was less focused and rigorous than Fisher's *Trial of the Constitution*, yet at the same time more erudite and expansive. Where Fisher zeroed in on the Article V amending clause, Wilson ranged far and wide over the constitutional system as a whole. He executed intellectual pirouettes that Fisher would have never dreamed of. One was an extended riff on the Darwinian revolution and its political implications. The U.S. Constitution, Wilson wrote, was a product of the Newtonian age, in which the universe was seen as stable and harmonious. The Founders had created a form of government in which the three branches revolved around each other much like the stars and planets in Newton's system of celestial mechanics, held in place by a system of mutual attraction and repulsion. Darwin, however, believed in something more dynamic, a violent, unstable world in which species appeared and disappeared and mountains rose and crumbled into the sea. Government in a post-Darwinian world was not supposed to just remain suspended in a state of perfect equilibrium; rather, it was supposed to *do* something—advance, develop, gather its strength for the tasks ahead, struggle, and fight. It should be able to grow and respond quickly to changing circumstances.

Echoing a line that was becoming increasingly common in academia, Wilson argued that the Constitution had taken an early stage in English political development and frozen it in place. For Wilson, the relevant period was the quarter century between the Glorious Revolution of 1688–89 and the arrival of George I, the first of the Hanovers, in 1714, when Parliament had never seemed more ambivalent about the political power that was increasingly falling into its lap. Following restoration of the monarchy in 1660, the legislative branch had hunkered down under Charles I's son, King Charles II, but had then risen in revolt when his more autocratic brother, James II, assumed the throne. In 1688, James was tossed out, overthrown by a coup d'état, and replaced by William of Orange, who was brought to rule in conjunction with his wife, Mary, James's daughter. Parliament, which wasn't sure whether it had invited William to take power or had merely acceded to his demands, found it all very confusing. It was betwixt and between, at odds with the new monarch just as it had been with the old one, yet afraid to rule on its own. For Wilson, Parliament's predicament in those awkward years was too all similar to Congress vis-à-vis the president. Yet where the British had moved on to different forms of constitutional arrangements, the Americans had taken the "Old Whig" theories of the day—the belief that liberty depended on a clear separation of legislative and executive functions, that conflict between the two branches was inevitable and desirable, and so on—and rendered them permanent. Wilson commented:

> It is extraordinary the influence the early Whig theory of political dynamics has had among us. . . . It is far from being a democratic theory. It is, on the contrary, a theory whose avowed object . . . is to keep government in a sort of mechanical equipoise by means of a standing amicable contest among its several organic parts, each of which it seeks to make representative of a special interest of the nation. It is particularly intended to prevent the will of the people as a whole from forming at any moment an unobstructed sweep and ascendancy. And yet in every step we have taken with the intention of making our governments more democratic, we have punctiliously kept to Whig mechanics.[18]

For all its modern wheeling and dealing, Congress was caught in a time warp. Its structure was essentially that of the seventeenth century and, consequently, more feudal than modern. "Each Standing Committee," Wilson observed acidly, "is the court-baron and its chairman lord-proprietor."[19] Bills had to travel a long and circuitous route, with petty potentates demanding tribute every step of the way. The process was as exhausting as it was inefficient.

Woodrow Wilson was hardly the first person to notice that Congress was composed of a multitude of political baronies, but he was among the first to notice a connection between political fragmentation and institutionalized irresponsibility. The American system was predicated on the assumption that concentrating power encourages its abuse—that power corrupts and absolute power corrupts absolutely, as Lord Acton put it. Yet Wilson argued the inverse: "the more power is divided, the more irresponsible it becomes."[20] Concentrated power can be watched, tamed, held to account, and harnessed. In contrast, the artificial separation of legislative and executive functions was a godsend for the self-serving and the corrupt. Because Congress passed laws for others to carry out, it could not be held accountable for the results. Because it was subject to rules laid out more than a century earlier by the Founders, it could not even be held responsible for its own conduct. Congress was free to go on passing laws forever with little concern for anything beyond the next round of elections.

Thus, Acton had gotten it backward: *incomplete* power corrupts absolutely. Rather than being broken up and scattered, Wilson argued that modern government rested on the belief that various governmental functions should be closely integrated. "No living thing can have its organs offset against each other as checks, and live," he declared, echoing Bentham. "On the contrary, its life is dependent upon their quick cooperation, their ready response to the commands of instinct and intelligence, their amicable community of purpose."[21] Rather than placing the navigator in one part of the ship, the captain in another, the helmsman in a third and seeing to it that they all worked at cross-purposes, modern democratic theory called for them to be placed in a single room so they could coordinate their actions in case an iceberg loomed suddenly ahead.

Modern democratic theory also called for clarity, a system in which accountability was so readily apparent that the individual citizen could tell at a glance who was responsible for what action and who was not. Yet by dividing American government, the Constitution had created the opposite. "Nothing about the system is direct and simple. Authority is perplexingly subdivided and distributed, and responsibility has to be hunted down in out-of-the-way corners," Wilson added (this time echoing, perhaps unconsciously, Tom Paine's complaint about the as yet only partially unified British system in 1776, which he described as "so exceedingly complex that the nation may suffer for years together without being able to discover in which part the fault lies")[22].

What was to be done? Here Wilson turned a bit vague. Sidney George Fisher had looked to a liberated Congress to smash through the bonds of the Article V amending clause and bring the Constitution down to earth, but Wilson saw Congress as being altogether too powerful to begin with. Calling upon Congress to take total power, he seemed to believe, would magnify its faults and entrench them all the more deeply. Although many radicals were coming to see the Supreme Court as the great mover and shaker of American politics, Wilson believed that the Court's independence vis-à-vis the elective branches was limited.[23] Instead, he looked to the third branch, the executive. With Congress hopelessly fragmented and irresponsible, he declared, "there is but one national voice in the country, and that is the voice of the President. His isolation has quite unexpectedly been his exaltation."[24] In an era of generalized moral squalor and plunging morale, the presidency was the only power center that seemed to be capable of lifting itself up out of the mire and providing real leadership.

There was a bit of Andrew Johnson's idea of the president as sole national spokesman in all this, not to mention Bolingbroke's Patriot King. The irony, of course, is that Wilson, some twenty-five years later, became the personification of his own program when, on the suggestion of a magazine editor in New York, the Democratic bosses in New Jersey plucked him out of obscurity as president of Princeton and nominated him for governor. Wilson won and quickly set about cleaning up one of the most corrupt political machines in the nation. Two years later, national Democratic Party leaders did the same. Wilson not only defeated Alabama governor Oscar Underwood, a leader of the party's Southern wing, for the nomination, but emerged victorious in a three-way race with the Republicans' Taft and Bull Mooser Teddy Roosevelt. Serene, cerebral, and aloof, the son of one Presbyterian minister and the grandson of another, Wilson was the very image of the stern, demanding, morally uplifting schoolmaster-*cum*-national leader. Shortly after taking office, he resurrected the old Federalist tradition, abandoned by Jefferson, of addressing Congress in person at the start of every year. The symbolism was striking: rather than an executor of Congress's wishes, the president now appeared before the House and Senate as the people's representative summoning them to action. Congress represented bits and pieces of the nation, while the president represented the whole. He set the tone, laid out the agenda, and mobilized the people. He led, while they followed.

After an impressive first term, in which he created the Federal Reserve Bank, persuaded Congress to pass various social reforms, and all in all imposed a degree of unity on federal operations not known since Reconstruction, Wilson then attempted to forge order out of chaos on an international scale by plunging into World War I. The results were an ungainly combination of cynical backroom politics and high-minded rhetoric. Wilson met privately with Lloyd George and Clemenceau and helped deal out the fate of various nations and peoples as if they were cards in a deck. He joined in the Allied crusade against the infant Soviet republic, while at the same time he was electrifying public opinion with his Fourteen Points for a just peace. ("Did Meester Veelson know that in the peasants' wargrimed houses along the Brenta and the Piave they were burning candles in front of his picture cut out of the illustrated papers?" John Dos Passos asked sarcastically.) On returning home in mid-1919, however, he ran into a congressional buzz saw over his proposal for a League of Nations, the linchpin on which the entire Versailles system depended. Despite a nationwide speaking tour by Wilson to drum up public support, Senator Henry Cabot Lodge—ironically, Wilson's editor forty years earlier at the *International Review*—saw to it that it went down in defeat. Wilson by this point had been crippled by a stroke, while the nation was torn by race riots and an anti-Bolshevik hysteria even more ferocious than that which followed World War II. Unfamiliar with the vagaries of divided government, Europeans had thought Wilson spoke for the U.S. government during the Versailles Treaty negotiations and were astonished when it turned out that he spoke for just one part of it, the executive branch. Rather than resolving the contradictions inherent in the Madisonian system, Wilson had merely raised them to a new level.

Wilson's *Congressional Government* set the tone for better than half a century. A steady flow of books, pamphlets, and articles followed, all dedicated to the theme of America the dysfunctional. Urban government was corrupt, Congress was unrepresentative, politics in general were a swindle, while the economy was controlled by a coterie of super-rich industrialists and financiers. Even those on top admitted that the constitutional machinery had broken down. "It is true we have at present irresponsible government, so divided that nobody can tell who is to blame," House Speaker Thomas B. Reed conceded in 1897.[25] Joseph Bailey, a Democratic senator from Texas, noted a few years later that "we have fallen to the point that even when in the cheap playhouses of the country, where cheap playwrights stage cheap plays, the audience applauds when senators are described as grafters."[26] In 1892, the newly organized Populist Party put out a call for a national system of initiative and referendum, the popular election of senators (not adopted until 1913), and other proposals for constitutional change.[27] The Socialist Party, established in 1901, followed suit with a call for a graduated income tax (which the judiciary had declared unconstitutional), equal suffrage for women, and abolition of the Senate and the presidential veto.[28] In 1912, Teddy Roosevelt, the Progressive standard-bearer, endorsed a Colorado proposal allowing voters to pass on any state law declared unconstitutional by a state court.[29] Essentially, the people would become the final court of appeals over and above the judiciary, an idea with obvious implications for the nation as a whole.

Besides Wilson, four other constitutional critics stand out amid this period of growing turmoil: James B. Thayer, a Harvard law professor; James Bryce, author of *The American Commonwealth;* Herbert Croly, author of the highly influential *Promise of American Life;* and Charles Beard, the Columbia University historian whose *Economic Interpretation of the Constitution* caused a storm when it appeared in 1913.

Bryce was an Englishman, but his two-volume study, published in 1888, proved at least as influential in this country as in his own. Like Tocqueville half a century earlier, he was a stranger in a strange land, one whose mission was to gather information on the exotic new breed of *homo Americanus* for the edification of the folks back home. Unlike Tocqueville, he didn't hail from a country still reeling from violence and revolution but from one that was confident it had solved the problem of government once and for all and was increasingly optimistic about the future. For Bryce, what was fascinating about America was that it was built around constitutional principles that were the opposite of those in the United Kingdom yet, according to all the usual political and economic indices, was a raging success nonetheless.

Reading Bryce's calm, measured prose nowadays, one gets the impression that he thought of the American Republic as a looking-glass world in which all the rules one thought of as normal were stood on their head. In Britain, Parliament's power was unlimited. Theoretically, it was free to deal with any topic under the sun. In America, by contrast, Congress's power was severely limited, with the result that it "tends to avoid all really grave and pressing questions, skirmishing around them, but seldom meeting them in the face or reaching a decision which marks an advance." Yet rather than being embarrassed, Americans regarded this arrangement as the most natural thing in the world. When asked about Congress's incapacity to deal with the most pressing problems of the day, Bryce went on, "an American . . . replies that at this moment some of the graver questions do not lie within the competence of Congress, and that in his country representatives must not attempt to move faster than their constituents."[30]

This was very curious. So was the question of fragmented responsibility, the problem that had obsessed Woodrow Wilson a few years earlier:

> In England, if a bad Act is passed or a good bill rejected, the blame falls primarily upon the ministry in power. . . . But in the United States the ministry cannot be blamed for the cabinet officers do not sit in Congress; the House cannot be blamed because it has only followed the decision of its committee; the committee may be an obscure body, whose members are too insignificant to be worth blaming. The chairman is possibly a man of note, but the people have no leisure to watch sixty chairmen.[31]

Where British politicians took pride in the efficiency and responsiveness of their governing institutions, Americans took a perverse pleasure in the opposite. Since government was intrinsically threatening, a well-oiled governing apparatus, in their eyes, was more dangerous than one that was constantly tying itself up in knots. Government was continually falling short, yet somehow, to Americans, it was *right* that it should continually fall short.

Throughout *The American Commonwealth*, Bryce was very much the levelheaded British utilitarian, with a characteristically utilitarian impatience with inefficiency and delay. If a policy was beneficial, it should be implemented; if not, it should be removed. Yet, as a student of American government, he understood that there might be a thousand reasons why, under the U.S. system, a beneficial policy could not be implemented—states' rights, the strange workings of Congress, some obscure constitutional restriction, and so forth. It didn't make sense, yet Bryce shrank from passing judgment. Rather than warning Americans that one day they would have to come to grips with the contradictions inherent in the idea of divided, limited government, he decided to hedge his bets:

> The Americans surpass all other nations in their power of making the best of bad conditions, getting the largest results out of scanty materials or rough methods. . . . The national inventiveness, active in the spheres of mechanics and money-making, spends little of its force on the details of governmental methods, and the interest in material development tends to diminish the interest felt in politics.[32]

Somehow, a lack of initiative in the political sphere had led to a superabundance of initiative in the economic. This was high heresy in terms of utilitarianism, which was based on the assumption that government had to be rational and efficient *in order* for society to be productive. Yet America was doing so well with a government that looked like it might have been designed by Lewis Carroll that Bryce hesitated to say it was wrong.

Yet this proto-Reaganite argument—limited government leads to unlimited private-sector growth—was no more correct in the late nineteenth century than it would be in the late twentieth. As Bryce also noted, there was clearly one area in which the United States *was* paying a price for its dysfunctional form of government. This was the area of urban affairs, which he called America's "one great failure."[33] Rather than diminishing, it would grow larger and larger over the ensuing decades to the point where it would become the part that swallowed the whole. Despite his final hesitation, Bryce had put his finger on a major flaw, the inability of the U.S. system to manage the everyday workings of society so that little problems did not grow up to be great big ones.

James Thayer was not nearly as major a figure as Bryce, but he rates a mention because he put his finger on another crucial flaw in American democracy, the contradiction between a society that extolled civil liberties in the abstract while violating them on a daily basis in practice. In an article in the *Harvard Law Review* in 1893, he argued that by placing civil liberties in the hands of the courts, the Bill of Rights had deprived the political branches—that is, the president and Congress—of primary responsibility for their protection. By making them not responsible, it had rendered them *ir*responsible, thereby undermining political support for the very rights it was designed to protect. Congress felt free to disregard civil liberties because civil liberties were not its concern. Observed Thayer:

It has been often remarked that private rights are more respected by the legislatures of some countries which have no written constitutions than by ours. No doubt our doctrine of constitutional law has had a tendency to drive out questions of justice and right, and to fill the mind of legislators with thoughts of mere legality, of what the Constitution allows. And moreover, even in the matter of legality, they have felt little responsibility; if they are wrong, they say, the courts will correct it.[34]

In assuming that Congress would behave in an abusive manner, the Constitution and the Bill of Rights had ensured that congressional abuses would continue.

Although Thayer did not draw the connection, the same point could be made about the people at large, namely, that they had been rendered lazy and complacent when it came to protecting civil liberties for the same reason. They could stand by and watch while blacks were lynched and union organizers jailed, confident that as long a certain piece of parchment was safely ensconced in the national archives, all was well. Unlike people with less exalted constitutions, they did not have to take to the streets in defense of the persecuted as had the Dreyfusards in France. Instead, they could observe from the sidelines while the courts exercised responsibility for the protection of civil liberties. Just as the legislature had grown fat and flabby as a consequence, so had the general population.

Herbert Croly's *The Promise of American Life*, which became something of a Progressive Bible following its publication in 1909, devoted only a few scattered pages to the Constitution. Yet they were an extremely important few pages both for what they said about his own attitude and the attitude of the generation of reformers he was addressing.

Croly began on an ironic note. American reformers, he wrote, had more in common with the country they were seeking to change than they realized. Like American politics in general, the growing reform movement was personality oriented and dominated by a few outsize individuals. Reformers were as reverential as any chamber of commerce booster when it came to the Constitution. Like the Puritans of old, they tended to look upon reform as a process of purification in which old values were restored rather than new ones created. They were "Old Believers" who saw the struggle for reform in almost metaphysical terms as "a fight between law and its violators, between the Faithful and the Heretic, between the Good and the Wicked."[35] For all their rejection of the society around them, Croly went on, they had wound up embracing the same

> insidious tradition of conformity—the tradition that a patriotic American citizen must not in his political thinking go beyond the formulas consecrated in the sacred American writings. They adhere to the stupefying rule that the good Fathers of the Republic relieved their children from the necessity of vigorous, independent, or consistent thinking in political matters—that it is the duty of their loyal children to repeat the sacred words and then await a miraculous consummation of individual and social prosperity.[36]

Croly's beef was not so much with the sacred Constitution as with sacredness per se. The concept was crippling because it took questions involving the structure of society and the nature of government and moved them out of the range of critical inquiry. It promoted an attitude of veneration and awe when what were really needed were skepticism and analysis. The people, in a sense, were reduced to arguing over wallpaper and furnishings when in fact it was clear that the dwelling as a whole was no longer suited to their purposes. A bit farther on in his book, Croly paused to consider the intense controversies surrounding the Supreme Court, noting quite sensibly that if the Constitution was a little less unyielding, the Court would be considerably less powerful:

> The fault of the American system . . . consists not in the independence of the federal judiciary, but in the practical immutability of the Constitution. If the instrument which the Supreme Court expounds could be altered whenever a sufficiently large body of public opinion has demanded a change for a significantly long time, the American democracy would have much more to gain than to fear from the independence of the federal judiciary.[37]

The Constitution must open itself up to change if democracy was to move forward. This was an important point, yet Croly faltered as he neared the finish line. The Constitution "is not all it should be," he summed up toward the end of his book, "but it is better than any substitute upon which American opinion could now agree. Modifications may and should be made in details, but for the present not in fundamentals."[38] Croly thus wound up supporting the very orthodoxy he had earlier reviled. After denouncing constitutional conformity as stupefying, he had turned around and embraced . . . constitutional conformity. His argument spoke volumes about the lack of democracy at the core of Progressivism. Despite the title of his book, his outlook was actually pessimistic since it assumed that the American people did not have the ability to reshape their society as they saw fit. For lack of an alternative, constitutional conformity would have to continue.

Finally, there is Charles Beard, perhaps the most famous American historian ever to ply the trade, whose *Economic Interpretation of the Constitution* caused a sensation when it was published in 1913. Beard was in many ways an admirable figure. His effort to demythologize the Founding Fathers and show that they were creatures of economic self-interest as much as any modern politician certainly took courage. His decision to throw over his faculty position at Columbia and support himself by his writings was a testament to his belief in the intelligence of the reading public. As an academic involved in urban reform and other problems, he was the model of the intellectual fully engaged with the affairs of his day.

Unfortunately, he was something less than the model of a conscientious scholar. Beard's thesis—that the men who drafted the Constitution and saw it through to ratification included a large number of Revolutionary War bondholders who wanted a strong central government primarily because it would make good on its debts—was crude and inaccurate. Although sometimes characterized as Marxist, it had nothing to do with the subtleties of Marx's thinking and everything to do with American prairie populism, which tended to see an Eastern banker lurking behind every tree. Conservative historians invested vast energy in the fifties in demolishing Beard's thesis, yet the fact is that Beard's contemporaries had pretty much reduced it to shreds within months of its release. Reviewing it in the *American Political Science Review*, the historian John Latané pointed out that four of the leading opponents of the Constitution in 1787 (Elbridge Gerry, Luther Martin, Oliver Ellsworth, and William S. Johnson) had collectively four times as much invested in war bonds as six of the Constitution's biggest supporters (Madison, Hamilton, Washington, James Wilson, Gouverneur Morris, and Charles Pinckney). Rather than pursuing their own immediate economic interests, the four opponents of ratification were guilty of doing the opposite. They were wrong given the range of options available at the time, but they were not corrupt. In the *History Teacher's Magazine*, the great constitutional scholar E. S. Corwin noted that Beard's financial data were meaningless—"the most unmitigated rot," is how he put it—since they were based on figures compiled in 1790 and therefore reflected bonds purchased after the Philadelphia convention as well as before. A more careful study of the data revealed that only seven delegates were bondholders prior to the Philadelphia convention and that, once again, it was the mercurial Elbridge Gerry—who refused to sign the final document and argued against ratification back home in Massachusetts—who was among the biggest bondholders.[39]

The relationship between money and politics was not as simple as Beard seemed to think. His statement that the ratification battle was "a deep-seated conflict between a popular party based on paper money and agrarian interests and a conservative party centered in the towns and resting on financial, mercantile, and personal property interests generally" contained just enough truth to be seriously misleading.[40] Heavily indebted backwoods farmers were indeed suspicious of the Constitution, but so were many big planters and slave owners. By the same token, urban artisans, America's very own *sans-culottes*, who were anything but conservative, were among the Constitution's most ardent supporters. By reducing the Founders to crude economic actors, Beard had stripped the process of its intellectual dimension. The contradictions inherent in seventeenth- and eighteenth-century ideology, the split between Court and Country, the rejection of political sovereignty—none of it mattered, apparently, since the Federalists were simply speculators in search of a buck.

Nonetheless, the response to Beard's book spoke volumes about the nature of America's civic religion. In a speech before more than a thousand prominent lawyers and politicians at New York's Waldorf-Astoria, William Howard Taft denounced *An Economic Interpretation* as muckraking gone mad. In Marion, Ohio, home of future president Warren G. Harding, the editors of the *Ohio Star*, who knew of Beard's book only from reviews and press reports, ran the memorable headline: "SCAVENGERS, HYENA-LIKE, DESECRATE THE GRAVES OF THE DEAD PATRIOTS WE REVERE." "If correctly represented," the paper added scrupulously, Beard and his book were "libelous, vicious and damnable." All good citizens, it declared, "should rise to condemn him and the purveyors of his filthy lies and rotten aspersions."[41] The New York Bar Association assembled a committee to investigate and summoned Beard to appear, while the Columbia board of trustees lectured him like a schoolboy.[42] Under intense pressure, Beard resigned his professorship in 1917.

If nothing else, Beard had exposed the intolerance at the heart of the American political system. Those who dissented too forcefully risked bringing the wrath of the priests and their flock down about their heads. Obviously, Beard was not to be fed to the lions or sent to the gulag, but he was driven from the classroom. Tolerance had its limits.

Of course, these are only the highlights of a great debate that waxed and waned from the gilded age through the Progressive era, the Republican triumph of the 1920s, and the New Deal. Robert La Follette, the Progressive senator from Wisconsin, spent years railing against the rigidity and unresponsiveness of Article V, with the result that between 1911 and 1929, some eighteen proposals were introduced in Congress to change the amending process, mostly with the intent of making it more liberal.[43] William MacDonald, a prominent journalist and editor, published a book in 1921 arguing that the Constitution had shown a distinct tendency "to widen the gulf between government and people, to discourage serious political thinking and debate save in moments of grave crisis, to increase the flower of corrupt machine politics, and to cultivate an easy-going indifference to abuses."[44] W. Y. Elliott, a professor of government at Harvard, complained in 1935 of "the dead hand of the past" that was holding America "in the grip of a fatal inertia,"[45] and Henry Hazlitt, who would later become famous as a champion of free-market economics, wrote that the structure of American government was "hopelessly antiquated."[46]

All were accurate as far as they went, but none quite came to grips with the problem of what made the constitutional order so intractable. In repeatedly complaining that the system was inefficient and unresponsive, they missed the point. The system was *supposed* to be inefficient and unresponsive. That, it was argued, was its saving grace. Where critics complained that it was antiquated, latter-day Madisonians praised it as the one immutable element in an all too mutable world. It was what held America in place, what caused it to stop from dashing off into the arms of the Klan, the Wobblies, or the mob. The amazing growth of the constitutional system and the nation it gave rise to made the critics seem petty and irrelevant. One did not argue with success, no matter how illogical a system might appear on paper.

Politically, the system appeared to loosen up under Theodore Roosevelt and Woodrow Wilson, but then entered a freeze beginning in the period of 1918–1920 that was even deeper than the last. William Howard Taft's appointment as chief justice in mid-1921 brought protests from the *Nation* and *New Republic*, both of which wondered why a president whom the voters had repudiated in 1912 because he was too conservative should now be given unchecked power over national policy as head of the Supreme Court. Yet Taft, who welcomed the appointment as an opportunity to wield "power without worry," was undeterred.[47] Under his reign, the court staged its famous "carnival of unconstitutionality," in which minimum wage laws, child labor laws, and various other business regulations were all struck down. As one constitutional historian put it:

> Congress was strapped by restrictive interpretations of the Commerce Clause and the Tenth Amendment, and the states were even more severely limited by Due Process requirements under the Fourteenth Amendment. A safe zone for business was created in which neither nation nor state could act.[48]

Never had constitutional dictatorship bitten so deeply or popular democracy been so thoroughly vanquished. The people were as powerless as they had been in trying to deal with the slavery issue in the 1840s and 1850s. The 1932 elections were thus as revolutionary as those of 1860, while those of 1936, when Franklin D. Roosevelt was swept back into office with sixty-four percent of the popular vote and a huge majority in Congress, corresponded roughly to those of 1866, when Republican congressmen were returned to office in overwhelming numbers to finish the job Lincoln had begun. Where the 1866 elections had put Congress on a collision course with an unelected president, those of 1936 put Congress and the White House on a collision course with an unelected Supreme Court.

The 1937 Court-packing crisis was thus another seminal constitutional event, not too different in its own way from the impeachment crisis in 1868. With the backing of Congress, FDR set out to tame the judiciary just as Radical Republicans had set out to tame the executive. But with all the foxiness of a politician born and raised in America's convoluted constitutional system, he launched an attack that was both devious and oblique. Furious over the Court's efforts to gut his program during his first term—the Court had struck down no fewer than a dozen New Deal initiatives[49]—he nonetheless held back from criticizing the justices during his reelection campaign, limiting himself to a few bland remarks to the effect that the Constitution was not meant to be a dead hand "blocking humanity's advance," but "a living force for the expression of the national will with respect to national needs."[50] During his State of the Union address the following January, however, he let loose with a stream of abuse that brought Congress to its feet. A month later, he dropped his bombshell, a complicated scheme to reshape the Court, in which the president would be empowered to appoint one new justice for every member who stayed on past the age of seventy. Attempting to portray himself as more constitutional than the Court, Roosevelt described his proposal as an effort to help the aged and infirm justices cope with a growing workload. No one was fooled. Frustrated by his inability to appoint justices of his own, the president was obviously looking for a way to offset the Court's slim conservative majority.

The plan was too clever by half. Interestingly, Benjamin Cohen, a member of Roosevelt's kitchen cabinet, had suggested instead a constitutional amendment giving Congress the power to override Supreme Court decisions through a simple majority vote. But Roosevelt was not interested. One reason was the sheer difficulty of pushing through an amendment, particularly one so radical. "Give me ten million dollars," he told a meeting of the cabinet in early February 1937, "and I can prevent any amendment to the Constitution from being ratified by the necessary number of states."[51] The other reason was undoubtedly institutional. Empowering Congress to override the Supreme Court would also have given it an edge over the executive branch, which Roosevelt was loath to do. While lowering the Supreme Court a notch, a Court-packing bill, on the other hand, would keep the other two branches on par with one another. "If these measures achieve their aim," Roosevelt told Congress, "we may be relieved of the necessity of considering any fundamental changes in the power of the courts or the Constitution of our government"—which was unfortunately the case.[52]

The rest of the story is well known—the tidal wave of letters to Congress and the White House opposing the plan, the growing nervousness among liberals over the threat to judicial independence, and finally the administration's decision to put the Court-packing scheme on hold for the duration. Roosevelt and his brain trust had clearly underestimated the widespread attachment to constitutional procedure and the widespread alarm that would greet any effort by one branch to invade the turf of another. Reverence for the Ancient Constitution had penetrated deep into America's bones and was not easily dismissed. Somehow, the administration had to figure out a way to get out from under the Supreme Court without upsetting this secular religion, to transform the substance of the constitutional system while leaving the form intact.

The solution was to change the Supreme Court from within. Despite its rocky reception on Capitol Hill, the Court-packing scheme had gotten the high court's attention and ultimately forced it to take several steps to the left. The process began some eight weeks after the Court-packing proposal was unveiled when the Court stunned observers by narrowly upholding a state minimum-wage law that was essentially indistinguishable from one it had struck down as unconstitutional a year earlier. "Switch in time saves nine," was how FDR brain truster Abe Fortas described the about-face. Other pro–New Deal rulings followed—a decision upholding a farm debtor relief program, another upholding a collective bargaining law, and finally, in mid-April, a decision sustaining the National Labor Relations Act, which greatly expanded Congress's power to regulate interstate commerce. Judicial resistance had collapsed. With Justice George Sutherland's resignation in January 1938, Roosevelt finally got the opportunity he had been waiting for to appoint a Supreme Court justice of his own. Other resignations followed, so that by the time of his death in 1945, he had filled every seat on the Court except one.

The Court was thus remade. Yet liberalism was remade as well. For decades, liberals had devoted themselves to attacking the very idea of a secretive judicial priesthood that gazed into the entrails of a dead document in deciding which acts of Congress should be struck down and which should be sustained. But now that they had stormed the inner sanctum, liberals discovered virtues in a high priesthood that they had previously overlooked. Where previously they had argued for judicial restraint so that the New Deal's work could go forward unimpeded, they now argued that the Court could be used to actively promote liberal values. After decades in the wilderness in which they repeatedly assailed the idea of the immutable Constitution, they now concluded that if the purpose was to protect civil liberties, then perhaps immutability wasn't such a bad thing after all.

Everything had changed, yet everything remained the same. America still embraced an essentially eighteenth-century ideology that held that majority rule was dangerous and anarchic and therefore had to be held in check by a permanent body of unchanging law. Where conservatives had sought to restrain the power of the majority so as first to protect slavery and then private property in general, liberals now did the same in the interests of protecting individual liberty. Yet the results were self-defeating. As James B. Thayer had warned, hedging and checking the power of the political branches had mainly served to render popular government petty and incompetent. The more aggressive the courts became, the more adept Congress and the president became at ducking the hard issues and seeing to it that they wound up in the judiciary's lap. Racial integration was, in a very real sense, the most sweeping constitutional change that the American

Republic had ever undertaken, yet the elected branches had had nothing to do with it. President Eisenhower only reluctantly intervened in support of court-ordered school integration in Little Rock, Arkansas, in 1958, four years after the original *Brown v. Board of Education* decision, while Congress resisted passing major civil rights legislation until 1965. In the face of this new wave of judicial activism, working people meanwhile retreated into sullen silence. Civil liberties were not something the people had created themselves, but something imposed on them from above. Given the new restraints being placed on its power, the majority settled down into an attitude best described as sullen acquiescence. In the 1968 presidential race, George Wallace, the right-wing populist, stunned observers by drawing nearly ten million votes, thirteen percent of the total. Thereafter, Republicans and Democrats competed with one another for the support of a deeply alienated population chafing under the rule of "limousine liberals" and "pointy-headed intellectuals." Despite the best efforts of groups like the ACLU to hold it together, civil liberties began to crumble without a strong base of popular support. By the 1980s, the judicial revolution that had begun in 1937 was a spent force.

7

POSTWAR AMERICA: THE NEW ISOLATIONISM

WILLY, *shaking Bernard's hand:* Good-by, boy.
CHARLEY, *an arm on Bernard's shoulder:* How do you
  like this kid? Gonna argue a case in front of the
  Supreme Court.
BERNARD, *protesting:* Pop!
WILLY, *genuinely shocked, pained, and happy:* No! The
  Supreme Court!
                              —Arthur Miller,
                              Death of a Salesman (1949)

THE ONLY THING more dangerous than total defeat is total victory. To describe the United States as the world's leading superpower in 1945 is an understatement. To a great extent, it was the only power, at least the only one left standing on its feet. With its twenty to twenty-five million war dead, the Soviet Union was a heap of ruins from the Baltic to the Black Sea. Germany, with its bombed-out cities and 13.6 million dead or missing, promised to be a basket case for generations to come. In France, national income as of 1946 had plunged to half the prewar level, while in Japan it was down forty-three percent from the level of the mid-thirties. In Italy, massive international aid was the only thing standing in the way of mass starvation. In Britain, where a new Labour government had taken office two months after V-E Day, John Maynard Keynes presented the cabinet with a hair-raising document warning that with its gold and foreign currency reserves depleted and its industrial base weakened, the country was facing nothing less than a "financial Dunkirk." Indeed, within a year, the Labourites would be forced to institute bread rationing for the first time in British history.

In the United States, by contrast, real GNP was up more than fifty percent over the same period, the landscape was unscathed, war deaths were under three hundred thousand, and money piling up in workers' bank accounts would soon be used to fuel the most astounding consumer boom in history. Where Europe's share of global manufacturing had fallen to the lowest level since the industrial revolution, America now controlled better than half the world's remaining industrial capacity and almost two-thirds of its gold supply. It also enjoyed a monopoly on nuclear weapons, which added a whole new dimension to its military advantage.[1]

Victory like this can't help but go to a nation's head. From an American point of view, two things seemed clear. One was that regardless of how much damage the other Allied powers had inflicted on the German war machine (in fact, roughly three out of four Axis casualties in the European theater were inflicted on the Eastern Front), it was America that had won the war. The other was that America had won the war because it deserved to. Victory was not merely the result of certain military, industrial, and geographical advantages, but of political and moral ones as well. The United States was freer, its society healthier, its government more soundly designed. As its politicians never tired of proclaiming, it was triumphant not only as a nation, but as a system and as an ideal. And, of course, the most basic institution of all, the font of all that political wisdom and good health, was the Constitution, a document whose durability and irreproachability was the key to everything that was sturdy and self-reliant about the society it had helped create.

This was just one of the many things that made the America of the 1940s seem like a different country from the America of before the war. For more than a century, liberals and radicals of various stripes had raged against the Constitution as a ball and chain around the ankle of American democracy, a restraint on the people's ability to grow and develop and manage their own affairs. Now the same document was magically transformed into an American Gibraltar, the foundation of the nation's stability and strength. In the late 1930s, during the heyday of the Popular Front, a fellow-traveling young journalist named Max Lerner had made a name for himself by attacking the Supreme Court as a "praetorian guard" for the propertied elite, one whose function it was "to strike down radical state legislation that might hurt hegemony of the corporation."[2] After the war, the same Max Lerner, by now an esteemed liberal columnist, was hard at work praising the Court as a bulwark of freedom and democracy. "Marshall, Taney, Miller, Harlan, Holmes, Hughes, Brandeis, Stone, Cardozo, Black, Frankfurter, Douglas, Warren," he intoned. "It would be hard to find a governing group in any society to match these men in talent, character, vision, and statesmanship."[3] Roger Taney's inclusion in this pantheon was particularly striking. For generations, liberal brows had darkened at the mere mention of his name. But now he had been rehabilitated. The Court was so great that all who sat on it were ennobled, including the long-ago author of the *Dred Scott* decision, who had struck down barriers to slavery, disenfranchised free blacks, and helped tip the scales in favor of civil war.

This is what complete and total triumph does to a nation—it dulls controversy, reinforces complacency, and bathes the most dubious institutions in a golden glow. No longer "nine old men," the Supreme Court, as Arthur Miller's play indicated, was now a moral touchstone. It was a symbol of all that was solid, serious, and good about America as opposed to the materialist will-o'-the-wisp that Willy Loman was forever chasing. The Court was admirable not because it was popular, but because it was *un*popular, that is, because it was stern and unbending, an institution over society rather than in it. The Court's elitism, the very thing that made it an object of widespread contempt during the New Deal, was now the quality most in its favor. Congress benefited from the golden glow as well. Joseph McCarthy was a product of the same system of institutionalized irresponsibility that reformers had been complaining about for generations. Yet what liberals seemed to notice most was not how the system had allowed the senator from Wisconsin to go on a five-year rampage, but how it had finally brought him to heel in the televised Army-McCarthy hearings in 1954, when it was decided that he had at last gone too far by impugning the honor of the U.S. Army. The system was slow to respond, yet once it started moving, liberal intellectuals told themselves, the results were impressive. It had produced the richest, stablest, freest society in history. As Max Lerner declared in 1957:

> Americans have never taken seriously the various projects for a thorough "modernizing" of government, to make it more logical or orderly. They have left well enough alone. It was Lord Bryce who is reported to have said that "Providence has under its special care children, idiots, and the United States of America." Which may be another way of saying that, given the industrial development and power of America, even a halting, stumbling, and outdated political system can be a success. America has the Midas touch; everything that a rich nation touches turns to gold.[4]

America was victorious now and would be victorious forevermore. While lesser nations reconfigured their political systems so as to make them more rational and efficient, America, thanks to some divine dispensation, was free to carry on with the same stumbling, outdated system indefinitely.

America during this period presented a paradox. Before the war, the United States had pursued an isolationist foreign policy. Yet, because of the long dissident tradition of constitutional criticism, it had been open in some respects to foreign ideas in the area of politics and statecraft. After 1945, as the greatest imperial power since ancient Rome, it was deeply immersed in the affairs of other nations. Yet thanks to this awesome postwar complacency, it was intellectually closed. "American experience is the key to the future," exulted *Life* magazine publisher Henry Luce in 1945. "America must be the elder brother of nations in the brotherhood of man."[5] Needless to say, it was not Big Brother's job to learn from others, but to teach.

Thus while Europeans picked themselves out of the rubble and constructed new state forms to take the place of the old discredited ones, Americans buried themselves in the old forms ever more deeply. From a U.S. perspective, West Europeans were either seen as pawns in the great game with Russia or, with their myriad parties and factions and their frequent changes of government, as excitable children to be kept in line but otherwise ignored. Yet the outcome some two or three decades later turned out very different than Lerner, Luce, et al. had foreseen. In Western Europe, the political recovery, like the economic recovery, started off slowly but then began gaining in confidence and speed. By the late fifties, it had worked up a full head of steam. America, meanwhile, followed a reverse trajectory in which the golden age of the forties and fifties gave way to the urban explosions of the sixties and the economic and political malaise of the seventies. By the nineties, America seemed old and tired, while the Europeans still retained a measure of their vigor and youth. Somehow, after half a century, America, with its hollowed-out tenements and rubblized cities, had wound up resembling nothing so much as Germany of 1945. Where once it had the Midas touch, it had now turned into an anti-Midas, in which everything it touched turned into dross.

This is the great reversal of the post–World War II era, a phenomenon that is as much the riddle of the late twentieth century as America's descent into paralysis and civil war was the great riddle of the mid-nineteenth. The about-face was the result of many factors, one of which was undoubtedly constitutional. Something about the American political structure had caused it to blow its enormous lead, while something about the West European structure had caused those societies to pull out far ahead. But what?

Perhaps the best place to start in a survey of postwar constitutional development is with a book called *The Genius of American Politics*, which an up-and-coming historian named Daniel J. Boorstin published to positive reviews in 1953. Boorstin, a professor at the University of Chicago who would later be named Librarian of Congress, was a former Communist Party member who, like so many others of his generation, had begun drifting rightward following the Hitler-Stalin nonaggression pact of 1939. Subpoenaed by the House Un-American Activities Committee shortly before his book was released, Boorstin assured HUAC that while party members should be barred from teaching, repentant ex-Communists like himself were perfectly safe and should be left alone.[6] *The Genius of American Politics* was proof of his sincerity. An extended hymn of praise to the American constitutional system, it was an attempt to turn the tables on the system's critics by arguing that whether or not what they had to say was true, it was all beside the point. Yes, wrote Boorstin, American politics lacked a rational structure. Yes, they were nonideological. But what had ideology and rationalism ever done for Europeans except to deliver them into the arms of the totalitarians? Where Old World intellectuals were forever cooking up theories, Americans had taken a different tack. Rather than forcing institutions to conform to manmade schemes, they had allowed them to develop according to their own internal laws and dynamics, free from human interference.

Consequently, Boorstin wrote, where Europeans were still half-buried in rubble, "dying of poverty, monopoly, aristocracy, and ideology," Americans were strong, prosperous, and free.[7] He continued:

> If we have learned anything from our history, it is the wisdom of allowing institutions to develop according to the needs of each particular environment; and the value of both environmentalism and traditionalism as principles of political life, as ways of saving ourselves from the imbecilities, the vagaries, and the cosmic enthusiasms of individual men.[8]

Instead of overthrowing governments and creating new republics on the ruins of the old, Americans were content to work within the confines of a Constitution whose essence had not changed since 1787.

Rather than revamping government from top to bottom, they were content to leave the same structure in place and allow it to adapt to changing circumstances slowly over time. They did so not because they were smarter or cleverer than Europeans, Boorstin continued, but because they lived in a part of the globe that had been specially blessed. Their "genius" was to realize that gifts from above were not to be tampered with or improved upon, but to be treasured and conserved. As a result, said Boorstin,

> it is not surprising that we have no enthusiasm for plans to make society over. We have actually made a new society without a plan. Or, more precisely, why should we make a five-year plan for ourselves when God seems to have had a thousand-year plan ready for us?[9]

For a traumatized ex-Communist like Boorstin, the appeal of this sort of fatalism was obvious. Trusting to institutions to develop on their own meant that Marxism, utilitarianism, or whatever other "ism" Euro-intellectuals had to offer were unimportant and could be safely ignored. Given the trouble he had gotten into as a consequence of his own cosmic enthusiasms in the 1930s, it meant the freedom to bypass political theory altogether and even the intellect. As Boorstin saw it, intelligence and wisdom were very different things. One was individual, innovative, and corrosive. The other was communal, traditional, bound up with the species, the nation, and the soil, all of which he lumped under the general heading of "the environment." One tore things down, while the other stood back and permitted them to blossom and develop:

> Our geography and history have led us to an unspoken assumption . . . that institutions are not and should not be the grand creations of men toward large ends and outspoken values; rather they are organisms which grow out of the soil in which they are rooted and out of the traditions from which they have sprung.[10]

Intelligence, in short, was dangerous. Applied in too lavish doses, it was likely to make things worse. Somehow, the individual had to acquire a sixth sense as to when to interfere and when to leave it to geography and the environment to do the work alone.

The Genius of American Politics was an example of how, in an age of *I Love Lucy* and Milton Berle, America had come full circle back to the awesome conservatism of certain late-eighteenth-century thinkers. Although Boorstin didn't mention him, the resemblance to Edmund Burke's *Reflections on the Revolution in France* was remarkable. Just as Boorstin lashed out at the imbecilities and cosmic enthusiasms of deracinated intellectuals, Burke, shocked by the events transpiring under his gaze in Paris, had blasted away at the "petulant, assuming, short-sighted coxcombs of philosophy" who, in his view, had hijacked the French nation and were steering it away from the wisdom of their forefathers.[11] Where Boorstin argued for "conservation and reform rather than . . . invention,"[12] Burke had praised the British for choosing "our nature rather than our speculations, our breasts rather than our inventions."[13]

The resemblance was not just coincidental but the product of similar beliefs operating in similar circumstances. Where Britain in 1790 was embarking on a prolonged crusade against Jacobinism and Bonapartism, which people like Burke saw as two sides of the same coin, America in 1953 was in the early stages of an even longer crusade against Communism, the Soviet Union, and radicalism in general, all of which people like Boorstin saw as stemming from the same thing—an excess of ideology, an undue reliance on the individual intellect as opposed to the wisdom of the group, and so on. Rather than stooping to their opponents' level by using rational arguments to counter what they saw as rationalism run amok, both Boorstin and Burke invoked tradition as an alternative to rational debate. For Burke, aimless chatter about *liberté, égalité,* and the Rights of Man were irrelevant next to a constitution as old and sturdy as a British oak. For Boorstin, Marxism, existentialism, and the rest paled in comparison to an American tradition that was even stronger and more powerful. Brit-

ain was great because it was Britain, whereas America was great because it was America. Intellectuals could never grasp the secret of
either because, being intellectuals, they lacked *faith*. Their minds were
too corrosive. European intellectuals, whom both Boorstin and Burke
held in contempt, were doubly disadvantaged because . . . well, because
they were European intellectuals.

Of course, nostalgic conservatism of this sort is possible in any country
with a tradition and a past to look backward to. America was in a
profoundly conservative mood after the war, but then so were many
Britons, Frenchmen, Japanese, and Dutchmen, all of whom could
come up with any number of reasons why it was better to bury oneself
in the past rather than face up to the need for modernization and
change. The one place where this was impossible, though, was Germany. As the one country assigned to take the rap for Nazism—as if
no one else shared in the responsibility—Germany, or at least that
portion under Western control, functioned as a kind of ground zero
for the West European political revolution. It was where the past had
been most thoroughly discredited, where prewar institutions were the
most suspect, and where fundamental change was the least possible to
avoid. Under the Allied occupation, Nazism was verboten both east
and west of the Elbe. But even milder forms of German nationalism,
with its traditional suspicion of liberal democracy and Western individualism, were forbidden as well. Burke had advised the Frenchmen
of his day to build on "old foundations" rather than experimenting
with newfangled political inventions, yet such advice was useless in a
society in which few foundations were left to build upon.[14]

The construction of a postwar West German state thus took place
in what, from an American perspective, was an anti-universe, one in
which the past was suspect, traditionalism was impossible, and all sur-
viving institutions were guilty until proven innocent. For the U.S.
military authorities in West Berlin, the solution seemed simple
enough. Since Germans lacked legitimate institutions of their own,
they would lend them some of theirs. Not long after arriving in Berlin,

General Lucius D. Clay, the conservative Atlantan appointed to head up the U.S. military occupation, went to work on a plan for a new German government that would be even more Jeffersonian than the American. By mid-1947, he was ready with a rough outline for a German federation complete with checks and balances, separation of powers, a limited central government, and a strong judiciary—a mini–United States on the North Sea. But when he laid it out for the Germans, he was taken aback by the response. Conservative politicians like Konrad Adenauer were receptive, but leftists like Kurt Schumacher, the sickly yet iron-willed leader of the Social Democrats, were staunchly opposed.

The result over the next two years was a political high comedy in which conservative Americans and German Social Democrats engaged in an elaborate test of wills to see whose constitutional vision would prevail. Clay, the son of a senator and a distant relation of Henry Clay, was a plainspoken, feet-on-the-desk type whom an admiring American journalist once described as "by birth and inclination an old-fashioned Jeffersonian liberal." Just as Jefferson enjoyed greeting European diplomats in his robe and slippers, Clay enjoyed throwing German journalists off balance by offering them a cigarette upon welcoming them into his office—most definitely not the sort of behavior German civilians were used to on the part of high-ranking military officers. Constitutionally, he was a true-blue believer in Jeffersonian decentralism; the best system, he once maintained, was the one that had existed around 1910, before Woodrow Wilson had ruined things by introducing a note of regulation and centralization. As a Southerner, Clay was also steeped in Reconstruction lore, and he now vowed to give the Germany "the kind of occupation the South would have had if Abraham Lincoln had lived."[15]

Schumacher, by contrast, seemed like a nightmare out of Germany's dark past, at least in the eyes of an American like Clay. Rigid, dogmatic, prickly as a hedgehog, he was deeply suspicious of the Americans, the French, the Soviets, or anyone else who threatened to get in the way of his vision of a unified, socialist Germany. The fact that he was visibly dying—he had lost an arm as a soldier in World War I and suffered the amputation of a leg shortly after the Allied occupation—did nothing to soften his personality. Quite the contrary, knowing that his enemies would be around after he had departed seemed to excite him to new levels of anger and bitterness. American officials openly loathed him, especially in comparison with the witty, rosebud-tending Konrad Adenauer, leader of the Christian Democrats, who had been an old-fashioned political boss in Cologne before the Nazis and consequently was someone they found more *sympathique*. Dean Acheson, Truman's secretary of state, later told of being charmed by Adenauer when they met "in a small private room in a very Victorian Bonn hotel, where we drank the delicious wines of the Rhineland," and of then being taken to meet Schumacher, who astonished him by launching into "an unrestrained" attack on his former host. "Breaking off this futile interview as soon as politeness permitted," Acheson continued, "I went on to a reception which the Chancellor was giving for me."[16]

Ideologically, Schumacher and the Americans were on different planets. Where Clay saw centralism, statism, and Stalinism as more or less flowing from the same source, the Social Democratic Party (commonly known by its German initials SPD) was hardly less centralist than the Soviets. Indeed, as a rising SPD politician in the 1920s, Schumacher had devoted one of his first speeches to denouncing "bourgeois particularism," meaning regional autonomy, and praising "socialist centralism."[17] Where Clay believed that American-style checks and balances were the obvious solution to the problem of German authoritarianism, the SPD believed that separation of powers was one of the things that had gotten Germany into trouble in the first place. The party's reasoning was simple. The Weimar Constitution had been an awkward blend of egalitarian and authoritarian elements. On one hand, a highly democratic form of proportional representation allowed as many as thirteen parties to gain a toehold in parliament, although only a half dozen were big enough to have any influence. On the other hand, the constitution gave the president enormous latitude to declare a state of emergency and rule by executive fiat. In times of legislative deadlock, the baton had passed all too easily into the hands of an authoritarian chief executive, with the result that after mid-1931, emergency rule had become the norm. The Social Democrats thus found themselves increasingly shut out of the centers of power. Had power been more firmly concentrated in parliament's hands, the party believed its clout would have been greater—perhaps great enough to prevent Hitler's accession to power.

None of which made any sense to Clay, who, as a good Jeffersonian, believed firmly in separation of powers and doubted that the SPD was democratic at all. As he once put it, the party was "close to a totalitarian party in operation and lack[ed] the democracy which comes from local pride."[18] The SPD's claims to have been anti-Nazi were similarly suspect. The Social Democrats were German, and weren't all Germans guilty of Hitler's crimes? From the SPD point of view, of course, things were the reverse. The party was intensely proud of its own anti-Nazi credentials and dubious of the Americans'. As Schumacher told a Social Democratic conference in 1946: "We fought the Nazis . . . before anyone else in the world bothered about it. . . . [W]e opposed the Nazis at great cost when it was still fashionable for the rest of the world to bid for their good will."[19] As a leader of the SPD's militant wing in the early thirties, Schumacher had indeed been among those advocating a last-ditch effort to prevent the Nazis from seizing power—a stance that earned him ten years in Dachau following Hitler's accession to power. Had he known of it, Schumacher would undoubtedly have pointed out that Clay himself had visited Germany as part of an official military delegation shortly after the Nazi takeover and had pronounced himself "rather pleased" with what he saw. "The Hitler regime had re-established law and order, and the public works program was very impressive," he later wrote, adding, of course, that such benefits had occurred "before the persecution of the Jews," which was obviously untrue.[20]

Thus, two very different men peered at one another from across the divide—a socialist versus a Jeffersonian, a defeated German versus a victorious American, a hard-bitten anti-Nazi versus a pragmatic conservative who believed that even Hitler had had his good side. With the Berlin Airlift, the conflict began to heat up. The Americans wanted a West German state with which to counter the Soviet-sponsored regime in the east. Yet the more they pressed for an agreement, the more Schumacher's Social Democrats dug in their heels. Schumacher thought little of Clay's ideas, which he characterized as "hyper-federalism." Instead of a loose-knit federation, he wanted a centralized parliamentary democracy with a flexible constitution, a subordinate judiciary, and *lander* (as the individual German states are known) that would be clearly subservient to the central government. He also wanted an "equalization of burdens" law, a mechanism by which the central government would be able to take tax revenue from the richer *lander* and distribute it among the poorer. It was the equivalent of Washington ordering Louisiana to share its oil revenue with dirt-poor Mississippi, an idea that Clay found little short of shocking. "Of course this right to transfer funds would completely destroy any state power and therefore make for . . . highly centralized government," he complained, not inaccurately. Schumacher's demand that the Bundestag, the West German lower house, be given virtually unlimited legislative authority alarmed him as well. It meant "leaving to the states power only to legislate . . . when the federal government has not exercised its prior power." "To my mind," he added, "we could not possibly accept the German proposal under our policy directive calling for a decentralized government as the German government would be as highly centralized as proposed by the Soviets."[21]

Matters came to a head in early 1949. Although Clay could count on support from the French, who did not care what kind of government West Germany had as long as it was weak and divided, the Labour government in Britain clearly sympathized with the SPD's desire for a strong, left-wing, parliamentary state. Hoping for signs of a compromise, Clay was devastated in April when the SPD's executive committee passed a resolution accusing the United States of trying to use superior force to ram through an unjust settlement. Democracy, the party leadership declared, could be achieved "only through the will of the German people, not . . . through mere constitutional constructions which rest on foreign orders." Rather than a rigid constitution festooned with rules and restrictions, the resolution called for a flexible document pared to "its essentials," with a dominant lower house, a weak upper house lacking in power to significantly "narrow the sovereignty of the people," and "maintenance of German legal and economic unity in all spheres, especially in that of legislation"— a euphemism for strong, centralized control. "In addition," the resolution stated, "the uniformity of social conditions of life in all parts of the federation, especially a uniform social order, must be guaranteed through a proper equalization of finance and of burdens." In other words, no states' rights, autonomy, or whatever else the Americans might call it. Rather, the central government would ensure that the same legal and economic conditions prevailed from one end of the country to the other.[22]

The effect of the SPD resolution was explosive. With the Soviets and the West at each other's throats over Berlin, the Americans saw their best-laid plans for a new regime in the west crumbling before their eyes. Anguished telexes flew back and forth between Washington and Clay's military headquarters. State Department suggestions that a compromise on the part of the United States might be in order roused Clay to anger. If Americans "bow to the arrogance and defiance of Schumacher, . . . [we] make him the top hero in Germany for his defiance," he responded. When Washington insisted, Clay shot back: "I see four years' work being destroyed. . . . All I can say is that it is most unfair to ask me to take an act which is entirely inconsistent with my deep conviction." Finally, General Omar Bradley dispatched a cable reminding Clay that a soldier's duty was to carry out orders whether he agreed or not. With that, Clay's temper snapped. "American philosophy expressed at Nuremberg," he declared, "found no excuse for a soldier carrying out political orders which he professed not to believe in."

This, of course, was absurd. Bradley was not asking Clay to fire up the crematoria at Auschwitz, merely to say yes to a revenue-sharing arrangement among the West German states. Yet in Clay's view—and the view of the American constitutional tradition in general—Stalinism and Nazism both flowed from the basic idea of centralized, sovereign government. To say yes to one was to say yes to the other, which is why Clay had gotten himself up in such a high moral dudgeon.

Nevertheless, Clay did eventually come around. Under pressure from Washington, he agreed to a compromise that gave in to the socialists on all major points.[23] As a result, Schumacher wound up with the strong parliamentary state he had always wanted. The powers of the upper house, the Bundesrat, were whittled down to the point where it was little more than a coordinating body. Rather than the states' rights favored by Clay, the *lander* were reduced to mere appendages of the national government in Bonn. Where the Americans had wanted voting for the lower house to be by districts just as it was back home, the Germans wound up with a much more equitable form of proportional representation, in which seats were essentially doled out according to each party's share of the national tally. The Germans also wound up with an amending clause that was stern—constitutional amendments could be approved solely by a vote of two-thirds of both houses—but not impossible. As a consequence, the "Basic Law," as it was formally known, would be amended more than thirty times over the next thirty-five years, for reasons large and small, while the U.S. Constitution would be amended only six.

Unfortunately for Schumacher, victory slipped out of his hands a few months later when Adenauer's Christian Democrats edged out the SPD in elections for the new Bundestag and entered into a coalition government with the middle-of-the-road, laissez-faire Free Democrats. Adenauer, the wily old fox of German politics, had not been displeased with the American constitutional proposals, since they would have allowed him to preserve his regional power base in Cologne. But now that the SPD-crafted constitution had given him sway over the entire West German federation, he was hardly displeased either. For the Social Democrats, however, the results couldn't have been more cruel. Cut off from their traditional stronghold in the Soviet-controlled east, they could only watch in frustration as the lean and efficient government machinery they had designed and fought for was taken over and put to use by members of the right wing. For Schumacher, whose motto was "a new Germany, not a reconstruction of the old," it meant standing by and watching as the old prewar conservatives, the same men who had handed power over to Hitler in 1933, once more took the helm.[24]

Still, the Basic Law was a real accomplishment, a democratic political framework in a country whose very name was synonymous with authoritarianism. Like the U.S. Constitution, the West German constitution also included a bill of rights. But where America's First Amendment was framed in negative terms ("Congress shall make no law . . ."), the Basic Law's language was positive. "Everyone shall have the right freely to express and disseminate his opinions," declared Article Five. "Freedom of the press and freedom of reporting by means of broadcast and films are guaranteed." Civil liberties were not something that would be brought about by limiting and restricting government. Rather, they would be achieved *through* government. Rather than the enemy of democracy, government was to be an instrument of democracy.

This is not to say that utopia had arrived by virtue of West Germany's new up-to-date structure of government. Quite the contrary, social democratic theory rejected the very idea of a constitutional utopia. The Basic Law was not a magic solution, "a machine that would go of itself," as James Russell Lowell had famously described the U.S. Constitution in 1888.[25] Rather, it was a mechanism by which the people could manage their own affairs. Ultimately, the only assurance that democracy would be maintained lay with the people—and, according to Social Democratic theory, especially with the workers—themselves.

Change and reconstitution was the norm in Western Europe throughout the postwar period. (It was also the norm in Eastern Europe, although there the story is somewhat more complicated.) Sweden, which had been neutral in the war, scrapped a much patched-over constitution that was nearly as old as the American one and substituted a revamped, up-to-date document under Prime Minister Olaf Palme in 1976. Where the old constitution had been issued in the name of the king, the new one began with a flat-out declaration that "all power in Sweden emanates from the people." If popular sovereignty was a fact in Sweden, then why not say so up front? Denmark abolished its upper house of parliament and approved a new constitution in 1953, while the Dutch, not to be outdone, did the same in 1972 and then another in 1983. France adopted a new constitution in 1958 (its six-teenth since the revolution), and Portugal adopted one in 1976 that was heavily revised in 1982 and again in 1989. A bit farther afield, Australians began debating dropping their allegiance to the British Crown as part of a general reorientation to the burgeoning economies of Asia, while New Zealanders revamped their voting laws by dropping a "first past the post" British system and adopting one based on pro-portional representation instead.[26]

The new buzzword in certain European political circles was "transparency," meaning a government apparatus whose workings were clear, simple, and instantly apparent to the typical voter. Rather than conference committees, pocket vetoes, filibusters, and all the other maneuverings that Americans had come to see as the essence of politics, the idea was that debate should be open and up front, con-centrated in a single chamber, with no artificial distinction as to leg-islative and executive functions. The people who made the laws would carry them out and would be instantly answerable for their actions. Since responsibility would be clear from the beginning, there would be minimal opportunity for excuses or passing the buck. The one thing democracy could not tolerate was complex and tangled lines of authority.

The one exception to all this change and restructuring in Europe was Great Britain, which, all too unfortunately, had come through the war with a renewed sense of tradition and national solidarity. George VI had never been terribly popular before 1939, but his radio addresses during some of the darkest hours of the conflict had turned him into an object of genuine mass affection. By V-E Day, consequently, the British were in a contradictory mood. They were hungry for change, yet wanted the old, traditional patterns of government restored. After five years as prime minister, Winston Churchill was swept from power by a huge margin and the Labour Party under Clement Attlee swept in. It was the most dramatic parliamentary election in British history, a quasi-revolutionary transformation that left politicians gasping for breath. But where Labour clearly had a mandate to build up a British welfare state nearly from scratch, it did not have, or at least members did not *think* it had, a mandate for a thorough reordering of the political structure. Where radical socialists had consoled themselves during the barren years of the Great Depression with thoughts of tossing out the king and abolishing the House of Lords, Labour now confined itself to more modest constitutional adjustments. Inequities in the electoral laws were ironed out, including a bizarre medieval relic that allowed Oxford, Cambridge, and certain other university graduates to vote twice in parliamentary elections. So was another provision that allowed bankers and brokers in the City of London financial district to do the same. But that was as far as it went. The lords continued to doze on their upholstered benches, while the monarchy remained in place. The class system was shaken but not toppled. In 1951, Labour held on to a small majority in terms of the popular vote but lost its parliamentary majority because much of its strength was concentrated in a relatively small number of urban seats. But where a truly radical party would have demanded that the electoral system be changed so as to more closely reflect the will of the people, Labour turned over the reins without protest. Being a good sport in British politics meant not only playing by the rules, but not questioning them as well.

Kurt Schumacher had called for a new Germany, but Labour dedicated itself to rebuilding the old family mansion on a somewhat fairer and more equitable basis. This was what left-wing critics would later deride as "royal socialism," in other words, a fairer deal for British workers within the confines of the existing class structure. Criticism like this was easy to dismiss in the high-growth fifties as so much left-wing carping, but less so in the stagnant seventies and eighties as Britain began falling behind the Continent and the awesome West German industrial machine began pulling out ahead. By the early nineties, constitutional reform was no longer a topic just for a few quasi-Marxist theoreticians but of mass concern. Pressure for change emanated from both the Left and the Right—from the Murdoch-controlled press, which was having a field day with the troubles and scandals besetting the royal family; from Labour Party modernizers who argued that Britain had to take a lesson from the Germans constitutionally if it was ever to catch up with them economically; and from more extreme leftists who argued that the monarchy was not simply an innocent diversion, but the linchpin of an entire class system. Labour circles buzzed with demands for proportional representation or a bill of rights, while it seemed impossible to pick up a copy of the *Guardian*, the superbly literate left-of-center daily, without reading that "Britain's pre-democratic state structures" were creaking "under the strains of their incapacities."[27] In December 1994, the Labour Party's shadow home secretary caused a small ruckus when he proposed that the number of members of the royal family on public stipend be pared from forty to a mere half dozen.[28] The goal was not merely to reduce expenses. Rather, slimming down and reining in the royal family was seen as the first step toward reining in an over-towering class structure that was squeezing the breath out of society at large. Rather than surrendering to tradition, the idea was that the people would take control not only of the monarchy, but of the state in general, revamping it from top to bottom so as to render it more responsive, more efficient, more Germanic or Scandinavian.

The strategy, in other words, was to rethink government the way it had been rethought on the Continent, to catch up with the great constitutional transformations that had been under way since the forties and perhaps even to surpass them. Where Britain had once gloried in its isolation from the rest of Europe, the goal now was to avoid becoming the odd man out, an offshore Ruritania filled with dukes, princes, and ladies-in-waiting yet with a declining industrial base, a growing underclass, and the worst educational system in Northern Europe. Yet Britain was hobbled by a curious constitutional paradox. Thanks to a highly centralized form of government, the House of Commons, at least in theory, could abolish the monarchy with less effort than it takes to get a highway bill through Congress. Yet given a deep-seated resistance to change that, if anything, had been strengthened by the war, the chances of it undertaking even the minor structural adjustments needed to keep up with its neighbors seemed dim. Britain's famous unwritten constitution turned out to be a double-edged sword. Because Parliament was subject to no formal, constitutional restraints, the House of Commons' power was essentially unlimited. Yet because the unwritten constitution had been married to the notion of tradition and historical continuity, it had once again become immobilized. The House of Commons could make any structural change it wanted to, except that by the mid-nineties it didn't seem to want to make any at all.

But at least Britons—*some* Britons, that is—were talking about constitutional change. This was more than what one could say about the Americans, for whom the idea of genuine popular sovereignty was more remote than ever. "If it ain't broke, don't fix it" might sum up the postwar American attitude toward their Constitution, except that the very idea of brokenness was unthinkable in a system considered to be in perfect working order even when it was at its most inefficient. What's more, even if it could somehow be determined that the constitutional system had broken down, who would do the fixing? With its requirement for approval by two-thirds of the House and Senate and three-fourths of the states, the amending process was long and tortuous. By forcing the electorate to deliberate in their capacity both as citizens of the nation and citizens of the individual states, Article V fairly guaranteed that the amending process would be even more fragmented than the legislative process. There was little opportunity for the people as a whole to reform the Constitution in toto in a way that was thoroughgoing and consistent. The postwar period actually saw a record number of amendments being approved—six as opposed to a mere dozen for the previous century and a half. But all were minor and peripheral: an amendment limiting the president to two terms in office, another giving Washington, D.C., residents the right to vote in presidential elections, and so on. None addressed the issue of an obsolete and undemocratic political structure. Indeed, one amendment was so antique that even constitutional scholars were taken aback. This was the twenty-seventh, prohibiting congressmen from voting salary increases for themselves until after the next election, which Madison had drafted as part of the Bill of Rights shortly after the Constitution was ratified. The amendment had been approved by a few state legislatures and had then lapsed into a two-century slumber before being rediscovered in the late 1970s. It then resumed its long trek through the state legislatures, picking up the thirty-eighth legislative endorsement needed for ratification in 1992. The experts were amused, yet the public remained largely in the dark. So incomplete was the people's power that an amendment had become virtually an indelible part of the Constitution without most of them even knowing what it said.

Yet the United States was in no mood for criticism in this period, particularly from abroad. A strange brouhaha in 1953 shows just how deeply the United States had withdrawn by that point into the protective folds of its constitutional religion. The incident arose when ex–Prime Minister Clement Attlee ventured some tepid criticism of the American system during a parliamentary debate. He asserted that when a British prime minister goes before the House of Commons and states his policy, "it is the policy of the government." But when an American president says something, it is not at all the same. For instance, Attlee continued,

President Eisenhower makes a great speech. It is the President's speech. He speaks for the Administration, but in

America power is divided between the Administration and Congress. . . . Therefore, the government in America are not really master in their own house. . . . We do find on occasion that there is one policy being run by the Treasury, another by the State Department, and perhaps another by the Pentagon. . . . One of the disadvantages of the American system of democracy is that it is sometimes hard to find where executive power lies.[29]

This was all quite mild and ordinary, nothing that any number of journalists and academics had not said on any number of occasions before the war. Yet in its postwar mood of deep, dark conservatism, the American mind had closed tighter than a drum. The press, consequently, was livid. The McCormick newspaper chain denounced Attlee as a "presumptuous political hack," the Scripps-Howard chain called him "the old fluff," the *New York Daily News* described him as "an ignoramus," and the Hearst chain dismissed his remarks as "stupid and insulting."[30] The U.S. Constitution had risen to a point where it was simply beyond criticism, not unlike the British constitution of some two centuries earlier. By definition, it was perfect. No one was allowed to say otherwise.

8

THE DISASTER
OF WATERGATE

WATERGATE, the great drama of postwar American politics, could
have been an opportunity for Americans to dig themselves out of their
constitutional hole, but instead it proved an occasion to bury themselves deeper. The reason can be summed up in a single word: faith.
The crisis was a resounding victory for America's civic religion of
constitution worship. Barbara Jordan, the black Democrat from Texas,
summed up the mood on the House Judiciary Committee during the
impeachment hearings when she proclaimed in ringing, preacherlike
tones: "My faith in the Constitution is whole, it is complete, it is total,
and I am not going to sit here and be an idle spectator to the dimi-
nution, the subversion, the destruction of the Constitution."[1] Virtually
the entire nation applauded at what was seen as an effort to defend

the rule of law against a president who believed, as he would later tell interviewer David Frost, that when the president does something, "that means that it is not illegal."[2] Yet what the United States needed at that moment was not another outburst of religious fervor but the cooler intellectual virtues of criticism, skepticism, and analysis. The system was emerging from the worst constitutional crisis since the Court-packing episode in 1937. Clearly, something had gone badly awry and needed to be fixed. Yet faith was a diversion from the hard work of analysis and repair. Rather than delving into the machinery, Congress and the press found it easier to heap all blame on a single individual, drive him from the temple, and then set to work patching up the holy shrine. With the Constitution restored, everything would soon be in working order—or so it was believed.

Yet it wasn't. Post-Watergate, the story of American politics was one of breakdown, failure, and loss of control—deepening paralysis on Capitol Hill, a growing sense of frustration and alienation out in the hinterlands, and strange political outbreaks like the Proposition 13 tax revolt in 1978, H. Ross Perot's bizarre presidential bid in 1992, the Oklahoma City bombing in 1995, and the proliferation of armed, right-wing militias. Where Watergate had indeed been a two-bit burglary aimed at gathering dirt on Nixon's opponents by rifling through Democratic files, the Iran-contra episode, which exploded into public view in 1986, was something very different, a highly professional operation in which top White House officials used off-the-books arms sales to evade congressional oversight and engage in covert activities around the globe. Yet Congress's response the second time around was a flop—weak, divided, and confused. For various reasons, Ronald Reagan was not nearly as convenient a scapegoat as Richard Nixon had been, the religious aura that had surrounded Watergate proved impossible to duplicate, and the ancient impeachment machinery could not be hauled into place in time to be effective. As a result, the perpetrators for the most part got off, Reagan was able to leave office with his popularity undiminished, while American democracy suffered a body blow from which it has yet to recover. If Watergate had been a real victory, it would have strengthened Congress's ability to combat lawlessness on the part of the executive branch. Instead, it left it weakened and disarmed.

While religious faith proved useful in drumming up opposition to Nixon, it promoted a sense of constitutional fatalism that in the end proved debilitating. By constitutional fatalism, I mean the widespread belief that the ways of Washington are permanent and unchanging, that the average citizen is powerless to alter the essential structure of government, and that power will always be divided precariously between an executive and legislative branch. Five years after the Nixon resignation, a fourteen-year veteran of Congress named Lloyd Meeds summed up the conventional wisdom on Capital Hill:

> There's nothing wrong with Congress that isn't wrong with this country. Congress, particularly the House of Representatives, is a mirror of what's happening and of the views that are being expressed in households all across the country today. And to expect Congress, particularly the House, with its short tenure of two years, to be better or worse than the country as a whole is to expect something that our Founding Fathers never intended, and something that is never going to happen.[3]

Congress was incapable of leading, incapable of governing, incapable even of managing its own affairs. Rather, it was only capable of carrying out instructions dictated by the Founding Fathers some two centuries earlier. To expect it to do anything more was simply impossible. As Bentham had once observed, no dictatorship was more terrible, more unyielding, than a dictatorship of the past.[4]

This sense of constitutional fatalism is uniquely American. Outside of Iran and a few other fundamentalist strongholds, the prevailing belief is that if institutions are not working, they should simply be fixed. This reflects a modern view that humans control their own destiny and that they fashion institutions for the betterment of their condition. If the institutions do not make things better, then it is up to the people to create new ones that will. Yet a system predicated on the notion that it is foolish "to expect something that our Founding Fathers never intended" is the very opposite, one in which institutions rule and the people obey.

The three branches of government have succumbed to this post-Watergate enfeeblement in various ways, although ultimately the outcome has been the same. Each has gotten sillier with every passing year, more intellectually limited, more ineffectual and broken down. The consequences have been disastrous for those who believe that government is necessary to improve society and a godsend for those latter-day Jeffersonians who argue that government is at most a necessary evil that in many cases fouls things up and makes them worse. Here is a rundown of the damage Watergate has wrought.

Congress: From self-congratulation to self-loathing

For those in search of a historical analogy, the event Watergate most resembles is the Glorious Revolution of 1688–89, when Parliament threw out James II and invited his son-in-law, William of Orange, to take his place. Like Watergate, the Glorious Revolution was both a triumph of constitutionalism and a political evasion. In between James's departure and William's accession, members of both houses got together in a special convention to pass a rather curiously worded resolution declaring that with "King James II . . . having endeavored to subvert the constitution of the kingdom . . . and withdrawn himself out of the kingdom, the throne is thereby vacant." The resolution contained a stunning non sequitur: James had subverted the constitution *and* he had vacated the throne, yet no effort was made to connect the two, to explain what one had to do with the other. The reason was obvious. Parliament had *forced* James out of office. Yet rather than open the door to a repetition of the revolutionary disorders of the 1640s, the landowners and good bourgeois who now ran Parliament preferred to play down their own role. *They* had not made him leave town, the resolution suggested. Rather, he had left on his own.

This was Parliament's way of assuring everyone that separation of powers had not been violated, the monarchy was still intact, and the legislative branch had not overstepped its constitutional bounds. All William had to do was to assume the throne for the status quo ante to be restored.

Something of the same process occurred during Watergate. As the crisis came to a head, congressmen went out of their way to stress that they were not invading the president's turf or upsetting the balance of power but merely acting out roles laid down centuries earlier by the Founders. They weren't forcing Richard Nixon out of office; rather, it was the Constitution that was the prime mover. As a result, the air at the impeachment hearings was so thick with constitutional piety it was difficult to breathe. House Judiciary chairman Peter Rodino, in ordinary times a Democratic hack from the devastated city of Newark, New Jersey, invoked the Emperor Justinian, King John, and Edmund Burke before winding up with a plea to his fellow committee members to see to it that the Constitution was left "as unimpaired for our children as our predecessors left it for us"—in other words, to restore conditions to their former purity. Elizabeth Holtzman, a liberal Democrat from Brooklyn, excoriated Nixon for never once stopping to ask himself, "What does the Constitution say? What are the limits of my power? What does the oath of office require of me? What is the right thing to do?"[5]—as if all a political leader had to do was hold to the ancient law for the country to be restored to health.

The people, in whose name all this was occurring, remained safely offstage, just as they had in 1688–89. Every day, the vigil outside the White House grew a little larger as the resignation grew nearer. Yet those who participated did so not as actors so much as passive observers at a historical spectacle, not unlike a coronation or a royal funeral. On the day of the resignation, a couple of *Washington Post* editors took to the field to assess the popular mood and reported back that conditions were safely under control:

There was no chorus of jubilation in Washington and no cries for vengeance or retribution. There was an absence of turmoil, mobs, violence, massive protests. The crowds that began gathering at the White House on Tuesday remained quiet, solemn and patient. They were witnesses to history, yes, and someday they would tell their grandchildren about it. But now . . . they seemed more preoccupied by personal feelings of sorrow and sadness.[6]

They were worshipers in an official church, bowing their heads as the preachers intoned the holy trinity of the Founders, the Constitution, and the Supreme Court. Alexander Cockburn, the acerbic left-wing columnist, captured the mood nicely when he observed shortly after the resignation:

On the word front, the sky is still dark with clichés coming home to roost. The nightmare of Watergate is slowly receding, the long national trauma is over, the country's profound need for rest has been appeased, a catharsis has taken place, a curtain is falling on a tragedy almost Greek in its dimensions, agony is giving way to peace, the nation's wounds are being healed, the healing has begun, the Constitution has worked, the system has worked, pretty well everything you've ever heard of has worked, except the economy.[7]

The tragedy *was* almost Greek in its dimensions, which is to say that the people watched in wonder, not unlike an audience at a performance of *Oedipus Rex*, as the law proceeded inexorably on its path. The constitutional machinery was unstoppable—its will would be done. The mood changed a month later when Gerald Ford granted Nixon a blanket pardon for all Watergate-related crimes. Protesters jeered and held up signs saying "Justice Died 9/9/74," while Anthony Lewis, the fourth estate's high priest of constitutionalism, worked himself up into a fine frenzy in the *New York Times* accusing the president of "frustrat[ing] the process of law and the Constitution."[8] Yet Ford was not to blame since he had based his actions on the same holy text. Taking his cue from Elizabeth Holtzman, he had asked himself in effect, "What does the Constitution say? What are the limits of my power?"—and had concluded, not unreasonably, that Article II, Section 2, gave him the power to spare his predecessor from any threat of criminal prosecution. All Ford had done was to take the document at its word. Rather than criticizing the Constitution for giving the chief executive such sweeping powers, liberals preferred to criticize the president for using them. Yet the position was untenable, which is why the protests soon died away.

Congress had thrown out an unpopular, authoritarian president. Yet rather than stepping in to fill the vacuum, it embarked on a series of wrongheaded reforms and fairly disintegrated. The old seniority system, in which aging political bosses on Capitol Hill had shooed rank-and-file congressmen out of their way like kindergartners, was overthrown. Now *no one* told rank-and-file congressmen what to do, with the result that they became a classic herd of independent minds, as easily scattered as a flock of sheep. In bypassing the old party organizations and placing federal matching funds directly in the hands of the candidates, the campaign-spending reforms inspired by Watergate helped transform members of Congress from Democratic or GOP foot soldiers into self-contained political entrepreneurs, each with his own fund-raising staff, pollsters, and campaign strategists. Instead of looking out for the party's interests, members now looked out for their own interests and those of their constituents. Reelection rates rose from their already sky-high levels, while committees and subcommittees proliferated as each member demanded a barony of his own to preside over as lord of the manor. By the late seventies, things had reached the point where Representative Morris Udall could joke that when passing some junior Democrat whose name he had forgotten, he would simply call out, "Good morning, Mr. Chairman," knowing that half the time he'd be right.[9] Creation of the Congressional Budget Office in 1974 gave legislators the analytical tools they needed to compete with the executive on an equal footing. Yet rather than using this power to exercise leadership, Congress used it to become more ornery, more "independent," and more undisciplined. Congress piled on staff, doubling the level of legislative employment between 1973 and 1984.[10] Yet work on Capitol Hill slowed to a crawl.

"Paradoxically," observed journalist Hedrick Smith, "reform opened up a razzle-dazzle political circus."[11] The more "open" Congress became after Watergate, the more fragmented and irresponsible it grew. Information, advice, and requests for help poured into Congress from all sides. Between 1972 and 1985, the volume of mail descending on Capitol Hill increased fifteenfold, and, by 1987, the number of registered lobbyists in Washington had reached an astounding twenty-three thousand, a sixtyfold increase over the level of 1961.[12] Yet all Congress seemed able to do with its newfound power was tie itself in knots. "The new power game has not only multiplied the centers and circles of power," Smith noted, "but it has led to a more piecemeal, jumbled, adversarial brand of politics."[13] Power on Capitol Hill could be used to obstruct, delay, divide, or advance one's own career—everything and anything, that is, but run government in a systematic, logical fashion.

This was indeed strange. Conceivably, Congress could have taken matters in hand and gotten its own house in order just as it had the executive's. But this would have required a vastly different mind-set, a willingness to rethink the separation of powers doctrine from top to bottom. Yet Watergate had strengthened separation of powers, not weakened it. Considering the penalty that Nixon had suffered for violating the doctrine, it was inconceivable that Congress would do the same.

Gerald Ford, of course, lasted a scant eighteen months in office, while Jimmy Carter's presidency proved to be one of the more disastrous of the century. Populist touches like walking to his inauguration and wearing a cardigan sweater while delivering a televised address fell embarrassingly flat. Attempts to work with Congress rather than against it proved naive. Carter started off his administration with the usual high-minded rhetoric about working hand in hand with the powers that be in the legislative branch. Yet he was soon sounding almost Nixonesque as he raged against "powerful and ravenous wolves" on Capitol Hill who were tearing his energy program to shreds:[14]

I learned the hard way that there was no party loyalty or discipline when a complicated or controversial issue was at
stake—none. Each legislator had to be wooed and won individually. It was every member for himself, and the devil take
the hindmost![15]

The upshot, of course, was the collapse of Democratic hopes, the
election of Ronald Reagan in 1980, and, a few years later, the Iran-
contra episode. Reagan restored the presidency to a measure of its
former strength and, ironically, restored a measure of discipline to the
Democrats in Congress, who always do better when they are under
siege than when they are in charge. A series of brutal foreign-policy
wars erupted when Reagan, the most popular president in decades,
insisted on funding a right-wing guerrilla army in Nicaragua for which
there was little popular support. In 1983, Democratic members of
Congress pushed through the so-called Boland Amendment prohibiting either the Department of Defense or the CIA from using funds
"for the purpose of overthrowing the Government of Nicaragua or
provoking a military exchange between Nicaragua and Honduras."
Instead of backing off, the administration responded by creating an
offshore operation to circumvent Congress and funnel arms to the
contras by other means.

In hindsight, the administration's response was all too predictable.
The tension between the executive and legislative branches was as
unbearable as it had been under Nixon. Rather than persuading them
to stay on their side of the fence, Watergate had merely taught the
president's men a lesson to be less sloppy the second time around, to
craft their operations with lawyerly precision. Since presidential "de-
niability" was key, the organizers made sure to keep "the Enterprise,"
as the Iran-contra conspiracy was known, far away from the Oval Office. Since the president could not be held accountable for what he
did not know, the participants made sure that he would know as little
as possible. Where the Boland Amendment prohibited the Defense
Department or CIA from aiding the contras, it did not expressly

permit other administration officials from inducing other national governments to do so in return for certain favors or gifts, a loophole that members of the Enterprise were quick to exploit. By the mid-1980s, they were brokering eight-figure arms deals with countries like Saudi Arabia and Brunei, arranging third-party payments, and even laying plans to recruit a militia in Lebanon. Rather than relying on a bunch of paunchy ex-detectives and Bay of Pigs veterans à la Nixon's White House Plumbers, the group was carefully structured with a tightly knit group of presidential appointees—CIA chief William Casey, National Security Advisor Robert McFarlane, and his deputy, Admiral John Poindexter—serving as a board of directors, the ever energetic Colonel Oliver North in charge of day-to-day supervision, and retired Major General Richard Secord serving as chief operating officer.[16]

The result was a legal device for the circumvention of congressional prerogatives, not only in terms of foreign policy but conceivably in domestic policy as well. The executive branch had liberated itself from legislative control. Even when the operation was disbanded in November 1986 after the press got a tip about secret arms sales to Iran, the damage was contained. Nicaragua's left-wing government was toppled, while Oliver North succeeded in turning the tables on Congress by engaging in a highly popular show of defiance before a special House-Senate investigating committee formed to look into the scandal. Not only did George Bush, Reagan's designated successor, succeed in getting himself elected in 1988, but, four years later, he pardoned former Defense Secretary Caspar Weinberger and five other accused Iran-contra conspirators, sparing them the vengeance of the courts. Ultimately, only one member of the conspiracy wound up doing jail time, a low-level operative named Thomas G. Clines. Like a group of crack commandos, the Iran-contra conspirators had accomplished their mission and then slipped away with a minimum of casualties.

Why was Congress's response so ineffectual? Clearly, the legislative branch was exhausted after a dozen years of battling nonstop with the executive. It had compromised itself politically by voting military aid for the Nicaraguan contras just weeks before the scandal broke. Reagan was far more popular than Nixon could ever have imagined being, which made him much more difficult to attack. But more importantly, though, Congress was, in the strict meaning of the term, incompetent. It lacked the know-how to deal with this latest challenge from the executive or the tools. For a variety of reasons, impeachment, the centuries-old blunderbuss that is the legislature's only real weapon for keeping the executive in line, was unsuited to the task. The conspiracy's engineers made sure there would be no physical evidence linking the president to the conspiracy, no Watergate-style "smoking gun." Reagan had let it be known that he wanted the contras kept together "body and soul" but otherwise left it to his underlings to fill in the blanks. Moreover, even if evidence could have been found, there was precious little time. Reagan was midway through his second term when the scandal broke. By the time the impeachment machinery could be hauled into place, he would be finished with three-fourths. By the time the hearings concluded, he would be all but out the door. Dragging an aging and still-popular president before a Senate tribunal to answer for crimes committed by overenthusiastic underlings would be a public-relations disaster, a prospect which few "responsible" Democrats on Capitol Hill could contemplate without a shudder.

This was precisely why the British Parliament had abandoned impeachment as a means of controlling the executive in the late eighteenth century—because it was clumsy, inefficient, and ill-suited to the tasks of modern government. It was a quasi-criminal procedure when what was really needed were more supple and effective *political* controls. Congress, consequently, was stymied. The investigation it eventually launched turned out to be a farce. Where the original Senate Watergate panel had been small and compact—just seven members plus majority and minority counsel—the joint committee assembled in the wake of Contragate was huge and unwieldy. The twenty-six senators and representatives who took part insisted on keeping their staffs separate, while members from the House further divided themselves up along party lines. Determined to make the most of their moment in the spotlight, virtually every last member demanded a shot at questioning witnesses. Some pounced and badgered like small-town prosecutors, while others sat back and let the witnesses have the floor. When Oliver North launched his counterattack, the members were stunned. North admitted to misleading legislators "with the purpose of hopefully avoiding . . . a shut-off of help for the Nicaraguan resistance" but added that it was not his fault but Congress's for leaking sensitive data in the first place.[17] He was forced to lie to Congress for its own good and for the good of the nation.

No military officer had dared use language like this since McClellan during the Civil War, yet the flood of pro-North telegrams that quickly followed left the members in a daze. North was defying the people's representatives, yet he seemed all the more popular for doing so. In an especially eerie moment following a day at the witness table, he appeared in full uniform at the balcony of a federal office building to wave to the hundreds of fans who had gathered below. The scene seemed less like Washington, D.C., in the 1980s than Buenos Aires during the rise of Juan Perón. "What would happen if a German Oliver North appeared before the Bundestag?" Marion Donhoff, an editor of the German weekly *Die Zeit*, asked at the time. "He would be ridiculous and we would all laugh at him."[18] No one, however, was laughing in Washington.

In January 1994, a revealing postmortem appeared in the *New York Times*. Following the release of independent prosecutor Lawrence E. Walsh's final report on the Iran-contra affair, reporter David E. Rosenbaum summed up all the ways Iran-contra had differed from Watergate. Reagan was "a short-timer," he wrote; consequently, impeachment proceedings "could not possibly have been completed before he was out of office." North, Poindexter, and the other conspirators refused to testify without grants of immunity, which, once granted, "meant that they could never be successfully prosecuted." As long as there was no hope of implicating the president, "the public was not much interested"—and so on. What was to be done? According to the *Times*'s front-page news analysis, the answer was very little. "The American political system may not be designed to cope when a popular Administration has run off course and impeachment is out of the question," the article concluded.[19] Because it was not *designed* to cope, the system was incapable of defending itself against an out-of-control presidency. The people were the victims of a pre-modern system that was unequipped to deal with the problems of the late twentieth century.

A newspaper article has no official standing. Yet, as a glimpse into the nature of America's constitutional culture, the *Times* piece was highly revealing. Because there was nothing to be done, there was nobody to blame either. Because Congress had not been programmed to deal with a situation that no one had foreseen in 1787, it could not be held responsible. Since the Founders were blameless by definition, they could not be held responsible either. Therefore, nobody was at fault. The failure to respond adequately to Iran-contra was just one of those things.

In the wake of the Iran-contra debacle, Congress continued to spiral downward. As public dissatisfaction grew and the anti-Washington mood deepened, twenty-year veterans of Capitol Hill tried to pass themselves off as antigovernment outsiders in order to hoodwink voters into returning them to office. In 1992, a Republican newcomer named Jack Quinn from Buffalo, New York, ran for Congress on a promise "to curtail spending for pork-barrel programs." Following his election, he promptly presented the House Ways and Means Committee with a wish list of $58.7 million in road projects he wanted approved for the folks back home. Few people on Capitol Hill so much as blinked.[20] When Bill Sarpalius, a conservative Democrat, launched a last-ditch effort to defend something called the Federal Helium Reserve, a $1.3-billion underground storage facility that just happens to be located in Sarpalius's district in Amarillo, Texas, he won praise for his performance. "No one ought to begrudge Bill Sarpalius his defense of this boondoggle," offered one of his colleagues on the Hill. "It's his job as a congressman to defend it."[21] A House freshman summed up the mood of resignation when she arrived in Washington in early 1993. "You have to have low expectations," she said. "Institutions like this move at a glacial pace."[22] Rather than changing Washington, the people's representatives had no choice but to adapt.

On the Senate side, conditions were possibly even worse. Twice as many filibusters took place during the 1991–92 session as in the entire nineteenth century.[23] Important measures no longer required fifty-one votes to pass, consequently, but sixty, the amount needed under Senate rules to cut off debate. In 1993, Bob Kerrey, a liberal Democrat from Nebraska, took to the Senate floor to castigate President Bill Clinton for caving in to congressional pressure and not giving the legislative branch the discipline it so obviously craved. Referring to the proposal for a broad-based energy tax, which the White House had dropped due to resistance in Congress, he declared:

> You have the right idea, Mr. President, with the BTU tax, and when we came after you with both barrels blazing, threatening to walk if you did not yield, you should have let us walk. You should have said to us that at least we'd be exercising something other than our mouths. Instead we find ourselves with a bill that asks Americans to pay 4.3 cents a gallon more. If they notice, I'll be surprised. If they complain, I will be ashamed. . . .[24]

This was the sound of an institution that was so lost in the wilderness it had given up hope of ever finding its way home. Left to its own devices, said Kerrey, Congress was incapable of generating anything but "disdain, distrust, disillusionment." Instead of making nice, Clinton should have given it a taste of the lash.

In mid-1994, shortly before his retirement, David L. Boren of Oklahoma, a powerhouse on the Senate Finance Committee, summed up a typical fourteen-hour day on Capitol Hill spent

> running from one room to another and one office building to another because four of my committees were meeting at the

same time; lunching just off the Senate floor while waiting for my amendment to come up; dashing to the Capitol steps for photos with three groups from home and back to my office for five appointments on pending legislation or projects—all followed by three or four hours of returning new phone calls, answering dozens of new letters, and reading a pile of urgent action memos from staff members asking directions on issues or constituent problems. Those days usually ended at 10 P.M. with dinner at my desk.[25]

If all this mad dashing to and fro had led to better government, it might have been justified. Yet, as Boren cheerfully admitted, the opposite was the case: "At the end of certain days, I sometimes asked myself what I had really done to help solve the major problems facing our country. My honest answer: not much."[26] If anything, Boren was too kind, both to himself and the institution he served. As a zealous champion of oil and other corporate interests, he had been chiefly known in recent years for sabotaging Bill Clinton's energy tax and helping to destroy health-care reform—in other words, not for what he had accomplished but for what he had caused *not* to be accomplished.

This, of course, was all prior to the great deluge of November 1994, when a furious electorate threw out the Democrats en masse and placed both houses under the control of the Republicans for the first time since 1946. Except that the consequences were so wretched, the outcome was heartily deserved. Under the Democrats, congressional bloat had reached astounding proportions. Where Woodrow Wilson had complained in 1885 that some sixty-odd legislative committees on Capitol Hill were strangling Congress, by 1994 the number of committees and subcommittees (the latter a relatively new wrinkle on Capitol Hill) had risen to close to three hundred. As recently as 1914, there had been more senators than senate employees, while as recently as 1935 there had been only two employees for every member of the House.[27] Yet by 1994 the number of legislative-branch employees stood at some thirty-seven thousand, roughly seventy workers for every elected politician.[28] With so many committees and subcommittees picking and clawing over individual bills—more than one hundred had a hand in formulating the 1992 defense budget, for instance, while forty claimed jurisdiction over energy legislation—the bills themselves grew both longer and more ineffective. The 1994 Crime Bill, the focus of the Clinton administration's attention for much of the year, totaled more than fourteen hundred pages, a great Christmas tree of a bill filled with initiatives, giveaways, and programs like midnight basketball games for the underprivileged. It had something for everyone, that is, except those who would like Congress to address society's growing list of ills in a coherent, intelligent, systematic manner.

The Presidency: The magic of personality

The German sociologist Max Weber once divided democracies up into two types, charismatic and rational. After a visit to America in 1912 in which he was able to catch a glimpse of the ever frenetic Theodore Roosevelt at work, he concluded that the United States was most definitely the former, a "leader-democracy" characterized by "a highly emotional type of devotion . . . and trust." Where rational politics spoke the language of programs and ideas, American politicians appealed on the basis of feelings and emotions, on their ability to persuade voters that they shared their thoughts and feelings without having to put them into words. Teddy Roosevelt's supporters backed him not merely because he promised to champion a progressive agenda, but because his vigor, sense of adventure, and all-around feistiness were what they thought the nation needed. They voted for the man rather than the program—or, rather, for the man as the embodiment of his program. The system, Weber concluded, favored the individual who "is most spectacular, who promises the most, or who enjoys the most effective propaganda measures in the competition for leadership."[29]

Unfortunately, TR came in second that year, ahead of Taft, the incumbent, but behind the comparatively colorless Woodrow Wilson, who as a Democrat enjoyed the solid support of the South as well as the party's big-city bosses up North. Nonetheless, Weber's thesis still held. At its most basic, the idea of a charismatic presidential system boiled down to a matter of arithmetic. In a modern parliamentary system, members grouped themselves in parties and batted arguments back and forth like a shuttlecock in a multisided game of badminton. Because the debates took place in the open, the public could follow each development as it unfolded every inch of the way—the effectiveness with which the ruling party defended its program, the nature of the opposition's attack, the quality of the arguments, and so forth. In a charismatic system, something of the same back-and-forth debate took place—but behind closed doors. Advisers and courtiers jockeyed for influence. Various ideas rose and fell. Yet, aside from occasional news leaks, the only thing the public saw was the spectacle of a single individual wrestling with his conscience.

Citizens were thus shut out. Since voters had little way of holding the president accountable in a system as fragmented as the American one, they only thing they had to go on was the quality of his performance—how he looked, how he talked, the success with which he was able to persuade a diverse electorate that he had each and every person's interests most at heart.

Needless to say, the process since 1912 has acquired layers of complexity that Weber could never have imagined. Instead of the candidate with the most outsize personality, elections by the 1970s were being won by the candidate with the most powerful public-relations machinery, the most adept pollsters, and, of course, the campaign contributors with the deepest pockets. As special interests proliferated, the presidential art of being all things to all people grew ever more arcane. Candidates traveled the country appealing to veterans, union members, corporate executives, and environmentalists, trying to figure out ways to appease one group without alienating the rest. Voters were increasingly aware that what they were witnessing was a sophisticated form of performance art. Yet rather than turning away in disgust, many of them gave themselves up to the spectacle. "*Is* he a phony?"

asked the columnist Richard Reeves of Jimmy Carter in 1976. "Of course he is. He's a politician, an actor, a salesman. What I like is that the product he's peddling is one of the most interesting I've seen in a long time."[30] Politics were phony, yet at the same time somehow real. "The political process . . . [is] freighted with fakery, contorted by compromise, mired in code," observed the *Village Voice* about Bill Clinton, not without a measure of admiration, in 1992. "The trick is to choose the lies that are true."[31] When pollsters asked voters in early 1993 what they thought the president-elect would do once he took office, only seven percent said he would try to keep all his campaign promises, while only thirty-six percent thought he would try to keep most. Yet seven out of ten were optimistic as to what the next four years would bring.[32] Clinton lied more often than not on the campaign trial, the voters believed. Yet they were willing to forgive and forget because they figured that was what a candidate had to do to play the game.

Not that parliamentary leaders do not also try to reconcile irreconcilable differences. Yet nowhere are voters, politicians, and journalists quite so self-deluded as they are in the United States. Nowhere, moreover, is policy making more anarchic or the structure of government, particularly the executive branch, more baroque. With its separate staffs for the president, the vice president, the first lady, and lately even the vice president's spouse, the White House plays host to nearly as much palace intrigue as the Romanovs, with an overall level of efficiency not much better than medieval. As a bemused British journalist observed in the 1960s:

> The president can be lonely as a king. For this and other reasons he must have intimates on which he can depend. These are the White House staffers—the King's Men. Only in Washington, and perhaps in such equally exotic places as Amman and Pnom Penh, do men of this ilk still wield so much power. The imperious Adenauer got by with a state secretary and some office help. De Gaulle needs only de Gaulle. In

Britain, . . . [t]he Prime Minister requires and gets only four private secretaries, career civil servants all. . . .[33]

By contrast, Richard Nixon regularly traveled with an entourage of two hundred: staff members and their spouses, valets and dog handlers, half a dozen navy mess stewards, several chauffeurs, eight switchboard operators, plus a hairdresser for his wife.[34]

Yet the paradoxical thing about such pomp and circumstance is that it actually serves to mask the *lack* of power at the heart of the presidency. As Harry Truman once groused: "They talk about the power of the president, they talk about how I can just push a button to get things done. Why, I spend most of my time kissing somebody's ass."[35] Since power in the U.S. system is mercurial, a president must take great care in coaxing it into his corner. He must cajole, persuade, but never bark an order, at least not in public. He must be a leader, yet at the same time a good ol' boy. He must wield power while somehow seeming not to, a trick that only the greatest Zen masters of American politics have come close to achieving.

To understand how this works, it is helpful to compare Ronald Reagan and Margaret Thatcher, who for much of the 1980s presided over the Western alliance as a kind of conservative diumvirate. Both were fierce anti-Communists and fervent free-marketeers, but otherwise they were as different as night and day. Thatcher was not only personally unpopular throughout her dozen years in office, but disdainful of the very idea of popularity. Her style was austere and aloof, which is why left-leaning papers like the *Guardian* took to calling her "Nanny" with such relish. Rhetorically, she was about as ambiguous as a traffic sign. British journalists who are alert to such things said her accent was that of a pretentious petty-bourgeois striver. Yet to American ears, every syllable was crisp and clear, every vowel well-rounded, every word precise and unmistakable. Whether or not people liked it, she insisted, changes had to be made. "There is no alternative"—TINA, as the press soon dubbed it—became her favorite phrase. "Remember, George, this is no time to go wobbly," she remonstrated with President Bush during the Persian Gulf crisis. Her power base in Parliament was secure, and she saw no reason not to use it to the utmost.

Ronald Reagan's approach was the opposite. Liberals loathed him as a B-movie actor who was still living in a Hollywood dream world, yet, characteristically, they missed the point. A stint as a B-actor, as it turns out, is a perfect apprenticeship for the role of an American president. The reason has to do with the nature of a good B-actor, which, in the glory days of the Hollywood studios, was an ability to more or less play the same part from movie to movie. The B-actor *becomes* the character he is playing and the character becomes him, a Pirandellian process in which the line between illusion and reality is blurred. As a result, Ronald Reagan was never more sincere than when he was reading a script, never more himself than when he was putting on a show. Where Thatcher took a palpable delight in administering bitter medicine, Reagan preferred to wrap his message in a gauzy, soft-focus image of America as "a shining city upon a hill" that once was and could be again. The fact that this image was false to the core was irrelevant. Voters, or at least a portion of them, recognized it as such but liked it all the same. The important thing was not whether it was real, but whether the president thought it was real and wanted them to as well. As *Time* magazine gushed at the height of his popularity in 1986, Reagan "is a Prospero of American memories, a magician who carries a bright, ideal America like a holograph in his mind and projects its image in the air. . . . Reagan, master illusionist, is himself a kind of American dream."[36]

Of course, the trouble with illusions is that the bubbles always burst, which is why the American presidency is inherently unstable. Almost invariably the same pattern asserts itself: the postinaugural honeymoon as the first family settles into the White House with pets and kids; the blues that set in soon after as Congress begins gnawing away at the administration's proposals; the writhing under the knife as the pundits try to figure out what went wrong; and, finally, the desperate attempts to get the old magic going again in time for the next election. Failure is the norm, success the exception, and bursts of activity are followed by long periods of crippling gridlock. After the lassitude of the Eisenhower years, John F. Kennedy was elected on a promise to get the country moving again, yet spent most of his three years in the White House stalemated by Congress. "The Constitution . . . give[s] all advantage of delay," he complained in 1962. "It is very easy to defeat a bill in Congress. It is much more difficult to pass one."[37] Lyndon Johnson proved brilliant at managing affairs on Capitol Hill (until he was brought down by Vietnam), while Richard Nixon's position during his first term as a minority president elected with just forty-three percent of the vote and facing a hostile Congress was all but impossible. Nixon tried to mask his helplessness by lashing out at others—invading Cambodia, bombing the North Vietnamese, siccing his attack dog Spiro Agnew on the liberal intelligentsia, and, in 1969, declaring a war on drugs. Instead of reasoned argument, he was an example of how the structure of the presidency encourages self-righteousness, bombast, and violent behavior.

The Supreme Court: Robert Bork and the Constitution's revenge

The story of the Supreme Court since Watergate has been one of breakdown as well, in this case of a school of liberal constitutional thought that rode into power with FDR's judicial revolution in 1937 and reached its apogee during the reign of Earl Warren and William O. Douglas in the fifties, sixties, and early seventies. According to liberal iconography, the breakdown was wholly the fault of a right wing determined to return the country back to the days of segregated drinking fountains and back-alley abortions. This is true to a point, but it overlooks the fact that the liberal edifice was already beginning to crumble on its own. The Court had taken on so much responsibility that it was buckling under the strain. It was simply not up to the tasks it had been assigned.

The problem can be said to have started with *Brown v. Board of Education* in 1954. The official view, of course, is that the Court listened to the arguments, retired to its chambers, and then decided in its heart of hearts that *Plessy v. Ferguson*, the separate-but-equal ruling of 1896, had been wrong and that integration was the way to go. This is the traditional view of the Court wrestling with its conscience *in camera*, cut off from the rest of the society. But the truth is more prosaic. By the 1950s, the sort of raw bigotry that was still widespread in the South was an international scandal. Soviet propagandists were having a field day with it, and the new crop of leaders in newly de-colonized Asia and Africa were disgusted and appalled. "Some of these attacks against us are based on falsehood or distortion," noted Dean Acheson, Truman's secretary of state, "but the undeniable existence of racial discrimination gives unfriendly governments the most effec-tive kind of ammunition for their propaganda warfare."[38]

Something had to be done, yet, as in previous instances, the sys-tem's political organs were blocked. The executive and legislative branches lacked both the legal authority and political will to act on their own, while a constitutional amendment, the normal remedy for a ruling like *Plessy*, was out of the question. Congress could never have mustered the two-thirds majority to get one through, and backers could never have garnered the support of three-fourths of the states. The Supreme Court was the only way out.

The result was the greatest constitutional change since Recon-struction, yet one that did not alter a single word in the document itself. *Brown* did not trigger a social revolution—that was the job of civil rights protesters who took to the streets to hurry integration along beginning in the late fifties. But it signaled that the political structure was beginning to shift. If the United States was to combat the Soviet menace, take charge of the Free World, win the space race, and all the rest, the Supreme Court alone would have to shoulder responsibility for seeing that the state was modernized. In the wake of *Brown*, other groundbreaking decisions followed: *Baker v. Carr* (1962), which required the states to reapportion legislative districts in accordance with the principle of one person–one vote; *Griswold v. Connecticut* (the same year), which struck down state laws against birth control; and finally *Roe v. Wade* (1973), which established a constitutional right to an abortion during the first trimester of pregnancy. Given the paralysis in the White House and Congress, Justice William Brennan wrote in 1962 that the judicial branch was now "the sole practicable avenue open to a minority to petition for redress of grievance."[39] William O. Douglas expanded the Court's role again the same year when he declared in *Griswold* that even though the Constitution did not explicitly grant a blanket right of privacy, such a right could be found in various "penumbras" and "emanations" arising out of the Bill of Rights. In its ability to make up new law as it went along, the Supreme Court was now the sovereign lawmaking body.

Of course, Douglas did not claim to be making *new* law, but merely to be discovering *old* law that had long been implicit in the Bill of Rights. This is what English kings claimed to be doing in interpreting the Ancient Constitution in the Middle Ages, even when clearly departing from past practice. Yet the Court found itself caught up in a crippling contradiction. If the Constitution was a "living" document, as liberal jurists and law professors liked to say it was, then obviously Supreme Court justices enjoyed considerable leeway in interpreting it to suit the needs of modern society. But if their latitude was all but unlimited, as Douglas's astonishing language seemed to suggest, then what was the point of having a constitution at all? With its detailed elucidation of federal powers and responsibilities, the Constitution was a document that demanded to be taken literally rather than figuratively. Although Hamilton had argued that it amounted to a grant of unlimited authority, everything about it, as the Jeffersonians had pointed out, suggested the opposite. And if Congress and the presidency were subject to constitutional limits and constraints, why not the Supreme Court as well?

The liberal judiciary was wide open to attack. The fact that the Court had agreed to tackle problems like abortion or desegregation that the elected branches were eager to avoid made it all the more vulnerable. It was all by itself in the social vanguard and thus became a magnet for the slings and arrows of the conservatives. No matter how well-intentioned, moreover, all too many social reforms initiated by the judiciary were proving less than successful out in the field. After *Brown*, public school integration actually declined, while the federal judicial takeover of the Boston public schools in 1974 proved particularly disastrous. Within ten years, white enrollment had plummeted better than seventy percent, leaving the city school system more segregated than when the integration plan had started.[40] Black children were more isolated, and racial relations as a whole had never been more poisonous.

The problem of de facto segregation in cities like Boston was not beyond hope. Government could have solved it if it had brought all its forces to bear—legislative, executive, and judicial as well as federal, state, and municipal. In order to reign in white flight and breathe new life into urban economies, transportation policies could have been reversed so that jobs and business flowed into the cities rather than out to the suburbs. Municipal governance could have been reformed to prevent the suburbs from stealing away the best jobs and most affluent citizens from the urban core. Yet this would have involved coordinated policy making that was quite beyond the power of the federal judiciary acting on its own. With judges pulling in one direction and elected officials at all levels pulling in another, failure was inevitable.

Robert Bork, the ultraconservative Supreme Court nominee in 1987, in a sense was the Constitution's revenge. In the face of an ever more inventive process of judicial interpretation, he called for a return to the purity of the original text. Where liberals argued that the Constitution was an ongoing collaborative process involving not just the Founders but successive generations of voters, legislators, and judges who had either amended or interpreted it, Bork argued that the Founders still reigned supreme. It was their Constitution, he said in essence; our job was to live up to their legacy, not twist it absurdly out of shape for reasons of political expediency.

Bork had about him a bit of the religious revolutionary who seeks to strip away centuries of church teachings and return to the purity of the Bible. As Protestant theologians had argued in the sixteenth and seventeenth centuries, the Bible was not something that had to be "explained" by church fathers; rather, any literate plowman could open it up and read it for himself. Similarly, Bork argued in his best-seller, *The Tempting of America*, that the Constitution was accessible to any modern-day American with a command of written English. Where scholars of a liberal or radical bent had tried to open up constitutional studies by bringing in "utilitarianism, contractarianism, Mill, Derrida, Habermas, positivism, formalism, Rawls, Nozick, and the literature of radical feminism," as Bork described it, his instinct, not unlike Edmund Burke's or Daniel Boorstin's, was to bar them all at the door.[41] The text, the whole text, and nothing but the text was all that was needed. "The American design of a constitutional Republic," he wrote, "is . . . a 'complete and self-supporting scheme,' as Hilaire Belloc said of Catholicism"—that is, closed to outside influences.[42] Everything a modern interpreter needed to know could be read within the five thousand words that comprised its length and breadth.

This was almost breathtakingly authoritarian. Yet rather than the authority of a jack-booted dictator, the authority Bork was seeking to reestablish was that of a group of Country gentlemen who had lived some two centuries earlier. "The orthodoxy of our civil religion . . . holds that we govern ourselves democratically," he added, "except on those occasions, few in number though crucially important, when the Constitution places a topic beyond the reach of majorities."[43] Yet why should *any* topic be placed beyond the reach of the democratic majority, particularly when it concerned something as basic as the political structure of the state? Bork's answer was solipsistic: the people should not ask why but should obey because, well, because they were the people and the Founders were the Founders. Bork confessed that he always found it "discouraging" when law students or even law professors would ask, "But why should we be ruled by men who are long dead?"[44] Yet what Bork clearly found discouraging about the question was not that it was unreasonable but that it was all *too* reasonable, namely, that it was based on rationality rather than a quasi-religious faith in the Founders' infinite wisdom. With his somewhat medieval cast of mind, Bork—a Catholic who is as conservative in his theology as in his politics—regarded any tendency to question matters of faith as a sort of *trahison des clercs*. Like Boorstin or Burke, he regards the free-ranging intellect as dangerous and corrosive, failing to realize, of course, that such questioning is at the heart of the modern condition.

Nonetheless, Bork would not have gotten as far as he had if he did not have a few points in his favor. The American constitutional tradition *is* authoritarian, which is to say it is based on deference to an original vision crafted in Philadelphia in 1787. Therefore, Bork's approach was not inconsistent with the document he was defending. His argument that judges should not take it upon themselves to clarify what the Constitution means but should leave it to the voters and their representatives to do so through the amending process was actually a good deal more modern than the liberal view that the judges should have wide leeway in interpreting the sacred text. A Social Democrat like Sweden's Olaf Palme would not have disagreed with Bork, which is why Palme's government, rather than making do with a much patched-over constitution dating from 1809, thought it important to clarify matters by drafting a new constitution in 1975. Yet, as Palme undoubtedly would also have pointed out, there is no way the people can exercise their judgment as long as a fiendishly difficult amending clause makes them a prisoner of the very constitution they supposedly control. Bork's complaints about a self-aggrandizing legal priesthood composed of judges, lawyers, and law school professors were not off the mark either. But as Herbert Croly had pointed out in *The Promise of American Life*, the best way to curb the priesthood was to render the Constitution more flexible and open to democratic change, which would mean overthrowing the tyranny of the Founders, not reinforcing it.

Bork lost the battle for confirmation, but he did not lose the larger ideological war. The next two nominees, David Souter and Clarence Thomas, were more or less in the Bork mold, while Bill Clinton's next two appointments to the high court proved surprisingly conservative as well. Ruth Ginzburg was Thomas's colleague on the D.C. Court of Appeals and, as Thomas himself has pointed out, was one of the first to congratulate him when he was named to the top bench. Stephen Breyer, an appellate judge from Boston, was eminently bland and middle-of-the-road, so much so that Senator Howard Metzenbaum, the liberal Democrat from Ohio, was moved to complain that Clinton had nominated Breyer solely to appease Orrin Hatch, the hard right's point man on the Senate Judiciary Committee—a charge Clinton made no effort to deny. "You know, this country got started by people who wanted a good letting alone from government," the president offered by way of explanation. "I think he [Breyer] understands that."[45] As one law professor said of the nominee: "He'll come up with solutions that the liberals will like and conservatives will accept and respect."[46] Translation: Robert Bork would not be unduly put out by the results. What's historically significant about the Breyer and Ginzburg appointments, commented another law professor, an unrepentant liberal,

> is not so much what they accomplish but what they mark: the collapse of the liberal position on constitutional law. The idea behind the Warren Court, that the court could be in the vanguard, has died. It's just dead and it's hardly possible to imagine Clinton nominating someone who believes in it.[47]

The theory of the "living" Constitution had simply keeled over from exhaustion.

9

THE CIVIL LIBERTIES CHARADE

AMERICANS, in some respects, are even prouder of the Bill of Rights than they are of the original Constitution. Rather than an afterthought, the Bill of Rights is now seen as the heart and soul of a constitutional system in which civil liberties are seen as representing the highest ideal. But there are at least two problems with this reverential view. One is that for the first century and a half of its existence, the Bill of Rights was not what we think of it today, a legal guarantee of individual liberties, but solely a restraint on a minuscule federal government whose role paled next to that of the states. Thus, while the First Amendment declares that "Congress shall make no law respecting an establishment of religion . . . or abridging the freedom of speech," there was nothing to stop the states from doing so, which is why established churches were a fact up and down the Atlantic seaboard until the 1820s or why abolitionist propaganda could be banned throughout the South beginning in the 1830s. Indeed, in *Barron v. Baltimore* (1833), the Supreme Court specifically declared that the Bill of Rights was intended to provide "security against the apprehended encroachments of the general [i.e., federal] government—not against those of the local governments." Only in 1868, with the passage of the Fourteenth Amendment declaring that "no State shall . . . abridge the privileges or immunities" of any citizen, did the federal government acquire the legal leverage to subject the states to the Bill of Rights. And even then, thanks to the setbacks of the post-Reconstruction era, the process did not even begin to get under way until the 1920s.

Thus, for most of the history of the Republic, state and local government could, and did, abridge with impunity those rights we now regard as sacrosanct. But the second problem with this reverential view of the Bill of Rights is that even after the judicial revolution of the 1960s, the state of civil liberties in the United States is abysmal—not just abysmal in relation to some ideal existing in the collective mind of the ACLU, but in relation to the real-life practices of societies of comparable economic and political development. In comparison with Western Europe, Canada, and Japan, the police in America are more violent; the criminal justice system is more grossly overloaded and hence less fair to the mass of poor defendants who come before it; and American politicians are unique in their regard for mass imprisonment as a solution to a growing array of social problems. Just as there was nothing in the advanced industrial world in the 1920s that quite compared with the lunacy of Prohibition, there is nothing in today's world, outside of a few benighted countries like Iran, that quite compares to the brutality of the U.S. war on drugs. Whereas the death penalty had either been abolished or was in retreat throughout the advanced industrial world by the mid-1990s, prisoners in the United States were being executed at a rate of about one every eleven days.[1] Where all but seven countries in the world, all of them Third World

Moslem nations, drew the line at executing murderers for crimes committed under the age of eighteen, the United States executed nine between 1984 and 1995.[2] In no other economically advanced society do the police go about with automatic weapons, bullet-proof vests, helicopters, and even armored vehicles. And in no other comparable society would officers successfully defend themselves against charges of police brutality on the grounds that official department policy required them to repeatedly club a speeder as he lay face down on the pavement, as four accused officers did in the Rodney King case.

Finally, since social policy is never entirely separate from civil liberties, in no other society would the authorities criminalize the possession of hypodermics as part of an ever wider crusade against drugs despite abundant evidence that dirty needles, an inevitable feature of the drug scene when clean needles are prohibited, are responsible for thousands of new AIDS cases per year. No society of comparable socioeconomic development, to put this as simply as possible, would so cavalierly deprive so many of its citizens of the greatest civil right of all, the right to life itself.

This is another puzzle for late-twentieth-century Americans—to figure out how their society can extol civil liberties on one hand and violate them so egregiously on the other, to try to understand how their politicians can worship the Bill of Rights while instituting policies that would cause more advanced societies to blush in embarrassment. The answer, once again, has to do with the problem of constitutional faith. Piety and thoughtlessness turn out to be two sides of the same coin, like religion and hypocrisy. Societies that worship at constitutional shrines spend less time *thinking* about politics and the consequences of their actions, while those that take a less exalted view of civil liberties, which treat them more or less like any other social amenity, such as clean water or high-quality public education, often try harder to make them *work*. In the end, perhaps, the issue is a little like sex. Societies that claim to put women on a pedestal and subject them to an elaborate code of politesse invariably treat them less well in practice than more egalitarian societies that treat them as one of the boys. Just as the last thing women need is to be shut away in a greenhouse like some delicate flower, the last thing civil liberties need is to be enshrined in some holy temple. They are better served instead by being brought down to earth, debated politically, and adapted to the needs of modern society.

Deep into *Law's Empire*, his much heralded 1986 foray into legal philosophy, New York University law professor Ronald Dworkin made a curious concession. America, he said, "is a more just society than it would have been had its constitutional rights been left to majoritarian institutions." This is something law professors have been telling their students for generations. But then, in a footnote, Dworkin added a qualification:

> I offer no argument for this flat claim; a further book would be necessary to do so. It would have to take into account, among other things, that the Supreme Court's record has been spotty, that the institutions I call "majoritarian" have not always—some would say never—represented either the opinions or the interests of the majority of citizens, and that the Court has sometimes exercised the power . . . to make these institutions more majoritarian than they would otherwise have been.[3]

Rather than taking the Bill of Rights as a given, as law professors are generally wont to do, Dworkin was suggesting that perhaps the system's claims were not absolutely beyond dispute and that further exploration might actually be warranted. It was a small but significant crack in the ideological edifice, rather as if the pope, or at least one of his better-known cardinals, had suggested that church teachings were not utterly beyond dispute as well.

This is a question worth exploring, and even if Dworkin was too busy to bother, others are not. Rather than an entire book, all it requires is a quick look around Great Britain, where Dworkin also happens to hold a seat as professor of jurisprudence at Oxford. The

United Kingdom, as it turns out, is a laboratory-pure example of the sort of "majoritarian" state he alludes to, one in which there is no Supreme Court to serve as a restraint on government, no formal Bill of Rights, and a Parliament that, if it wanted to, could wipe out civil liberties at a stroke. If unchecked power is the very definition of tyranny, as Madison said it was in the Federalist Papers,[4] then Parliament, still the classic example of unchecked, sovereign power, should be terrorizing minority neighborhoods and locking up everyone from backyard pot growers to young men sipping beer on sidewalk stoops.

Yet the curious thing is that it isn't—rather, the United States is. Ever since Margaret Thatcher's rise to power in the late seventies, British liberals have been bemoaning the damage done to civil liberties due to the ever growing concentration of power in the hands of the most right-wing government of the twentieth century. The complaints are quite valid, yet, from an American perspective, need to be taken with a grain of salt. Just as crime in the most economically depressed neighborhood in Glasgow or Liverpool does not compare to crime in Detroit or the South Bronx, civil liberties violations, even during the darkest days of Thatcherism, simply do not compare with what Americans have gotten used to on almost a daily basis. British civil libertarians were up in arms over the strong-arm tactics that Thatcher used to impede mass picketing in the 1984–85 coal miners' strike. But such methods were in a different league from the Pinochet-like mass firings and arrests that the Reagan administration used to crush the air traffic controllers' strike in 1981. Prosecutions of journalists for violations of Britain's Official Secrets Act are an international scandal, yet they hardly compare to the American treatment of dissidents of one stripe or another, from Mark Hampton, the Black Panther who died in a fusillade of police gunfire in Chicago in 1969, to the Branch Davidians, eighty-one of whom needlessly perished in a federal assault in 1993.

Over the *longue durée* of the twentieth century, moreover, the discrepancy is even more striking. Despite the absence of a Bill of Rights and judicial review, the British somehow found it within themselves *not* to throw thousands of radicals in jail immediately after World War I; *not* to make hundreds of thousands of arrests as part of an absurd crusade against alcohol; *not* to hound thousands of accused Communists out of jobs and into jail in the forties and fifties; and *not* to arrest millions more people as part of a neo-Prohibitionist war on drugs. The United States did all these things and more despite being blessed with the most glorious Constitution and Bill of Rights since the dawn of creation. Despite the existence of sizable black communities in Liverpool and London, the British also somehow found it within themselves not to lynch a dozen or more blacks a year through the early 1930s. In 1950, when a British court found Czech-born physicist Klaus Fuchs guilty of passing atomic secrets to the Soviets, it sentenced him to just fourteen years in prison on the not unreasonable grounds that Fuchs's employer, the Soviet Union, had been a wartime ally at the time the violation occurred. Three years later, when Julius and Ethel Rosenberg were found guilty in a federal court in New York of passing along much less important secrets during the same period, Judge Irving Kaufman launched into a hysterical tirade accusing them of responsibility for the Korean War and then sentenced both to death. Although the FBI had evidence that Julius was no more than a low-level espionage operative at most while Ethel was probably ignorant of the whole affair, it stood by and said nothing while both went to the electric chair.[5]

Where the United States spent much of the twentieth century careening between "hysteria, repression, and remorse," as Arthur Schlesinger Jr. once put it,[6] British officials somehow kept an even keel. Political debate in Britain is livelier than in the States, the range of political opinion is broader, yet violence does not seem to be forever bubbling up from below. Britain and America share a common history, yet something about their makeup, their constitution, causes them to function according to very different principles.

Any comparison of British and American civil liberties should probably begin with World War I, when state power in both societies expanded

217

dramatically, along with government's capacity to abuse. During the war itself, the two countries were not all that far apart. Both bombarded their citizens with propaganda, punished dissidents, and jailed conscientious objectors, although repression in the United States had a somewhat fiercer edge, if only because it was more decentralized, spontaneous, and uncontrolled. After the war, however, the two societies diverged. In Britain, the end of the war, not surprisingly, brought a return to normalcy, an opportunity to loosen up and allow passions to subside. In America, it brought the opposite, a buildup of passions so violent that by 1919, the country seemed ready to explode.

Needless to say, the cause was not Germany this time around, but the new Bolshevik regime in Russia. As a prosperous, heavily middle-class country far removed from the revolutionary battleground, America would seem to be the most immune to the threat (or promise) of Communism. Yet it was the most terrified. As British journalist A. C. Gardiner recalled:

> No one who was in the United States as I chanced to be, in the autumn of 1919, will forget the feverish condition of the public mind at that time. It was hag-ridden by the spectre of Bolshevism. It was like a sleeper in a nightmare, enveloped by a thousand phantoms of destruction. Property was in an agony of fear, and the horrid name "Radical" covered the most innocent departure from conventional thought with a suspicion of desperate purposes. "America," as one wit of the time said, "is the land of liberty—liberty to keep in step."[7]

Constitutional safeguards, such as they were, fell by the wayside amid the general frenzy. In February 1919, a jury in Hammond, Indiana, took just two minutes to acquit a man who had gunned down an alien for yelling, "To hell with the United States." In May, an audience in Washington, D.C., erupted in shouts and applause as an enraged sailor fired three shots into a man who had failed to rise for the "Star-Spangled Banner" during a victory loan program. Early in

1920, a clothing salesman in Waterbury, Connecticut, drew a six-month sentence for remarking to a customer that Lenin was one of the "brainiest" politicians in the world.[8] The red flag was banned in thirty-two states (this at a time when Socialist-voting farmers in Oklahoma were in the habit of riding to town on Saturday nights with red banners streaming from their pickups), some fourteen hundred people were arrested under various state antisedition and criminal syndicalism laws, and another ten thousand people were rounded up by federal agents during the Palmer Raids in January 1920. Many of the victims were indeed genuine radicals, while others were simply ordinary people swept up in the madness, such as several unfortunate individuals in Hartford, Connecticut, who had come to the local jailhouse to inquire after friends, only to find themselves under arrest as Bolshevik sympathizers as well.[9]

To repeat, this was all quite exceptional. British Communists were more numerous during this period and enjoyed far more influence in the working class, yet the governing class somehow avoided mass hysteria about reds under the bed. Where Congress repeatedly barred Victor Berger, a rather conservative member of the Socialist Party elected from Milwaukee, from taking his seat in 1919–20, leftists were amply represented in the British Parliament, and the Labour Party was just three years away from forming its own government. In France, leftists were four years away from doing the same, while a nominal socialist, Friedrich Ebert, was already at the head of the new German government. Indeed, the one West European country where postwar events followed anything like a similar trajectory was Italy, where the radical right went from strength to strength after the war until Mussolini was able to seize power in 1922.

Moreover, America was repressive not only when it came to big-ticket items like arresting radicals and crushing strikes, but when it came to the petty details of everyday life as well. As Raymond Fosdick, a longtime servant of the Rockefellers who was an authority on international police practices, put it in 1920: "The willingness with which we undertake to regulate by law the personal habits of private citizens is a source of perpetual astonishment to Europeans." American society, he wrote, was marked by a strange contradiction:

> With an intolerance for authority and an emphasis upon individual rights more pronounced, perhaps, than any other nation, we are, of all people, not even excepting the Germans, pre-eminently addicted to the habit of standardizing by law the lives and morals of our citizens.[10]

Fosdick cited an incident in Baltimore as an illustration. After repeated violations of the city's stringent blue laws, the police launched a crackdown one Sunday, arresting 113 people and handing out more than two hundred summonses:

> Two men were arrested for balancing their books in their own homes. Selling a child a stick of candy constituted a heinous offense. . . . One man was arrested for painting the gate in his backyard. Police did not hesitate to approach a man who happened to be smoking a cigar and question him as to how he came into its possession.[11]

Yet what was even more astonishing was the fact that the citizens did not revolt but merely grumbled and snickered as they went on their way. One reason, no doubt, was the sheer difficulty of rebelling in a society in which the lines of authority were so tangled and diffuse that it was often difficult to know just whom to rebel against. But another undoubtedly had to do with the absence of full-throated democratic debate. Lacking a central forum in which such issues could be thrashed out in full, Americans were reduced to fighting the great battle over Sunday blue laws in a piecemeal fashion in a thousand different locales, which is why the issue could drag on for decades without being fully resolved.

In Britain, where there was full-scale national debate, the attitude was much more laissez-faire. By southern European standards, the British were prim and uptight; by American standards, they were amazingly tolerant and loose. "The liberty of the people is still believed in," George Orwell noted in 1940 in his famous essay, "The Lion and the Unicorn"—not only political liberty, but the personal liberty to drink, gamble, and do all those other things that are forever drawing disapproving glances from middle-class reformers:

> One thing one notices if one looks directly at the common people, especially in the big towns, is that they are not puritanical. They are inveterate gamblers, drink as much beer as their wages will permit, are devoted to bawdy jokes, and use probably the foulest language in the world. They have to satisfy these tastes in the face of astonishing, hypocritical laws (licensing laws, lottery acts, etc etc) which are designed to interfere with everybody but in practice allow everything to happen.[12]

The licensing laws were an attempt to reduce drinking by limiting pub hours and other such measures. They were indeed hypocritical, which is to say they were ineffectual, contradictory, and halfhearted. But hypocritical half-measures were a far sight better than the draconian methods employed in the United States, where police smashed stills, raided speakeasies, and arrested some 750,000 people for alcohol-related offenses during twelve and a half years of Prohibition.[13] Orwell went on to note that "the common people are without definite religious belief, and have been so for centuries. The Anglican Church never had a real hold on them, it was simply a preserve of the landed gentry, and the Nonconformist sects only influenced minorities."[14] Americans, by contrast, were, and are, among the most pious people in the world, not only in terms of religion but in terms of civic institutions as well.

Prohibition is especially relevant to this discussion because it was instituted not just by an act of Congress, but by a constitutional amendment. As such, it illustrates all the pitfalls of the United States amending process. Congressmen voted for the Eighteenth Amendment never dreaming it would be approved by the states, yet opponents were caught short by the speed with which it raced through the individual legislatures. The result was an amendment approved by a supermajority, yet which nonetheless proved vastly unpopular when it was actually implemented. This is not to say parliamentary democracies are incapable of such blunders. They are. But the difference is that once they have gotten themselves in trouble, they can get themselves out just as easily through a simple majority vote. Under the Constitution, however, Prohibition could be repealed only by the same laborious method by which it had been adopted. With their usual timidity, the Republicans and Democrats conspired to keep the issue off the table as long as possible in Congress, while the forces of repeal were reduced to doing a slow crawl through the then-forty-eight states. Ultimately, the Crash in combination with Roosevelt's landslide victory in 1932 shook up the system so that repeal could be hurried along. Yet in the end it was clear that rather than protecting the people from rule by an "interested and overbearing majority," as Madison put it, the Constitution had prolonged such rule long after the majority had melted away into nothingness.

The consequences for civil liberties were, as usual, awful. In addition to the thousands of arrests, Congress and the states ratcheted up penalties so that sentences grew longer. Thus, by the late twenties, a Lansing, Michigan, man had been sentenced to life for possession of fourteen ounces of gin, while a forty-eight-year-old mother of four also drew a life sentence for various other infractions related to Prohibition.[15] Whatever their private misgivings, lawmakers felt they had no choice but to enforce Prohibition to the hilt as long as it was the law of the land. In Britain, where the people were too much "addicted" both to drink and the notion that what an individual did on his own time was his business alone, a comparable situation would have been all but inconceivable. The government could try to limit drinking, but to ban it outright was too extreme for anyone but the Americans.

By the early thirties, another civil liberties matter looming large in the American mind was the issue of race. At first glance, any comparison with Britain in this regard would seem invalid for the simple reason that Britain, racially speaking, is a much more homogeneous society (although in the past, other kinds of "racial" differences, such as those between Celts and Anglo-Saxons, have loomed just as large). Yet Britain has not been quite as lily-white over the centuries as Americans might suppose. From virtually the moment England entered the trans-Atlantic slave trade in the mid-sixteenth century, transplanted Africans began washing up on English shores in increasing numbers. By 1596, Queen Elizabeth was complaining to the lord mayor of London about "divers blackamoores" settling in the city,[16] while by the eighteenth century London's black population had swelled to an estimated fifteen thousand—some of them slaves brought over by their masters from the West Indies, others free and independent sailors who had entered on their own.[17] In terms of its racial makeup, London during this period was much closer to Philadelphia or Boston than it is to either city today.

What was different, however, was the atmosphere, which was far more liberal than anything black people had encountered, north or south of the Mason-Dixon line, in the soon-to-be United States. Although slavery was not declared illegal until 1772, large numbers of English slaves were already taking advantage of lax local laws by the 1750s to run away from their masters and take refuge in London's many back alleys. Within a few years, these same runaways had become so bold as to return to their masters to demand wages for work they had previously performed for free. In 1768, things reached the point where a judge was moved to complain that planters

> bring them [i.e., blacks] to England as cheap servants having no right to wages; they no sooner arrive here than they put themselves on a footing with other servants, become intoxicated with liberty, grow refractory, and either by persuasion of others or from their own inclinations, begin to expect wages according to their own opinion of their merits; and as there are already a great number of black men and women who

made themselves troublesome and dangerous to the families
who have brought them over as to get themselves discharged,
these enter into societies and make it their business to corrupt
and dissatisfy the mind of every black servant that comes to
England.[18]

Yet there was little that those in power could do, or felt they could
do, to keep such "refractory" elements in line. As no less an authority
than Blackstone observed in his *Commentaries*, "The spirit of liberty
is so deeply implanted in our constitution, and rooted in our very soil,
that a slave or a negro, the moment he lands in England, falls under
the protection of the laws, and so far becomes a freeman. . . ."[19] In
the 1850s, around the same time that the Supreme Court was declaring even free blacks to be ineligible for U.S. citizenship in *Dred Scott*,
an American sailor named Herman Melville landed in Liverpool and
was instantly struck by the difference in attitudes:

At first, I was surprised that a coloured man should be treated
as he is in this town; but a little reflection showed that, after
all, it was but recognizing his claims to humanity and normal
equality; so that, in some things we Americans leave to other
countries the carrying out of the principle that stands at the
head of our Declaration of Independence.[20]

Needless to say, race relations in America followed a somewhat
different course. Given the large number of slaves who had run away
to join the British forces during the Revolutionary War, the South
wound up more racially stratified after independence than before. In
New York, blacks, who had long been in the habit of voting for upper-
crust Federalists, were effectively disenfranchised when white populists
began pushing to the fore in the 1820s. In South Carolina, the state
legislature during this period embarked on a policy of interning black
British sailors while their ships were docked in Charleston harbor to
prevent them from spreading dangerous ideas to American slaves. Britain protested that the jailings were a violation of rights guaranteed by

treaty, yet local planters insisted that they be enforced.[21] The gap between the two societies thus opened wider. The Civil War promised some relief, but the failure of Reconstruction plunged America back into the dark ages. By the early 1890s, lynchings were running at better than two hundred a year,[22] and race riots, which in those days were almost invariably instigated by whites, reached a peak of frenzy in the strange and twisted year of 1919 when major outbreaks occurred in a half-dozen cities from Omaha to Washington, D.C.[23] In 1920, Raymond Fosdick reported a conversation with a chief of detectives in an unnamed Southern city, in which he was told: "We have three classes of homicides. If a nigger kills a white man, that's murder. If a white man kills a nigger, that's justifiable homicide. If a nigger kills another nigger, that's one less nigger."[24] This was a uniquely American kind of mass violence—grassroots, spontaneous, almost Jeffersonian.

The federal government made no effort to intervene. This was the case not only during the Republican reign of the 1920s, but during the New Deal as well. The early thirties, for instance, saw both a resurgence in lynch-mob terrorism and renewed pressure on Washington to intercede. In a particularly gruesome incident in October 1934, a mob dragged a black man accused of killing a white woman out of a jail cell in southern Alabama, transported him to Marianna, Florida, where the crime had allegedly occurred, and then proceeded to stab, kick, mutilate, shoot, and finally hang him in the courthouse square in a night-long orgy of sadism. As many as four thousand people witnessed the spectacle, while press and radio not only provided a blow-by-blow account, but actually advertised the lynching in advance. Yet the police refused to step in. The NAACP sent the Roosevelt administration an urgent appeal asking the Justice Department to prosecute the lynchers under the Lindbergh Law, which made kidnapping across state lines a federal offense, yet Attorney General Homer Cummings refused on the grounds that it would alienate Southern support in Congress.[25] A few months later, Walter White, the NAACP's national director, succeeded in obtaining an audience with FDR himself in which he implored the president to declare himself in favor of antilynching legislation that had just been introduced in Congress. Replied the president:

> I do not choose the tools with which I must work. Southerners, by reasons of seniority rules in Congress, are chairmen or occupy strategic places in most of the Senate and House committees. If I come out for the anti-lynching bill now, they will block every bill I ask Congress to pass to keep America from collapsing. I just can't take the risk.[26]

In effect, FDR was saying that blacks had to be thrown overboard so that the New Deal could proceed. Seniority rules, the committee system, the Southern stranglehold on Congress—all were intractable. In Britain, the constitution made it all but impossible to deny freedom to black people, while America's immutable Constitution made it all but impossible to grant it. In late 1937, a Gallup Poll found that public support for antilynching legislation had risen to seventy-two percent nationwide and fifty-seven percent in the South, yet Roosevelt still refused to speak out in favor. As a consequence, the measure died the following year in the face of a Southern filibuster.[27] Racism, obviously, was still widespread in America. But whatever their personal prejudices, the great majority of even white Americans wanted such barbaric practices to end. They wanted to modernize and move forward, yet the government they had allegedly created refused to let them.

Impediments to action like these were incomprehensible from a British point of view. Since Parliament was sovereign, it had the power to step in wherever abuses needed correcting. Allowing several thousand people to torture and kill a black man in full view of the police was unthinkable. Yet in America it was constitutionally unthinkable that Congress might actually invade local prerogatives and put such atrocities to a halt.

The question, though, is: why? Why did the United States consistently violate civil liberties it professed to uphold?

Any attempt at an answer brings us back to James Bradley Thayer, the Harvard law professor who argued in 1893 that overreliance on judicial review and the Bill of Rights had tended "to drive out questions of justice and right, and to fill the mind of legislators with thoughts of mere legality, of what the Constitution allows." Handing over primary responsibility for the protection of civil liberties to the courts meant removing primary responsibility from the legislature, which in turn meant allowing the legislative branch to behave as *ir*-responsibly as it wished—to rage against pointy-headed liberals, to rant about Communist infiltrators, to take to the Senate floor to accuse blacks of engaging in a "diabolical effort to despoil the womanhood of the Caucasian race," as Mississippi's Theodore Bilbo did during the antilynching debate in 1938,[28] all without any thought to the consequences in terms of democratic values. That was someone else's concern. The legislature's job was to dodge the issues, demagogue, and cater to the basest passions of its audience, confident in the belief that the Supreme Court would tap it on the shoulder and let it know when it had stepped out of line and was in danger of upsetting the delicate balance. Since the Supreme Court could never *penalize* Congress for its various transgressions, there was nothing to stop it from coming up with new and ingenious ways to violate civil liberties whenever the old ways were overturned, which it invariably did.

Civil liberties were depoliticized, while politics were de-liberalized. Both suffered as a consequence—civil liberties by never being shaped, updated, and refined by the political branches so as to meet the needs of modern society, and politics by being devitalized and debased. But the problem was also one of institutionalized fragmentation. Thanks to its essential design, Congress was incapable of dealing with social problems in a coherent, comprehensive manner. Rather, its responses were narrow, short-lived, episodic. It would become irritated, lash out, and then lose interest as some other issue hove into view. Then, when it discovered some time later that the original problem had not gone away but had actually gotten worse, it would strike out again, this time a little more angrily than before. Eventually, if the problem proved really intractable, it would work itself up into a fury, breaking down doors, sending out the police, locking people up for longer and longer periods.

The best example is the most recent, the war on drugs, an all-consuming crusade that by this point completely dwarfs the war on alcohol of the 1920s. Although it didn't shift into high gear until the reign of Richard Nixon, the drug war had its first stirrings nearly a century earlier in San Francisco, where a crackdown on Chinese opium dens began in the 1870s. Thereafter, the crusade picked up momentum with every passing decade. In the 1880s, Congress took the first steps to reduce the availability of smoking opium nationwide. In 1914, it passed the Harrison Narcotics Act, the first step toward the criminalization of all coca and opium derivatives. In 1937, Harry J. Anslinger, the longtime chief of the Federal Bureau of Narcotics, succeeded in having marijuana added to the list of proscribed substances, while, in the 1960s, New York governor Nelson Rockefeller persuaded the state legislature to up drug penalties to a maximum of life in prison for possession of more than two ounces of any illegal substance, including marijuana.[29] In 1969, Richard Nixon followed suit by proclaiming a national antidrug crusade in a nationwide television address.

The result by the 1990s was a collective obsession involving some 1.25 million drug arrests per year,[30] total government expenditures of about $30 billion annually,[31] and an overall incarceration rate, driven in great measure by the antidrug frenzy, that by 1993 was forty percent higher than that of South Africa, four and half times greater than that of the Canadians, six times greater than that of France or Germany, and ten times greater than that of the Dutch. Only Russia was higher—by about seven percent.[32] Yet what was most remarkable about the antidrug crusade was not that it had grown so large, but that it had done so with virtually no debate as to strategy or goals. The most basic policy questions were at stake—whether, for instance, drugs were evil per se or merely dangerous to the degree they affected health, productivity, or crime; whether society should try to ban all drugs or concentrate its efforts on the more potent substances; and so on. In his famous treatise *On Liberty*, John Stuart Mill had written in 1859 that while no one had a right to harm others, "over himself, over his own body and mind, the individual is sovereign."[33] While many Americans were willing to admit by the 1960s that might be the case with sex, was it also the case with drugs?

These were all vitally important questions that Congress should have discussed yet scrupulously avoided. As early as the 1880s, for example, evidence was accumulating that the crackdown on drugs had led to a surge in smuggling and criminal racketeering, in this case on the part of Chinese criminal societies known as tongs.[34] Following passage of the Harrison Narcotics Act, a Congressional investigating committee found that the drug market had gone deep underground, where, rather than contracting, it had put down roots and was beginning to spread.[35] The drug war was also a major factor in encouraging users to switch from smokable opium to injectable morphine, which was not only more concentrated and potent but, because it was more compact, was easier to smuggle as well. Heroin, another opium by-product, displaced morphine in the early twenties chiefly because it was two to three times as potent per weight and therefore even more portable.[36] These were findings that should have given officials pause. Yet, in each instance, the official response was to redouble the antidrug effort and widen the field.

"To find out whether a people is free it is necessary only to ask if there is an opposition and, if there is, to ask what it is." Thus wrote W. Ivor Jennings, an authority on the British constitution in the early sixties.[37] By this token, given the almost complete absence of debate and opposition, Americans were enslaved to a growing drug habit. They were hooked on the thrill of busting down doors and arresting addicts, of locking them away for years at a time, of entertaining deep, dark fantasies about Fu Manchu–like drug kingpins using sex, drugs, and jazz in various combinations to subdue society. In the 1920s, an ex-congressman from Alabama named Richard Pearson Hobson made a fortune on the lecture circuit scaring the daylights out of middle-class citizens with tales of vampirelike heroin pushers scheming to take over America and forcing innocent white girls into prostitution.[38] Harry Anslinger's "Reefer Madness" campaign a decade later was an immense hit (even though the movie of that title would later reduce college audiences to paroxysms of laughter), while a *New York Times* editorial charged quite seriously during the Korean War that Chinese Communists were flooding the country with heroin in order to sap its fighting morale.[39] No story was too outrageous, too farfetched, to be believed. In 1962, the same year that he was postulating the existence of a constitutional right of privacy in *Griswold v. Connecticut*, Supreme Court justice William O. Douglas let loose in another opinion with a tirade on drugs that was a classic example of what Richard Hofstadter would soon call the paranoid style in American politics. Declared Douglas:

> To be a confirmed drug addict is to be one of the walking dead. . . . The teeth are rotted out, the appetite is lost, and stomach and intestines don't function properly. The gall bladder becomes inflamed; eyes and skin turn a bilious yellow; in some cases membranes of the nose turn a flaming red; the partition separating the nostrils is eaten away—breathing is difficult. Oxygen in the blood decreases; bronchitis and tuberculosis develop. Good traits of character disappear and bad ones emerge. Sex organs become affected. Veins collapse. . . .[40]

Barely a word of it was true. Opiates did not rot the teeth, block the intestines, or do any of the other things Douglas described. Notwithstanding their addictive properties, they were actually rather benign in their physiological effects, as nineteenth-century physicians, who prescribed them for a wide range of maladies, well knew.[41] Rather, if addicts were poor, lonely, and in ill health, it was likely as not due to the consequences of being fired from their jobs, thrown into the streets by their families, or herded off to jail by the police, all the result of drug criminalization rather than drug use.

As John Erlichman, Nixon's domestic policy chief, explained:

"Narcotics repression is a sexy political issue. Parents are worried about their kids using heroin, and parents are voters. This is why the Nixon White House became involved."[42] But it was in the 1980s that the fallout from the drug war became most damaging. Where earlier antimarijuana efforts had encouraged the growth of a new breed of smuggler who was more professional, more businesslike, and better capitalized, a major crackdown on pot smuggling launched in South Florida in 1982 produced something even worse: a wholesale shift by these same *narcotraficantes* out of pot and into a substance that had the advantage of being more compact, portable, potent, and pricey—cocaine. This was the same effect that had been noticed decades earlier when the drug market shifted first to morphine and then to heroin, but this time the changeover was even more dramatic. In short order, the marijuana supply contracted, while the coke supply exploded. Cocaine prices, an index of growing abundance, plummeted from upwards of $60,000 a kilogram in Miami to as little as $9,000 in 1987.[43] Formerly a high-priced drug for the Hollywood and rock-music elite, cocaine reemerged in the mid-eighties in a new, smokable form known as crack as the low-priced high of the ghetto poor.

Crack was indeed a destructive substance, as anyone who has witnessed its effects firsthand can attest. Yet the epidemic was to a great extent manufactured in Washington. Rather than pausing to consider where the drug war was heading, Congress responded as it usually did in such situations by closing its eyes, stopping up its ears, and bellowing for more. The death of basketball star Len Bias in 1986 was an occasion for renewed frenzy on Capitol Hill. "It's mob mentality in there," gasped one congressman as the House voted overwhelmingly to approve a multibillion-dollar drug bill.[44] When reporters dared to question how a bag of crack displayed by George Bush on nationwide TV in September 1989 had come to be purchased across the street from the White House—federal narcotics agents, it turned out, had lured the dealer to the location in order to drum up publicity for the president's speech—Bush turned petulant. "I don't understand," he snapped. "I mean, has somebody got some advocates here for this drug guy?"[45] When TV newsman Sander Vanocur asked the three major candidates during the 1992 presidential debates whether the time hadn't come to consider some less punitive approach, he met with a solid wall of obduracy. Bush was adamant ("we've got to keep fighting this war against drugs"), H. Ross Perot was belligerent ("we've got chemical warfare being conducted against our children on the streets in this country all day, every day, and we don't have the will to stamp it out"), while Bill Clinton was characteristically touchy-feely:

> Like Mr. Perot, I have held crack babies in my arms, but I know more about this, I think, than anybody else up here because I have a brother who is a recovering drug addict. I'm very proud of him, but I can tell you this: if drugs were legal, I don't think he'd be alive today. I am adamantly opposed to legalizing drugs. He is alive today because of the criminal justice system.[46]

As an intelligent man, Clinton should have known the danger of extrapolating from a single case. Whatever his brother's experiences, they were no more conclusive than the experience of a single drunk during Prohibition. Yet it was impossible to run for office and discuss drug policy intelligently at the same time. The system would not allow it. When Surgeon General Joycelyn Elders suggested in 1993 that legalization at least merited official study, Clinton, a man otherwise known for studying any problem to death, scotched the idea immediately. When Elders suggested a year later that masturbation "perhaps should be taught" as part of a comprehensive sex-education program dealing with sex and AIDS, he fired her. While the comment was "rational" and "fully consistent with conservative demands that the schools teach 'abstinence' as the only sure-fire protection against AIDS," the *New York Times* concluded in an editorial that it was also inopportune—"a reckless act of indifference to Mr. Clinton's political fortunes."[47] Rationality, as always in the American system, was inconvenient and unwise.

The results for civil liberties implications have been far worse than even in the 1920s. Between 1980 and 1989, total drug arrests increased more than two and a half times to a level that, proportional to the U.S. population as a whole, was *ten times greater* than the average rate of alcohol-related arrests during Prohibition.[48] Where nonviolent drug offenders incarcerated in federal prisons served an average of four years each in 1980, by 1988 the figure was closer to six. Where the proportion of first-time drug offenders who wound up behind bars stood at just twenty-seven percent in 1980, by 1987 it stood at forty-three percent.[49] By the early nineties, tens of millions of Americans had had to submit to workplace drug tests regardless of whether there was any evidence that they were using drugs or that drug use might in any way impair their work. Although some employers resisted instituting such tests, the 1988 Anti-Drug Abuse Act, which prohibited the award of a federal contract to any company that did not take certain specified steps to achieve a drug-free workplace, was a powerful incentive to get in line.[50] The courts permitted police helicopters to swoop down over private property to look for marijuana plants and allowed cops to perform "consensual" searches of luggage on crowded interstate buses in which passengers have little real choice but to agree.[51] By 1993, state and federal forfeiture laws had allowed police and federal agents to seize some thirty-three thousand yachts, homes, cars, and bank accounts in cases in which "probable cause" had been found linking them with drug deals. Although the Supreme Court ruled in December 1993 that such wholesale property seizures were unconstitutional, it was too late to benefit Donald Scott, a businessman in Malibu, California, whose two-hundred-acre ranch had been the target the year before of a raid conducted by the Los Angeles Sheriff's Department and a half-dozen other agencies. Acting on a tip that marijuana was growing on Scott's property, thirty-two police and other government officials swooped down on the house and burst through the door. When Scott came downstairs with a drawn gun, the officers ordered him to put down the weapon, which he did. But a shot rang out anyway, killing him on the spot. A report by the Ventura County District Attorney subsequently charged that in commencing the investigation and organizing the raid, the L.A. Sheriff's Department had been "motivated, at least in part, by a desire to seize and forfeit the ranch for the government"—a seizure that might have netted the department more than $4 million. No drugs were found, meanwhile, not even a seed.[52]

Invading a citizen's home and shooting him to death is serious deprivation of civil liberties indeed, which is why West Europeans have been anxious to avoid a repeat of the American experience. When Conservative prime minister John Major proposed raising the maximum penalty for possession of marijuana and other soft drugs from five hundred to twenty-five hundred pounds (about $4,000), a pittance by American standards, he was criticized by, of all people, prosecutors and the police on the grounds that it would lead to more people being imprisoned without cutting into drug use.[53] Small-scale possession of pot has been decriminalized in Germany and Spain, drug use of all sorts has been effectively decriminalized in Italy and the Netherlands, while the Swiss have begun experiments in the creation of a semilegal "grey" market for heroin.[54]

In the end, the country the United States most resembles when it comes to drug policy is Iran, a nation with some of the harshest drug laws in the world and, not coincidentally, one of the highest rates of drug addiction as well. The shah banned opium smoking in 1955, the Ayatollah Khomeini banned all other stimulants in 1979, and in 1989, the Islamic government announced a policy of executing anyone found with thirty grams or more of heroin, a little over an ounce, or five kilograms or more of opium. By June 1990, more than eleven hundred drug offenders had been executed, according to Amnesty International, mostly by public hanging. Yet all this repression merely drove prices, and hence smuggling, to sky-high levels, so that by the early nineties, drug trafficking was the country's biggest economic activity after oil production. Rather than admit responsibility, officials resorted to predictably zany theories to explain the surge. As a top Iranian antidrug official put it in the early nineties, it was all the fault of the CIA, Zionism, and that old chestnut, the international Masonic conspiracy. As crazy as this sounds, it was not all that different in spirit from the explanation advanced by the Republican Party in 1984, which declared in its national platform that the drug epidemic in the United States was the work of various "Communist dictators" seeking "to undermine our free society."[55] Theocratic societies—Iran follows Islam, while the United States follows the civic religion of the Founding Fathers and the Constitution—tend to have notably weak grips on reality.

Just as civil liberties are inseparable from social policy, they are also bound up with the issue of public health. Perhaps the most nightmarish aspect of America's drug habit has been the system's response to the question of needles and AIDS. Sharing needles, which is what heroin users do when hypodermics are illegal and therefore in short supply, is a devastatingly effective means of transmitting the human immunodeficiency virus. Addicts poke themselves with a syringe, draw back to make sure they've found a vein, and press down on the plunger. Then they pass it on to someone else who does the same. The infection leaps from user to user like a spark of electricity. Given the speed with which HIV can spread under such circumstances, the rational thing, it would seem, would be to recalibrate public policy so as to encourage addicts to engage in less dangerous behavior. If society can't stop them from shooting up, then at least it can encourage them to shoot up more safely. After all, addicts not only hurt themselves when they contract HIV. They also pose a threat to their sexual partners and whatever children they may conceive. Given the virus's long incubation period, the threat may exist for years before the infected individual develops symptoms of AIDS. He may have kicked drugs, cleaned himself up, gotten married, and gotten himself a job—and still be a walking Typhoid Mary.

This is the sort of horror that any halfway sensible politician would go to great lengths to avoid. Yet ever since the dimensions of the needle-borne AIDS epidemic became apparent in the mid-eighties, American policy has been to bury its head in the sand. In Los Angeles, the city board of supervisors in 1985 pronounced itself shocked when it learned that local health workers had begun distributing a pamphlet instructing junkies on how to avoid contracting the AIDS virus and ordered it withdrawn.[56] In New York, where half of the city's estimated 250,000 intravenous drug users were believed to be infected by 1985, the city health commissioner, Dr. David J. Sencer, proposed changing state law to allow needles to be sold over the counter, only to be overruled by the city's five district attorneys, including Brooklyn DA Elizabeth Holtzman—the same Elizabeth Holtzman who, as a member of the House Judiciary Committee, had lectured Richard Nixon on the subject of constitutional morality some eleven years earlier. As a consequence, Mayor Ed Koch pronounced Sencer's clean-needles proposal an idea "whose time has not come and, based upon the response, will never come."[57] In 1989, Drug Czar William Bennett denounced clean-needle proposals as "pernicious," and a White House spokesman declared that President Bush was "opposed to the exchange of needles under any condition"[58]—regardless, in other words, of what the empirical evidence might be. A year later, then–New York mayor David Dinkins canceled an $861,000 program to educate junkies on the danger of AIDS,[59] and in early 1994 Lee Brown, Dinkins's former police chief and now drug czar under Bill Clinton, came out against clean needles as well. "The culmination of all the research that I've seen at this point," Brown said in an interview, "tells me that the position we will take until additional research changes our mind is not to take a stance supporting needle exchange."[60] It was an example of a bureaucrat using tortuous prose to justify mindless devotion to the status quo.

The result was like banning condoms in order to discourage gay sex. More than 146,000 new AIDS cases were reported in the United States during an eighteen-month period beginning in January 1993, twenty-eight percent of them—nearly forty-one thousand—due to dirty needles.[61] Most, if not all of them, could have been prevented had clean needles been available. In Britain, the response could not have been more different. In 1985–86, the same time that alarms were going off about needle-borne AIDS in the United States, health officials in Edinburgh, Scotland, were shocked to discover that between fifty and eighty-five percent of the intravenous drug users in their city were HIV-positive as well. Rather than covering their eyes, though, they responded with what, by government standards, was blinding speed. By the fall of 1986, the Scottish Health Department had issued a report recommending that intravenous drug users be supplied with clean needles and taught how to use them to prevent the spread of HIV. A few months later, the government in London endorsed the report's proposals and announced that it was instituting them on a nationwide basis. By April 1987, fifteen clean-needle programs were in place in various places around the country, while by December 1988 there were more than one hundred.[62]

There was nothing particularly brave or heroic about the British effort. It was simply a matter of reasonable people taking reasonable precautions to prevent a bad situation from getting worse. In Liverpool, which has one of the worst drug problems in Britain and was thus the focus of much of the effort, locally transmitted HIV cases among intravenous drug users plummeted to near zero as a result by December 1988.[63] By 1990, new cases of needle-borne HIV in Edinburgh were down to a handful as well. As an American reporter summed it up, "The specter of AIDS jolted the Government, freeing public money to attack the problem and encouraging doctors to begin treating addicts more like patients than criminals."[64] Yet in America, where the incidence of AIDS is roughly eighty times greater per capita than in Britain, the specter of AIDS jolted government into doing the opposite—that is, into closing its eyes to the growing danger and immersing itself even deeper in an increasingly counterproductive strategy.

Why? The curious thing about the British effort was that it occurred not under a Labour government, which might be expected to be more enlightened about such matters, but under Margaret Thatcher, whom British leftists revile as a latter-day Attila the Hun for ripping up the social fabric. Yet when it came to a fundamental threat to the national health, Thatcher's government was incapable of *not* taking certain elementary precautions to protect the general health, just as the American government, regardless of who was at the helm, was incapable of a rational response. Confronted with the same problem, the two societies reacted in diametrically opposite ways. Leadership was not the issue since Thatcher, Ronald Reagan, and George Bush were, according to the usual political indices, cut from pretty much the same cloth. Rather, the difference had to do with something deeper, the structure, or constitution, of the two societies. For all its pomp and artifice, the British state was more up-to-date, more reasonable, better able to respond to the needs of its citizens, while the American system was simply unequipped to deal with the problems of the modern world.

1 0

The Unraveling
Social Fabric

I AM STANDING in the Alsterarkaden in the old city of Hamburg,
Germany, a covered walkway alongside a canal overlooking the ornate
city hall, the red-brown Saint Petri church, and the tree-lined city
square. Normally, the square stands empty except for strollers, but on
this occasion it is dotted with a dozen or so white canvas literature
booths as part of a festival against racism sponsored by the local Social
Democrats, who have run Hamburg ever since the war. Notwithstanding a vaguely punkish rock band playing at the far end of the square,
the scene is quite elegant, indeed far more elegant than anything New
York has to offer. The sun is setting, the outdoor cafés are buzzing,
and the streets are crowded with well-dressed shoppers who seem
strangely unaffected by the staggering prices displayed in the clothing

store windows. Looking out on the Rathausmarkt, it's hard to imagine that a half-century ago, this was little more than a field of rubble. "Operation Gomorrah," unleashed by the RAF under General Arthur "Bomber" Harris in the summer of 1943, created an intense firestorm that killed some forty-five thousand civilians and was hot enough to melt forks and spoons and destroy brick. The lovely northern European cityscape before me thus had to be reassembled, stone by stone, from a heap of debris.

What is the connection between a city and a constitution? Between the way a society looks and the way it functions politically? In America, where scores of cities like Hamburg have been *dis*assembled brick by brick over the same period, the question is rarely asked. The reason is a reigning ideology that assumes that society is composed of various building blocks that are separate and distinct. The Constitution is one such building block, politics another, urban decay a third. Experts who hotly debate problems in one area rarely pause to consider how they connect to problems in another. Yet they are very much related. Downtown Hamburg is not spiffy and elegant due to divine intervention or some innately German drive for neatness and order. Rather, Germans struggled *politically* after the war to create a mechanism that would allow them to put it back together. By the same token, urban America, with its bombed-out neighborhoods, armies of crack addicts, and staggering crime rates, is not in this sad state due to changing demographics, race, or some warp in U.S. character that causes middle-class Americans to eschew urban living for the wide-open expanses of suburbia.

Rather, it's because the people failed to create a political framework that would allow them to prevent cities from falling apart. Americans allowed themselves to be saddled with a system of government so antique, so lacking in up-to-date skills, as to be incapable of keeping a modern city in anything like proper running order. The notion that Americans preferred suburban living after World War II is one of those myths that are continually concocted to justify the status quo. Rather, there is every reason to believe that given an idea of what they

were getting into, they would have opted for more balanced transportation and development policies that would have preserved and
improved the cities while opening the countryside to more modest
and attractive kinds of development. The problem, though, is that they
were never presented with such options. Instead, whether by design
or default, Americans were presented with a fait accompli in the form
of a massive postwar de-urbanization policy that was implemented after only the most cursory, piecemeal discussion. Free choice did not
exist, only a series of highly *limited* choices between making do in
crowded city apartments or moving far afield into heavily subsidized
housing that, in the case of the first Levittown, was springing up in
the potato fields of Long Island some fifty miles from New York. The
choices were limited because democracy was limited. But if the choices
had been different—if, for example, the people had had greater control over various government agencies that were busily subsidizing
suburban development, if they had been made aware of the social costs
of rampant de-urbanization, or if government had been more creative
in tackling the problems of postwar development—they would no
doubt have chosen differently as well.

Although the connection between America's unique Constitution and
its unique urban crisis is rarely made nowadays, a century ago it was
something of a commonplace. "There is no denying that the government of cities is the one conspicuous failure of the United States,"
wrote James Bryce in the 1880s, adding:

> What Dante said of his own city may be said of the cities of
> America: they are like the sick man who finds no rest upon
> his bed, but seeks to ease the pain by turning from side to
> side. Every now and then the patient finds some relief in a
> drastic remedy, such as the enactment of a new charter or the
> expulsion in an election of a gang of knaves. Presently, how-
> ever, the weak points of the charter are discovered, the State
> Legislature begins to interfere by special acts, or a "public

service corporation" begins to reduce the virtue of officials; civic zeal grows cold and allows bad men to creep back into the chief posts.[1]

The problem was our old friend fragmentation—fragmented laws, fragmented political control, a fragmented political mentality—which made a systematic analysis of the growing urban crisis all but impossible. From Bryce's point of view, urban governance in the United States was an insane jumble of conflicting jurisdictions and divided responsibilities. If New York City's mayor

> has failed to keep the departments up to their work, he may argue that the city legislature hampered him and would not pass the requisite ordinances. Each house of a two-chamber legislature can excuse itself by pointing to the actions of the other, or of its own committees. . . . The various boards and officials have generally little intercommunication; and the fact that some were directly elected by the people make them feel themselves independent both of the mayor and the city legislators.[2]

Urban government was national government writ small. Despite hordes of baby-kissing, glad-handing politicians, the system was unresponsive, tangled, and confused. The more politicians tried to satisfy voters individually, the more they failed to serve them collectively. Overlapping jurisdictions had led to an impenetrable thicket of laws and regulations. "The enactments . . . have been modified, superseded, and repealed so often," said a New York judge in an essay Bryce had reprinted in his book, "that it is difficult to ascertain just what statutes are in force at any particular time."[3]

Contemporary urban historians like Jon Teaford of Purdue University and Kenneth Jackson of Columbia have zeroed in on the period around the turn of the century as the point in which the American system began shifting on its axis in relation to urban development. Previously, despite the awesome corruption and inefficiency of urban government, immense forces were combining to squeeze Americans into the big cities. At some point, though, centrifugal forces began doing the opposite, driving residents away, particularly those in the middle class, and causing them to wall themselves off in suburban enclaves. Initially, big cities had what people in outlying communities most wanted: sewerage, electricity, and gas lines, as well as police and fire protection, all at reasonable tax rates. Later, when such amenities became available in the suburbs as well, cities seemed to have all the things that middle-class Americans *didn't* want: noise, congestion, immigrants, and crime. In 1887, residents of Hyde Park, Cicero, and Lake View, Illinois, clamored to be annexed by Chicago so they could partake of the city's "perfect police, fire, postal system, and all the blessings of civilization that a big city can avail itself of."[4] In 1890, residents of Jamaica, Queens, who were without sewers, and residents of Flushing, who were without electric lights, gazed enviously at the still-separate city of New York across the East River, where residents had both.[5] In Indianapolis, gas rates, tax rates, and streetcar fares were all lower in the city than in the surrounding suburbs.[6] Yet, over the next two decades, the relationship reversed. Rather than clamoring to be annexed, suburbanites began clamoring for the right to go their own way. Rather than consolidation, fragmentation became the order of the day.

Americans were not unique in this respect. The first stirrings of de-urbanization could be felt in other societies as well as a result of the automobile and the rise of consumerism. Around the turn of the century, middle-class suburbanites outside of Birmingham and other British cities also began clamoring for self-determination. The reasons were similar, a desire to escape urban social problems and retreat behind hedges and lawns. But the official response was different. Where American politicians fell over themselves catering to the new suburbanites, British authorities said no. In 1904–5, a British government agency known as the Local Government Board issued a ruling forbidding middle-class communities from breaking away from larger cities in order to form their own districts. The reason, the board explained, was that "the sub-division of administrative districts often leads to increased expenditure, and in the case of areas having a small population and low assessable value, this increase in expenditure is not generally accompanied by a corresponding increase in administrative efficiency."[7] In 1911, MPs favoring the consolidation of the greater Birmingham area into a single urban unit argued "that municipal authorities can deal with the pressing and crying evils existing in the slums of cities" only by annexing tax-rich suburbs. Parliament agreed, and consolidation was approved.[8] Although hardly a radical bastion, the House of Commons recognized that suburbanites should not be permitted to reap the benefits of living close to the big cities without shouldering a fair share of the costs.

Parliament resisted such tendencies for a variety of reasons, not least of which was the lingering legacy of Benthamism. If the greatest good for the greatest number meant anything, it was that the interests of society as a whole predominated over those of any single person or group. In the United States, the dominant point of view was not utilitarian but individualistic. Regardless of the social consequences, the right of the individual or community to go its own way was sacrosanct. The eminent legal authority Thomas Cooley asserted unequivocally in 1868 that "the American system is one of complete decentralization, the primary and vital ideal of which is that local affairs shall be managed by local authorities."[9] Unless it could somehow be proven that local self-determination was unconstitutional, municipal fragmentation was unstoppable. State legislators thus cheered the forces of municipal secession on. As Teaford has documented, municipal subdivisions began breaking away around the turn of the century in ever growing numbers; the more crowded and urbanized the county, the greater the fragmentation. By 1910, Minnesota had 645 municipalities, eighteen of them in Minneapolis's Kennepin County. Michigan had 459 the same year, twenty of them in Detroit's Wayne County. Pennsylvania had 880, including sixty-five in Pittsburgh's Allegheny County; Massachusetts had 354, including thirty-two within a ten-mile radius of downtown Boston; and so on.[10]

For the cities, the consequences were, to use a Capitol Hill expression, like being nibbled to death by ducks. They found themselves besieged by leafy, middle-class communities that skimmed off the most affluent citizens and the cleanest and most profitable businesses, leaving them with the dregs. Although well-to-do suburbanites still went downtown to shop, visit the doctor, or take in a concert, their property at home was beyond the reach of city tax assessors. In effect, they were given a license to avail themselves of city services without paying for them in return—in plain English, to steal. In 1906, meat-packing companies in East Saint Louis, now one of America's prime urban disaster areas, came up with a clever legal trick. Fed up with local regulation and taxes, they broke away and formed a municipality of their own, which they promptly dubbed National City. According to Teaford:

> The packing companies built about forty frame houses next to the factories and moved in a sufficient number of employees to meet the population requirement for incorporation. . . . The National City mayors were basically officers of the ruling companies. . . . National City's municipal tax assessor was an employee of the meat packers and legally served his industrial masters. Though the Swift, Armour, and Morris properties were worth millions, the National City assessor valued these plots at only $117,000.[11]

Other manufacturers resorted to similar gambits in Pittsburgh, Chicago, Milwaukee, Denver, and Minneapolis–Saint Paul. The result was a carnival of legalized tax evasion in which not just big corporations participated, but individual homeowners intent on reaping the greatest benefits while paying the least by way of taxes did as well. State legislators should have been able to see where these beggar-thy-neighbor policies were leading, yet they did nothing to get in the way. "From New England to the Pacific Northwest," said Teaford, "state legislators deferred to the right of the local unit to determine its fate."[12] Instead of exercising responsibility, politicians gave tiny batches of citizens carte blanche to carve up the political landscape.

The structure of American politics provided no basis for a national discussion of where all this was heading. Congress was institutionally unequal to the task. It was too fragmented, too parochial, too much given to log rolling and deal making for anything like a coherent debate to take place. Moreover, Congress's legal authority was limited. Urban policy was not one of the federal government's enumerated powers under the Constitution but a prerogative of the states, one they could be counted on to guard jealously. After the civil rights revolution of the 1960s, Congress would find a way to intervene, albeit indirectly, but for now it was as unlikely to say no to municipal fragmentation as it was to say no to the design of a new city hall.

What's more, if fragmentation was desirable at one level, why not at another? If the Founders had solved the problem of America's volatile politics by splitting the polity horizontally between the federal government and the states and vertically among the three branches, why not solve America's urban problems by splitting up the cities as well? If big cities meant big problems, then smaller municipal units might mean smaller problems that were more tractable.

Needless to say, it didn't work. Rather than making cities better, the strategy made them worse. Urban areas were left with the lion's share of social problems yet, because of their stagnant or eroding tax bases, were deprived of the means with which to solve them. Not surprisingly, urban economies deteriorated.

This connection between fragmentation, declining taxes, and an increasingly unfavorable urban outlook is important because of the common perception in America that everything was fine in the cities until "they" came along—"they," of course, being blacks and Hispanics. Cities were clean and prosperous and neighborhoods stable and safe, until an alien element arrived, bringing with it drugs, violence, and poverty. Or so it seemed to the refugees from Brooklyn and the Bronx who, by the fifties and sixties, were flooding out onto Long Island, New Jersey, and Westchester. In reality, as historians like Teaford and Jackson have shown, the writing was on the wall for American cities long before the minority influx. As early as the 1920s, when it was still overwhelmingly white, Newark, New Jersey, was discovering that, hemmed in at a scant twenty-four square miles, it was too small to generate the tax revenues needed to support a modern industrial city. Plenty of tax revenue was available, but it lay just beyond reach in well-to-do enclaves like Belleville and Short Hills. In 1927, a prominent local businessman bragged:

> Great is Newark's vitality. It is the red blood in its veins—this basic strength that is going to carry it over whatever hurdles it may encounter, enable it to recover from whatever losses it may suffer, and battle its way to still higher achievement industrially and financially, making it eventually perhaps the greatest industrial center in the world.[13]

Yet such boasts were beginning to sound hollow with the suburban exodus already well under way. By 1925, more than forty percent of all attorneys with offices in Newark were living outside the city in one of the affluent suburbs. By 1947, the figure would rise to sixty-three percent, and by 1965 it would hit seventy-eight percent. By 1932, more than eighty-six percent of the officers and board members of Newark's chamber of commerce lived in the suburbs as well.[14] Back in 1900, Newark's mayor had begun talking about annexing a handful of nearby suburbs in order to expand the city's tax base. "By exercise of discretion," he explained, "we can enlarge the city from decade to decade without unnecessarily taxing the property within our limits, which has already paid the cost of public improvements."[15] Yet by 1940, when Newark was showing clear signs of deterioration, the *National Municipal Review* reported that affluent suburbanites were determined to keep Newark at arm's length due to a mixture of snobbery and fear of the city's growing "foreign-born and Negro population."[16]

In America, snobbery and fear ran unopposed. Everything encouraged them; nothing stood in their way. In the 1930s, the Home Owners Loan Corporation, one of the constellation of New Deal alphabet agencies created by FDR, drew up a system of guidelines to determine which neighborhoods were worthy of federal mortgage guarantees and which were not. The guidelines were frankly racist and anti-Semitic. New upscale neighborhoods filled with white, Christian professionals were given the highest rating, upscale Jewish neighborhoods were ranked somewhere in the middle, while older black neighborhoods were grouped at the very bottom. In northern New Jersey, the system ensured that far more federally guaranteed mortgages flowed to Newark's affluent suburbs than to Newark itself, while, in Brooklyn, the Federal Housing Administration refused to approve a mortgage if a single family on the block was black. In a particularly notorious example, the FHA refused to insure mortgages in a white neighborhood in Detroit that had grown up in what the administration felt was uncomfortable proximity to a black enclave along Eight Mile Road. Finally, in 1941, an enterprising developer came up with a solution: a concrete wall between the two groups that would hold race mixing to a minimum. The FHA took another look and approved the mortgage guarantees—but only for whites.[17]

What did the Constitution have to do with such practices? Obviously, America was not the only society drifting in the direction of racism and anti-Semitism in the 1930s. But what was different about the United States was the subterranean nature of the shift. Rather than right-wing parties hurling anti-Semitic invective in the open as they did in the Reichstag or the French National Assembly, federal bureaucrats in the United States implemented such policies in the vitally important area of housing in such a way that they would not come to light for decades to come. Opportunities to publicize such abuses and debate them nationally were therefore nil. Few people in Congress were willing to rock the boat about anything so sensitive. And while a small, antiracist party might have been willing, there were no small parties to be found on Capitol Hill—not because public support was lacking, but because the American voting laws and the very structure of the electoral system served to keep them out. Since debate was limited, democratic control of the bureaucracy was limited as well.

Rather than taking control of their destiny and democratically shaping society as they wanted it to be, Americans stood by and allowed the federal bureaucracy to do the shaping for them. Instead of acting, they were acted upon, with devastating consequences for the urban fabric.

The same thing could be said for transportation policy, which in the United States has been no less an agent of urban destruction. Americans were hardly the only people in the world to fall madly in love with the automobile, although, initially at least, they were the only ones with the means to see that their love was fulfilled. By World War I, Americans were producing and consuming cars at a rate the rest of the world found staggering. Downtown Los Angeles was already paralyzed by traffic by the early 1920s, a time when Germans were still going about by streetcar, bicycle, or on foot.[18] The urban consequences were nothing short of revolutionary. Trains and trolleys had funneled people and goods downtown where rail lines converged. But automobiles reversed the flow by encouraging people and businesses to relocate out on the periphery where traffic was lighter and parking more abundant. Urban geography thus turned inside out. Downtown property values fell as the old urban core became less accessible, while property values out along the highways rose. The old city centers emptied out as the outlying areas filled up.

None of this was unique. As the postwar economic miracle gathered force in northern Europe, officials began seeing evidence of a similar inversion. In West Germany, home of the Volkswagen, Mercedes-Benz, and Porsche, Hamburg and other cities began taking on that vacant, listless appearance that Americans knew all too well from back home. Yet the response in this case was also different. Beginning in the sixties, officials began restricting auto access to the old urban centers, holding down development out on the periphery, and designing residential streets with speed bumps and lots of little twists and turns in order to achieve what German urban planners call "traffic calming." Rather than straightening and widening roads so that traffic would flow quickly and smoothly, the idea was to narrow them so that drivers would be encouraged to slow down and make room for pedestrians and cyclists.

In America, on the other hand, virtually no effort was made to interfere with a process widely regarded as natural and inevitable. Instead, everything was sacrificed to the divine automobile. Highway planners hacked their way "with a meat ax" through dense urban neighborhoods, as New York's Robert Moses once put it,[19] and sturdy old brick buildings were demolished to make way for parking lots. Railroads plunged into bankruptcy. Although Lewis Mumford and a few other intellectuals protested, they had little impact on the people who really counted—the politicians, the developers, and the overwhelming mass of voters.

What was curious about America's massive switch to auto transport is that it was accompanied by an equally massive shift in terms of public finance. In the bad old days of the railroad monopolies, railroads had taken care not only of the engines and cars but of the track beds as well. To be sure, government helped by providing free rights-of-way and real-estate grants. Yet rail travel was still to a great extent self-supporting. With the automobile, government not only provided land for a new network of highways, but also built and maintained them. Where railroad companies had formerly paid property and business taxes to the communities they passed through, roads and highways paid nothing at all. Indeed, the impact on urban finance was doubly ruinous since downtown officials felt obliged to accommodate a surging tide of motor vehicles by widening streets and leveling entire blocks to make way for municipal parking lots. Urban population fell, pedestrian traffic declined, and the tax base deteriorated—yet business *still* flowed to the suburbs.

In one sense, this was most un-Jeffersonian. Government was replacing a private transportation infrastructure with one that was publicly owned. It was instituting policies that undermined municipal finances and made a mockery of local control. Yet what made such policies seem ultimately justified is that they were taken in order to foster an illusion of private transport and individual mobility. Government used quasi-Hamiltonian means to pseudo-Jeffersonian ends, to make it seem that when an American put his key into the ignition, he was driving under his own power and paying his own way, when in fact he was reaping the benefits of an enormously expensive middle-class welfare system.

The results may have been popular for a time, but they were not democratic. Instead of encouraging voters to revamp government, it encouraged them in the belief that they could outrun society's growing list of ills by heading out onto the highway and pressing the accelerator to the floor. A utilitarian society would have tried to make the people understand that there were vast costs associated with the car, that the auto had to be understood as a cog in a national transportation system in which railroads, coastal shipping, cycling, and even walking had to be coordinated and balanced so as to achieve maximum efficiency overall. Jacking up gas taxes is rarely popular. But if it serves to moderate highway demand, reduce congestion and pollution, and speed up the flow of goods, then it might enjoy political support. But such policies are possible only when the electorate can be made to see society as a whole, not when the political landscape is allowed to fracture into thousands of self-serving pieces.

Sociologist Robert C. Wood inadvertently illustrated the pitfalls in the American approach to social policy in a classic 1961 study, *1400 Governments*, when he wrote:

Essentially, two major competing definitions of the "best" transportation network are involved in the political process at the present time. The rail and transit agencies, and the interest groups clamoring for mass transportation, proceed from the postulate that the best transportation network is the one which moves the greatest number of people most rapidly in the shortest period of time. . . . The automobile-oriented agencies, on the other hand, . . . define transportation needs in terms of what it takes to satisfy the preferences of individual highway users. . . . What matters is not a determination of which set of assumptions is "right" according to the criterion of some outside party. What matters is which agencies possess the financial and political capability to translate their own goals into operating programs.[20]

Americans, in other words, were incapable of grasping a concept like collective efficiency. Instead of sorting through such problems politically as a group, they were only able to approach them individually. Since who is "right" is irrelevant, whoever lassos the most votes in favor of naked self-interest wins.

Given that transportation policy has nothing to do with maximizing efficiency, as Robert Wood assured us it does not, it is not very surprising that, in general, efficiency has plummeted. Growing auto dependence has led to crippling congestion in places like Long Island, Los Angeles, the Chicago suburbs, and various points in between. Rather than making it easier to go from Point A to Point B, an increasingly monocultural transportation system has made it more difficult. As with so many other areas of social policy, the result of all those individual units pushing and straining has been to cause conditions to deteriorate for all.

What should the United States have done instead? The answer is that it should have reined in municipal fragmentation, put a brake on runaway suburban development, and raised fuel taxes to cover the full cost of driving, including the cost of highway construction and maintenance, highway services, and environmental damage from air pollution and noise. The closer the *price* of driving came to matching the *cost* for society as a whole, the greater the level of overall efficiency. Rather than allowing taxis and other vehicles to use city streets for free in midtown Manhattan, for example, where commercial office space rents for about $30 a square foot per year, it should have charged them the full commercial value of the roadway they take up for perhaps twelve hours a day.

This is essentially the direction Europeans have been heading in since the 1960s. Where U.S. gasoline prices have been stuck at around a dollar a gallon since the 1970s, the Germans have pushed them up to around $4 by boosting fuel taxes, and the Scandinavians have hiked them to $5 or more. People in those countries still drive too much, but they drive far less than motorists in the United States. Rather than caving in to municipal fragmentation, former West Germany slashed the number of local governing units by up to eighty-five percent beginning in the 1960s.[21] The Germans have also discouraged hangarlike shopping malls strung out along the highways on the grounds that they encourage auto dependence and rob downtown shopping areas of their vitality.

Such efforts are what make central Hamburg so attractive. Private car traffic has been largely pushed out of the old city, which is why, to a Manhattanite, the streets seem oddly calm and quiet. A number of major shopping streets have been paved over and turned into pedestrian arcades so mothers can wheel children in strollers without having to worry about taxicabs careening onto the sidewalk as they occasionally do in New York. Rather than empty and windblown, as pedestrian streets invariably turned out to be when a few American cities tried them in the 1970s, Hamburg's are lively and vibrant, crowded with strollers, tourists, and people hurrying to work, without a boarded-up storefront in sight. In the sixties, the prevailing wisdom was that Germans were not Italians and had no taste for lolling about in sidewalk cafés. Yet in the seventies it was discovered that northern Europeans were just as capable of idling over a cup of cappuccino as those in the south. Café life proliferated.

This is not to say that Hamburg is completely free of the pathologies of late-twentieth-century life. Pushing auto traffic out of the central city has meant pushing it onto a ring of inner suburbs, with predictably undesirable social and environmental consequences. While the city is clean, in places it's also corporate and sterile, also the result of pushing undesirable activities out of the urban center. Still, there are far fewer homeless than in New York and, needless to say, no bombed-out slums or ultraviolent housing projects echoing with the sound of automatic weapons. Skinheads, who have gotten such enormous publicity in the United States, are fairly uncommon, at least in the old city. Even the seediest areas seem fairly nice by American standards. Residents complain about the rising volume of violent crime, yet the murder rate is still about a seventh of that of New York City.[22]

But if the results are impressive, it's not because of nationality or ethnicity but because of structure. Political democracy in Germany is sufficiently broad that it allows urban policy to be debated, developed, and implemented in a halfway sensible fashion. Amazingly enough from an American perspective, German municipalities do not steal companies away from their neighbors by bombarding them with tax breaks, and wealthy suburbs do not ban the construction of three-bedroom apartments on the grounds that they might attract working families with children and thereby add to municipal expenses. The government, tyrannical as it sounds, does not allow it. Bureaucrats in Hamburg all seem to have the same reaction when told about the jurisdictional squabbles and tangled lines of responsibility that characterize urban governance in the United States. They smile, shake their heads, and then launch into a detailed explanation of how the federal government in Bonn harmonizes policy at the local level so that wrinkles can be ironed out as soon as they occur. When an American points out that it all seems remarkably calm and rational, they seem perplexed, as if to ask, what else should government be—crazy and mixed up?

Since World War II, municipal fragmentation in the United States has gone from the baroque to the rococo. As developers have pushed the suburban frontiers ever outward, countless new townships and villages have sprung up where once there were only cornfields and pine barrens. At last count, the United States had some eighty-three thousand governmental units—the federal government, the fifty state governments, plus a bewildering variety of fauna and flora below, everything from counties and townships to library boards, school boards, flood-control districts, sewer districts, and so on, all with the power to assess and collect taxes. If all these strange hybrids were merely cogs in a large and intricate machine, the arrangement might make sense. Yet each is a self-contained feudal duchy, quick to raid its neighbors for businesses and tax assets, and even quicker to file suit when it feels that its ancient constitutional rights are somehow being infringed. In some areas, government units overlap like layers in a wedding cake. In Los Angeles, for instance, it was not unusual for a homeowner in the 1970s to receive an annual property-tax bill with as many as twenty itemized charges—a city tax, a county tax, one or two school taxes, plus a dozen or more taxes from special districts for flood control, parks, and the like.[23] Since no citizen could possibly keep tabs on twenty governmental units, the system added up to a modern version of taxation without representation, which is one reason the Proposition 13 tax revolt exploded with such fury in 1978. In New York, as Robert Wood noted, there are some fourteen hundred governments in the greater metropolitan area—the city itself, the five boroughs, seventeen other counties in three states, plus hundreds of towns, villages, and school districts. While the number of government units nationwide has either held stable in recent decades or even declined due to the consolidation of one-school rural school districts, in built-up urban and suburban areas they have expanded. According to one Census Bureau study, the number of municipalities in such areas rose better than eleven percent in one ten-year period (1962–72), while the number of special districts rose by better than thirty percent.[24]

The results are chaotic. Yet this is only the tip of the iceberg. Beneath those thousands of government units are thousands more *administrative* units—481 Law Enforcement Planning Regions created by the federal government in the 1960s; 975 Community Action Agencies; 419 Cooperative Area Manpower Planning System Councils; fifty-six Local Development Districts; 247 Air Quality Regions, and so on ad infinitum, each answerable to a separate part of the bureaucracy.[25] Within New York City alone, more than thirty "business improvement districts" have sprung into existence since 1984, each one a minigovernment in its own right, with power to levy business taxes and hire employees.[26] There are also community school districts and city council districts to add to the stew. Manhattan's Fourteenth Street, all two and half miles of it, slices through four police precincts, five sanitation districts, five community planning districts, three congressional districts, four state senate districts, three state assembly districts, and three city council districts—a veritable urban jungle.[27]

If this were Britain, it would be very easy to imagine a special parliamentary commission being created to study the problem of tangled and overgrown municipal government and to come up with recommendations for sorting it out. And indeed the British Parliament has been fiddling with local government on an almost continuous basis ever since passage of the Municipal Corporations Act of 1835. As the *Financial Times* reported of the latest such effort, the idea was to make local government "cheaper and easier for voters to understand" by having "all local services . . . provided by a single, all-purpose unitary authority"—an eminently sensible idea regardless of what one thinks of the specific proposal.[28] But this is not the way America works, or, rather, fails to work. Since transportation is both a federal and state prerogative, it either winds up the victim of a tug-of-war between contending jurisdictions or falls between the cracks. Since municipal governance is entirely a state responsibility, the feds have no basis to step in to prevent local fragmentation. Conceivably, Washington could use its enormous economic clout to push the states and municipalities in a more rational direction, but Congress is too much a collection of squabbling local interests itself to come up with something so reasonable and consistent.

As international-affairs expert David Calleo remarked in a book geared to British students of American government:

> Metropolitan areas . . . encompass so many separate territorial authorities, each chosen by a different electorate, that they seem reminiscent of the old Holy Roman Empire. . . . Looking at the American system as a whole, one cannot help but

be struck by its astonishing incoherence. . . . There has never been an American Richelieu or Colbert to put all the governing powers of the nation within a single rational system of administration. . . . Nor, indeed, has there ever been a Bentham to inspire a bureaucratic elite with the authority and competence to bring local authorities under a uniform network of regulation and inspection.[29]

What is a citizen to do? No one, obviously, has time to keep up with the doings of the school board, the city council, the local mosquito abatement commission, and all the rest, not to mention the state legislature, the governor, Congress, and of course the various comings and goings of the president himself. One would have to be a little cracked even to try. Rather, since meaningful representation is impossible, a typical citizen has three choices. He can give up and tune out in front of the TV set. He can vote with his feet by moving to a jurisdiction where the public amenities are better and the taxes lower. Or, if he can't move but still doesn't like how things around him are shaping up, he can go on the warpath against government in general. The first means retreating into the privacy of one's home, the second means turning oneself into a consumer of government services rather than a citizen, while the third means joining up in one of the mindless populist revolts that have been contorting the American landscape ever since Proposition 13.

Unfortunately, none of them works. The couch potato is affected by political forces outside his door whether he likes it or not, while the political "consumer" finds himself choosing from an increasingly unappetizing bill of fare as conditions deteriorate across the board. What is the point of fleeing to the suburbs, when the suburbs are hardly less congested, crime-ridden, and unattractive than the city? As for the populist tax rebel, no matter how emotionally satisfying such revolts may seem at the time, the effect, as events in California since 1978 have shown, is simply to impoverish government services and widen economic disparities by cutting off funds to poorer neighborhoods. The poor get poorer and hence angrier, which only seems to make the middle class angrier as well. With its riot-torn cities, brutal police, and nervous middle-class whites huddling in their suburban *laagers,* California is a perfect example of where know-nothing suburban revolts of this sort will lead.

Not surprisingly, the problem is getting worse. Every new social disturbance, be it a pogrom in Crown Heights, a riot in L.A., or something a bit less momentous, causes new fissures to open up in the political structure. More than an occasional political reaction, nimbyism (from "not in my backyard") has become a way of life based on just saying no to all the diversity and uncertainty of the outside world. The more events spin out of control, the more determined the suburban middle class becomes to close the gates and seal the door. In Durham, North Carolina, residents forced the rerouting of a proposed jogging path and nature trail near their neighborhood on the grounds that it might attract a bad element. In Overland Park, Kansas, residents just said no to basketball and volleyball courts on the grounds that they might attract unruly youths. In affluent North Miami Beach, residents have opposed laundromats, telegram offices, car washes, pawnshops, or any other business that might draw outsiders. In a well-to-do section of North Dallas, they even went on the warpath against the opening of a new multiplex movie theater on the grounds that, as one mother explained, it might attract gangs. Yet the desire to stop the world and freeze it in place is counterproductive as well. "People right now are opposed to any change, and that creates absolute instability as we go out and try to promote economic development in the city," a Dallas city council member observed.[30]

This is the new America, land of the fearful, home of the reclusive. Attitudes like these are irrational in one sense, yet all too rational in the context of a fundamentally irrational constitutional system. Movie theaters *do* draw traffic and sometimes even crime. Since government has proved incapable of dealing with either, suburbanites cannot be faulted out of hand for seeking to bar them at the door. By failing to deal with social breakdown, the system has wound up encouraging them to withdraw into their castle fastness. Since safety comes from walling oneself off, absolute safety comes from walling oneself off absolutely. Barring nature hikers may seem a little extreme, but why take chances?

Of course, not every middle-class American is a suburban isolationist. In a few urban centers, a counterethic has grown up based on embracing diversity rather than rejecting it. While the new urban pioneers don't exactly seek danger out, they don't barricade themselves behind triple-locked doors either. Rather, they bravely sally forth, dodging traffic, picking their way around overturned garbage cans, constructing a mental map of the city showing which areas are safe and which are not. On the extremes of the movement, a few people have learned not just to deal with urban chaos, but to enjoy it. A *Village Voice* cover illustration a few years ago showed a young urbanite gaily striding down the crumbling, violent, crack-ridden streets of the Lower East Side. A promo for the *Voice*'s annual entertainment guide, the clear message was that urban collapse can be exciting if only one has the right attitude.[31] The city was breaking down, exploding in crime and conflict. Yet rather than a nightmare, it was possible to see the city as a postmodern fun house with a thrill around every corner.

This urban counterethic may seem hip and cutting edge. Yet in a curious way it's as passive and conservative as anything found in the suburbs. It is predicated on the assumption that urban collapse is natural and inevitable and that all the individual can do is go along for the ride. But social decay is not inevitable. Political fragmentation, the narrowing of the tax base, and the abandonment of mass transit are not just things that happen, like thunderstorms in August. Rather, people *make* them happen. And just as they make them happen, they can make them *un*happen by adopting different policies. The postmodern notion that decay is something one can ride out and enjoy turns out to be merely a variation on the theme of premodern fatalism. What would be truly radical, on the other hand, would be to recognize that cities can be just as spiffy and clean as people want them to be, that the people should no more accept urban deterioration than they should accept poverty or starvation. The notion that freedom and urban decay are somehow interconnected, while an efficient, well-functioning urban environment is necessarily repressive and authoritarian, is a variation on the eighteenth-century Country belief that democracy and disorder go hand in hand. In fact, people are more free when the urban machinery functions properly and crime is under control. Kids can drink beer in grunge-rock clubs until 3 A.M. knowing that when it comes time to take the subway home, the trains will be on schedule and the stations clean and safe. The notion that urban decay makes one wild and free is a myth, just like the notion that artists do their best work when starving in an unheated garret. Real urban breakdown, like real poverty, inhibits freedom and discourages creativity and is not the least bit fun at all.

Who benefits from fragmentation? In a revealing article in an economics journal published by a branch of the Federal Reserve, Glenn H. Miller Jr., a Fed vice president, posed the question whether there were perhaps too many governments in the Fed's Tenth District. Considering that the Tenth District, which includes seven western and midwestern states, has more than fourteen thousand governmental units, per capita nearly two and a half times the national average, one might think the answer was yes. Yet Miller's answer was the opposite. The more government units, he reasoned, the more easily residents and businesses can shop around for "the jurisdiction that best fits their tax and public services preferences." The result is heightened competition with the public sector, which in turn

lead[s] local governments to provide the preferred services and to provide them efficiently. Such competition is greater the larger is the number of governments in the specific geographic area. And, because the competition between jurisdictions associated with decentralization increases efficiency, the overall size of the local public sector is reduced. . . .[32]

More government units, in other words, implies greater efficiency, greater freedom of choice, and less government overall.

Needless to say, this sort of economic analysis couldn't be more wrongheaded. The real result of government pileup is not heightened efficiency, but heightened *in*efficiency, stepped-up bureaucracy, and a decline in real freedom. The Tenth District may have more government units per capita, yet with their fast-food joints, strip malls, and suburban developments, those units wind up looking remarkably the same. Rather than more freedom of choice, a homeowner looking for a community in which to relocate actually winds up with less. Every overlapping jurisdiction meanwhile results in wasteful redundancy, which eats up tax money and results in a lower quality of service overall. Social breakdown, which municipal fragmentation encourages, imposes costs that are just as significant as an increase in one's utility or tax bill.

The free-market assault on government that has become all the rage since the 1980s is a reprise of John C. Calhoun's parting blast at mass democracy a decade before the Civil War. Where Calhoun saw democracy as a form of totalitarianism, free-market economists see it as a form of economic monopoly. In both cases, their real beef is with popular sovereignty, which, by definition, adds up to a monopoly on power. But where antidemocrats see this as something frightening, those in favor see it as the opposite. The majority wants power not just for its own sake, but because power is necessary in order to achieve change. As Bagehot observed in 1867:

All men need great results, and a change in Government is a great result. It has a hundred ramifications; it runs through society; it gives hope to many, and it takes away hope from many. It is one of those marked events which, by its magnitude and its melodrama, impress men even too much.[33]

The absence of popular sovereignty means that great changes never occur. Hopes are vanquished as society drifts, which is as good an explanation as any for America's current political malaise. Thus, the remarkable thing about American society is not only how noisy and chaotic it can be, but how tired and overgrown the whole affair is beginning to look. Institutionalized chaos has led to stagnation and despair.

THE TERMINAL CRISIS

AMID RISING INTERNATIONAL trade tension, Karel van Wolferen, a Dutch journalist residing in Japan, made a big splash in 1989 with a book entitled *The Enigma of Japanese Power*, which aimed to explain that country's inscrutable political system for the benefit of a mystified, frustrated West. As a citizen of the Netherlands, van Wolferen was used to the rational modern state as it exists in northern Europe, yet what he had found in his years in Japan was very different. True, it had a parliament, a prime minister, a cabinet, and all the other trappings of a modern democracy. But van Wolferen had concluded that it was all for show. Real power lay with a group of godfathers and political fixers who eschewed public debate and preferred to settle disagreements through a ritualized process of compromise and conciliation behind closed doors. Regardless of what happened in parliament or other political forums, *real* Japanese decision making took place on a different plane according to quite different rules.

For van Wolferen, the problem was how to describe this parallel power structure that somehow managed to be everywhere and nowhere at the same time. "System" was the best he could come up with. The word was useful, he wrote, because it

> hints at something beyond the range of the potentially corrective powers of democratic politics . . . something that cannot be reasoned with, although it may occasionally be duped. As it happens, the Japanese are rarely allowed to forget the existence of socio-political arrangements that are infinitely stronger than any kind of might the individual could ever bring to bear on them and have, at best, only a dim notion that ideally one should have recourse to democratic processes as a means of changing them.[1]

The system was nebulous, foglike, yet paralyzing. The purpose of politics in Japan was not to structure debate in order to solve problems and move society forward, but to provide an illusion of progress, debate, and problem solving so that the system could continue undisturbed. When it comes to domestic policy making, van Wolferen went on, "this System without a core works reasonably well, even though areas of social malfunction tend to go on malfunctioning for lack of decisive action."[2] But as long as the problem areas did not get out of hand, the system was secure. Westerners were frustrated by a system that turned its back on foreign influences. But for the average Japanese, the arrangement was not without its advantages.

All of which may be a bit one-sided but does not seem entirely implausible. But the curious thing about van Wolferen was that while he was obviously well-schooled in Dutch and Japanese politics, he was apparently unfamiliar with much of what lay in between. If he had been better informed, he could not have helped noticing a certain large land mass where the political characteristics were not all that different from the ones he was describing. Like Japan, this great middle kingdom had also grown up in relative isolation and had developed a nonrational form of politics very different from those in northern Europe. Debate was muted and contorted by what locals called "the system," while "areas of social malfunction" were also allowed to fester for generations for lack of concerted action that might threaten the status quo. Like Japan, this middle kingdom was intensely conservative, not so much in the sense of being right wing but in its intense devotion to an immovable constitutional system as the supreme moral and political value. Government was ruled by certain ancient principles that, as far as the people were concerned, were untouchable. Life was incomprehensible without them. As van Wolferen said of the Japanese, they had "only a dim notion that ideally one should have recourse to democratic processes as a means of changing them."

The great middle kingdom, of course, is the United States. What makes the United States even more inscrutable—what caused van Wolferen and other pundits to miss the obvious similarities—is that, unlike Japan, its mysteries are all on the surface. It has a Constitution, which, as Robert Bork has pointed out, is intelligible to anyone with a command of written English. Its politics are some of the loudest in the world, with more squabbles, disputes, policy papers, and byzantine maneuvers at various levels than one can shake a stick at. And it has a noisy, cantankerous citizenry to boot, one that is ready to complain about everything from drugs to traffic at a drop of a hat—all of which would seem to make America an open book. If the Japanese are reserved, distant, formal, Americans are the reverse—loud, demanding, in-your-face.

Yet the American system is a case of hiding in plain sight. Its mysteries are deeper by virtue of being right in front of one's nose. A marvel of eighteenth-century engineering, the political system is structured in such a way that the greater the pressure on it to move, the more it tends to freeze in place. Although at times the resultant tensions seem intolerable, what holds it together is an underlying belief that change is frightening, efficiency in government is dangerous, and that every society needs an anchor to keep it from sailing away. The people may rage and scream for change, but at the same time they are grateful that something is holding them in place—because if they were allowed to go forward unimpeded, who knows where they might end up?

This is the enigma of American power. Other countries have their quirks, hidden recesses, and strange byways, even model democracies like the Scandinavian countries or the Netherlands. Yet none, not even Italy, is quite so defiant of rationality. "I have a saying, which is that you can't be wealthy and stupid for more than one generation," Romano Prodi, a rising political star of the Italian center-left, declared in early 1995.[3] Yet no country is more devoted than we are to the absurd proposition that trusting to the intelligence of a bygone generation is the key to muddling through all difficulties.

There are, of course, differences between the American and Japanese systems, chief of which is the fact that the American system by this point is so much older. Where in the past it has been highly effective in smoothing over differences and promoting social harmony, this is no longer the case. After years of neglect and halfhearted nonsolutions, "areas of social malfunction" such as racism, urban decay, the drug war, and a chronically malfunctioning transportation system have been turned into monsters that are now threatening to swallow up the whole of society. Where the United States, despite its fragmented political system, once seemed to be "a purposeful giant bent on economic conquest" (as van Wolferen described Japan), it now seems befuddled and confused. As recently as the early sixties, public opinion polls found that seventy percent or more of the people trusted Washington to do the right thing all or most of the time. Yet by 1992 the percentage had plunged to a little over twenty percent, while by 1994 it was down even more.[4] In August 1994, a *Time* magazine–CNN poll found that whereas ninety percent of the respondents said they wanted a government that promotes change, ninety-one percent said they had little or no faith in the ability of Washington to solve problems and get things done.[5] Americans wanted change, they needed change, yet they believed, not inaccurately, that their government was the last thing capable of providing it.

The 1990s are shaping up as the decade of the great unraveling, the period in which America's Ancient Constitution finally proved unable to cope with the problems of modernity and came unstuck. In hindsight, the process started in 1991 when George Bush's approval rating hit an astounding ninety percent in the aftermath of the Persian Gulf War but then began heading south as the recession began to bite. The turnabout left Bush, the apostle of status-quo politics, in a terrible fix. On one hand, as the inheritor of the Reagan mantle, he had no choice but to call on Americans to "stay the course" and stick with the policies of the previous ten years. On the other hand, it was clear that such a slogan would not go down well with a people who, after years of deficit spending and gridlock on Capitol Hill, were hungry for an alternative. A few years earlier, an iconoclastic MIT economist named Paul Krugman had marveled at the American people's "lack of protest" over a "basically dreary economic record" extending back over decades.[6] Yet by the early nineties it was clear that the mood was beginning to shift. Voters were turning restless and irritable. They were beginning to protest. Homelessness, crime, the mess on Capitol Hill, even traffic were contributing to a case of badly jangled nerves.

The effect on politics was curious. While George Bush's ratings entered a free fall and a southern governor named Bill Clinton began pulling out ahead in the early Democratic primaries, voters allowed their attention to wander to a couple of quirky political characters out on the periphery who, according to the experts, had no chance of winning but seemed all the more interesting as a consequence. The first such figure was Paul Tsongas, the Massachusetts Democrat whose hound-dog expression perfectly suited his downbeat call for economic sacrifice to eliminate the deficit and whose way of mumbling and swallowing his words contrasted appealingly with Clinton's glib, carefully crafted TV performances. The second, of course, was H. Ross Perot, the Texas billionaire who, like a corporate white knight in the midst of a takeover battle, had stepped into the middle of the campaign with an offer to lead a citizens' crusade to clean up Washington and put an end to gridlock once and for all.

Both were symptomatic of a deep malaise (to use a popular Washington buzzword) that had settled on the electorate and would not let go. Thanks to his jug ears and five-dollar haircut, Perot was even more untelegenic than Tsongas, which, perversely, made him all the more attractive. Where other politicians shucked and jived, Perot was far and away the most plainspoken candidate to hit the campaign trail since Harry Truman. He was contemptuous of the political system as it existed in Washington, contemptuous of the conventional wisdom that said an outsider could never win, and contemptuous of the accepted rules. He was also contemptuous of the notion that Washington was a great mass crushing the citizenry under its weight, which was impossible to budge. As he put it during one of the presidential debates when asked if he was capable of getting government to function, there was nothing the people couldn't accomplish if they were of a mind to:

> Can we govern? . . . I love that one. The "we" is you and me. You bet your hat we can govern because we will be in there together and we will figure out what to do and you won't tolerate gridlock, you won't tolerate endless meandering and wandering around, and you won't tolerate non-performance. And believe me, anybody that knows me understands I have a very low tolerance for non-performance also. Together we can get anything done.[7]

This was a theme that Newt Gingrich would use to great effect in 1994, the theme of the people as an unstoppable power who would bend government to their will. Rather than clamoring or complaining, they had the power to give orders and see to it that they were carried out.

This was explosive because it suggested that "we the people" were superior to the process in Washington, not subordinate to it. The powers that be in Washington were nearly paralyzed in response. Early into Perot's campaign, for instance, House Republican leader Bob Michel observed, not imperceptively, that Perot

> isn't the first, and isn't going to be the last, to say that democracy isn't working and that if you trust me with power, I'll solve your problems. That message, sometimes sinister, sometimes downright silly, has been heard all over the world at various times in this century. Their siren call has enchanted good, decent people who are attracted to such simplicity and ignorance because of genuine grievances with their government. Ross Perot is the wake-up call for all those who believe that democratic government must be made to work and who are willing to spell out ways it can work, in the old-fashioned American way, before the election.[8]

The last line, however, was the giveaway. Government either had to be made to work "the old-fashioned American way," Michel was admitting in effect, or it would not work at all. Yet it was precisely the old-fashioned way that had gotten American politics into such trouble in the first place, a truth Michel couldn't bring himself to utter, yet which Perot, surprisingly, could.

Indeed, beginning in the late eighties when his national profile began to grow, Perot began speaking out politically in a way that no one other than a few radicals and academics had in America for decades. The United States, he repeated, was no longer the greatest country in the world. It had grown "complacent and arrogant after the war" and had surrendered its lead "at a time when we had an incredible edge."[9] "We're daydreaming of our past while the rest of the world is building its future," he said on another occasion. "We're living in the past and standing still."[10] Where standard-issue campaign rhetoric called for describing every two-bit burg as a shining city on the hill, Perot was very possibly the first major American candidate in history willing to say what ordinary Americans knew to be true—that U.S. cities were inordinately ugly, barren, and depressing.

> Go to Rome, go to Paris, go to London. Those cities are centuries old. They're thriving. They're clean. They work. Our oldest cities are brand new compared to them and yet . . . go to New York, drive through downtown Washington, go to Detroit, go to Philadelphia. What's wrong with us?[11]

More astonishing, however, was the criticism meted out for that holy of holies, the Constitution. "Our Founders built a beautiful ship of state," he declared at one point, "but the barnacles have latched on and the hull has rusted. It's time for a scrubdown from top to bottom."[12] Why, he mused on another occasion, were Japan and Germany winning the industrial race? Because "they got new constitutions in 1945. We gave them to them."[13] Sounding much like Woodrow Wilson (whom he undoubtedly never read), he declared in an interview that the Constitution was woefully obsolete:

> Keep in mind our Constitution predates the industrial revolution. Our founders did not know about electricity, the train, telephones, radio, television, automobiles, airplanes, rockets, nuclear weapons, satellites, or space exploration. There's a lot they didn't know about. It would be interesting to see what kind of document they'd draft today. Just keeping it frozen in time won't hack it.[14]

This was remarkable—not only that Perot said it, but the fact that the voters did not recoil in horror at seeing their national icon called into question. Vice President Dan Quayle, for one, tried to stir up public outrage by accusing Perot of having "contempt" for the Constitution, yet the effort fell flat.[15] Rather than being outraged, voters seemed to like what they heard. Given the emptiness of most politicians, it was refreshing to have an antipolitician like Perot who was willing to speak the truth.

Perot was that rarest of commodities, a genuine radical, one who was willing to question society's most basic assumptions in a fundamental way. Of course, the flip side of his radicalism was authoritarianism, a belief that he was uniquely suited to the job of picking up American society and putting it back on track. Where Sidney George Fisher had looked to Congress to transform the system during the Civil War, Perot looked to a new and even more charismatic version of the presidency. The people would not cut the Gordian knot of American politics themselves. Rather, they would trust Perot to do it for them, knowing that he shared their innermost desires and ambitions.

Perot gave full vent to his egomania on the campaign trail. Where Clinton told economically hard-hit voters "I feel your pain" so often it became a national joke, Perot stared straight into the TV cameras at one point and, without a hint of embarrassment, told viewers: "I'm doing this because I *love* you."[16] Perot was not just for the people or of the people. He *was* the people. His identification with the nation was complete.

Rather than popular sovereignty, Perot was advancing the theory of sovereignty of the leader as the personification of the people. Like every would-be strong man, he was contemptuous of ideas, philosophy, words, and debate. Washington, he declared in March 1992, "has become a town filled with sound bites, shell games, handlers, media stuntmen who posture, create images, talk, shoot off Roman candles, but don't ever accomplish anything. We need deeds, not words, in this city."[17] He would stride into that great "talkerie" on Capitol Hill like a latter-day Coriolanus and browbeat the members into submission. The people would beat down everything in their path, acting, of course, through the essential agency of Ross Perot himself. Perot promised to depart after a single term, but, then, that is what dictators often promise when they take power, even those who wind up holding on for life.

Needless to say, Perot's prescription would not have worked. Contrary to mythology, authoritarianism does not result in order. Rather, a system in which all power flows from a single, decidedly erratic individual inevitably winds up being more disordered than whatever it may have replaced. As a businessman with a decidedly uneven track record, Perot would have been lost in the complexities of modern government. His proposal for "electronic town halls," reminiscent of Napoleon III's penchant for plebiscites and referenda, was a joke. Such meetings would either have resulted in cacophony with nameless citizens shouting at each other across the airwaves, or they would have been arranged in such a way as to tell the president precisely what he wanted to hear. The people, meanwhile, would have no chance to work through the problems themselves, using their own intellects and their own resources. Instead, they would stand by and watch as Perot worked his way through them in their behalf—and no doubt made a fearful botch of it. Shutting the political parties out of the loop, which the Perot program would have accomplished, would have been a giant step backward. America's problem was not an excess of political partisanship, as Perot seemed to think, but a shortage. Where parties in other countries had grown into political factories-*cum*-universities, in which ideas were hammered out, policy forged, and leaders trained, America's were still stuck at a mid-nineteenth-century point of development in which they were little more than mutual-aid societies for aspiring politicians. Yet rather than moving American politics forward, Perot would have moved them back to a point where party development was even more rudimentary. The people would have been more shut out of the political process than ever.

Of course, the American system did not choose that particular road to ruin. Instead, with the election of one William Jefferson Clinton, it chose another.

Bill Clinton was a product of an antiquated political system that, after losing steam for decades, seemed to have reached the final stage of exhaustion. Virtually a case study out of Alan Ehrenhalt's 1991 book, *The United States of Ambition*, which dealt with the rise of the full-time, self-supporting, entrepreneurial candidate, Clinton began his ascent up the greasy pole in high school by becoming president of his junior class, joining half a dozen student clubs and bands, and picking up a slew of awards for things like "youth leadership" from local civic and business groups. As everyone's ideal of a well-scrubbed American youth, he was in such demand as a public speaker that his high school principal had to step in and limit his appearances.[18] As a participant in something called Boys' Nation, a national get-together in which teenagers act out the roles of real, live senators and congressmen on Capitol Hill, he made the famous lunge for John F. Kennedy's outstretched hand that was memorialized on film and shown before the Democratic National Convention in 1992. At Georgetown University, he ran for president of the freshman class on a platform of improving the homecoming float and then left for Oxford on a Rhodes scholarship, where he dabbled on the edges of the antiwar movement in such a way as not to impair his political prospects back home.[19]

This was a portrait not only of a political animal, but a certain *kind* of political animal. Where it's possible to imagine a budding politician in Britain or Germany setting out to build a career while still in his teens, the first steps would undoubtedly have been taken in a different milieu. In the case of the former, rather than running for freshman class president, he would more likely have cut his teeth by participating in the ideological battles that are perennially breaking out in the National Union of Students or by joining one of the party youth groups, which is how Margaret Thatcher got her start at Oxford.[20] Rather than perfecting the unctuous manner demanded by groups like the Rotarians or Elks, he would more likely have tried to develop the proper techniques for rousing the troops and leading them into battle. Rather than learning how to ingratiate himself, he would have learned how to debate. Clinton, however, was a product of one of the most depoliticized, de-ideologized systems in the world, with the result that the skills he honed were those of the backslapper, jawboner, and joke teller.

Indeed, it was precisely those skills that first drew him national

273

attention. In 1988, the journalist David Osborne marveled at how Clinton, a rising star in the Democratic firmament,

> thrives on the handshaking and elbow-rubbing that are the backbone of politics in Arkansas, and people bask in his warmth. Rather than wearing him down, the personal contact seems to rev him up. He is as comfortable and natural telling jokes with the good ol' boys as discussing international economic problems with a group of professors. Among governors today, he is virtually unparalleled at either.[21]

This was extremely important because it seemed to show that Clinton possessed the all-important common touch, which meant that he had a way of making vaguely liberal Democratic nostrums palatable to farmers, blue-collar workers, and Southerners in general.

Yet Clinton, someone who was in love with the process of politics rather than the substance, was also notoriously slippery—a hollow man who had come of age in a system of hollowed-out politics. As he wrote in his now-famous letter to the head of the University of Arkansas ROTC program in 1969: "I decided to accept the draft in spite of my beliefs for one reason: to maintain my political viability within the system."[22] Beliefs had to be jettisoned so viability could be maintained. (In fact, Clinton only accepted the draft after it became clear that, thanks to a high lottery number, he would not be chosen.) In an astute article in 1994, Garry Wills took a second look at Clinton's love of backslapping and elbow rubbing and found it all rather shallow and empty. Clinton, he noted, was sensational in his ability to become one with whatever audience he was addressing. But it was at the cost of completely losing himself in the ecstasy of each individual encounter:

> The very concentration that closes Clinton in on one person, on one situation, seals him off from all others. He can be great, moment by moment; but the moments are disjunct. He adapts so well to the present that he disregards any bearing it might have on the past or the future.[23]

He was like a child, forever living in the present as he stuffed his mouth with Big Macs and take-out pizza. "Clinton is an omnidirectional placater," Wills continued. "He wants to satisfy everyone, which is a sure-fire way of satisfying no one."[24] According to one famous story from the mid-eighties, he vetoed a bill one evening allowing tax credits for private contributions to Arkansas colleges and had someone slip it under the locked door of the state clerk's office. Then, after calling up the state's university presidents and learning that they in fact favored the bill, he sent a state trooper to fish it out with a coat hanger so he could change it from vetoed to approved. Fed up with Clinton's shilly-shallying, J. Bill Becker, the embattled chief of the Arkansas state AFL-CIO, described him in 1990 as "the kind of man who'll pat you on the back and piss on your leg."[25] Rather than waxing indignant over George Bush's call for a constitutional amendment to ban flag burning, Clinton urged his fellow Democrats to "get on the right side" of the issue by denouncing flag burning while also opposing a flag-burning amendment—an example of his penchant for splitting differences in order to head off disagreement and debate.[26]

This is what it took to be elected president in November 1992, although it was not what it took to serve successfully as president beginning in January 1993. Clinton benefited in the campaign from two quirks in the American political structure. One was the hallowed Country notion that by virtue of being untainted by power, a politician from the hinterlands was somehow better equipped to run the federal government than one who had spent years in the center of action. The idea would have been unfathomable in London, Paris, or Bonn, yet in the eighteenth-century American system, it was almost axiomatic. The other quirk had to do with the chasm between governing and campaigning. Unlike Britain, where the opposing party forms a shadow cabinet whose job it is to dog the real cabinet every step of the way, letting voters know exactly what it would do as an alternative, a typical American politician withdraws from governing as he heads out onto the campaign trail, immerses himself in the minutiae of fund-raising, and then fine-tunes his campaign pitch so as to appeal to the widest swath of the electorate as possible. Governing is no more than an afterthought. Bill Clinton won in '92 because he was the best prepared (he had been laying the groundwork for a presidential bid since the mid-eighties) and went down most easily with the largest number of voters. He aroused very little by way of enthusiasm, but at least he was *acceptable* to the plurality of voters needed to put him over the edge.

Once elected, however, these selfsame qualities proved crippling. Without a strong party behind him, he had no means to enforce discipline on Capitol Hill. At a time when congressional incumbents were routinely reelected with sixty or seventy percent of the vote, his forty-three percent of the total was most unimpressive. Indeed, Democratic lawmakers could argue with considerable credibility after the '92 elections that he had swept into office on *their* coattails, not they on his. The lack of real popular enthusiasm turned out to be an impediment as well, as did his inexperience with the ways of Washington. The vagueness that had served him so well proved embarrassing when the time came to turn campaign promises into concrete proposals for action. "There's a mandate for change, but not a mandate for a program," Harry C. McPherson, White House counsel under LBJ, tartly observed for the benefit of the *New York Times*. Clinton, he added, "has got to put together a program pretty quickly that will win the assent of the American people"—as if that had not been his job as a candidate running for election.[27]

Clinton became that rare president who sees his administration fall apart before he even takes office. By mid-January 1993, with the inauguration still several days away, he was busily backtracking on campaign promises to cut taxes for the middle class, to halve the budget deficit within four years, to trim White House staff by twenty-five percent, and to admit Haitian boat people seeking political asylum, an issue he had used to particular effect in savaging George Bush on the campaign trail. Once he took office, matters turned even worse. Following a tense meeting over the issue of gays in the military, Clinton wavered for several days before going back on his campaign promise and agreeing to a humiliating compromise in which his administration wound up enforcing the very antigay rules he had vowed to repeal. A few weeks later, Democratic chieftains on Capitol Hill nixed his proposals for campaign-spending reform. In March, they persuaded him to back off his proposal to upgrade the absurdly low fees charged to western ranchers for the privilege of grazing their livestock on federal land. In early May, he dropped his proposal for a free, comprehensive childhood vaccination program. In June, he withdrew Lani Guinier from consideration for the post of the Justice Department's chief of civil rights, while a few days after that he backed off from his proposal for a broad-based BTU energy tax that would have had the combined effect of boosting federal revenue, moderating energy consumption, and encouraging efficiency.

His administration was in a headlong retreat before it could even walk. Yet none of it was entirely his fault. The *system*, rather, was disintegrating as senators and representatives scattered in every conceivable direction but the one that made sense. Clinton's humiliating retreat on gays in the military was not due merely to a failure of nerve. Rather, the battle was lost when Sam Nunn, the chief of the Senate Armed Services Committee and one of the most powerful barons on Capitol Hill, entered the fray on the side of the military. The BTU tax died when Senators David Boren of Oklahoma and John Breaux of Louisiana, both Democrats who worried about what would happen to oil drillers back home if America ever succeeded in curbing its gargantuan energy appetite, combined against it. Grazing fees were different—Clinton probably did not have to give in to a handful of senators from the sparsely populated Far West. But by this point his administration was already suffering from shell shock. As Arkansas journalist John Brummett told it in *Highwire*, his account of Clinton's first year in office, the trouble began in mid-March when Max Baucus, a Montana Democrat, led a delegation of western senators to the White House to request that they be consulted before a new schedule of grazing fees went into effect. Instead of acceding to the request, the president's office went them one better by dropping the idea entirely. Rather than rustle feathers, the White House staffer assigned to study the matter had decided that it was more trouble than it was worth, and higher-ups had agreed. As Brummett put it: "A group of senators had asked only for a dialogue; a few days later they were handed a convincing victory that cost them nothing."[28] Baucus responded by issuing a press release crowing that he and his western colleagues had talked tough with the president and forced him to back down.

With that, Clinton's credibility on Capitol Hill was shot. Yet, left to their own devices, the credibility of the Democrats on Capitol Hill was nil as well. When the Republicans controlled the White House, the Democrats had shown a certain esprit de corps, but now that one of their own was president, they had degenerated into a shapeless blob, just as they had under Carter. In fact, the two branches were dragging each other down together. The more abuse Clinton took on Capitol Hill, the more legislators and the press felt he deserved it. The more assiduously legislators looked out for their constituents' interests, the more contempt voters felt for the job they were doing as a whole. The North American Fair Trade Agreement sparked such an orgy of deal making on Capitol Hill that even the Mexicans were shocked.[29] The protracted 1993 budget negotiations had a similar effect. "Forget policy," the *Wall Street Journal* reported at one point. "The budget negotiations are about votes—and, of course, money."[30] One congressman wanted money to expand a nuclear assembly plant in his home district. Another wanted to make sure his constituents got a piece of Pentagon helicopter contracts. Senate majority leader George Mitchell wanted a provision benefiting the Maine boat industry, and so on. "Once David Boren became a political capitalist," one congressman remarked following the Oklahoma senator's defection on the energy-tax issue, "this place became a Mideast bazaar."[31]

Of course, the Democrats' real Waterloo, the focus of Clinton's first two years in office, was health care. Health-care reform was simply too much for Congress to handle: too sweeping, too complex, too fundamental. In the late forties, Aneurin Bevin, minister of health in

Clement Attlee's postwar Labour government, had created the National Health Service with the help of a few civil servants plus occasional input from the British Medical Association. In 1993, when Clinton tapped his old Oxford chum Ira Magaziner to design an American health plan, Magaziner recruited more than five hundred experts, whom he divided into thirty-four subgroups to examine everything from cost controls to ethics. A Canadian-style single-payer system, in which the government would act as insurer for all citizens, would have been simpler. But it would also have been more radical and hence more disturbing to the status quo, which was why Clinton was opposed. Instead, Magaziner used his immense pool of talent to assemble a more "moderate" package that tried to distribute the burden of health-care reform up and down the line, from the insurance companies to the doctors and hospitals. The problem with such an approach, however, was complexity: the more broadly the burden was distributed, the more complicated the mechanisms needed to ensure that no one would suffer more than his fair share of the pain. Complexity was not so bad from the health-care industry's point of view, since with its armies of lawyers and financial strategists, it would always find a way to turn such a system to its advantage. But a complex plan would also be easy to nitpick to death on Capitol Hill. It presented a target for congressional Republicans that was almost too soft and easy.

Thus, simplicity and complexity were *both* dangerous. No matter what kind of proposal Magaziner came up with, the odds of getting it through the congressional meat grinder were slim. As it was, Magaziner's proposal, set forth in thirty three-ring binders, was so convoluted that even Hillary Clinton was alarmed.[32] A flowchart of how it was supposed to work looked like a circuit board from inside a TV set. Republicans took one look at it, pronounced it worthy of Rube Goldberg, and pounced on it with ill-concealed glee. As the debate got under way, Democratic senators began peeling away to formulate their own health-care proposals so that before long a half-dozen plans were circulating on Capitol Hill, each more complicated and flawed than the next. One needed a doctorate in public health in order to keep up with the relative strengths and weaknesses of each, which is why individual senators, whose postgraduate training is chiefly in the arts of fund-raising and prevarication, were quickly lost. In the end, the whole game collapsed due to general exhaustion.

Clinton's few remaining defenders in the press argued that he had fallen short merely because he had aimed so high. A national health system was an ambitious goal, one that had defeated Harry Truman back in 1948, so perhaps Clinton should not have felt so bad that it had defeated him as well. Yet every advanced industrial nation had created comprehensive health-care systems decades earlier with far less fuss and bother. Health care was considered an essential responsibility of modern government, yet it was beyond Congress's competence. Individual senators and representatives found it easy to make broad promises on the campaign trail yet inordinately difficult to say yes to anything that might adversely affect their constituents or campaign contributors. Representative Paul McHale, a freshman Democrat from Pennsylvania, opposed forcing employers to contribute to their workers' health-care insurance because it might sink small businesses in his district, opposed anything that might erode health benefits for union retirees, and opposed anything smacking of "socialized" medicine—yet insisted that Congress come up with something regardless. "There will be no excuse for inaction," he proclaimed.[33] Like every other Democrat in Washington, he wanted to eat his cake and have it too, which is why Congress wound up with neither.

What had happened, simply enough, was that an entire form of politics had collapsed, one based on individualism, deal making, and buck passing. In its place, a new system arose, one that was far more ideological and partisan.

The guiding light behind this transition was, of course, Newt Gingrich, the Republican congressman from Cobb County, Georgia, a white, middle-class, heavily right-wing enclave outside Atlanta. Although Cobb County, according to *Common Cause Magazine*, received more federal money in 1992 than all but two other suburban districts, it didn't stop its man in Congress from attacking welfare and federal giveaways.[34] Gingrich had made his name in the House as a ferocious GOP attack dog, but once the '94 campaign got under way, he came up with a stroke of real genius. This was the "Contract with America." Although the press dismissed it as strategic blunder, the contract turned out to be remarkable not only because it spelled out the Republicans' aims clearly for all to see, but because it also forced the individual candidates to line up behind it. Following their victory, the Republicans, the party of rugged individualism and anticollectivism, thus wound up with something on Capitol Hill that had always escaped the Democrats—a collectivized mass. Voters had something they could line up behind as well. Instead of seeing themselves as atomized particles, voters—at least those who had hopped on the GOP bandwagon—could see themselves as part of a national movement.

The result was a political steamroller united both at the top and at the base. Congress had not seen anything quite like it in decades. Yet, although it may have been wishful thinking, within a couple of months journalists in Washington were already noticing signs of fragmentation around the edges. In late February, for instance, farm-belt Republicans in the Senate vetoed a House proposal to eliminate federal food stamps, while Republicans from the Northwest rose up against another GOP proposal to privatize the Bonneville Power Administration. "I normally agree with Scott Klug [a leading GOP budget cutter] on nine out of ten of his suggestions," declared one beleaguered Republican from Washington State—the exception, of course, being when he proposed cutting subsidies for her own district.[35] More such mutinies would likely erupt as additional sacred cows were gored. Still and all, Gingrich's achievement was not inconsiderable. If only for the moment, he had taken a fractured system and made it work. Where the House had previously taken a second seat to the Senate, he had helped to elevate it to number one. Indeed, for a time, the House seemed to be overshadowing the presidency as well, much as the House of Commons had eventually overshadowed the throne and the House of Lords. For the historically conscious, perhaps the most interesting moment came in early March when seventy-odd Republican House freshmen marched across the Capitol to the Senate as the Balanced Budget Amendment was coming to a vote. They were turned away at the door, but for a moment it seemed almost as if Cromwell's Ironsides had returned to chase the lords from their nest.[36]

Of course, all this institutional upheaval was in the service of the most right-wing program since the Republican landslide of 1946 made a ruin of Truman's first term. Where Evelyn Waugh had once complained that although conservative politicians talked big, he had never met one who would truly turn back the clock, he never met Newt Gingrich, who really *did* believe in switching the spool of history into reverse. America, Gingrich argued, is the story of paradise lost. "Until the mid-1960s," he said in one postelection interview, "there was an explicit long-term commitment to creating character. It was the work ethic. It was honesty, right and wrong. It was not harming others. It was vigilance in the defense of liberty." But then came the fall in the form of what he called the sixties' "counter-culture . . . a culture which is extraordinarily tolerant of violence, with a situation-ethics morality, in which your immediate concern about your personal needs outweighs any obligation to others."[37] Reviewing a televised history course that Gingrich teaches, Garry Wills pointed out in March 1995 that Gingrich was that strangest of phenomena, a professional historian who believes a historian's job is not to uncover the truth but to promote certain myths:

> Gingrich unabashedly states that the aim of history courses is to inculcate values, the values embodied in ancient myths—in Washington praying at Valley Forge, or Patrick Henry saying, "Give me liberty or give me death," or Nathan Hale saying, "I regret that I have but one life to lose for my country." Gingrich does not advert to the fact that none of those things,

in all likelihood, ever occurred—but one senses that he would not care if this were pointed out to him. It is the moral that matters, not the evidence.[38]

The Gingrich revolution was at its core yet another American flight from reality, from modernity, a retreat into a gauzy past in which children obeyed their parents, husbands and wives never divorced, homosexuality was closeted, and black people were compliant and untroublesome.

This is a past that never was, which is why Gingrich's effort to recapture it was doubly doomed. The Contract with America was thus incoherent. Its promise to eliminate the deficit *and* reactivate plans for a Star Wars antimissile defense system—a hideously expensive military boondoggle with no conceivable justification since the demise of the Soviet Union—was an affront to common sense. So was its promise to boost revenue while instituting a fifty-percent cut in capital gains taxes. Where the contract's proposal to reduce the number of legislative committees might be seen as a way of enhancing accountability on Capitol Hill, the call for a line-item veto was the opposite. By providing the executive branch with a fine instrument with which to punish its legislative enemies and control dissent, it would result in a massive power shift from Congress to the presidency, with the result that it would no longer matter very much whether the legislature was more accountable or not.

Gingrich assembled the contract together with Dick Armey, the Texas Republican who would subsequently become House majority leader, and GOP pollster Frank Luntz and then presented it to Republican candidates for their approval.[39] This was novel by American standards, but it was still a far cry from what a modern party does, which is to gather its members in a single room and jointly hammer out a workable program. If Gingrich and Armey had done that, some GOP backbencher would undoubtedly have stood up to point out the idiocy of promising to bring back Star Wars and cut the deficit at the same time, whereupon the members would have been forced to fight it on the spot. As it was, however, such programmatic inconsistencies went unacknowledged until after the elections, thereby ensuring that the Republicans would have to settle their differences on the House floor, where any resolution would be a good deal messier.

But the Gingrich revolution did prove one thing about the Madisonian system. Complaints that it is incapable of concerted action are not strictly accurate. It *is* capable of concerted action—when moving in reverse. Congress was beside itself with fear when Clinton tried to advance into new territory with the creation of a national health plan. Institutionally, though, it seemed much more sure of itself as it rallied to Gingrich's call to cut welfare, eliminate school lunch programs, and expand the death penalty, all of which involved moving backward in time rather than forward. If America is a deeply conservative country, as Gingrich never tired of repeating, then it is because the Ancient Constitution is a deeply conservative concept. It is built around the idea that society must maintain an unbroken bridge with the past rather than cutting its ties and striking off in the direction of something bold and new. As presently constituted, America grows nervous when straying too far from its roots, which is why after a period of experimentation it feels compelled to tuck its tail between its legs and hurry on home. The Clinton administration was incompetent and confused from the start, but even its brief half-stab at progress was enough to send the constitutional system into a panic. All those Republican House freshmen in early 1995 who could be seen sporting copies of the Federalist Papers were not all that different from Iranian mullahs waving copies of the Koran. At a time when the world was changing all around them, their only response was to close their eyes, fold their hands, and trust in the wisdom of the patriarchs.

THE END IS NIGH (WE HOPE)

IT'S THE YEAR 2020, and the state of California has all the troubles of Job that it had in the 1990s, only more so. It is more ill-governed than ever before, its crumbling highway system more overloaded, and, with a minority population nearing thirty percent, ever more racked by racial conflict.[1] Even the mudslides are worse due to lax enforcement of regulations against overbuilding. The financially strapped government in Washington, which seems to lose a few points off its collective IQ with each passing year, is too mired in difficulties of its own to be of any assistance. Representatives from the lily-white Rocky Mountain states, the last bastion of rugged individualism, regard California with the same baleful skepticism once reserved for New York. They love lecturing Californians about all the mistakes they've made along the way, about their overly liberal welfare policies, their overly powerful labor unions, or their too big cities. California, they say, should stop complaining and feeling sorry for itself. It has too many Asians in San Francisco, too many blacks and Mexicans in L.A. and San Diego, too many liberals, tree huggers, sun worshipers, and assorted other cultists in between. If its heart isn't in the United States, say the Montanans, Wyomingites, and Dakotans—all 3.3 million of them[2]—it should get its ass out.

Remarkably, California resolves to do just that. As the breach with Washington grows, much of the state's ire settles on the U.S. Senate, as irresponsible and unrepresentative a body in the twenty-first century as it was in the nineteenth or twentieth. California has forty-eight million people by this point, nearly twice as many as Texas, its nearest rival. Yet it has the same two seats as Vermont or Wyoming, which are tied for last place with just 658,000 people each.[3] One rancher in Wyoming, in other words, has seventy-three times the clout in the Senate as a typical Californian threading his way through traffic. And since the Senate also approves treaties and advises and consents on presidential appointments, including those in the judiciary, that means that Wyomingites enjoy disproportionate clout in these other two branches as well. This is worse than in the 1990s, when the ratio between the most and least populous state was sixty-six to one, and far, far worse than in the early days of the Republic when it was a mere ten to one (six to one, if slaves were ignored). Yet if the situation was annoying in the 1790s, by now it is intolerable. As an increasingly influential group of California-Firsters points out, no other country puts up with such legislative discrepancies. Either they've revamped their upper houses to make them more representative or, as in the case of Britain, they've pared their powers nearly to zero. Yet the United States has done neither, with the result that the still-formidable U.S. Senate is about as representative as the British House of Commons during the heyday of the rotten-borough system in the late eighteenth century.

With that, California issues an ultimatum. No taxation, the state legislature declares, without equal representation. Either Washington reforms the Senate in accord with the principle of one person–one vote, or California leaves. With a 750-mile coastline, ample cultural links throughout the Pacific Rim, and some of the best deepwater ports in the world, the top honchos in Sacramento figure the state has more than enough resources to make it on its own. Korea, Japan, and Singapore have done more with less, so why not California? The choice, they figure, is Washington's. If it changes, California will stay. If not, it will go. . . .

Not only is the American constitutional system pre-utilitarian and pre-Darwinian (as Woodrow Wilson argued), it is also pre-Gödelian. Kurt Gödel, of course, was the Austrian-Jewish mathematician who developed his famous incompleteness theorem at the University of Vienna in 1931. Shorn of its abstruse terminology, the theorem boils down to the proposition that every system of logic contains a contradiction that its laws are unable to resolve. No matter how elaborate or complete, each contains a loose thread that, if pulled hard enough, will cause the entire system to unravel. An example in the system of logic that we call everyday common sense is the famous Cretan Paradox, which declares: all Cretans are liars, saith the Cretan. It was the subject of a wonderful *Star Trek* episode in which Captain Kirk adopts the role of the Cretan in order to disable a relentlessly logical android bent on holding him and his crew captive. Everything I say is a lie, Kirk declares. To which the android replies: "You say you are lying, but if everything you say is a lie, then you are telling the truth. But you cannot tell the truth because everything you say is a lie"—and so on and so forth until smoke starts streaming from the robot's ears.[4]

In a sense, the Constitution is a self-contained, self-reinforcing system of logic as well, what Sidney George Fisher called a "finality" unto itself and Robert Bork, quoting the Catholic writer Hilaire Belloc, described as a "complete and self-supporting scheme." If so, then Article V, the amending clause, is its dangling thread, as Gödel, something of a student of the U.S. Constitution himself, was well aware.[5]

California's demand for reform of the U.S. Senate would plunge the system into the same sort of quandary as that confronting the android in *Star Trek*. The federal government would have basically three choices, each more unpalatable than the last. Washington, for instance, could respond to the California ultimatum simply by saying good-bye and good riddance. If California wishes to depart the Union, it might declare, then the rest of the country is better off without it. But if California were to go, Texas, New York, and any number of the other large states would undoubtedly follow. They would be no more inclined to put up with such an inequitable system in the Senate than their cousin out west, particularly since California had just shown that the system could be successfully defied. This would leave the United States as a scattered archipelago of underpopulated states stretching from Maine and New Hampshire to Idaho, Nevada, and maybe Alaska—hardly a viable configuration for a modern nation-state.

As an alternative, Washington could burst into a collective chorus of the "Battle Hymn of the Republic," airlift troops to Sacramento, and order California to stay put or suffer the consequences. Militarily, there is no question it would succeed, although there is no doubt that in terms of public relations it would be disastrous. Rather than suppressing a slaveholders' revolt, the case in 1861–65, the federal government would be using overwhelming force to crush a revolt in defense of equal representation, an idea that most of the rest of the world regards as a basic axiom of political democracy. The United States would look brutal and obdurate, much as Pakistan did when it tried to stop Bangladesh from going its own way in 1971. Since world opinion is nothing to be sneezed at these days, Washington would likely have to back down as well.

The third option—to reform the Senate along more democratic lines—would seem to be the most civilized. But it would also be unconstitutional. The language in Article V is clear and unequivocal. After outlining how the Constitution may be amended, it concludes with the proviso that, notwithstanding any of the above, "no State, without its consent, shall be deprived of its equal suffrage in the Senate." Where two-thirds of each house of Congress plus three-fourths of the states are enough to repeal the Bill of Rights, they are not enough to reform the Senate according to the principle of one person–one vote. A constitutional convention would not be able to touch it as well. Rather, the consent of all *fifty* states would be required. Considering how much the demographic microstates would have to lose in such an eventuality, the chances of a reform like this passing are something on the order of finding a decent bagel in Missoula, Montana. For all intents and purposes, the barrier would be insurmountable. As long as Wyoming, the Dakotas, et al. stick to their guns, they would each have two senators, same as California or New York, in perpetuity. There would be no way to reform the unreformable, no way to change the single most immutable element in the entire Madisonian Constitution.

Thus, the constitutional system would find itself caught in an impossible situation—damned if it did and damned if it didn't. It couldn't say good-bye to California, couldn't rein it in, and couldn't take steps to satisfy its concerns. Not unlike the *Star Trek* android, it would find itself babbling ever more incoherently until smoke poured out its ears and it lapsed into a coma.

On the other hand, it is possible to conceive of a fourth alternative. Imagine that a group of top representatives are sitting around one evening when the stunning news arrives from California. They race over to the White House for a high-level huddle with the president, his press secretary, pollster, and chief of staff, plus Chief Justice Clarence Thomas and a few other establishment luminaries. After a few minutes of discussion, the group realizes that its options are zero and that there is no way out of the bind—no way that the federal government can agree to California's ultimatum and no way that it cannot. After a few moments of uncomfortable silence, the Speaker of the House raises his hand. "I wonder," he says, "if anyone here remembers *Federalist* No. 40." An unusually blank expression settles over the president's face. "I meant to read it in college," he says, "but was up to my ears in elections for the prom committee and never got around to it."

"In that case," the Speaker begins, "let me tell you what it says. It's the one in which Madison grapples with the problem of how to reconcile the provision in Article VII, which said the proposed new constitution would go into effect when ratified by nine out of the thirteen states, with the provision in the Articles of Confederation that said that any constitutional change must be approved by all thirteen."

"Yes?" the president asks politely.

"Well, it was a ticklish situation because the Articles were still the law of the land, which meant that the problem before Madison was how to justify *violating* the old constitution in order to put a new one in its place." The Speaker fishes out a dog-eared copy he just happened to be carrying in his briefcase and begins leafing through. "Oh, yes, here it is. After mulling the question over, Madison concludes that the idea of 'subjecting the fate of twelve States to the perverseness or corruption of a thirteenth' was an 'absurdity,' as 'every citizen who has felt for the wounded honor and prosperity of his country' well knows."

"I don't see where this is leading."

"The parallel is obvious. Madison was trapped, you see, by a law that might have made a modicum of sense when it was adopted but that made no sense years later even though it was still in effect. What's more relevant, though, is how he made his escape. Since the law requiring unanimous approval was an absurdity, he said, the law was null and void. Here are Madison's exact words: 'As this objection, therefore, has been in a manner waived by those who have criticized the powers of the convention, I dismiss it without further observation.' Everyone knew the provision was idiotic, so Madison simply waved it away, just like that."

The Speaker notices that everyone is staring at him with curious expressions.

"The point," he resumes nervously, "the point is that we can do the same. If Madison could dismiss the unanimous-consent provision with a wave of his hand, so can we. We're trapped by a constitutional provision that says that a certain constitutional change must be approved by all fifty states, in effect, which is as absurd today as it was in the days of the Founders. Law and logic are at odds, and since we can't repeal logic, we'll have to repeal the law."

"But you would have no authority," the president interjects.

"Neither did Madison."

"You would be acting illegally."

"So were the Founders, at least according to the Articles of Confederation, although I should add that when the Constitution was declared a year later to have been ratified under the terms of Article VII—the *new* Article VII, that is—the result, essentially, was to repeal the old law according to the provisions of the new one, thereby rendering their violation of the law null and void. It's as if a bank robber had succeeded in passing a law retroactively legalizing holdups."

"The Founders—criminals?" sputters the chief justice. "How absurd!"

The president, worried about what the crisis will do to his approval rating, rolls his eyes and calls on his pollster. The Speaker, seeing that there is no point in arguing any further, slips out the door and heads over to his office on the Hill. He rounds up a few of his colleagues from the House majority and then, just as the sun begins rising behind the Washington Monument, puts the finishing touches on the most important press release of his career. In a few hours, it declares, members of the House will begin debating a historic resolution repealing the equal state representation provision in Article V as the first step toward a thorough reorganization of American government. Because repeal would drastically alter the power both of the Senate and the states, the part of the amending clause requiring approval by two-thirds of the Senate and three-fourths of the states will not be applied. Instead, the House alone will vote the resolution up or down on the basis of a simple majority. Assuming it passes, the announcement continues, the Constitution will be considered to have been amended. Since the House will be acting in the name of the American people, the members will then take the extraordinary step of submitting to a special election within three weeks' time. If the people approve of what the House has done, they can vote the members who approved the amendment back into office. If they disapprove, they can vote them out and leave it to a new crop of representatives to sort out the mess.

At the press conference a few hours later, a reporter raises his hand and asks if it isn't all more than a little, well, unconstitutional. This is the one question the Speaker has been dreading. After all, he took an oath to preserve and protect the Constitution, and while it's one thing to change it through unprecedented means, it's quite another actually to violate it. He hesitates, trying to come up with an appropriate response, when one of the younger members steps up to the mike.

"Absolutely not," she begins. "We don't think it's unconstitutional at all. The reason is that the Constitution, we believe, contains two amending clauses. One is Article V, which, as everyone knows, is slow and difficult and, in this case, absolutely useless. But we believe there is another amending clause that is superior, and that's the Preamble. In declaring that 'we the people' are ordaining and establishing this constitution and everything in it, the Preamble says that we are doing so for a certain purpose, which is to establish justice, insure domestic tranquility, form a more perfect union, and so on. Implicit in this is the right of the people to change anything in the Constitution that runs counter to that purpose. Article V is no exception. We think it is painfully obvious that the idea that California and Wyoming should have the same two votes in the Senate is unjust, that it is not promoting domestic tranquility, and that if allowed to stand, it will end up blowing the Union to smithereens. We believe that the Article V amending clause is in violation of the Preamble. Therefore, we the people have a right in our collective capacity to change it. Rather than working through Article V, we have a perfect right to go around it.

If the people are sovereign, then the people cannot be constrained by any provision that 'we the people' made ourselves."

This no doubt sounds farfetched, but in fact it's not completely implausible as a way out of the nation's constitutional bind.[6] Clearly, some sort of extraconstitutional solution would be required to solve the problem of Article V, and clearly the House is the only institution with anything approaching the moral authority to do it. The Senate couldn't, obviously. Nor, given that their authority is under the Constitution rather than over it, could the courts. While the president conceivably could take it into his hands to excise a troublesome line in the Constitution, he would be assuming extraconstitutional powers in doing so, which would be disastrous for democracy. The House, on the other hand, could excise it in the name of popular sovereignty. By calling a special election, it would underscore that it was not engaging in a crude power play but was acting in behalf of the democratic majority—although in the event of a sufficiently loud roar of approval from the populace, it would perhaps not have to submit to an election for several years.

If voters did give the thumbs-up to the House's democratic coup d'état, the results would be the most far-reaching political transformation in America since the Constitution was itself adopted in 1787–88. Article V's equal suffrage clause is the keystone of the arch; precious little of the Constitution would be left standing once it was removed. By repealing the unrepealable, the House would establish its authority not only over the Constitution, but over everything else *under* the Constitution as well. In effect, it would become the new American parliament, which is essentially what Sidney George Fisher was calling on it to become in 1862. Since it could change the Constitution at a stroke, it could abolish the Senate or reduce it to a largely ceremonial body à la the House of Lords. As the new center of gravity in Washington, it would have little choice but to reduce the president to semi-figurehead status along the line of the German presidency or the Austrian. By overthrowing the old immutable Constitution, it would effectively rob the judiciary of much of its power, just as Herbert Croly had predicted in 1909. The Supreme Court, conceivably, could still cite the Constitution in overturning an act of Congress. But since the House could now change the Constitution at a stroke, such a ruling would be meaningless. In effect, the House would become a new super–supreme court since it would now have the power to override anything the Supreme Court might decide.

The House would also be supreme over itself, which is to say it could reorganize itself on whatever basis it wished. It could increase its membership or reduce it, retain the present system of "first past the post" voting, in which the top vote-getter in any given district is the winner, or adopt a system of proportional representation, in which seats are doled out on the basis of each party's share of the national tally. Rather than serving as part of the government, the House would be the whole show, which means that in addition to passing legislation, it would have the job of executing it. To do so, it would no doubt wish to elect some kind of executive committee to take care of day-to-day governance—in other words, a cabinet, as it's commonly known, with a prime minister at its head.

In a sense, the United States would wind up with something it never had before: a government. Rather than an endless soccer game in which power is always in motion, total authority would, for the first time, rest with a single institution. So would total responsibility, meaning that the House would be answerable for each and every step the new government might take, large or small. No longer would there be endless opportunities for buck passing among the three branches for the simple reason that the branches would no longer exist, at least not as rival power centers. The fact that the House's coup d'état would be technically illegal would make it all the better by underscoring the power of the people to make or break the law. It would demonstrate that the people, by virtue of their sovereignty, are incapable of behaving illegally since it is now the people, and not some long-ago race of giants known as the Founders, who determine what the law says.

The results would not only be politically and legally revolutionary, but intellectually as well. Not just the Constitution would be toppled, but so would checks and balances, separation of powers, and the deeply inculcated habit of deferring to the authority of a group of eighteenth-century Country gentlemen. Instead of relying on a previous generation's judgment and analysis, the people would have no choice than to rely on their own. The old notion that people were wiser and more farsighted in the eighteenth century than they are today would, of necessity, be reversed. So would the old idea that reform involved a process of cleansing, purification, and a return to some original ideal. Instead of a return to the old, the people, by virtue of having cut their ties to the past, would now understand reform as a search for something new. The traditional American distrust of political power, rooted in the ideology of the eighteenth-century Country opposition, would undoubtedly disappear as well. When power is wielded by others—judges in long black robes, politicians in distant Washington, and so on—it's scary. But when wielded by the people themselves, in as simple and unencumbered a fashion as possible, it is simply a tool for getting things done. Rather than dispersing power, the people would have reason to see that it was concentrated in their own hands. Rather than an object of fascination and fear, it would become an object of utility.

Other changes would be unleashed as well. The creation of a more flexible kind of government would result in a different kind of politics, one that was more free-ranging and less constrained by deference to the past. Instead of suffering under the terrible Republican-Democratic duopoly as they have since the mid-nineteenth century—a record of political stagnation without parallel in virtually any other country—Americans would almost surely want to organize new parties, many of which would likely have a realistic shot at wielding real power in a newly reconstituted House of Representatives. If the House were to move to proportional representation, it would open the door even further—to perhaps five or six major parties as in Germany or maybe even a dozen as in Israel. Political power, conceivably, might still remain in the hands of politicians determined that business in the

United States still be done the old way as much as possible. But given the pent-up desire for change in America, a desire that has been building for decades and decades as politics have become more degraded and social problems more acute, it would more likely be in the hands of people willing to think big and engage in precisely the kinds of broad schemes and projects that Madison disapproved of in the 1780s.

Indeed, perhaps the most important thing about fundamental change of this sort would be change itself. In a country in which the very idea of freedom rests on the denial of constitutional change, people have a dim idea of what political change even means. As David Calleo has pointed out, the United States has never known anything like the clean sweep of the Meiji Restoration in Japan or the 1832 revolution in government in Britain. When the Radical Republicans tried to remake the South from top to bottom, they were halted in their tracks after less than a decade and were then excoriated by generations of historians as tyrants and fanatics for so much as trying. Yet the rise of an all-powerful House would clear the way for precisely the sort of sweeping transformation that had previously been impossible. For the first time in their history, the American people would have an opportunity to turn their collective intelligence on the problem of government as a whole, not just as part of a plan developed by a group of merchants and planters in Philadelphia two centuries earlier. Freed of its eighteenth-century constraints, the government could reach into every last corner of society, leaving no stone unturned. It could reform federalism, cut back on states' rights, or, for that matter, break them up into *départements* the way the Jacobins broke up the old French provinces, which was Hamilton's idea in the 1790s. The ultimate result is, of course, unknown. But the important thing is that it would be up to the people as a whole to decide, not the states or municipalities. Hopefully, the days when an affluent suburb could raid its neighbors for jobs and businesses while barring poor people at the door would be at an end. Rather than separate powers able to thumb their noses at the rest of society at will, they would be tamed and subservient. Rather than a political landscape pockmarked with more local potentates than the Holy Roman Empire, the new House would undoubtedly want to create a society that was fairer, more uniform and consistent, more democratic—to do to the United States, as David Calleo pointed out, what Richelieu and Colbert had done to seventeenth-century France.

Inevitably, given the current state of politics, any talk of equalizing political conditions from one end of society to the other conjures up images of an Aldous Huxley–style dystopia in which Americans wear the same clothes, live in the same homes, and eat the same foods. This is ironic since it is precisely the semicontrolled anarchy of the U.S. Constitution that has resulted in unprecedented homogeneity, at least for the suburban middle class, across the length and breadth of the land. Traveling cross-country, one sees the same subdivisions, fast-food joints, and shopping malls in a California suburb as in Paramus, New Jersey. Real popular sovereignty would allow Americans to decide what aspects at the community level they want to be the same (railroad stations, for example, or schools) and which ones they want to be different.

The new order would also be more democratic. Where the malapportioned U.S. Senate was a hot topic in the late nineteenth century, it has been all but forgotten by the late twentieth. Yet the disparities are worse than ever. Nine states account for more than half the total U.S. population, yet they account for less than twenty percent of the Senate vote. By the same token, a Senate majority can be gotten from twenty-six states representing less than one American in five. Twenty-one states, representing as little as one citizen in nine, are enough to filibuster any piece of legislation to death, while thirteen states, representing as little as 4.5 percent of the population, are enough to stop a constitutional amendment in its tracks. This is a minority veto run amok. In other respects, the arrangement is deeply unfair as well. Because they are predominantly rural, the twenty-six smallest states have fewer blacks (in fact, about half the national average), fewer Asians, fewer gays, and, of course, fewer urban dwellers in general.[7]

Violations of one person–one vote have been barred at the state or municipal level ever since *Baker v. Carr* in 1962. Yet they are, for the moment, beyond challenge at the federal level.

Disparities like these are not just unfair—they are stupid and lazy. No comparable country puts up with anything like them, yet Americans seem oblivious. On the rare occasion when they do think about them, New Yorkers, Californians, et al. seem to just shrug. Commenting on how the Senate Republican minority had filibustered Clinton's economic-stimulus package in April 1993, the journalist Sidney Blumenthal observed matter-of-factly in the *New Yorker:*

> The Senate, of course, was designed to be unrepresentative; it incorporates the principle of the equality of states, not the equality of citizens. The forty-three Republicans do not represent forty-three percent of the people. Because they are clustered in the smaller states, the Senate Republicans represent less than a third of the population.[8]

That little phrase "of course" sums up all that is fatalistic and unthinking in the American character, as presently constituted, that is. It represents uncritical obedience to the dictates of the Founders—to the notion that if the framers *wanted* the Senate to be unrepresentative, that's the way it shall be forevermore. A conscious decision, on the other hand, to abolish such disparities would mean the opposite. It would signal a determination to think through the problems of government ourselves, to take responsibility for where society is heading, and to put an end to drift and gridlock.

Needless to say, taking control of one's destiny can also be dangerous. Just as there is nothing to stop a young person who gets his own apartment and credit card from behaving irresponsibly, there is nothing to stop a nation either. By abolishing separation of powers and checks and balances, the House would liberate itself from judicial review. Even if the Bill of Rights were to remain in place, citizens would have no assurance that the House would abide by its provisions other than its own pledge to do so. Yet what the House promises one day, it can unpromise the next; it could thus abolish free speech and a free press at a stroke, with little more than a yelp of protest from the courts. The only thing that could stop them would be the people themselves, who would recognize that real majority rule is impossible outside of a framework of free and vigorous criticism and debate. The people would want to preserve democracy not for the sake of various beleaguered minorities, the justification presently cited by the ACLU, but for the sake of the majority, namely, its own. A demos that allowed democracy to be squashed would be a demos no longer, merely a collection of atomized prisoners of the status quo.

For a people who like their guarantees in writing, this may not sound like much. Yet the development of a modern, mass democratic consciousness, of a modern democratic *movement*, is the only assurance that democracy in the United States can even survive. Americans must stop thinking of democracy as a legacy of the Founders and a gift of the gods, something that allows millions of voices to cry, "me! me! me!," while politicians and judges divide up the spoils according to some time-honored formula. Rather, they'll have to think of it as an intellectual framework that *they* create and continuously update, one that allows them to tackle the problems of the modern world not as individuals but as a society. If democracy is to survive, it must grow. And if it is to grow, it must detach itself from pre-democratic eighteenth-century norms and take its place in the modern world.

On the other hand, a young person who does not leave home will be stuck in a stage of attenuated adolescence forever. The same thing is true for Americans as a whole if they fail to emancipate themselves from dependence on a two-century-old legacy. "We're still Jefferson's children," Ronald Reagan once declared in a moment of ersatz piety.[9] And as long as they continue to worship at the shrine of the Founders, Americans will remain in that childlike state indefinitely.

The alternative to taking responsibility and assuming risk is accepting the certainty of decline. There are any number of alternatives that one could imagine to the scenario of a democratic clean sweep sketched out above, none of them very pleasant. Rather than focusing their ire on the federal government, it's all too possible that Californians (not to mention Texans, New Yorkers, Pennsylvanians, etc.) might decide that it is more satisfying to fight among themselves along racial or geographic lines. The vast unfairness of the present arrangement in Washington might all too easily become lost in the mass of petty politics that is life in America, in which a scandal on the local school board often looms larger than the scandalous inequality of the U.S. Senate. Fragmentation, after all, is what has allowed the system to survive the last two centuries, and it may be what allows it to limp along for two centuries more. Not unlike the British, Americans may opt for a variation on the theme of muddling through, in which the devil you know (complacency) is to be preferred over the one you don't (change). Small adjustments may be instituted to keep California from boiling over—a bit of military pork here, a federal boondoggle there, a tacit understanding that even if it is to have only two votes in the Senate, its wishes nonetheless will be accorded extra weight. Perhaps Congress will approve the division of the state into three parts so that residents will wind up electing six senators rather than the present two. It would not eliminate the disparities but would at least make them more tolerable. All the old problems would remain—gridlock, the absence of a coherent, systematic policy to deal with social problems, and so on—yet at least it would keep the ship of state from going to pieces when it is still miles from shore.

On the other hand, it would also mean continued long-term decline, and Americans do not seem to be the sort of people to put up with long-term decline. They are too volatile, too imbued with a sense of their own greatness, too angry with themselves and with each other. Checks and balances may persist in Washington, but, if so, political tension will undoubtedly rise to even more dangerous levels. For those who know their German history, there is already a whiff of Weimar in the air. Just as the prewar German constitution was pulled apart by unresolved tension between the executive and legislative branches, the American system seems to be coming apart in a not-dissimilar way as well. True, the United States is not fragmented among a dozen or so political parties as Weimar was. Rather, thanks to the attenuated two-party system, it is fragmented among some 535 representatives and senators, each of whom recognizes no authority but his or her own. While Newt Gingrich has succeeded in imposing a remarkable degree of discipline on this motley crew, it is at the cost of increasing fragmentation below—between blacks and whites, the federal government and the states, the cities and suburbs, and so forth. H. Ross Perot's bizarre 1992 presidential bid is meanwhile an illustration of the authoritarian potential that has long been latent in the executive branch. "Presidential power is the power to persuade," political scientist Richard Neustadt once proclaimed.[10] But what happens if an H. Ross Perot transforms that power into the power to give orders and have Congress snap to attention?

The problem with the Constitution as it has developed over two centuries is that rather than engaging in a fundamental reordering, Americans have tried to democratize a predemocratic structure. As originally conceived, only one ruling institution—the House—was to be popularly elected and even then only by a fraction of what we now regard as the proper electorate (i.e., only, for the most part, by property-owning white males). The other ruling institutions—the Senate, the presidency, and the courts—were to be only indirectly chosen. But then Andrew Johnson helped democratize the presidency, the Seventeenth Amendment democratized the upper chamber to a degree by providing for the direct election of senators, and the furious confirmation battles over Robert Bork and Clarence Thomas have opened up the judiciary to an unprecedented level of popular pressure and inspection as well. The effect of separation of powers under such conditions has been to divide popular democracy against itself in such a way as to send the collective temperature shooting up to the boiling point. The electorate, as a consequence, is locked in a desperate internal struggle, which, as long as Madisonian checks and balances remain in effect, can never end. The results are tortuous, yet ultimately only two outcomes are possible. Either the body politic will keel over from exhaustion or it will explode.

Yet the more tension builds up, the more fragmented the national intellect seems to become and the less people seem to have an idea of the constitutional issues at stake. A century ago, when a growing number of critics were snapping at the Constitution's heels, Constitution worship could at least be justified on the grounds that the country's performance as a whole was so spectacular that something about the arrangement had to be proper and right. There was just no arguing with success. As James Russell Lowell observed shortly after the Constitution's first centennial:

> After our Constitution got fairly into working order it really seemed as if we had invented a machine that would go of itself, and this begot a faith in our luck which even the civil war itself but momentarily disturbed. Circumstances continued favorable, and our prosperity went on increasing. I admire the splendid complacency of my countrymen, and find something exhilarating and inspiring in it. We are a nation which *struck ile*, but we are also a nation that is sure the well will never run dry.[11]

Now consider a passing remark made by Robert M. Solow, the Nobel Prize–winning economist at MIT, in the course of a book review in the *New Republic* in August 1994:

> When Europeans express to me their astonishment at the inconsistencies and the hesitations of American economic policy, I have to remind them that our political system is very different from what they are used to. We have no party discipline. A president, even if he has a formal majority in Congress, cannot count on getting his way. In a very large and federally organized system like ours, legislators have distinct and urgent regional and industrial interests to pursue, in order to keep their own voters happy. So a president is very often in a position of bargaining with members of his own party. . . . We ask for "chaos" and we get it.[12]

Where Lowell saw the Constitution as something sleek and powerful, Solow, a century later, sees it as a kind of gridlock machine, a device for the perpetuation of political chaos. Optimism has given way to pessimism, and what one generation saw as a blessing is now seen as a burden or maybe even a curse. Yet what has *not* changed is the sense that, come what may, there is little to be done to alter the national fate. Where Lowell claimed to be inspired by the country's splendid complacency, Solow can only note that, having chosen chaos, the nation must live with its decision.

Needless to say, America did not choose chaos or anything else for that matter. Given that only about five percent of the U.S. population actually cast ballots for delegates to the various state ratifying conventions between 1787 and 1790, the great majority were not consulted at all about the Constitution that was being made in their name.[13] Even among white males, only a small minority participated in the ratification process. Since then, no Americans have been able to vote on the Constitution as a whole at all, either directly via a referendum or through their representatives in Congress. Although a majority might still vote for the Constitution were a referendum held today, a constitution submitted to the people to be voted up or down would automatically be a very different constitution than the one we have today, which does not even recognize the possibility.

Rather, what the people have been presented with since ratification is a fait accompli, one they have so far accepted without protest. Instead of choosing chaos, they've submitted to it, which is a very different thing. Where Americans have fought wars, gone on strike, demonstrated against Vietnam, and engaged in a thousand other causes and protests over the years, what they have never done is to take charge of their society as a whole. Rather, they've elected to drift. As Solow indicates, chaos has been the result, chaos, moreover, which can only deepen the longer this popular abdication of responsibility persists.

On April 19, 1995, the contradictions deep within America's constitutional structure exploded all too literally when a massive bomb tore through an eight-story federal office building in downtown Oklahoma City, killing 169 people. Within days, attention zeroed in on the burgeoning militia movement as the ideological source from which the accused bomber, a Desert Storm veteran named Timothy McVeigh, had apparently imbibed many of his political ideas. Images flashed around the globe of thousands of weekend Rambos parading about with Chinese- and Russian-made automatic rifles, camouflage uniforms stretched tight over their middle-aged paunches. The militia members looked like standard, middle-American gun nuts yet were actually something more interesting—militant constitutional fundamentalists. They were motivated not so much by love of weaponry as devotion to the eighteenth-century Country principle embodied in the Second Amendment that an armed populace is the surest check on the power of tyrannical government—a view which, whatever liberals might believe, is closer to the thinking of the Founders than the modern position of the ACLU.[14] As Garry Wills noted: "The modern militia movement, far from thinking itself outside the law, believes it is the critical force making for a restoration of the Constitution."[15] The militia members love the Constitution because they loathe the federal government. They were determined, consequently, to force Washington to withdraw to its old Madisonian boundaries, if necessary through force of arms.

The militias are the most dramatic symptom yet of the growing American retreat from the problems and uncertainties of the late twentieth century to a Jeffersonian never-never land of the early nineteenth. As an international phenomenon, the militia movement is *sui generis*. Other countries have their skinheads and neo-Nazis, yet none, at least in the advanced industrial world, has thousands of armed, Constitution-waving traditionalists demanding a return to ancient rights and liberties. Indeed, in order to come up with anything comparable, it is necessary to return once again to the by-now-familiar terrain of the seventeenth and eighteenth century, when English-speaking society was swept by another wave of what Walter Bagehot labeled "the documentary superstition." The fact that the document in question was the Holy Bible rather than a written constitution was inconsequential: the effects were very much the same. Like the Constitution, the Bible was seen both as divine writ and "the supreme law of the land" (to quote today's Article VI)—supreme not only religiously, but intellectually, morally, and every other way as well. The more political institutions fell, the more its authority rose, until it seemed, as Milton put it in 1642, that "all wisdom is enfolded" within its pages.[16]

The parallels between the "Bibliolatry" of Milton's day and the "Constitutionolatry" of ours are striking. English Bible mania reached a peak in the tumultuous decade of the 1640s, when political institutions were tumbling right and left and people needed something solid to grab on to—just as Americans seem to need something solid to hold on to today. The more unsettled conditions became, the more power and influence passed from bishops and professional theologians into the hands of half-educated "mechanic preachers" who held forth in alehouses and roamed through the ranks of Cromwell's New Model Army, firing up the troops with the glory of God. In the unsettled 1990s, similarly, influence seems to be passing from federal judges and law professors to homespun constitutional exegetes whose paranoid writings are now flooding the Internet and stirring up militia members in places like Idaho and Montana. In the mid-seventeenth century the Bible ceased to be a force for conservatism and order and became instead a revolutionary document filled with warnings about the impending downfall of wicked kings and corrupt priests. In the late twentieth, the Constitution is increasingly viewed, at least by the militias and like-minded groups, as a quasi-revolutionary document whose central message is that what the people giveth in the form of a limited grant of power to federal judges, bureaucrats, congressmen, et al., the people can just as easily taketh away. In the 1640s religious zealots regarded kings and bishops as products of the Fall and promised to sweep them all away; in the 1990s constitutional zealots regard the FBI, the IRS, and the Bureau of Alcohol, Tobacco, and Firearms as products of the fall from the Jeffersonian Eden of the early nineteenth century and promise to sweep them away as well.

The Puritan revolution disintegrated in the 1650s for a number of reasons, not least of which was the problem of interpretation. The trouble with the Bible was that it was a grab bag of books and lyrics cobbled together over centuries by various scribes and priests, "a huge bran-tub," to quote Christopher Hill, out of which any number of paradoxes and heresies might be drawn.[17] It could be used to support a doctrine of turning the other cheek to royal authority or one of militant resistance, to justify and defend economic inequality or (as modern liberation theologians argue) to demand an equalization of wealth and a leveling of incomes. After more than a decade of self-proclaimed messiahs parading naked through the streets while awaiting a sign from above, it began to dawn on Englishmen (not to mention Scots, Germans, Frenchmen, etc.) that the Bible could be used to justify anything, no matter how loony. As a result documentary superstition began crumbling under its own weight. In 1657 members of Parliament actually laughed out loud at a colleague who quoted the Bible at excessive length, something that ten years earlier would have been unthinkable. Following his restoration to the throne in 1660, the "Merrie Monarch," Charles II, cultivated an attitude of blithe indifference toward all things religious, while Anglican authorities taught that restorationist theology must be balanced, moderate, and in conformity with the new scientific doctrine of people like Isaac Newton. Instead of rearing up in indignation, a majority of Englishmen seemed to sigh with relief. By 1663 one observer noted that anti-Scripturism "grows . . . rife, and spreads fast," while in 1697 a character in a stage play, reminded that the Bible requires one to return good for evil, replied dryly: "That must be a mistake in the translation."[18]

The question some three and a half centuries later is whether U.S. Constitution mania is following a similar trajectory—whether, after one last mass upsurge, it too will keel over from exhaustion and be replaced by something more skeptical and sophisticated. Like the Bible, the Constitution is an ideological grab bag that can be used to prove nearly anything and its opposite—that racial segregation, for example, is permissible (*Plessy v. Ferguson*) or impermissible (*Brown v. Board of Education*), that federal prerogatives are sharply limited or essentially unconstrained, and so forth. Amendments have been piled on willy-nilly over the years, while theories of interpretations have been cooked up to serve the political needs of the day, all with little regard for internal consistency. Jeffersonian and Hamiltonian interpretations trotted out by highly trained legal specialists have been true to the extent that they reflect certain specific aspects of the Constitution but incorrect to the degree they purport to speak for the document as a whole. When it comes to something as fundamentally incoherent as the U.S. Constitution, all interpretations are false to the extent that they imply a consistency and intelligence that simply don't exist.

The *difference* between Bible and Constitution mania is simply the difference between the seventeenth century and the twentieth. In the 1640s people fell back on Holy Scripture because, in a prescientific age, they had no better tools at hand to understand the political earthquake that was going on all around them. If kings were falling and bishops were being chased from their pulpits, then it was clear that ancient biblical prophecies were at long last being fulfilled. Yet today we know that history is progressive rather than cyclical, that biblical prophecies are irrelevant, and that new thinking is required to fit new circumstances. This makes the long-established American tendency to fall back on the wisdom of the Founders in times of stress all the more inappropriate. In a high-tech age, there is simply no excuse for blind worship of a group of preindustrial *philosophes*. The longer it persists, the more disaster looms.

In fact, disaster is already upon us. The flip side of the growth of the militias is the deep depression that has settled over the rest of American politics generally. The authority of the Supreme Court has been undermined, perhaps permanently, by the bruising battles over Clarence Thomas and Robert Bork; the Clinton presidency may well be the weakest in the history of the republic while, after a brief burst of energy in early 1995 under Newt Gingrich, Congress seemed once more to be sinking into paralysis. Although few seemed to care, the most remarkable thing about the Republicans' Contract With America as it neared its first anniversary was how little of it had been passed. Of the document's original ten items, just two—a proposal to subject Congress to the same employment and environmental regulations as the other branches of government and a ban on unfunded federal mandates—had become law. Two others—a tax cut and a bid to rein in liability lawsuits by corporate stockholders—seemed likely to squeeze through the Senate in the fall of 1995, although in reduced form, while the six others were either moribund, hopelessly stalled, or completely dead.[19] These included such items as term limits, a balanced budget amendment, and a line item veto, all of which had been highly useful in motivating the troops yet none of which had ever made much sense. In more sophisticated countries, a majority party that accomplished less than forty percent of what it set out to do would be a laughing stock. Yet in America, as GOP presidential hopefuls began trooping through Iowa, the pundits seemed oblivious. Indeed, Gingrich appeared the most indifferent of all. Rather than analyzing why his legislative program had hopped the tracks, he seemed more interested in promoting his new best-seller, *To Renew America*, a compilation of the speaker's thoughts and ruminations in which he speculates on the possibilities of sex in outer space ("Imagine weightlessness and its effects and you will understand some of the attractions"[20]), calls for a real, live Jurassic Park ("It may not be at all impossible, you know"[21]), and advises that the solution to the drug problem is simply to lop off smugglers' heads ("I strongly favor a mandatory death penalty for entering our territory with a commercial quantity of illegal drugs"[22]).

Particularly revealing was the following gem about the future evolution of the American state:

While the Industrial Revolution herded people together into gigantic social institutions—big corporations, big unions, big government—the Information Revolution is breaking up these giants and leading us back to something that is—strangely enough—much like de Tocqueville's 1830s America.²³

In essence, Gingrich was proposing to break up the structure of American politics beyond even the present level of fragmentation and return it to its embryonic pre–Civil War state. His answer to the problem of a dysfunctional national government was to all but dismantle it. The 1830s, needless to say, were a time not of freedom but of biting constitutional dictatorship, a period in which Americans were prevented from acting nationally to institute internal improvements, create a pro-industrial economic policy, or tackle the growing slavery problem in any concerted, effective way. It was a decade in which abolitionists were dragged through the streets and murdered, antislavery materials were censored from the mails, free blacks were increasingly disenfranchised, and unfree ones were subject to ever more rigorous controls. Like the militias, Gingrich regards this period as a paradise lost, yet for a majority of Americans it would be the opposite—a kind of pre-democratic hell.

Amid all this gathering political nonsense and decay, it is thoroughly unsurprising that public dismay continues to sound new depths. By mid-1995, pollsters were discovering, for instance, that 58 percent of Americans believed that people like themselves had little say in what government did; that 59 percent could not think of a single elected official currently in office whom they admired; and that 79 percent said they trusted the federal government to do the right thing no more than some of the time.²⁴

Deep demoralization of this sort is dangerous for any democracy, especially one as old and sclerotic as the United States. Americans are hungry for change yet fearful of it. They are uncertain as to what change even means—whether it involves going forward or returning to some misty past. They are tyrannized by tradition in the form of an immutable constitution yet are unsure of how or even whether to rebel. The problem, ultimately, is a system of politics predicated on the belief that individual rights are at odds with majority rule and that the advancement of one is possible only if severe limits are placed on the other. It is an essentially pessimistic view shared by the ACLU, the militias, and virtually all others in between. Yet it is quite false. The most fundamental freedom of all is the freedom of the democratic majority to alter the society around it as it sees fit, without any traditions or constitutional restraints to get in its way. This is the freedom on which all other freedoms depend. There can be no assurance that the people will use this freedom wisely, just as there can be no assurance that they will make wise use of free speech or a free press. But there is total assurance that in the absence of such freedom, politics will atrophy, society will die, and civil liberties will go with it. This is the lesson of the great Soviet experiment, when an absence of political democracy reduced socialism to an empty shell, and it is the lesson of the American experiment as well.

Appendix

THE CONSTITUTION
OF THE UNITED STATES

WE THE PEOPLE OF THE UNITED STATES, in order to form
a more perfect Union, establish justice, insure domestic tranquility,
provide for the common defence, promote the general welfare, and
secure the blessings of liberty to ourselves and our posterity, do ordain
and establish this Constitution for the United States of America.

ARTICLE I
Section 1

All legislative powers herein granted shall be vested in a Congress of
the United States, which shall consist of a Senate and House of Representatives.

NOTE: The historical text has been edited to conform to contemporary usage.

Section 2

The House of Representatives shall be composed of members chosen every second year by the people of the several States, and the electors in each State shall have the qualifications requisite for electors of the most numerous branch of the State Legislature.

No Person shall be a Representative who shall not have attained to the age of twenty-five years, and been seven years a citizen of the United States, and who shall not, when elected, be an inhabitant of that State in which he shall be chosen.

Representatives and direct taxes shall be apportioned among the several States which may be included within this Union, according to their respective numbers, which shall be determined by adding to the whole number of free persons, including those bound to service for a term of years, and excluding Indians not taxed, three fifths of all other persons. The actual enumeration shall be made within three years after the first meeting of the Congress of the United States, and within every subsequent term of ten years, in such manner as they shall by law direct. The number of Representatives shall not exceed one for every thirty thousand, but each State shall have at least one Representative; and until such enumeration shall be made, the State of New Hampshire shall be entitled to choose three, Massachusetts eight, Rhode-Island and Providence Plantations one, Connecticut five, New York six, New Jersey four, Pennsylvania eight, Delaware one, Maryland six, Virginia ten, North Carolina five, South Carolina five, and Georgia three.

When vacancies happen in the representation from any State, the Executive Authority thereof shall issue writs of election to fill such vacancies.

The House of Representatives shall choose their Speaker and other officers; and shall have the sole power of impeachment.

Section 3

The Senate of the United States shall be composed of two Senators from each State, chosen by the Legislature thereof, for six years; and each Senator shall have one vote.

Immediately after they shall be assembled in consequence of the first election, they shall be divided as equally as may be into three classes. The seats of the Senators of the first class shall be vacated at the expiration of the second year, of the second class at the expiration of the fourth year, and of the third class at the expiration of the sixth year, so that one-third may be chosen every second year; and if vacancies happen by resignation, or otherwise, during the recess of the Legislature of any State, the Executive thereof may make temporary appointments until the next meeting of the Legislature, which shall then fill such vacancies.

No person shall be a Senator who shall not have attained to the age of thirty years, and been nine years a citizen of the United States, and who shall not, when elected, be an inhabitant of that State for which he shall be chosen.

The Vice President of the United States shall be President of the Senate, but shall have no vote, unless they be equally divided.

The Senate shall choose their other officers, and also a President pro tempore, in the absence of the Vice President, or when he shall exercise the office of President of the United States.

The Senate shall have the sole power to try all impeachments. When sitting for that purpose, they shall be on oath or affirmation. When the President of the United States is tried, the Chief Justice shall preside: and no person shall be convicted without the concurrence of two thirds of the members present.

Judgment in cases of impeachment shall not extend further than to removal from office, and disqualification to hold and enjoy any office of honor, trust, or profit under the United States: but the party convicted shall nevertheless be liable and subject to indictment, trial, judgment and punishment, according to Law.

Section 4

The times, places, and manner of holding elections for Senators and Representatives, shall be prescribed in each State by the Legislature thereof; but the Congress may at any time by law make or alter such regulations, except as to the places of choosing Senators.

The Congress shall assemble at least once in every year, and such meeting shall be on the first Monday in December, unless they shall by law appoint a different day.

Section 5

Each House shall be the judge of the elections, returns, and qualifications of its own members, and a majority of each shall constitute a quorum to do business; but a smaller number may adjourn from day to day, and may be authorized to compel the attendance of absent members, in such manner, and under such penalties as each House may provide.

Each House may determine the rules of its proceedings, punish its members for disorderly behavior, and, with the concurrence of two thirds, expel a member.

Each House shall keep a journal of its proceedings, and from time to time publish the same, excepting such parts as may in their judgment require secrecy; and the yeas and nays of the members of either House on any question shall, at the desire of one fifth of those present, be entered on the journal.

Neither House, during the session of Congress, shall, without the consent of the other, adjourn for more than three days, nor to any other place than that in which the two Houses shall be sitting.

Section 6

The Senators and Representatives shall receive a compensation for their services, to be ascertained by law, and paid out of the Treasury of the United States. They shall in all cases, except treason, felony, and breach of the peace, be privileged from arrest during their attendance at the session of their respective Houses, and in going to and returning from the same; and for any speech of debate in either House, they shall not be questioned in any other place.

No Senator or Representative shall, during the time for which he was elected, be appointed to any civil office under the authority of the United States, which shall have been created, or the emoluments whereof shall have been increased during such time; and no person holding any office under the United States shall be a member of either House during his continuance in office.

Section 7

All bills for raising revenue shall originate in the House of Representatives; but the Senate may propose or concur with amendments as on other bills.

Every bill which shall have passed the House of Representatives and the Senate, shall, before it becomes a law, be presented to the President of the United States; if he approve he shall sign it, but if not he shall return it, with his objections to that House in which it shall have originated, who shall enter the objections at large on their journal, and proceed to reconsider it. If after such reconsideration two thirds of that House shall agree to pass the bill, it shall be sent, together with the objections, to the other House, by which it shall likewise be reconsidered, and if approved by two thirds of that House, it shall become a law. But in all such cases the votes of both Houses shall be determined by yeas and nays, and the names of the persons voting for and against the bill shall be entered on the journal of each house, respectively. If any bill shall not be returned by the President within ten days (Sundays excepted) after it shall have been presented to him, the same shall be a law, in like manner as if he had signed it, unless the Congress by their adjournment prevent its return, in which case it shall not be a law.

Every order, resolution, or vote to which the concurrence of the Senate and House of Representatives may be necessary (except on a question of adjournment) shall be presented to the President of the United States; and before the same shall take effect, shall be approved by him, or being disapproved by him, shall be repassed by two thirds of the Senate and House of Representatives, according to the rules and limitations prescribed in the case of a bill.

Section 8

The Congress shall have power to lay and collect taxes, duties, imposts and excises, to pay the debts and provide for the common defense and general welfare of the United States; but all duties, imposts and excises shall be uniform throughout the United States;

To borrow money on the credit of the United States;

To regulate commerce with foreign nations, and among the several States, and with the Indian tribes;

To establish a uniform rule of naturalization, and uniform laws on the subject of bankruptcies throughout the United States;

To coin money, regulate the value thereof, and of foreign coin, and fix the standard of weights and measures;

To provide for the punishment of counterfeiting the securities and current coin of the United States;

To establish post offices and post roads;

To promote the progress of science and useful arts, by securing for limited times to authors and inventors the exclusive right to their respective writings and discoveries;

To constitute tribunals inferior to the Supreme Court;

To define and punish piracies and felonies committed on the high seas, and offences against the law of nations;

To declare war, grant letters of marque and reprisal, and make rules concerning captures on land and water;

To raise and support armies, but no appropriation of money to that use shall be for a longer term than two years;

To provide and maintain a navy;

To make rules for the government and regulation of the land and naval forces;

To provide for calling forth the militia to execute the laws of the Union, suppress insurrections, and repel invasions;

To provide for organizing, arming, and disciplining, the militia, and for governing such part of them as may be employed in the service of the United States, reserving to the States, respectively, the appointment of the officers, and the authority of training the militia according to the discipline prescribed by Congress;

To exercise exclusive legislation in all cases whatsoever, over such district (not exceeding ten miles square) as may, by cession of particular States, and the acceptance of Congress, become the seat of the Government of the United States, and to exercise like authority over all places purchased by the consent of the Legislature of the State in which the same shall be, for the erection of forts, magazines, arsenals, dock-yards, and other needful buildings;—And

To make all laws which shall be necessary and proper for carrying into execution the foregoing powers, and all other powers vested by this Constitution in the Government of the United States, or in any department or officer thereof.

Section 9

The migration or importation of such persons as any of the States now existing shall think proper to admit, shall not be prohibited by the Congress prior to the year one thousand eight hundred and eight, but a tax or duty may be imposed on such importation, not exceeding ten dollars for each person.

The privilege of the writ of habeas corpus shall not be suspended, unless when in cases of rebellion or invasion the public safety may require it.

No bill of attainder or ex post facto law shall be passed.

No capitation, or other direct, tax shall be laid, unless in proportion to the census or enumeration herein before directed to be taken.

No tax or duty shall be laid on articles exported from any State.

No preference shall be given by any regulation of commerce or revenue to the ports of one State over those of another: nor shall vessels bound to, or from, one State, be obliged to enter, clear, or pay duties in another.

No money shall be drawn from the Treasury, but in consequence of appropriations made by law; and a regular statement and account of the receipts and expenditures of all public money shall be published from time to time.

No title of nobility shall be granted by the United States: and no person holding any office of profit or trust under them, shall, without the consent of the Congress, accept of any present, emolument, office, or title, of any kind whatever, from any king, prince, or foreign state.

Section 10

No State shall enter into any treaty, alliance, or confederation; grant letters of marque and reprisal; coin money; emit bills of credit; make any thing but gold and silver coin a tender in payment of debts; pass any bill of attainder, ex post facto law, or law impairing the obligation of contracts, or grant any title of nobility.

No State shall, without the consent of the Congress, lay any imposts or duties on imports or exports, except what may be absolutely necessary for executing its inspection laws; and the net produce of all duties and imposts, laid by any State on imports or exports, shall be for the use of the Treasury of the United States; and all such laws shall be subject to the revision and control of the Congress.

No State shall, without the consent of Congress, lay any duty of tonnage, keep troops, or ships of war in time of peace, enter into any agreement or compact with another state, or with a foreign power, or engage in war, unless actually invaded, or in such imminent danger as will not admit of delay.

ARTICLE II
Section 1

The executive power shall be vested in a President of the United States of America. He shall hold his office during the term of four years, and, together with the Vice President, chosen for the same term, be elected, as follows

Each State shall appoint, in such manner as the Legislature thereof may direct, a number of electors, equal to the whole number of Senators and Representatives to which the State may be entitled in the Congress: but no Senator or Representative, or person holding an office of trust or profit under the United States, shall be appointed an elector.

The electors shall meet in their respective States, and vote by ballot for two persons, of whom one at least shall not be an inhabitant of the same State with themselves. And they shall make a list of all the persons voted for, and of the number of votes for each; which list they shall sign and certify, and transmit sealed to the seat of the Government of the United States, directed to the President of the Senate. The President of the Senate shall, in the presence of the Senate and House of Representatives, open all the certificates, and the votes shall then be counted. The person having the greatest number of votes shall be the President, if such number be a majority of the whole number of electors appointed; and if there be more than one who have such majority, and have an equal number of votes, then the House of Representatives shall immediately choose by ballot one of them for President; and if no person have a majority, then from the five highest on the list the said House shall in like manner choose the President. But in choosing the President, the votes shall be taken by States, the representation from each State having one vote; A quorum for this purpose shall consist of a member or members from two thirds of the States, and a majority of all the states shall be necessary to a choice. In every case, after the choice of the President, the person having the greatest number of votes of the electors shall be the Vice President. But if there should remain two or more who have equal votes, the Senate should choose from them by ballot the Vice President.

The Congress may determine the time of choosing the electors, and the day on which they shall give their votes; which day shall be the same throughout the United States.

No person except a natural born citizen, or a citizen of the United States, at the time of the adoption of this Constitution, shall be eligible to the office of President; neither shall any person be eligible to that office who shall not have attained to the age of thirty-five years, and been fourteen years a resident within the United States.

In case of the removal of the President from office, or of his death, resignation, or inability to discharge the powers and duties of the said office, the same shall devolve on the Vice President, and the Congress may by law provide for the case of removal, death, resignation or inability, both of the President and Vice President, declaring what officer shall then act as President, and such officer shall act accordingly, until the disability be removed, or a President shall be elected.

The President shall, at stated times, receive for his services, a compensation, which shall neither be increased nor diminished during the period for which he shall have been elected, and he shall not receive within that period any other emolument from the United States, or any of them.

Before he enter on the execution of his office, he shall take the following oath or affirmation:—"I do solemnly swear (or affirm) that I will faithfully execute the office of President of the United States, and will to the best of my ability, preserve, protect, and defend the Constitution of the United States."

Section 2

The President shall be Commander in Chief of the Army and Navy of the United States, and of the militia of the several States, when called into the actual service of the United States; he may require the opinion, in writing, of the principal officer in each of the executive departments, upon any subject relating to the duties of their respective offices, and he shall have power to grant reprieves and pardons for offences against the United States, except in cases of impeachment.

He shall have power, by and with the advice and consent of the Senate, to make treaties, provided two thirds of the Senators present concur; and he shall nominate, and by and with the advice and consent of the Senate, shall appoint ambassadors, other public ministers and consuls, judges of the Supreme Court, and all other officers of the United States, whose appointments are not herein otherwise provided for, and which shall be established by law: but the Congress may by law vest the appointment of such inferior officers, as they think proper, in the President alone, in the courts of law, or in the heads of departments.

The President shall have power to fill up all vacancies that may happen during the recess of the Senate, by granting commissions which shall expire at the end of their session.

Section 3

He shall from time to time give to the Congress information of the state of the Union, and recommend to their consideration such measures as he shall judge necessary and expedient; he may, on extraordinary occasions, convene both Houses, or either of them, and in case of disagreement between them, with respect to the time of adjournment, he may adjourn them to such time as he shall think proper; he shall receive ambassadors and other public ministers; he shall take care that the laws be faithfully executed, and shall commission all the officers of the United States.

Section 4

The President, Vice President, and all civil officers of the United States shall be removed from office on impeachment for, and conviction of, treason, bribery, or other high crimes and misdemeanors.

ARTICLE III
Section 1

The judicial Power of the United States, shall be vested in one Supreme Court, and in such inferior courts as the Congress may from time to time ordain and establish. The judges, both of the supreme and inferior courts, shall hold their offices during good behavior, and shall, at stated times, receive for their services, a compensation, which shall not be diminished during their continuance in office.

Section 2

The judicial power shall extend to all cases, in law and equity, arising under this Constitution, the laws of the United States, and treaties made, or which shall be made, under their authority; to all cases affecting ambassadors, other public ministers and consuls; to all cases of admiralty and maritime jurisdiction; to controversies to which the United States, shall be a party; to controversies between two or more States; between a State and citizens of another State; between citizens of different States; between citizens of the same State claiming lands under grants of different states, and between a State, or the citizens thereof, and foreign states, citizens, or subjects.

In all cases affecting ambassadors, other public ministers and consuls, and those in which a State shall be party, the Supreme Court shall have original jurisdiction. In all the other cases before mentioned, the Supreme Court shall have appellate jurisdiction, both as to law and fact, with such exceptions, and under such regulations, as the Congress shall make.

The trial of all crimes, except in cases of impeachment, shall be by jury; and such trial shall be held in the State where the said crimes shall have been committed; but when not committed within any State, the trial shall be at such place or places as the Congress may by law have directed.

Section 3

Treason against the United States, shall consist only in levying wear against them, or, in adhering to their enemies, giving them aid and comfort. No person shall be convicted of treason unless on the testimony of two witnesses to the same overt act, or on confession in open court.

The Congress shall have power to declare the punishment of treason, but no attainder of treason shall work corruption of blood, or forfeiture except during the life of the person attained.

ARTICLE IV
Section 1

Full faith and credit shall be given in each State to the public acts, records, and judicial proceedings of every other State. And the Congress may by general laws prescribe the manner in which such acts, records, and proceedings shall be proved, and the effect thereof.

Section 2

The citizens of each State shall be entitled to all privileges and immunities of citizens in the several States.

A person charged in any State with treason, felony, or other crime, who shall flee from justice, and be found in another State, shall on demand of the Executive authority of the State from which he fled, be delivered up, to be removed to the State having jurisdiction of the crime.

No person held to service or labor in one State, under the laws thereof, escaping into another, shall, in consequence of any law or regulation therein, be discharged from such service or labor, but shall be delivered up on claim of the party to whom such service or labor may be due.

Section 3

New States may be admitted by the Congress into this Union; but no new State shall be formed or erected within the jurisdiction of any other State; nor any State be formed by the junction of two or more States, or parts of States, without the consent of the Legislatures of the States concerned as well as of the Congress.

The Congress shall have power to dispose of and make all needful rules and regulations respecting the territory or other property belonging to the United States; and nothing in this Constitution shall be so construed as to prejudice any claims of the United States, or of any particular State.

Section 4

The United States shall guarantee to every State in this Union a Republican form of government, and shall protect each of them against invasion; and on application of the Legislature, or of the Executive (when the Legislature cannot be convened) against domestic violence.

ARTICLE V

The Congress, whenever two thirds of both Houses shall deem it necessary, shall propose amendments to this Constitution, or, on the application of the Legislatures of two thirds of the several States shall call a convention for proposing amendments, which, in either case, shall be valid to all intents and purposes, as part of this Constitution, when ratified by the Legislatures of three fourths of the several States, or by conventions in three fourths thereof, as the one or the other mode of ratification may be proposed by the Congress; provided that no amendment which may be made prior to the year one thousand eight hundred and eight shall in any manner affect the first and fourth clauses in the ninth Section of the first Article; and that no State, without its consent, shall be deprived of its equal suffrage in the Senate.

ARTICLE VI

All debts contracted and engagements entered into, before the adoption of this Constitution, shall be as valid against the United States under this Constitution, as under the Confederation.

This Constitution, and the laws of the United States which shall be made in pursuance thereof; and all treaties made, or which shall be made, under the authority of the United States, shall be the supreme law of the land; and the judges in every State shall be bound thereby, any thing in the Constitution or laws of any State to the contrary notwithstanding.

The Senators and Representatives before mentioned, and the members of the several State Legislatures, and all executive and judicial officers, both of the United States and of the several States, shall be bound by oath or affirmation, to support this Constitution; but no religious test shall ever be required as a qualification to any office or public trust under the United States.

ARTICLE VII

The ratification of the conventions of nine States shall be sufficient for the establishment of this Constitution between the States so ratifying the same.

Done in convention by the unanimous consent of the States present the seventeenth day of September in the year of our Lord one thousand seven hundred and eighty seven and of the independence of the United States of America the Twelfth. In witness whereof we have hereunto subscribed our names.

George Washington
President and Deputy from Virginia

New Hampshire: John Langdon, Nicholas Gilman

Massachusetts: Nathaniel Gorham, Rufus King

Connecticut: Wm. Saml. Johnson, Roger Sherman

New York: Alexander Hamilton

New Jersey: Wil. Livingston, Wm. Paterson, David Brearley, Jona. Dayton

Pennsylvania: B. Franklin, Thomas Mifflin, Robt. Morris, Geo. Clymer, Thos. FitzSimons, Jared Ingersoll, James Wilson, Gouv. Morris

Delaware: Geo. Read, Gunning Bedford Jun, John Dickinson, Richard Bassett, Jaco. Broom

Maryland: James McHenry, Dan. of St. Thos. Jenifer, Danl. Carroll

Virginia: John Blair, James Madison, Jr.

North Carolina: Wm. Blount, Richd Dobbs Spaight, Hu. Williamson

South Carolina: J. Rutledge, Charles Cotesworth Pinckney, Charles Pinckney, Pierce Butler

Georgia: William Few, Abr. Baldwin, Attest: William Jackson, Secretary

AMENDMENTS TO THE CONSTITUTION OF THE UNITED STATES

ARTICLE 1[1]

Congress shall make no law respecting an establishment of religion, or prohibiting the free exercise thereof; or abridging the freedom of speech, or of the press; or the right of the people peaceably to assemble, and to petition the Government for a redress of grievances.

ARTICLE II

A well regulated militia, being necessary to the security of a free State, the right of the people to keep and bear arms, shall not be infringed.

ARTICLE III

No soldier shall, in time of peace be quartered in any house, without the consent of the owner, nor in time of war, but in a manner to be prescribed by law.

ARTICLE IV

The right of the people to be secure in their persons, houses, papers, and effects, against unreasonable searches and seizures, shall not be violated, and no warrants shall issue, but upon probable cause, supported by oath or affirmation, and particularly describing the place to be searched, and the persons or things to be seized.

ARTICLE V

No person be held to answer for a capital, or otherwise infamous crime, unless on a presentment or indictment of a Grand Jury, except in cases arising in the land or naval forces, or in the militia, when in actual service in time of war or public danger; nor shall any person be subject for the same offence to be twice put in jeopardy of life or limb; nor shall be compelled in any criminal case to be a witness,

---

[1] Amendments I through X, often called the Bill of Rights, were ratified in 1791.

against himself, nor be deprived of life, liberty, or property, without due process of law; nor shall private property be taken for public use, without just compensation.

ARTICLE VI

In all criminal prosecutions, the accused shall enjoy the right to a speedy and public trial, by an impartial jury of the State and district wherein the crime shall have been committed, which district shall have been previously ascertained by law, and to be informed of the nature and cause of the accusation; to be confronted with the witnesses against him; to have compulsory process for obtaining witnesses in his favor, and to have the assistance of counsel for his defense.

ARTICLE VII

In suits at common law, where the value in controversy shall exceed twenty dollars, the right of trial by jury shall be preserved, and no fact tried by a jury, shall be otherwise re-examined in any court of the United States, than according to the rules of the common law.

ARTICLE VIII

Excessive bail shall not be required, nor excessive fines imposed, nor cruel and unusual punishments inflicted.

ARTICLE IX

The enumeration in the Constitution, of certain rights, shall not be construed to deny or disparage others retained by the people.

ARTICLE X

The powers not delegated to the United States by the Constitution, nor prohibited by it to the States, are reserved to the States, respectively, or to the people.

ARTICLE XI [1795]

The judicial power of the United States shall not be construed to extend to any suit in law or equity, commenced or prosecuted against one of the United States by citizens of another State, or by citizens or subjects of any foreign state.

ARTICLE XII [1804]

The electors shall meet in their respective states, and vote by ballot for President and Vice President, one of whom, at least, shall not be an inhabitant of the same state with themselves; they shall name in their ballots the person voted for as President, and in distinct ballots the person voted for as Vice President, and they shall make distinct lists of all persons voted for as President, and of all persons voted for as Vice President, and of the number of votes for each, which lists they shall sign and certify, and transmit sealed to the seat of the government of the United States, directed to the President of the Senate; the President of the Senate shall, in the presence of the Senate and House of Representatives, open all the certificates and the votes shall then be counted; the person having the greatest number of votes for President, shall be the President, if such number be a majority of the whole number of electors appointed; and if no person have such majority, then from the persons having the highest numbers not exceeding three on the list of those voted for as President, the House of Representatives shall choose immediately, by ballot, the President. But in choosing the President, the votes shall be taken by states, the representation from each State having one vote; a quorum for this purpose shall consist of a member or members from two thirds of the states, and a majority of all the states shall be necessary to a choice. And if the House of Representatives shall not choose a President whenever the right of choice shall devolve upon them, before the fourth day of March next following, then the Vice President shall act as President, as in the case of the death or other constitutional disability of the President. The person having the greatest number of votes as Vice President, shall be the Vice President, if such number be a majority of the whole number of electors appointed, and if no person have a majority, then from the two highest numbers on the list, the Senate shall choose the Vice President; a quorum for the purpose shall consist of two thirds of the whole number of Senators, and a majority of the whole number shall be necessary to a choice. But no person constitutionally ineligible to the office of President shall be eligible to that of Vice President of the United States.

ARTICLE XIII [1865]
Section 1

Neither slavery nor involuntary servitude, except as a punishment for crime whereof the party shall have been duly convicted, shall exist within the United States, or any place subject to their jurisdiction.

Section 2

Congress shall have power to enforce this article by appropriate legislation.

ARTICLE XIV [1868]
Section 1

All persons born or naturalized in the United States, and subject to the jurisdiction thereof, are citizens of the United States and of the State wherein they reside. No State shall make or enforce any law which shall abridge the privileges or immunities of citizens of the United States; nor shall any State deprive any person of life, liberty, or property, without due process of law; nor deny to any person within its jurisdiction the equal protection of the laws.

Section 2

Representatives shall be apportioned among the several States according to their respective numbers, counting the whole number of persons in each State, excluding Indians not taxed. But when the right to vote at any election for the choice of electors for President and Vice President of the United States, Representatives in Congress, the executive and judicial officers of a State, or the members of the Legislature thereof, is denied to any of the male inhabitants of such State, being twenty-one years of age, and citizens of the United States, or in any way abridged, except for participation in rebellion, or other crime, the basis of representation therein shall be reduced in the proportion which the number of such male citizens shall bear to the whole number of male citizens twenty-one years of age in such State.

Section 3

No person shall be a Senator or Representative in Congress, or elector of President and Vice President, or hold any office, civil or military, under the United States, or under any State, who, having previously taken an oath, as a member of Congress, or as an officer of the United States, or as a member of any State Legislature, or as an executive or judicial officer of any State, to support the Constitution of the United States, shall have engaged in insurrection or rebellion against the same, or given aid or comfort to the enemies thereof. But Congress may, by a vote of two thirds of each House, remove such disability.

Section 4

The validity of the public debt of the United States, authorized by law, including debts incurred for payment of pensions and bounties for services in suppressing insurrection or rebellion, shall not be questioned. But neither the United States nor any State shall assume or pay any debt or obligation incurred in aid of insurrection or rebellion against the United States, or any claim for the loss or emancipation of any slave; but all such debts, obligations, and claims shall be held illegal and void.

Section 5

The Congress shall have power to enforce, by appropriate legislation, the provisions of this article.

ARTICLE XV [1870]

Section 1

The right of citizens of the United States to vote shall not be denied or abridged by the United States or by any State on account of race, color, or previous condition of servitude.

Section 2

The Congress shall have power to enforce this article by appropriate legislation.

ARTICLE XVI [1913]

The Congress shall have power to lay and collect taxes on incomes, from whatever source derived, without apportionment among the several States, and without regard to any census or enumeration.

ARTICLE XVII [1913]

The Senate of the United States shall be composed of two Senators from each State, elected by the people thereof, for six years; and each Senator shall have one vote. The electors in each State shall have the qualifications requisite for electors of the most numerous branch of the State Legislatures.

When vacancies happen in the representation of any State in the Senate, the executive authority of such State shall issue writs of election to fill such vacancies: Provided, that the legislature of any State may empower the executive thereof to make temporary appointment until the people fill the vacancies by election as the legislature may direct.

This amendment shall not be so construed as to affect the election or term of any Senator chosen before it becomes valid as part of the Constitution.

ARTICLE XVIII [1919]

Section 1

After one year from the ratification of this article the manufacture, sale, or transportation of intoxicating liquors within, the importation thereof into, or the exportation thereof from the United States and all territory subject to the jurisdiction thereof for beverage purposes is hereby prohibited.

Section 2

The Congress and the several States shall have concurrent power to enforce this article by appropriate legislation.

Section 3

This article shall be inoperative unless it shall have been ratified as an amendment to the Constitution by the legislatures of the several States, as provided in the Constitution, within seven years from the date of the submission hereof to the States by Congress.

ARTICLE XIX [1920]

The right of citizens of the United States to vote shall not be denied or abridged by the United States or by any State on account of sex.

Congress shall have power to enforce this article by appropriate legislation.

ARTICLE XX [1933]
Section 1

The terms of the President and Vice President shall end at noon on the twentieth day of January, and the terms of Senators and Representatives at noon on the third day of January, of the years in which such terms would have ended if this article had not been ratified; and the terms of their successors shall then begin.

Section 2

The Congress shall assemble at least once in every year, and such meeting shall begin at noon on the third day of January, unless they shall by law appoint a different day.

Section 3

If, at the time fixed for the beginning of the term of the President, the President-elect shall have died, the Vice President-elect shall become President. If a President shall not have been chosen before the time fixed for the beginning of his term, or if the President-elect shall have failed to qualify, then the Vice President shall have qualified; and the Congress may by law provide for the case wherein neither a President-elect nor a Vice President-elect shall have qualified, declaring who shall then act as President, or the manner in which one who is to act shall be selected, and such person shall act accordingly until a President or Vice President shall have qualified.

Section 4

The Congress may by law provide for the case of the death of any of the persons from whom the House of Representatives may choose a President whenever the right of choice shall have devolved upon them, and for the case of the death of any of the persons from whom the Senate may choose a Vice President whenever the right of choice shall have devolved upon them.

Section 5

Sections 1 and 2 shall take effect on the 15th day of October following the ratification of this article.

Section 6

This article shall be inoperative unless it shall have been ratified as an amendment to the Constitution by the legislatures of three fourths of the several States within seven years from the date of its submission.

ARTICLE XXI [1933]
Section 1

The eighteenth article of amendment to the Constitution of the United States is hereby repealed.

Section 2

The transportation or importation into any State, territory, or possession of the United States for delivery or use therein of intoxicating liquors, in violation of the laws thereof, is hereby prohibited.

Section 3

This article shall be inoperative unless it shall have been ratified as an amendment to the Constitution by convention in the several States, as provided in the Constitution, within seven years from the date of the submission thereof to the States by the Congress.

ARTICLE XXII [1951]
Section 1

No person shall be elected to the office of the President more than twice, and no person who has held the office of President, or acted as President, for more than two years of a term to which some other person was elected President shall be elected to the office of the President more than once. But this article shall not apply to any person holding the office of President when this article was proposed by the Congress, and shall not prevent any person who may be holding the office of President, or acting as President, during the term within which this article becomes operative from holding the office of President or acting as President during the remainder of such term.

Section 2

This article shall be inoperative unless it shall have been ratified as an amendment to the Constitution by the legislatures of three fourths of the several States within seven years from the date of its submission to the States by the Congress.

ARTICLE XXIII [1961]
Section 1

The District constituting the seat of Government of the United States shall appoint in such manner as the Congress may direct: A number of electors of President and Vice President equal to the whole number of Senators and Representatives in Congress to which the District would be entitled if it were a State, but in no event more than the least populous State; they shall be in addition to those appointed by the States, but they shall be considered, for the purposes of the election of President and Vice President, to be electors appointed by a State; and they shall meet in the District and perform such duties as provided by the twelfth article of amendment.

Section 2

The Congress shall have the power to enforce this article by appropriate legislation.

ARTICLE XXIV [1964]
Section 1

The right of citizens of the United States to vote in any primary or other election for President or Vice President, for electors for President or Vice President, or for Senator or Representative in Congress, shall not be denied or abridged by the United States or any State by reasons of failure to pay any poll tax or other tax.

Section 2

The Congress shall have the power to enforce this article by appropriate legislation.

ARTICLE XXV [1967]
Section 1

In case of the removal of the President from office or of his death or resignation, the Vice President shall become President.

Section 2

Whenever there is a vacancy in the office of the Vice President, the President shall nominate a Vice President who shall take office upon confirmation by a majority vote of both Houses of Congress.

Section 3

Whenever the President transmits to the President pro tempore of the Senate and the Speaker of the House of Representatives his written declaration that he is unable to discharge the powers and duties of his office, and until he transmits to them a written declaration to the contrary, such powers and duties shall be discharged by the Vice President as Acting President.

Section 4

Whenever the Vice President and a majority of either the principal officers of the executive departments or of such other body as Congress may by law provide, transmit to the President pro tempore of the Senate and the Speaker of the House of Representatives their written declaration that the President is unable to discharge the powers and duties of his office, the Vice President shall immediately assume the powers and duties of the office as Acting President.

Thereafter, when the President transmits to the President pro tempore of the Senate and the Speaker of the House of Representatives his written declaration that no inability exists, he shall resume the powers and duties of his office unless the Vice President and a majority of either the principal officers of the executive department or of such other body as Congress may by law provide, transmit within four days to the President pro tempore of the Senate and the Speaker of the House of Representatives their written declaration that the President is unable to discharge the powers and duties of his office. Thereupon Congress shall decide the issue, assembling within forty-eight hours for that purpose if not in session. If the Congress, within twenty-one days after receipt of the latter written declaration, or, if Congress is not in session, within twenty-one days after Congress is required to assemble, determines by two thirds vote of both Houses that the President is unable to discharge the powers and duties of his office, the Vice President shall continue to discharge the same as Acting President; otherwise, the President shall resume the powers and duties of his office.

ARTICLE XXVI [1971]
Section 1

The right of citizens of the United States, who are 18 years of age or older, to vote shall not be denied or abridged by the United States or by any state on account of age.

Section 2

The Congress shall have power to enforce this article by appropriate legislation.

ARTICLE XXVII [1992]

No law, varying the compensation for the services of the Senators and Representatives, shall take effect, until an election of Representatives shall have intervened.

Notes

Introduction

1. E. L. Godkin, "The Constitution, and Its Defects," *North American Review*, (July 1864): 121–22.
2. James Madison, *Federalist* No. 63. In *The Federalist Papers*, ed. Clinton Rossiter (New York: New American Library, 1961), 384.

Chapter One: Conception

1. Samuel P. Huntington, *Political Order in Changing Societies* (New Haven: Yale University Press, 1968), see esp. pp. 93–133.
2. This concept of an unwritten constitution may be difficult for modern Americans to comprehend, although Colonial Americans, who were steeped in this tradition as much as their cousins across the sea, would have had no difficulty. In its "ancient" form, the unwritten constitution amounted to an all-purpose excuse for society to dig in its heels and just say no to any and all structural

change. In its modern form, it amounts to a belief that, despite the immense changes of the nineteenth and twentieth centuries, something about Britain has remained constant and continuous, not only the role of Parliament and the Crown, but the relationship of the individual and the state. In his famous essay, "The Lion and the Unicorn," written as bombs were crashing all around during the London Blitz, George Orwell referred to the English constitution as a "strange mixture of reality and illusion, democracy and privilege, humbug and decency, the subtle network of compromises, by which the nation keeps itself in its familiar shape." From a legal concept in the sixteenth, seventeenth, and eighteenth centuries, the unwritten constitution had evolved into an ethnic-communal concept of a people determined to resist foreign invasion and govern themselves according to their own principals and traditions. *The Collected Essays, Journalism, and Letters of George Orwell*, vol. 2, eds. Sonia Orwell and Ian Angus (New York: Harcourt, Brace & World, 1968), 63. For further information on the Ancient Constitution, a term that had all but disappeared by the early nineteenth century, see J. G. A. Pocock, *The Ancient Constitution and the Feudal Law: A Study of English Historical Thought in the Seventeenth Century* (Cambridge: Cambridge University Press, 1957), and Glenn Burgess, *The Politics of the Ancient Constitution: An Introduction to English Political Thought, 1603–1642* (University Park, PA: Pennsylvania State University Press, 1992).

3. Lawrence Stone, "The Results of the English Revolutions of the Seventeenth Century." In *Three British Revolutions: 1641, 1688, 1776*, ed. J. G. A. Pocock (Princeton: Princeton University Press, 1980), 66.

4. Lawrence Stone, *The Causes of the English Revolution, 1529–1642* (New York: Harper & Row, 1972), 58.

5. Philip Corrigan and Derek Sayer, *The Great Arch: English State Formation as Cultural Revolution* (Oxford: Basil Blackwell, 1985), 51.

6. Penry Williams, *The Tudor Regime* (Oxford: Clarendon Press, 1979), 38.

7. Ibid., 38.

8. J. P. Kenyon, *Stuart England* (London: Penguin Books, 1978), 35.

9. A. L. Rowse, *The England of Elizabeth: The Structure of Society* (London: Macmillan, 1951), 294–95.

10. Ibid., 307.

11. Huntington, *Political Order in Changing Societies*, 113; Katharine Q. Seelye, "At the Bar," *New York Times*, Apr. 7, 1995, p. A33.

12. Capsule biographies, including occupations, for British, German, and Canadian MPs can be found in *Vacher's Parliamentary Guide 1992; Amtliches Handbuch des Deutschen Bundestages: 12. Wahlperiode* (NDV Neue Darmstadter Verlagsanstalt, 1991); and the *Canadian Parliamentary Handbook/Repertoire parlementaire canadien 1992* (Borealis).

13. Christopher Hill, *God's Englishman: Oliver Cromwell & the English Revolution* (London: Weidenfeld and Nicolson, 1970), 26.

14. David Hackett Fischer, *Albion's Seed: Four British Folkways in America* (Oxford University Press, 1989), 17.

15. Huntington, *Political Order in Changing Societies*, 103.

16. John Phillip Reid, "The Jurisprudence of Liberty." In *The Roots of Liberty: Magna Carta, Ancient Constitution, and the Anglo-American Tradition of Rule of Law*, ed. Ellis Sandoz (Columbia, MO: University of Missouri Press, 1993), 184.

17. Huntington, *Political Order in Changing Societies*, 100.

18. Christopher Hill, *The Century of Revolution 1603–1714* (New York: W. W. Norton, 1966), 65.

19. Burgess, *The Politics of the Ancient Constitution*, 223–24.

20. Fischer, *Albion's Seed*, 56.

21. Stone, *The Causes of the English Revolution*, 105–6.

22. Bernard Bailyn, *The Origins of American Politics* (New York: Knopf, 1968), 41.

23. J. G. A. Pocock, *The Machiavellian Moment: Florentine Political Thought and the Atlantic Republican Tradition* (Princeton: Princeton University Press, 1975), 477.

24. Isaac Kramnick, *Bolingbroke and His Circle: The Politics of Nostalgia in the Age of Walpole* (Cambridge: Harvard University Press, 1968), 262.

25. Henry St. John, Viscount Bolingbroke, *The Works of Lord Bolingbroke*, vol. 1 (Philadelphia: Cavey and Hart, 1841), 304.

26. Ibid., vol. 2, 401.

27. Ibid., vol. 2, 93.

28. Ibid., vol. 1, 331.

29. Ibid., vol. 2, 397.

30. Quoted in John P. Diggins, "The Three Faces of Authority in American History." In *The Problem of Authority in America*, eds. Diggins and Mark E. Kann (Philadelphia: Temple University Press, 1981), 32. Originally published in Henry Adams, *The Great Secession Winter of 1860–61 and Other Essays*, ed. George H. Hochfield (New York: Sagamore, 1958), 194.

31. Jack P. Greene, introduction to *Great Britain and the American Colonies, 1606–1763*, ed. Jack P. Greene (Columbia: University of South Carolina Press, 1970), xiv.

32. Jack P. Greene, "The Seven Years' War and the American Revolution: The Causal Relationship Reconsidered." In *The British Atlantic Empire Before the American Revolution*, eds. Peter Marshall and Glyn Williams (London: Frank Cass, 1980), 87.

33. Pocock, *The Machiavellian Moment*, 511–13.

34. G. D. H. Cole and Raymond Postgate, *The Common People 1746–1946* (London: Methuen, 1971), 96–97.

35. Derek Jarrett, *Britain 1688–1815* (London: Longmans, 1965), 301.
36. Fischer, *Albion's Seed*, 826.
37. Bolingbroke, *Works*, vol. 2, 396.

Chapter Two: Birth

1. Thomas K. McCraw, "The Strategic Vision of Alexander Hamilton," *The American Scholar* (winter 1994): 43.
2. Gordon S. Wood, "Interests and Disinterestedness in the Making of the Constitution." In *Beyond Confederation: Origins of the Constitution and American National Identity*, eds. Richard Beeman, Stephen Botein, and Edward C. Carter III (Chapel Hill: University of North Carolina Press, 1987), 76.
3. Ibid., 74.
4. Rossiter, *The Federalist Papers*, 106.
5. Adrienne Koch, introduction to *Notes of Debates in the Federal Convention of 1787 Reported by James Madison* (New York: W. W. Norton, 1966), 79.
6. J. Allen Smith, *The Spirit of American Government* (1907). Excerpted in *The Case Against the Constitution: From the Antifederalists to the Present*, eds. John F. Manley and Kenneth M. Dolbeare (Armonk, NY: M. F. Sharpe, 1987), 7.
7. Madison, *Notes of Debates*, 57.
8. Kramnick, *Bolingbroke and His Circle*, 251.
9. Rossiter, *The Federalist Papers*, 322.
10. Madison, *Notes of Debates*, 37.
11. Ibid., 103.
12. Paul Finkelman, "Slavery and the Constitutional Convention: Making a Covenant with Death." In Beeman, Botein, and Carter, *Beyond Confederation*, 193.
13. R. R. Palmer, *The Age of the Democratic Revolution: A Political History of Europe and America, 1760–1800*, vol. 1 (Princeton: Princeton University Press, 1959–64), 492.
14. Rossiter, *The Federalist Papers*, 84.
15. Ibid.
16. Ibid., 79.
17. Ibid., 278.
18. George Ticknor Curtis, *Constitutional History of the United States from Their Declaration of Independence to the Close of Their Civil War*, vol. 2 (New York: Da Capo Press, 1974), 234.
19. Madison, *Notes of Debates*, 650.
20. McCraw, *The American Scholar*, 32.
21. Ibid., 46.
22. Madison, *Notes of Debates*, 139.
23. Ibid., 133.

24. Charles Sellers, *The Market Revolution: Jacksonian America 1815–1846* (New York: Oxford University Press, 1991), 127.

25. Palmer, *The Age of the Democratic Revolution*, vol. 2, 522.

26. "Notes on the State of Virginia," Query XIX. In *Thomas Jefferson: Writings*, ed. Merrill D. Peterson (New York: Library of America, 1984), 290–91.

27. Clinton Rossiter, *Alexander Hamilton and the Constitution* (New York: Harcourt, Brace & World, 1964), 141.

28. John Murrin, "Self-Interest Conquers Patriotism: Republicans, Liberals, and Indians Reshape the Nation." In *The American Revolution: Its Character and Limits*, ed. Jack P. Greene (New York: New York University Press, 1987), 228.

29. Ibid., 205.

30. Robert W. Tucker and David C. Hendrickson, *Empire of Liberty: The Statecraft of Thomas Jefferson* (Cambridge: Oxford University Press, 1990), 38.

31. Sellers, *The Market Revolution*, 77.

32. Rossiter, *The Federalist Papers*, 301.

33. John C. Miller, *The Federalist Era 1789–1801* (New York: Harper & Row, 1960), 242.

34. Rossiter, *Alexander Hamilton and the Constitution*, 195.

35. John W. Shy, "Force, Order, and Democracy in the American Revolution." In Greene, *The American Revolution*, 76.

36. Palmer, *The Age of Democratic Revolution*, vol. 2, 523.

37. McCraw, *The American Scholar*, 34.

38. Lord Acton, *The History of Freedom and Other Essays* (London: Macmillan, 1922), 582.

39. Rossiter, *The Federalist Papers*, 35.

40. Sellers, *The Market Revolution*, 72.

41. Ibid., 71.

42. Miller, *The Federalist Era*, 72.

43. John M. Murrin, "1787: The Invention of American Federalism." In *Essays on Liberty and Federalism: The Shaping of the U.S. Constitution*, eds. David E. Narrett and Joyce S. Goldberg (Arlington: Texas A&M University Press, 1988), 43.

44. Sellers, *The Market Revolution*, 62.

45. John B. Owen, *The Eighteenth Century 1774–1815* (New York: W. W. Norton, 1974), 316.

46. Sellers, *The Market Revolution*, 130.

Chapter Three: Breakthrough in Britain

1. Edmund Burke, *Reflections on the Revolution in France*, ed. Conor Cruise O'Brien (London: Penguin, 1986), 194–95.

2. Ibid., 192.
3. Cole and Postgate, *The Common People 1746–1946*, 155.
4. Burke, *Reflections on the Revolution in France*, 141.
5. Ibid., 181–82.
6. Asa Briggs, *The Age of Improvement 1783–1867* (New York: David McKay, 1962), 90.
7. Palmer, *The Age of the Democratic Revolution*, vol. 1, 150–51.
8. George Otto Trevelyan, *The Early History of Charles James Fox* (New York: AMS Press, 1971), 94–95.
9. Ibid., 294.
10. Charles Warren Everett, *The Education of Jeremy Bentham* (New York: Columbia University Press, 1931), xix; John Dinwiddy, *Bentham* (Oxford: Oxford University Press, 1989), 17–18.
11. Leslie Stephen, *The English Utilitarians*, vol. 2 (New York: Peter Smith, 1950), 86.
12. Bertrand Russell, *A History of Western Philosophy* (New York: Simon & Schuster, 1959), 777; John Maynard Keynes, *Works*, vol. 10 (New York: St. Martin's Press, 1971–89), 445.
13. Michel Foucault, *Discipline and Punish: The Birth of the Prison* (New York: Random House, 1979), 195–228.
14. Jeremy Bentham, *Works*, vol. 1 (New York: Russell & Russell, 1962), 227.
15. Samuel P. Huntington, *American Politics: The Promise of Disharmony* (Cambridge: Belknap Press, 1981), 34–35.
16. Bentham, *Works*, vol. 2, 501.
17. James Steintrager, *Bentham* (London: George Allen & Unwin, 1977), 112.
18. Bentham, *Works*, vol. 10, 66.
19. H. L. A. Hart, "Bentham and the United States of America," *Journal of Law and Economics* XIX, no. 3 (1976): 559.
20. Bentham, *Works*, vol. 3, 450.
21. Pocock, *The Machiavellian Moment*, 548.
22. Bentham, *Works*, vol. 2, 402–3.
23. Ibid., vol. 2, 442.
24. Dinwiddy, *Bentham*, 111.
25. Burke, *Reflections on the Revolution in France*, 170.
26. G. D. H. Cole, *The Life of William Cobbett* (Westport, CT: Greenwood Press, 1971), 192–93, 266; E. P. Thompson, *The Making of the English Working Class* (New York: Random House, 1966), 757.
27. Thompson, *The Making of the English Working Class*, 756.
28. Elie Halevy, *A History of the English People in the Nineteenth Century*, vol. 2 (London: Ernest Benn, 1965), 188–89.
29. *Mill on Bentham and Coleridge*, ed. F. R. Leavis (Cambridge: Cambridge University Press, 1980), 41–45.

30. Karl Marx, *Capital* (New York: International, 1967), 609–10n.
31. Chilton Williamson, "Bentham Looks at America," *Political Science Quarterly* 70 (December 1955): 550–51.
32. Bentham, *Works*, vol. 3, 447.
33. Palmer, *The Age of Democratic Revolution*, vol. 1, 301.
34. Dinwiddy, *Bentham*, 14.
35. Bentham, *Works*, vol. 11, 41.
36. Frances Trollope, *Domestic Manners of the Americans*, ed. Donald Smalley (New York: Vintage, 1960), 222.
37. Ibid., 227.
38. Charles Dickens, *American Notes: A Journey* (New York: Fromm International, 1985), 120.
39. James Walvin, *Black Ivory: A History of British Slavery* (London: Harper-Collins, 1992), 266.
40. William L. Mathieson, *British Slave Emancipation 1838–1849* (New York: Octagon Books, 1967), 45.
41. Ibid., 57.
42. Ibid., 119–120.

Chapter Four: Breakdown in America

1. Cole and Postgate, *The Common People*, 91.
2. Indeed, the one thing a sovereign people could not do was put an end to their own sovereignty by overthrowing the popular democracy that was the basis of their rule. For a discussion of some of the philosophical implications of sovereignty, see Peter Suber, *The Paradox of Self-Amendment: A Study of Logic, Law, Omnipotence, and Change* (New York: Peter Lang, 1990), esp. pp. 92–93.
3. Leonard D. White, *The Jacksonians: A Study in Administrative History, 1829–61* (New York: Macmillan, 1954), 511–12.
4. Theodore J. Lowi, *The Personal President: Power Invested, Promise Unfulfilled* (Ithaca: Cornell University Press, 1985), 24–25.
5. Bernard Schwartz, *From Confederation to Nation: The American Constitution, 1835–1877* (Baltimore: Johns Hopkins University Press, 1973), 88.
6. Phillip S. Paludan, *A Covenant with Death: The Constitution, Law, and Equality in the Civil War Era* (Urbana, IL: University of Illinois Press, 1975), 93.
7. Arthur Bestor, "The American Civil War as Constitutional Crisis," *American Historical Review* LXIX (January 1964): 340.
8. The president of the American Bar Association declared that Meese's doctrine shook "the foundations of our system," the ACLU's executive director branded it "a call to defiance," and Harvard Law professor Laurence Tribe

described it as "a grave threat to the rule of law." Sanford Levinson, *Constitutional Faith* (Princeton: Princeton University Press, 1988), 40.

9. Laurence Tribe, *American Constitutional Law*, 2nd ed. (Mineola, NY: Foundation Press, 1988), 549.

10. Robert H. Bork, *The Tempting of America: The Political Seduction of the Law* (New York: Free Press, 1990), 28.

11. Robert A. Burt, "What Was Wrong with *Dred Scott*, What's Right About *Brown*," *Washington and Lee Law Review* 42 (winter 1985): 11.

12. Schwartz, *From Confederation to Nation*, 124.

13. Henry Steele Commager, ed., *Documents of American History*, vol. 1 (New York: Meredith, 1968), 344.

14. Burt, "What Was Wrong with *Dred Scott*," 10.

15. Schwartz, *From Confederation to Nation*, 114.

16. Ibid., 114–15.

17. Don E. Fehrenbacher, *The Dred Scott Case: Its Significance in American Law and Politics* (New York: Oxford University Press, 1978), 235.

18. Alexis de Tocqueville, *Democracy in America*, vol. 1 (New York: Random House, 1990), 359.

19. Ibid., 64.

20. Schwartz, *From Confederation to Nation*, 126.

21. Ibid., 128.

22. Commager, *Documents of American History*, vol. 1, 385.

23. Kenneth Stammp, "The Concept of a Perpetual Union." In *The Imperiled Union: Essays on the Background of the Civil War* (New York: Oxford University Press, 1980), 20.

24. Ibid., 6–7.

25. Ibid., 15.

26. Ibid., 15.

27. Ibid., 16; Rossiter, *The Federalist Papers*, 244.

28. Stampp, *The Imperiled Union*, 9.

29. Ibid., 21–22.

30. Ibid., 34.

31. Commager, *Documents of American History*, vol. 1, 385.

32. Ibid., vol. 1, 363–64.

Chapter Five: Forward to the Past

1. John Milton, "Areopagitica," *Complete Poems and Major Prose*, ed. Merritt Y. Hughes (Indianapolis: Bobbs-Merrill, 1957), 744.

2. Godkin, *North American Review*, 123.

3. Mark E. Neely Jr., *The Fate of Liberty: Abraham Lincoln and Civil Liberties* (New York: Oxford University Press, 1991), 30.

4. Ibid., 23.
5. Richard N. Current, ed., *The Political Thought of Abraham Lincoln* (Indianapolis: Bobbs-Merrill, 1967), 16.
6. Eric Foner, *A Short History of Reconstruction, 1863–1877* (New York: Harper & Row, 1990), 4.
7. Commager, *Documents of American History*, vol. 1, 417–18.
8. Herman Belz, *Lincoln and the Constitution: The Dictatorship Question Reconsidered* (Fort Wayne, IN: Louis A. Warren Lincoln Library and Museum, 1984), 19.
9. Paludan, *A Covenant with Death*, 93.
10. Ibid., 19–21.
11. Ibid., 145.
12. Schwartz, *From Confederation to Nation*, p. 147. Historian Mark Neely puts the total number of political arrests by Union forces at more than twelve thousand during the course of the war. *The Fate of Liberty*, 113–38.
13. Commager, *Documents of American History*, vol. 1, 394.
14. T. Harry Williams, *Lincoln and the Radicals* (Madison, WI: University of Wisconsin Press, 1941), 57.
15. Commager, *Documents of American History*, vol. 1, 422.
16. Fawn M. Brodie, *Thaddeus Stevens: Scourge of the South* (New York: W. W. Norton, 1959), 166.
17. Ibid., 292.
18. Williams, *Lincoln and the Radicals*, 164.
19. Ibid., 273.
20. Ibid., 213.
21. Hans L. Trefousse, *Impeachment of a President: Andrew Jackson, the Blacks, and Reconstruction* (Knoxville: University of Tennessee Press, 1975), 6.
22. Foner, *A Short History of Reconstruction*, 32–33.
23. W. R. Brock, *An American Crisis: Congress & Reconstruction 1865–1867* (London: Macmillan, 1963), 36.
24. Bruce Ackerman, *We the People*, vol. 1 (Cambridge: Harvard University Press, 1991), 93.
25. Joseph B. James, *The Ratification of the Fourteenth Amendment* (Macon, GA: Mercer University Press, 1984), 7.
26. Schwartz, *From Confederation to Nation*, 200–1.
27. Foner, *A Short History of Reconstruction*, 82–83.
28. Brodie, *Thaddeus Stevens*, 219.
29. Trefousse, *Impeachment of a President*, 5–12.
30. Brock, *An American Crisis*, 120.
31. Ibid., 137.
32. Foner, *A Short History of Reconstruction*, 117.
33. Brock, *An American Crisis*, 158.

34. Brodie, *Thaddeus Stevens*, 279.
35. Trefousse, *Impeachment of a President*, 39.
36. Brodie, *Thaddeus Stevens*, 288.
37. Ibid., 314–15.
38. Ibid., 307.
39. Foner, *A Short History of Reconstruction*, 121.
40. Melvin I. Urofsky, *A March of Liberty: A Constitutional History of the United States* (New York: Alfred A. Knopf, 1988), 455.
41. Foner, *A Short History of Reconstruction*, 143.
42. Trefousse, *Impeachment of a President*, 135.
43. Ibid., 178.
44. Brodie, *Thaddeus Stevens*, 338.
45. Ibid., 292.
46. Ibid., 338.
47. Brodie, *Thaddeus Stevens*, 338.
48. *The Collected Works of Walter Bagehot*, vol. 4, ed. Norman St. John-Stevas (Cambridge: Harvard University Press, 1968), 427–28.
49. Ibid., vol. 4, 428.
50. Trefousse, *Impeachment of a President*, 154.
51. John F. Kennedy, *Profiles in Courage* (New York: Harper & Brothers, 1955), 144.
52. Trefousse, *Impeachment of a President*, 185–87.
53. Brodie, *Thaddeus Stevens*, 322.
54. Eric Foner, *Politics and Ideology in the Age of the Civil War* (Oxford: Oxford University Press, 1980), 224–25.
55. Brock, *An American Crisis*, 51n.
56. Foner, *A Short History of Reconstruction*, 245.
57. C. Vann Woodward, *Reunion and Reaction: The Compromise of 1877 and the End of Reconstruction* (Boston: Little, Brown, 1951), 6.
58. Ibid., 21.
59. Leland D. Baldwin, *Reframing the Constitution: An Imperative for Modern America* (Santa Barbara, CA: American Bibliographical Center-Clio Press, 1972), 65.
60. Louis M. Hacker and Benjamin B. Kendricks, *The United States Since 1865*, 3rd ed. (New York: F. S. Crofts, 1939), 72.
61. Woodward, *Reunion and Reaction*, 245.
62. Ibid., 23.
63. Urofsky, *A March of Liberty*, 495.

Chapter Six: Constitutional Orthodoxy Restored

1. Paludan, *A Covenant with Death*, 170–73.
2. Sidney George Fisher, *The Trial of the Constitution* (New York: Negro University Press, 1969), 39.
3. Ibid., 27.
4. Ibid., 38.
5. Ibid., 38–39.
6. Ibid., 57.
7. Ibid., 62.
8. Ibid., 41.
9. Ibid., 96.
10. Walter Dean Burnham, *Critical Elections and the Mainsprings of American Politics* (New York: W. W. Norton, 1970), 81.
11. Robert L. Zangrando, *The NAACP Crusade Against Lynching, 1909–1950* (Philadelphia: Temple University Press, 1980), 6–7.
12. Charles A. Beard, *American Government and Politics* (New York: Macmillan, 1930), 117.
13. Leland D. Baldwin, *The Stream of American History*, vol. 2 (New York: American Book Co., 1957), 28.
14. J. Allen Smith, "The Spirit of American Government." In Manley and Dolbeare, *The Case Against the Constitution*, 11.
15. Robert Sherrill, *Why They Call It Politics: A Guide to American Government* (New York: Harcourt Brace Jovanovich, 1972), 75.
16. Ibid., 148.
17. Thomas W. Wilson, "Cabinet Government in the United States," *International Review* 7 (August 1879): 160.
18. Woodrow Wilson, *Congressional Government: A Study in American Politics* (Boston: Houghton Mifflin, 1925), 203.
19. Ibid., 92.
20. Ibid., 93.
21. Ibid., 56.
22. Ibid., 331; Thomas Paine, *Common Sense*, ed. Isaac Kramnick (London: Penguin, 1986), 68.
23. Wilson, *Congressional Government*, 37–38.
24. Ibid., 202.
25. Gamaliel Bradford, *The Lesson of Popular Government* (New York: Macmillan, 1899), 364.
26. George E. Mowly and Judson A. Grenier, introduction to *The Treason of the Senate*, by David Graham Phillips (Chicago: Quadrangle Books, 1964), 28.
27. William M. Wiecek, *Constitutional Development in a Modernizing Society: The*

United States, 1803 to 1917 (Washington, DC: American Historical Association, 1985), 71.

28. Albert Fried, *Socialism in America: From the Shakers to the Third International* (Garden City, NY: Doubleday, 1970), 396–97.

29. Urofsky, *A March of Liberty*, 578.

30. James Bryce, *The American Commonwealth*, vol. 1 (New York: Macmillan, 1914), 148.

31. Ibid., 162–63.

32. Ibid., 174–75.

33. Ibid., 642.

34. James B. Thayer, "The Origin and Scope of the American Doctrine of Constitutional Law," *Harvard Law Review*, 7, no. 3 (1893): 155–56.

35. Herbert Croly, *The Promise of American Life* (Boston: Northeastern University Press, 1989), 145.

36. Ibid., 150.

37. Ibid., 200.

38. Ibid., 316.

39. Ellen Nore, *Charles A. Beard: An Intellectual Biography* (Carbondale: Southern Illinois State University Press, 1983), 63–64.

40. Charles A. Beard, *An Economic Interpretation of the Constitution of the United States* (New York: Macmillan, 1935), 292.

41. Nore, *Charles A. Beard*, 63.

42. Ibid., 78.

43. John R. Vile, *The Constitutional Amending Process in American Political Thought* (New York: Praeger, 1992), 147.

44. William MacDonald, *A New Constitution for a New America* (New York: B. W. Huebsch, 1921), 22.

45. William Yandell Elliott, *The Need for Constitutional Reform* (New York: McGraw-Hill, 1935), 207.

46. Henry Hazlitt, "Our Obsolete Constitution," *Nation*, Feb. 4, 1931, pp. 124–25.

47. Paul L. Murphy, *The Constitution in Crisis Times, 1918–1969* (New York: Harper & Row, 1972), 41–42.

48. Gerald Garvey, *Constitutional Bricolage* (Princeton: Princeton University Press, 1971), 120–21.

49. Leonard Baker, *Back to Back: The Duel between FDR and the Supreme Court* (New York: Macmillan, 1967), 111.

50. Urofsky, *A March of Liberty*, 683.

51. Baker, *Back to Back*, 9–10.

52. Garvey, *Constitutional Bricolage*, 135.

Chapter Seven: Postwar America: The New Isolationism

1. Paul Kennedy, *The Rise and Fall of the Great Powers: Economic Change and Military Conflict from 1500 to 2000* (New York: Random House, 1989), 357–68.

2. Max Lerner, *It Is Later Than You Think: The Need for a Militant Democracy* (New York: Viking, 1938), 93.

3. Max Lerner, *America as a Civilization: Life and Thought in the United States Today* (New York: Simon & Schuster, 1957), 448.

4. Ibid., 361.

5. Kennedy, *The Rise and Fall of the Great Powers*, 360.

6. C. P. Trussell, "Ex-Red Sees Peril in School Inquiries," *New York Times*, Feb. 27, 1953, p. 1.

7. Daniel Boorstin, *The Genius of American Politics* (Chicago: University of Chicago Press, 1953), 182.

8. Ibid., 186.

9. Ibid., 179.

10. Ibid., 6.

11. Ibid., 186.

12. Ibid., 179.

13. Burke, *Reflections on the Revolution in France*, 121.

14. Ibid., 121.

15. Delbert Clark, *Again the Goose Step: The Lost Fruits of Victory* (Indianapolis: Bobbs-Merrill, 1949), 36.

16. Dean Acheson, *Sketches From Life of Men I Have Known* (New York: Harbert & Brothers, 1959), 171–72.

17. Lewis J. Edinger, *Kurt Schumacher: A Study in Personality and Political Behavior* (Stanford: Stanford University Press, 1965), 39–40.

18. Jean Edward Smith, ed., *The Papers of General Lucius D. Clay*, vol. 2 (Bloomington: Indiana University Press, 1974), 1077.

19. Edinger, *Kurt Schumacher*, 147.

20. John Edward Smith, *Lucius D. Clay: An American Life* (New York: Henry Hale, 1990), 72.

21. Smith, *The Papers of General Lucius D. Clay*, vol. 2, 1067.

22. Ibid., vol. 2, 1118–19.

23. Ibid., vol. 2, 1120–28.

24. Although billed by the United States as a hero of the anti-Nazi resistance, Adenauer was among those prewar conservatives who toyed with the idea that the best way of "drawing the Nazis' teeth" was to bring Hitler into the government. In August 1932, less than six months before Hitler gained the chancellorship, he confided in a letter to a fellow politician that the pro-Catholic Center Party, which he headed, was ready for just such a course. In 1933, the

Center was among those conservative parties that actually voted Hitler emergency powers. Of course, once in office, the Nazis consolidated their dictatorship by kicking moderate conservatives like Adenauer out of power. Yet Adenauer was able to wrangle a pension from the authorities in Berlin and spend the next decade or so in not uncomfortable retirement. Terence Prittie, *Konrad Adenauer: 1876–1967* (London: Tom Stacey, 1972), 81–94.
25. Michael Kammen, *A Machine That Would Go of Itself: The Constitution in American Culture* (New York: Knopf, 1986), 18.
26. Martin Linton, "No Southern Comfort for Labour," *Guardian*, Nov. 9, 1993, p. 2.
27. Will Hutton, "Royal Reform Key to Real Recovery," *Guardian*, Dec. 14, 1992, p. 9.
28. Patrick Wintour, "Fury Over 'Slim Down Royals' Plan," *Guardian*, Dec. 5, 1994, p. 1.
29. "What Attlee Really Said," *New Republic*, June 8, 1953, p. 16.
30. Ibid.

Chapter Eight: The Disaster of Watergate

1. "Excerpts From Transcript of the Proceedings on Impeachment," *New York Times*, July 25, 1974, pp. 11–13.
2. "Transcript of the Frost-Nixon Interview," *New York Times*, May 20, 1977, p. A16.
3. Sherrill, *Why They Call It Politics*, 113.
4. "A despotism, though it were that of a Caligula or a Nero, might be to any degree less mischievous, less intolerable, than any such immutable law." Bentham, *Works*, vol. 2, 403.
5. "Excerpts from Transcript of House Judiciary Panel's Impeachment Proceedings," *New York Times*, July 25, 1974, p. 24.
6. Richard Harwood and Haynes Johnson, "A Solemn Change," *Washington Post*, Aug. 9, 1974, p. 1.
7. Alexander Cockburn, "Press Clips," *Village Voice*, Aug. 15, 1974, p. 8.
8. Robert A. Divine, *Since 1945: Politics and Diplomacy in Recent American History*, 2nd ed. (New York: John Wiley, 1975), 214; "The System Scorned," *New York Times*, Sept. 9, 1974, p. 35.
9. Hedrick Smith, *The Power Game: How Washington Works* (New York: Random House, 1988), 25.
10. Ibid., 24.
11. Ibid., 35.
12. Ibid., 29–31.
13. Ibid., 27.

14. Jimmy Carter, *Keeping Faith: Memoirs of a President* (New York: Bantam Books, 1982), 84.

15. Ibid., 80.

16. See Philip Bobbitt, *Constitutional Interpretation* (Oxford: Basic Blackwell, 1991), 67–69, for a fuller discussion of the enterprise's corporate structure. Bobbitt served as the Senate Democrats' legal counsel during the Iran-contra investigation.

17. "Iran-Contra Hearings: Day 2: The President's Knowledge and the Ayatollah's Money," *New York Times*, July 9, 1987, pp. A10–A11.

18. James M. Markham, "Washington's Course Worries Allies," *New York Times*, July 17, 1987, p. A8.

19. David E. Rosenbaum, "The Inquiry That Couldn't," *New York Times*, Jan. 19, 1994, p. A1.

20. Jackie Calmes, "Candidates of Change in 1992 Find Congress Reforms Them Instead," *Wall Street Journal*, May 6, 1994, p. A1.

21. Sam Howe Verhovek, "Deflate Government? Helium Didn't," *New York Times*, Sept. 21, 1993, p. A14.

22. Ibid.

23. Jackie Calmes, " 'F-Word' Threatens Clinton Capitol Hill Agenda, Though Wind Has Gone Out of Most Filibusters," *Wall Street Journal*, Aug. 16, 1994, p. A14.

24. John Brummett, *Highwire: From the Backwoods to the Beltway—The Education of Bill Clinton* (New York: Hyperion, 1994), 188.

25. David L. Boren, "Why I Am Leaving the Senate," *New York Times*, May 13, 1994, p. A31.

26. Ibid.

27. Godfrey Hodgson, *All Things to All Men: The False Promise of the Modern American Presidency* (New York: Simon & Schuster, 1980), 134–35.

28. Joseph A. Califano Jr., "Imperial Congress," *New York Times Magazine*, Jan. 23, 1994, p. 40.

29. Hodgson, *All Things to All Men*, 115–17.

30. Richard Reeves, "Carter's Secret," *New York*, Mar. 22, 1976, p. 30.

31. Richard Goldstein, "Sweet William: Sex and Sensibility: The Clinton Touch," *Village Voice*, Oct. 27, 1992, p. 33.

32. Adam Clymer, "Americans Have High Hopes for Clinton, Poll Finds," *New York Times*, Jan. 19, 1993, p. A13.

33. Louis Heren, *The New American Commonwealth* (New York: Harper & Row, 1968), 434.

34. Sherrill, *Why They Call It Politics*, 15.

35. Ibid., 9.

36. Lance Morrow, "Yankee Doodle Magic: What Makes Reagan So Remarkably Popular a President?" *Time*, July 7, 1986, p. 12.

37. Sherrill, *Why They Call It Politics*, 129.
38. Mary L. Dudziak, "Desegregation as a Cold War Imperative," *Stanford Law Review* 41 (1988): 111.
39. Urofsky, *A March of Liberty*, 951.
40. Gene I. Maeroff, "Boston's Decade of Desegregation Leaves Experts Disputing Effects," *New York Times*, Dec. 28, 1984, p. A1.
41. Bork, *The Tempting of America*, 134.
42. Ibid., 4.
43. Ibid., 153.
44. Ibid., 170.
45. Gwen Ifill, "President Chooses Breyer, an Appeals Judge in Boston, for Blackmun's Court Seat," *New York Times*, May 14, 1994, p. 1.
46. Akhil Reed Amar of Yale. Quoted in David Margolick, "Scholarly Consensus Builder: Stephen Gerald Breyer," *New York Times*, May 14, 1994, p. 1.
47. Linda Greenhouse, "Why Breyer's Hearing Was Meant to Be Dull," *New York Times*, July 17, 1994, sec. 4, p. 4.

Chapter Nine: The Civil Liberties Charade

1. "Execution Update," NAACP Legal Defense and Educational Fund, New York, Feb. 21, 1995.
2. "UN Member States and Their Positions on the Death Penalty for Crimes Committed by Persons Below 18 Years of Age," Amnesty International, London, Nov. 14, 1994.
3. Ronald Dworkin, *Law's Empire* (Cambridge: Belknap Press, 1986), 356, 449.
4. "The accumulation of all powers, legislative, executive, and judiciary, in the same hands, whether of one, a few, or many, and whether hereditary, self-appointed, or elective, may be justly pronounced the very definition of tyranny" (Federalist No. 47)—a definition that applies to today's House of Commons no less than it did to the Kremlin under the Soviets. Rossiter, *The Federalist Papers*, 301.
5. According to an FBI referendum, one of the questions agents hoped to put to Julius should he decide to confess before going to the chair was the following: "Was your wife cognizant of your activities?" After prosecuting Ethel as a full-fledged member of the conspiracy, the government was apparently unsure about the verdict even as it sent her to her death. Ronald Radosh and Joyce Milton, *The Rosenberg File: A Search for the Truth* (New York: Holt, Rinehart and Winston, 1983), 416–17.
6. Arthur M. Schlesinger Jr., *The Vital Center: The Politics of Freedom* (Cambridge: The Riverside Press, 1949), 196.
7. Robert K. Murray, *Red Scare: A Study in National Hysteria, 1919–1920* (Minneapolis: University of Minnesota Press, 1955), 17.

8. Stanley Coben, *A. Mitchell Palmer: Politician* (New York: Columbia University Press, 1963), 196.

9. Murray, *Red Scare*, 233–34; Arthur M. Schlesinger Jr., *The Age of Roosevelt: The Crisis of the Old Order 1919–1933* (Boston: Houghton Mifflin, 1957), 43.

10. Raymond B. Fosdick, *American Police Systems* (New York: The Century Co., 1920), 47–48.

11. Ibid., 51.

12. Orwell, *The Collected Essays*, vol. 2, 59.

13. Clark Warburton, "A History of Prohibition." In *The Politics of Moral Behavior: Prohibition and Drug Abuse*, ed. K. Austin Kerr (Reading, MA: Addison-Wesley, 1973), 46.

14. Ibid.

15. Larry Engelmann, *In Temperance: The Lost War Against Liquor* (New York: Free Press, 1979), 184.

16. James Walvin, *The Black Presence: A Documentary History of the Negro in England, 1555–1860* (London: Orbach & Chambers, 1971), 12.

17. Ibid., 15.

18. Peter Linebaugh, *The London Hanged: Crime and Civil Society in the Eighteenth Century* (Cambridge: Cambridge University Press, 1992), 355.

19. Walvin, *The Black Presence*, 24.

20. Hans Kohn, *American Nationalism: An Interpretive Essay* (New York: Collier Books, 1961), 120.

21. Ibid., 276.

22. Zangrando, *The NAACP Crusade Against Lynching*, 6.

23. Arthur I. Waskow, *From Race Riot to Sit-In, 1919 and the 1960s: A Study in the Connection Between Conflict and Violence* (Garden City, NY: Anchor Books, 1967), 12.

24. Fosdick, *American Police Systems*, 45.

25. Ibid., 122–24.

26. Joseph P. Lash, *Eleanor and Franklin: The Story of Their Relationship, Based on Eleanor Roosevelt's Private Papers* (New York: W. W. Norton, 1971), 516.

27. Zangrando, *The NAACP Crusade Against Lynching*, 148.

28. Ibid., 150.

29. Thomas Szasz, *Ceremonial Chemistry: The Ritual Persecution of Drugs, Addicts, Pushers* (Garden City, NY: Anchor Press/Doubleday, 1974), 22.

30. *Americans Behind Bars* (New York: The Edna McConnell Clark Foundation, 1992), 14.

31. The figure comes from the Drug Policy Foundation, a pro-decriminalization lobbying group in Washington, which bases its estimate on an analysis of federal, state, and local spending for police, prisons, and jails. The figure does not include ancillary costs such as robberies by users seeking money to buy drugs or murders and shootings arising from various disputes in the

underground drug market—all of which, legalization advocates maintain, are due not to the drugs themselves but to laws that criminalize drugs and drug users and foster a vast and extremely violent black market. Interview, Dave Fratello, DPF spokesman, Mar. 6, 1995.

32. Marc Mauer, *Americans Behind Bars: The International Use of Incarceration, 1992–1993* (Washington, DC: The Sentencing Project, 1994), 4.

33. *The English Philosophers From Bacon to Mill,* ed. Edwin A. Burtt (New York: Modern Library, 1939), 956.

34. Edward M. Brecher, *Licit and Illicit Drugs* (Boston: Little, Brown, 1972), 44.

35. Ibid., 51.

36. Ibid., 95.

37. W. Ivor Jennings, *The British Constitution* (Cambridge: Cambridge University Press, 1961), 78.

38. Edward Jay Epstein, *Agency of Fear: Opiates and Political Power in America* (New York: G. P. Putnam's Sons, 1977), 33.

39. Ibid., 33–34.

40. *Robinson v. California,* 370 U.S. 660. Quoted in Brecher, *Licit and Illicit Drugs,* 21.

41. Ibid., 22.

42. Richard Lawrence Miller, *The Case for Legalizing Drugs* (New York: Praeger, 1990), 101. Originally published in David J. Bellis, *Heroin and Politicians: The Failure of Public Policy to Control Addiction in America* (Westport, CT: Greenwood Press, 1981), 23.

43. Paul Eddy, Hugo Sabogal, and Sara Walden, *The Cocaine Wars* (New York: W. W. Norton, 1988), 98.

44. Brian J. Donnelly, D-Mass. Quoted in Elaine Shannon, *Desperados: Latin Drug Lords, U.S. Lawmen, and the War America Can't Win* (New York: Viking, 1988), 378.

45. Lewis H. Lapham, "A Political Opiate," *Harper's* (December 1989): 44.

46. "Transcript of First TV Debate Among Bush, Clinton, and Perot," *New York Times,* Oct. 12, 1992, p. A16.

47. "A Surgeon General's Untimely Candor," *New York Times,* Dec. 10, 1994, p. 22.

48. The U.S. population has approximately doubled since the 1920s. At 1.25 million, therefore, the volume of drug arrests in 1989 was about ten times greater per capita than the average sixty thousand alcohol-related arrests during Prohibition from 1920–33.

49. Edna McConnell Clark Foundation, *Americans Behind Bars,* 14.

50. Steven Wisotsky, "A Society of Suspects: The War on Drugs and Civil Liberties," Cato Institute Policy Analysis No. 180 (Washington: The Cato Institute, 1992), 12.

51. Ibid., 14–15.

52. Cynthia Cotts, "The Pot Plot," *Village Voice,* June 15, 1993, pp. 33–34.
53. Alan Travis, "Police and Lawyers Oppose Plan to Raise Soft Drug Fines," *Guardian,* Feb. 14, 1994, p. 7.
54. "Disarray on Drugs." Editorial originally published in *Le Monde,* reprinted in *Guardian Weekly,* May 8, 1994, p. 13.
55. Scheherazade Daneshkhu, "Traffickers Pay Price of Iran's Draconian Drug Crusade," *Financial Times,* Oct. 9, 1991, p. 4; "The Communist Connection," *New York Times,* Sept. 13, 1984, p. A17.
56. "Booklet on Drug Use and AIDS Assailed," *New York Times,* Aug. 23, 1985, p. A8.
57. Joyce Purnick, "Koch Bars Easing of Syringe Sales in AIDS Fight," *New York Times,* Oct. 5, 1985, p. B5.
58. Martin Tolchin, "2 Bush Aides at Odds on Giving Needles to Addicts," *New York Times,* Mar. 11, 1989, p. 7.
59. Catherine Woodard, "Needle-Cleaning Project Killed," *New York Newsday,* May 3, 1990, p. 2.
60. Francis Wilkinson, "A Separate Peace," *Rolling Stone* (May 5, 1994): 27.
61. "Recent Trends in Reported U.S. AIDS Cases" (Atlanta: Center for Disease Control and Prevention, Aug. 4, 1994): 1.
62. Allan Parry and Russell Newcombe, *Preventing the Spread of HIV Infection Among and From Injecting Drug Users in the UK: An Overview with Specific References to the Mersey Regional Strategy* (Liverpool: The Maryland Center, undated), 3–4.
63. Ibid., 9–10.
64. William E. Schmidt, "To Battle AIDS, Scots Offer Oral Drugs to Addicts," *New York Times,* Feb. 8, 1993, p. A3.

Chapter Ten: The Unraveling Social Fabric

1. James Bryce, *The American Commonwealth,* vol. 1, 654–55.
2. Ibid., 648.
3. Ibid., 646.
4. Jon C. Teaford, *City and Suburbs: The Political Fragmentation of Metropolitan America, 1850–1970* (Baltimore: Johns Hopkins University Press, 1979), 44.
5. Ibid., 59.
6. Ibid., 51.
7. Ibid., 66.
8. Ibid., 73.
9. Ibid., 5.
10. Ibid., 9.
11. Ibid., 16.
12. Ibid., 39.

13. Kenneth T. Jackson, *Crabgrass Frontier: The Suburbanization of the United States* (New York: Oxford University Press, 1985), 275.

14. Ibid.

15. Ibid., 277.

16. Lawrence H. Wendrich, "Greater Newark: A Quarter Century Vision," *National Municipal Review* XXIX, no. 10 (Oct. 1940): 657.

17. Jackson, *Crabgrass Frontier*, 209.

18. Robert Fishman, *Bourgeois Utopias: The Rise and Fall of Suburbia* (New York: Basic Books, 1987), 162.

19. Helen Leavitt, *Superhighway—Superhoax* (Garden City, NY: Doubleday, 1970), 53.

20. Robert C. Wood, with Vladimir V. Almendinger, *1400 Governments: The Political Economy of the New York Metropolitan Region* (Cambridge: Harvard University Press, 1961), 132–34.

21. Arthur B. Gunlicks, *Local Government in the German Federal System* (Durham, NC: Duke University Press, 1986), 57.

22. There were sixty-four murders in Hamburg in 1993 out of a population of 1.69 million, about 3.8 per 100,000. In the same year, New York, with 7.32 million, had 1,960 murders, a rate of 26.8 per 100,000. Source: Klaus Kamp, Statisches Landesamt, Freie und Hansestadt Hamburg.

23. Robert Kuttner, *Revolt of the Haves: Tax Rebellions and Hard Times* (New York: Simon & Schuster, 1980), 48–49.

24. Theodore J. Lowi, *The End of Liberalism: The Second Republic of the United States* (New York: W. W. Norton, 1979), 176.

25. Ibid., 176–77.

26. Douglas Martin, "Districts to Improve Business Proliferate," *New York Times*, Mar. 25, 1994, p. B3.

27. "One Street, Four Precincts, Three Council Districts . . . ," *New York Times*, Nov. 21, 1993, sec. 13, p. 6.

28. John Authers, "Up the Pole at the Town Hall," *Financial Times*, Oct. 20, 1993, p. 12.

29. Calleo, *The American Political System*, 19.

30. Scott McCartney, "Communities, Fearful of Importing Crime, Bar Routine Businesses," *Wall Street Journal*, Mar. 15, 1994, p. A1.

31. "A Guide to the Naked City: Eating, Shopping, & Looking for Love in All the Cheap Places," *Village Voice*, Nov. 17, 1992. Cover illustration by Ross MacDonald.

32. Glenn H. Miller Jr., "Are There Too Many Governments in the Tenth District?" *Economic Review*, Federal Reserve Bank of Kansas City (second quarter 1993): 73.

33. Walter Bagehot, *The English Constitution* (Ithaca: Cornell University Press, 1966), 72–73.

Chapter Eleven: The Terminal Crisis

1. Karel van Wolferen, *The Enigma of Japanese Power* (New York: Knopf, 1989), 43–44.
2. Ibid., 48.
3. Celestine Bohlen, "New Contender Rises From Italy's Center-Left," *New York Times*, Mar. 6, 1995, p. A3.
4. Jill Abrahamson and Daniel Pearl, "Congressman's Sojourn in Washington Teaches Bitter Political Lesson," *Wall Street Journal*, Dec. 15, 1993, p. A1.
5. "Government Garners Low Marks in Poll," *New York Times*, Aug. 21, 1994, p. 35.
6. Paul Krugman, *The Age of Diminished Expectations: U.S. Economic Policy in the 1990s* (Cambridge, MA: MIT Press, 1990), xi.
7. "Transcript of 3d TV Debate Between Bush, Clinton and Perot," *New York Times*, Oct. 20, 1992, pp. A20–A23.
8. George Grant and Susan Alder, *Perot: The Populist Appeal of Strong-Man Politics* (Wheaton, IL: Crossway Books, 1992), 123.
9. Ibid., 17.
10. Ibid., 3.
11. Ibid., 106.
12. Ross Perot, *United We Stand: How We Can Take Back Our Country* (New York: Hyperion, 1992), 23.
13. *Ross Perot Speaks Out: Issue by Issue, What He Says About Our Nation*, ed. James W. Robinson (Rocklin, CA: Prima Publishing, 1992), 15.
14. Grant and Alder, *Perot*, 109.
15. Official transcript of speech delivered at the Mayflower Hotel, Washington, D.C., on June 12, 1992, op. cit.
16. "Transcript of 3d TV Debate Between Bush, Clinton and Perot," *New York Times*, Oct. 20, 1992, pp. A20–A23.
17. Robinson, *Ross Perot Speaks Out*, 55. Perot made his remarks in an interview with the *Dallas Morning News* on March 22, 1992.
18. Michael Kelly, "The President's Past," *New York Times Magazine*, July 31, 1994, p. 25.
19. Charles F. Allen and Jonathan Portis, *The Comeback Kid: The Life and Career of Bill Clinton* (New York: Birch Lane Press, 1992), 26–27.
20. Hugo Young, *The Iron Lady: A Biography of Margaret Thatcher* (New York: Farrar Straus Giroux, 1989), 17–27.
21. David Osborne, *Laboratories of Democracy* (Boston: Harvard Business School Press, 1988), 87–88.
22. "A Letter by Clinton on His Draft Deferment: 'A War I Opposed and Despised,'" *New York Times*, Feb. 13, 1992, p. A25.

23. Garry Wills, "Clinton's Troubles," *New York Review of Books*, Sept. 22, 1994, p. 7.
24. Ibid.
25. Brummett, *Highwire*, 215.
26. Philip Martin. Introduction to *Bill Clinton As They Know Him: An Oral Biography*, by David Gallen (New York: Gallen Publishing Group, 1994), 11.
27. David E. Rosenbaum, "Looking Ahead: Clinton Could Claim a Mandate, But It Might Be Hard to Define," *New York Times*, Nov. 1, 1992, p. 30.
28. Brummett, *Highwire*, 102–105.
29. Michael Wines, "A 'Bazaar' Method of Dealing for Votes," *New York Times*, Nov. 11, 1993, p. A23.
30. David Rogers, "Budget Negotiators Confront Variety of Choices In Last-Minute Scramble for Coveted Provisions," *Wall Street Journal*, July 30, 1993, p. A10.
31. David Rogers and John Harwood, "No Reasonable Offers Refused as Administration Bargains to Nail Down Deficit Package in House," *Wall Street Journal*, Aug. 6, 1993, p. A12.
32. Elizabeth Drew, *On the Edge: The Clinton Presidency* (New York: Simon & Schuster, 1994), 192.
33. John Harwood, "How Clinton's Plan for Health Reform Lost 2 Moderate Voices," *Wall Street Journal*, Aug. 23, 1994, p. A1.
34. Peter Overby, "White-Picket Welfare," *Common Cause Magazine* (Fall 1993): 22.
35. Robert Pear, "G.O.P. Leaders in House Agree on Alternative to Food Stamps," *New York Times*, Mar. 2, 1995, p. A1; Timothy Egan, "A G.O.P. Attack Hits Bit Too Close to Home," *New York Times*, Mar. 3, 1995, p. A14.
36. Katharine Q. Seelye, " 'We Are Freshmen, Hear Us Roar' Falls Silent at Senate," *New York Times*, Mar. 3, 1995, p. A18.
37. Maureen Dowd, "G.O.P.'s Rising Star Pledges to Right Wrongs of the Left," *New York Times*, Nov. 10, 1994, p. A1.
38. Garry Wills, "The Visionary," *New York Review of Books*, Mar. 23, 1995, p. 6.
39. Dan Balz, "GOP 'Contract' Pledges 10 Tough Acts to Follow," *Washington Post*, Nov. 20, 1994, p. A1.

Chapter Twelve: The End Is Nigh (We Hope)

1. The U.S. Census Bureau projects the black, Asian, and American Indian population to reach twenty-nine percent in California by the year 2020, a nine-point increase over the level of 1993. The proportion of Hispanics is projected to reach thirty-six percent over the same period. Paul R. Campbell, *Population Projections for States, by Age, Race, and Sex: 1993–2000*, U.S. Bureau of the

Census, Current Population Reports, P25-1111 (Washington, DC: U.S. Government Printing Office, 1994), 17–23.

2. Ibid.

3. Ibid.

4. "I, Mudd," written by Stephen Kandel and David Gerrold, episode no. 41 of the original series.

5. Gödel, who had fled to the United States after the rise of Hitler and took a post at the Institute for Advanced Studies in Princeton, drove to Trenton with his friend Albert Einstein to apply for citizenship in 1948. The judge began by congratulating Gödel on escaping Nazism, adding, "but, fortunately, that [i.e., Nazism] is not possible in America." "On the contrary," Gödel replied, "I know how that can happen." He began to explain how Article V could be used to repeal democratic rights and install a Nazi state until a nervous Einstein succeeded in shutting him up so the hearing could continue. Hao Wang, *Reflections on Kurt Gödel* (Cambridge, MA: MIT Press, 1987), 115–16.

6. "Article V . . . should not be understood as binding the People themselves, who are the masters, not the servants—who are indeed the source—of Article V and the rest of the Constitution. Thus, although the Constitution empowers and limits government, it neither limits nor empowers the People themselves. Rather, the Constitution is predicated on their pre-existing power." Akhil Reed Amar, "Philadelphia Revisited: Amending the Constitution Outside Article V," *University of Chicago Law Review*, vol. 55, no. 4 (fall 1988): 1055.

7. These numbers are based on 1993 data. Campbell, *Population Projections for States*, 1, 17.

8. Sidney Blumenthal, "Bob Dole's First Strike," *New Yorker*, May 3, 1993, p. 40.

9. Hugh Sidey, "The Presidency: 'We're Still Jefferson's Children,' " *Time*, July 13, 1987, p. 14.

10. Richard E. Neustadt, *Presidential Power and the Modern Presidents: The Politics of Leadership from Roosevelt to Reagan* (New York: Free Press, 1990), 11.

11. Kammen, *A Machine That Would Go of Itself*, 18.

12. Robert M. Solow, "Advise and Dissent," *New Republic*, Aug. 1, 1994, p. 41.

13. Forrest McDonald, *E Pluribus Unum: The Formation of the American Republic* (Indianapolis: Liberty Press, 1979), 319.

14. For discussions of the historical background of the right to bear arms, see Sanford Levinson, "The Embarrassing Second Amendment," *Yale Law Journal 99* (December 1989), pp. 637–59, and Robert E. Shalhope, "The Ideological Origins of the Second Amendment," *The Journal of American History 69* (December 1982), pp. 599–614.

15. "The New Revolutionaries," *The New York Review of Books*, Aug. 10, 1995,

p. 52. For additional information about this resurgent constitutional funda-
mentalism, see Paul Glastris, "Patriot Games," *The Washington Monthly*, July
1995, pp. 23–26, and James A. Aho, *The Politics of Righteousness: Idaho Christian
Patriotism* (Seattle: University of Washington Press, 1990), 114–32.

16. Christopher Hill, *The English Bible and the Seventeenth-Century Revolution*
    (London: Penguin Books, 1994), 21.
17. Ibid., 41.
18. Ibid., 424–29.
19. "What Congress Has Done," *The Wall Street Journal*, Aug. 11, 1995, p. A6.
20. Newt Gingrich, *To Renew America* (New York: HarperCollins, 1995), 192.
21. Ibid., 190.
22. Ibid., 181.
23. Ibid., 57.
24. R. W. Apple Jr., "Poll Shows Disenchantment with Politicians and Politics,"
    The New York Times, Aug. 12, 1995, p. 1.

Bibliography

Reports and Journal Articles

Amar, Akhil Reed. "Philadelphia Revisited: Amending the Constitution Outside Article V," *University of Chicago Law Review* 55 (fall 1988).

Amnesty International. *When the State Kills . . . : The Death Penalty: A Human Rights Issue* (New York: Amnesty International USA, 1989).

———. "UN Member States and Their Positions on the Death Penalty for Crimes Committed by Persons Below 18 Years of Age," London, Nov. 14, 1994.

Bailyn, Bernard. "1776: A Year of Challenge—A World Transformed," *Journal of Law & Economics* 19 (October 1976).

Bestor, Arthur. "The American Civil War as Constitutional Crisis," *American Historical Review* LXIX (January 1964).

Burt, Robert A. "What Was Wrong with *Dred Scott*, What's Right About *Brown*," *Washington and Lee Law Review* 42 (winter 1985).

Campbell, Paul R. *Population Projections for States, by Age, Race, and Sex: 1993–*

2000, U.S. Bureau of the Census, Current Population Reports, P25-1111, U.S. Government Printing Office, 1994.

Centers for Disease Control and Prevention. "Recent Trends in Reported U.S. AIDS Cases," Atlanta, Aug. 4, 1994.

Dudziak, Mary L. "Desegregation as a Cold War Imperative, *Stanford Law Review* 41 (1988).

Edna McConnell Clark Foundation. *Americans Behind Bars*, New York, 1992.

Final Report of the Joint Committee on the Organization of the Congress. U.S. Government Printing Office, 1993.

Fiorina, Morris P. "The Decline of Collective Responsibility in American Politics," *Daedalus* 109 (summer 1980).

Godkin, E. L. "The Constitution, and Its Defects," *North American Review* (July 1864).

Hart, H. L. A. "Bentham and the United States of America," *Journal of Law and Economics* 19 (1976).

Hazlitt, Henry. "Our Obsolete Constitution," *Nation*, Feb. 4, 1931.

Hume, L. J. "Jeremy Bentham and the Nineteenth-Century Revolution in Government," *The Historical Journal* 10 (1967).

Levinson, Sanford. "The Embarrassing Second Amendment," *Yale Law Journal* 99 (December 1989).

Luhmann, Niklas. "Operational Closure and Structural Coupling: The Differentiation of the Legal System," *Cardozo Law Review* 13 (March 1992).

Koch, Edward I. "The Mandate Millstone," *The Public Interest* 61 (fall 1980).

Martig, Ralph R. "Amending the Constitution: Article Five: The Keystone of the Arch," *Michigan Law Review* 35 (1937).

Mauer, Marc. *Americans Behind Bars: The International Use of Incarceration, 1992– 1993*, The Sentencing Project, Washington, DC, 1994.

McCraw, Thomas K. "The Strategic Vision of Alexander Hamilton," *The American Scholar* (winter 1994).

Miller, Glenn H. Jr. "Are There Too Many Governments in the Tenth District?" *Economic Review*, Federal Reserve Bank of Kansas City, Second Quarter 1993.

NAACP Legal Defense and Educational Fund. "Execution Update," New York, Feb. 21, 1995.

Parry, Allan, and Russell Newcombe. *Preventing the Spread of HIV Infection Among and From Injecting Drug Users in the UK: An Overview with Specific References to the Mersey Regional Strategy*. The Maryland Center, Liverpool, undated.

Pocock, J. G. A. "Virtue & Commerce in the Eighteenth Century," *Journal of Interdisciplinary History* no. 3 (1972).

Powell, H. Jefferson. "The Original Understanding of Original Intent," *Harvard Law Review* 98 (March 1985).

Reconnection for Learning: A Community School System for New York. Mayor's Advisory Panel on Decentralization of the New York City Schools, McGeorge Bundy, chairman, 1967.

Richards, David A. J. "Revolution and Constitutionalism in America," *Cardozo Law Review* 14 (January 1993).

Shalhope, Robert E. "The Ideological Origins of the Second Amendment," *The Journal of American History 69* (December 1982).

Thayer, James B. "The Origin and Scope of the American Doctrine of Constitutional Law," *Harvard Law Review* 7 (1893).

Wendrich, Lawrence H. "Greater Newark: A Quarter Century Vision," *National Municipal Review* XXIX (October 1940).

Williamson, Chilton. "Bentham Looks at America," *Political Science Quarterly* 70 (December 1955).

Wilson, Thomas W. "Cabinet Government in the United States," *International Review* 7 (August 1879).

Wisotsky, Steven. "A Society of Suspects: The War on Drugs and Civil Liberties," Cato Institute Policy Analysis No. 180, Washington, DC, 1992.

Books

Acheson, Dean. *Sketches from Life of Men I Have Known.* New York: Harbert & Brothers, 1959.

Ackerman, Bruce. *We the People.* Cambridge, MA: Harvard University Press, 1991.

Acton, Lord. *The History of Freedom and Other Essays.* London: MacMillan, 1922.

Aho, James A. *The Politics of Righteousness: Idaho Christian Patriotism.* Seattle: University of Washington Press, 1990.

Allen, Charles F. and Jonathan Portis. *The Comeback Kid: The Life and Career of Bill Clinton.* New York: Birch Lane Press, 1992.

Amery, L. S. *Thoughts on the Constitution.* Oxford University Press, 1964.

Anzovin, Steven, and Janet Podell, eds. *Speeches of the American Presidents.* New York: H. W. Wilson, 1988.

Appleby, Joyce. *Capitalism and a New Social Order: The Republican Vision of the 1790s.* New York: New York University Press, 1984.

———. *Liberalism and Republicanism in the Historical Imagination.* Cambridge: Harvard University Press, 1992.

Arendt, Hannah. *On Revolution.* New York: Viking, 1963.

Ayling, S. E. *The Georgian Century, 1714–1832.* London: George G. Harrap, 1966.

Aylmer, G. E. *The Struggle for the Constitution: 1603–1689.* London: Blandford, 1963.

Backer, John H. *Winds of History: The German Years of Lucius DuBignon Clay.* New York: Van Nostrand, 1983.

Bagehot, Walter. *The English Constitution.* Ithaca: Cornell University Press, 1966.

Bailyn, Bernard. *The Origin of American Politics.* New York: Knopf, 1968.

Baker, Leonard. *Back to Back: The Duel between FDR and the Supreme Court.* New York: Macmillan, 1967.

Baldwin, Leland D. *Reframing the Constitution: An Imperative for Modern America.* Santa Barbara, CA: American Bibliographical Center-Clio Press, 1972.

———. *The Stream of American History.* New York: American Book Co., 1953–57.

Barone, Michael, and Grant Ujifusa. *The Almanac of American Politics.* Washington, DC: National Journal, 1991.

Beard, Charles A. *American Government and Politics.* New York: Macmillan, 1930.

———. *An Economic Interpretation of the Constitution of the United States.* New York: Macmillan, 1935.

——— and Mary Beard. *The Rise of American Civilization.* New York: Macmillan, 1929.

Beeman, Richard, Stephen Botein, and Edward C. Carter III, eds. *Beyond Confederation: Origins of the Constitution and American National Identity.* Chapel Hill: University of North Carolina Press, 1987.

Beer, Samuel H., Adam B. Ulam, Suzanne Berger, and Guido Goldman. *Patterns of Government: The Major Systems of Europe,* 3rd ed. New York: Random House, 1973.

Belz, Herman. *Lincoln and the Constitution: The Dictatorship Question Reconsidered.* Fort Wayne, IN: Louis A. Warren Lincoln Library and Museum, 1984.

———, Ronald Hoffman, and Peter J. Albert, eds. *To Form a More Perfect Union.* Charlottesville: University Press of Virginia, 1992.

Benn, Tony and Andrew Hood. *Common Sense: A New Constitution for Britain.* London: Hutchinson, 1993.

Bentham, Jeremy. *A Fragment on Government.* (orig. pub. 1776.) Cambridge: Cambridge University Press, 1988.

———. *Works.* New York: Russell & Russell, 1962.

Berlin, Isaiah. *Four Essays on Liberty.* Oxford: Oxford University Press, 1969.

Bobbitt, Philip. *Constitutional Interpretation.* Oxford: Basic Blackwell, 1991.

Bolingbroke, Viscount Henry St. John. *Historical Writings.* Chicago: University of Chicago Press, 1972.

———. *The Works of Lord Bolingbroke.* Philadelphia: Cavey and Hart, 1841.

Bollens, John C. *Special District Governments in the United States.* Berkeley: University of California Press, 1957.

——— and Henry J. Schmundt. *The Metropolis: Its People, Politics, and Economic Life.* New York: Harper & Row, 1965.

Boorstin, Daniel J. *The Americans: The Colonial Experience.* New York: Random House, 1958.

———. *The Genius of American Politics.* Chicago: University of Chicago Press, 1953.

Bork, Robert H. *The Tempting of America: The Political Seduction of the Law.* New York: Free Press, 1990.

Bradford, Gamaliel. *The Lesson of Popular Government.* New York: Macmillan, 1899.

Brecher, Edward M. *Licit and Illicit Drugs.* Boston: Little, Brown, 1972.

Briggs, Asa. *The Age of Improvement 1783–1867.* New York: David McKay, 1962.

Brock, W. R. *An American Crisis: Congress & Reconstruction 1865–1867.* London: Macmillan, 1963.

Brodie, Fawn M. *Thaddeus Stevens: Scourge of the South.* New York: W. W. Norton, 1959.

Browne, Ray B. and Glenn J. Browne, eds. *Laws of Our Fathers: Popular Culture and the U.S. Constitution.* Bowling Green, OH: Bowling Green State University Press, 1986.

Brummett, John. *Highwire: From the Backwoods to the Beltway—The Education of Bill Clinton.* New York: Hyperion, 1994.

Bryce, James. *The American Commonwealth.* New York: Macmillan, 1914.

Burgess, Glenn. *The Politics of the Ancient Constitution: An Introduction to English Political Thought, 1603–1642.* University Park, PA: Pennsylvania State University Press, 1992.

Burke, Edmund. *Reflections on the Revolution in France.* (orig. pub. 1790.) London: Penguin, 1986.

Burnham, Walter Dean. *Critical Elections and the Mainsprings of American Politics.* New York: W. W. Norton, 1970.

Burns, James MacGregor. *The Deadlock of Democracy: Four-Party Politics in America.* Englewood Cliffs, NJ: Prentice-Hall, 1964.

Burtt, Edwin A., ed. *The English Philosophers From Bacon to Mill.* New York: Modern Library, 1939.

Calleo, David P. *The American Political System: A Background Book.* London: The Bodley Head, 1968.

Carswell, John. *From Revolution to Revolution: England 1688–1776.* London: Routledge & Kegan Paul, 1973.

Carter, Jimmy. *Keeping Faith: Memoirs of a President.* New York: Bantam Books, 1982.

Chrimes, S. B. *English Constitutional History.* Oxford: Oxford University Press, 1965.

Clark, Delbert. *Again the Goose Step: The Lost Fruits of Victory.* Indianapolis: Bobbs-Merrill, 1949.

Clinton, Bill and Al Gore. *Putting People First: How We Can Change America.* New York: Random House, 1992.

Coben, Stanley. *A. Mitchell Palmer: Politician.* New York: Columbia University Press, 1963.

Cole, G. D. H. *The Life of William Cobbett.* Westport, CT: Greenwood Press, 1971.

——— and Raymond Postgate. *The Common People 1746–1946.* London: Methuen, 1971.

Commager, Henry Steele. *The American Mind: An Interpretation of American Thought and Character since the 1880s.* New Haven: Yale University Press, 1950.

———. *The Defeat of America: Presidential Power and the National Character.* New York: Simon & Schuster, 1974.

———. *The Empire of Reason: How Europe Imagined and America Realized the Enlightenment.* Oxford: Oxford University Press, 1982.

———. *The Era of Reform 1830–1860.* New York: Van Nostrand, 1960.

———. *The Search for a Usable Past, and Other Essays in Historiography.* New York: Knopf, 1967.

———, ed. *America in Perspective: The United States Through Foreign Eyes.* New York: Random House, 1947.

———, ed. *Documents of American History.* New York: Meredith, 1968.

Corrigan, Philip and Derek Sayer. *The Great Arch: English State Formation as Cultural Revolution.* Oxford: Basil Blackwell, 1985.

Corwin, Edward S. *The 'Higher Law' Background of American Constitutional Law.* Ithaca: Cornell University Press, 1955.

Croly, Herbert. *The Promise of American Life.* Boston: Northeastern University Press, 1989.

Current, Richard N., ed. *The Political Thought of Abraham Lincoln.* Indianapolis: Bobbs-Merrill, 1967.

Curtis, George Ticknor. *Constitutional History of the United States from Their Declaration of Independence to the Close of Their Civil War.* New York: Da Capo Press, 1974.

Cwiklik, Robert. *House Rules: A Freshman Congressman's Introduction to the Backslapping, Backpedaling, and Backstabbing Ways of Washington.* New York: Villard Books, 1991.

Dewey, Donald O. *Union and Liberty: A Documentary History of American Constitutionalism.* New York: McGraw Hill, 1969.

Dickens, Charles. *American Notes: A Journey.* 1842. New York: Fromm International, 1985.

Diggins, John P. and Mark E. Kann, eds. *The Problem of Authority in America.* Philadelphia: Temple University Press, 1981.

Dinwiddy, John. *Bentham.* Oxford: Oxford University Press, 1989.

Divine, Robert A. *Since 1945: Politics and Diplomacy in Recent American History,* 2nd ed. New York: John Wiley, 1975.

Draper, Theodore. *A Very Thin Line: The Iran-Contra Affairs.* New York: Hill and Wang, 1991.

Drew, Elizabeth. *On the Edge: The Clinton Presidency.* New York: Simon & Schuster, 1994.

Dworkin, Ronald. *A Bill of Rights for Britain.* London: Chatto & Windus, 1990.

———. *Law's Empire.* Cambridge, MA: Belknap Press, 1986.

Eadie, John W., ed. *Classical Traditions in Early America.* Ann Arbor: Center for Coordination of Ancient and Modern Studies, 1976.

Eddy, Paul, Hugo Sabogal, and Sara Walden. *The Cocaine Wars.* New York: W. W. Norton, 1988.

Edinger, Lewis J. *Kurt Schumacher: A Study in Personality and Political Behavior.* Stanford: Stanford University Press, 1965.

Eisenstadt, S. N., ed. *Max Weber on Charisma and Institution Building: Selected Papers.* Chicago: University of Chicago Press, 1968.

Elliott, William Yandell. *The Need for Constitutional Reform.* New York: McGraw-Hill, 1935.

Ely, John Hart. *Democracy and Distrust: A Theory of Judicial Review.* Cambridge: Harvard University Press, 1980.

Engelmann, Larry. *In Temperance: The Lost War Against Liquor.* New York: Free Press, 1979.

Epstein, Edward Jay. *Agency of Fear: Opiates and Political Power in America.* New York: G. P. Putnam's Sons, 1977.

Everett, Charles Warren. *The Education of Jeremy Bentham.* New York: Columbia University Press, 1931.

Fehrenbacher, Don E. *The Dred Scott Case: Its Significance in American Law and Politics.* New York: Oxford University Press, 1978.

Fischer, David Hackett. *Albion's Seed: Four British Folkways in America.* Oxford: Oxford University Press, 1989.

Fisher, Sidney George. *The Trial of the Constitution.* New York: Negro University Press, 1969.

Fishman, Robert. *Bourgeois Utopias: The Rise and Fall of Suburbia.* New York: Basic Books, 1987.

Foner, Eric. *Politics and Ideology in the Age of the Civil War.* Oxford: Oxford University Press, 1980.

———. *A Short History of Reconstruction, 1863–1877.* New York: Harper & Row, 1990.

Ford, Henry Jones. *The Rise and Growth of American Politics: A Sketch of Constitutional Development.* New York: Macmillan, 1898.

Fosdick, Raymond B. *American Police Systems.* New York: The Century Co., 1920.

Foucault, Michel. *Discipline and Punish: The Birth of the Prison.* New York: Random House, 1979.

Fried, Albert. *Socialism in America: From the Shakers to the Third International.* Garden City, NY: Doubleday, 1970.

Gallen, David. *Bill Clinton As They Know Him: An Oral Biography*. New York: Gallen Publishing Group, 1994.

Garvey, Gerald. *Constitutional Bricolage*. Princeton: Princeton University Press, 1971.

Gingrich, Newt. *To Renew America*. New York: HarperCollins, 1995.

Goldwin, Robert A. and William A. Schambra, eds. *How Democratic is the Constitution?* Washington and London: American Enterprise Institute for Public Policy Research, 1980.

Goodnow, Frank J. *Social Reform and the Constitution*. New York: Macmillan, 1911.

Gorer, Geoffrey. *The American People: A Study in National Character*. New York: W. W. Norton, 1948.

Grant, George and Susan Alder. *Perot: The Populist Appeal of Strong-Man Politics*. Wheaton, IL: Crossway Books, and Franklin, TN: Adroit Press, 1992.

Green, James R. *Grass-Roots Socialism: Radical Movements in the Southwest 1895–1943*. Baton Rouge: Louisiana State University Press, 1978.

Greene, Jack P., ed. *The American Revolution: Its Character and Limits*. New York: New York University Press, 1987.

———, ed. *Great Britain and the American Colonies, 1606–1763*. Columbia: University of South Carolina Press, 1970.

Gross, Robert A. *The Minutemen and Their World*. New York: Hill and Wang, 1976.

Gunlicks, Arthur B. *Local Government in the German Federal System*. Durham, NC: Duke University Press, 1986.

Hacker, Louis M. *Alexander Hamilton in the American Tradition*. New York: McGraw-Hill, 1957.

———. *The Shaping of the American Tradition*. New York: Columbia University Press, 1947.

——— and Benjamin B. Kendricks. *The United States Since 1865*, 3rd ed. New York: F. S. Crofts, 1939.

Halevy, Elie. *A History of the English People in the Nineteenth Century*. London: Ernest Benn, 1965.

Hardin, Charles M. *Constitutional Reform in America: Essays on the Separation of Powers*. Ames, IA: Iowa State University Press, 1989.

Harrison, Ross. *Bentham*. London: Routledge & Kegan Paul, 1983.

———. *Essays on Bentham: Studies in Jurisprudence and Political Theory*. Oxford: Clarendon Press, 1982.

Hart, Jennifer. *Proportional Representation: Crisis of the British Electoral System 1820–1945*. Oxford: Clarendon Press, 1992.

Hartrich, Edwin. *The Fourth and Richest Reich*. New York: Macmillan, 1980.

Hasler, P. W. *The History of Parliament: Volume I: The House of Commons 1558–1603*. London: Her Majesty's Stationery Office, 1981.

Havighurst, Alfred F. *Britain in Transition: The Twentieth Century.* Chicago: University of Chicago Press, 1979.

Hazlitt, Henry. *A New Constitution Now.* New Rochelle, NY: Arlington House, 1974.

Hennessy, Peter. *Never Again: Britain 1945–1951.* New York: Pantheon, 1993.

Heren, Louis. *The New American Commonwealth.* New York: Harper & Row, 1968.

Hill, Christopher. *The Century of Revolution 1603–1714.* New York: W. W. Norton, 1966.

———. *God's Englishman: Oliver Cromwell & the English Revolution.* London: Weidenfeld and Nicolson, 1970.

———. *The English Bible and the Seventeenth-Century Revolution.* London: Penguin Books, 1994.

———. *Puritanism and Revolution: Studies in the Interpretation of the English Revolution of the 17th Century.* London: Penguin, 1986.

Hodgson, Godfrey. *All Things to All Men: The False Promise of the Modern American Presidency.* New York: Simon & Schuster, 1980.

Hofstadter, Douglas R. *Godel, Escher, Bach: An Eternal Golden Braid.* New York: Vintage, 1980.

Huntington, Samuel P. *American Politics: The Promise of Disharmony.* Cambridge: Belknap Press, 1981.

———. *Political Order in Changing Societies.* New Haven: Yale University Press, 1968.

———. *The Soldier and the State: The Theory and Politics of Civil-Military Relations.* Cambridge: Belknap Press, 1957.

Jackson, Brooks. *Honest Graft: Big Money and the American Political Process.* New York: Knopf, 1988.

Jackson, Kenneth T. *Crabgrass Frontier: The Suburbanization of the United States.* New York: Oxford University Press, 1985.

James, Joseph B. *The Ratification of the Fourteenth Amendment.* Macon, GA: Mercer University Press, 1984.

Jarrett, Derek. *Britain 1688–1815.* London: Longmans, 1965.

Jennings, W. Ivor. *The British Constitution.* Cambridge: Cambridge University Press, 1961.

Jonas, Manfred. *The United States and Germany: A Diplomatic History.* Ithaca: Cornell University Press, 1984.

Jones, J. R. *Country and Court: England, 1658–1714.* Cambridge: Harvard University Press, 1978.

Kammen, Michael. *A Machine That Would Go of Itself: The Constitution in American Culture.* New York: Alfred Knopf, 1986.

Kayser, Elmer Louis. *The Grand Social Enterprise: A Study of Jeremy Bentham in His Relation to Liberal Nationalism.* New York: Columbia University Press, 1932.

Keir, David Lindsay. *The Constitutional History of Modern Britain Since 1485.* Princeton: D. Van Nostrand, 1966.

Kennedy, John F. *Profiles in Courage.* New York: Harper & Brothers, 1955.

Kennedy, Paul. *The Rise and Fall of the Great Powers: Economic Change and Military Conflict from 1500 to 2000.* New York: Random House, 1989.

Kenyon, J. P. *Stuart England.* London: Penguin Books, 1978.

Kerr, K. Austin, ed. *The Politics of Moral Behavior: Prohibition and Drug Abuse.* Reading, MA: Addison-Wesley, 1973.

Keynes, John Maynard. *Works.* New York: St. Martin's Press, 1971–89.

Knapton, Ernest John. *France: An Interpretive History.* New York: Scribner's, 1971.

Koh, Harold Hongju. *The National Security Constitution: Sharing Power After the Iran-Contra Affair.* New Haven: Yale University Press, 1990.

Kohn, Hans. *American Nationalism: An Interpretive Essay.* New York: Collier Books, 1961.

Kramnick, Isaac. *Bolingbroke and His Circle: The Politics of Nostalgia in the Age of Walpole.* Cambridge: Harvard University Press, 1968.

————. *Republicanism and Bourgeois Radicalism: Political Ideology in Late Eighteenth-Century England and America.* Ithaca, NY: Cornell University Press, 1990.

———— and Michael Foot, eds. *Thomas Paine Reader.* Harmondsworth, UK: Penguin, 1987.

Krugman, Paul. *The Age of Diminished Expectations: U.S. Economic Policy in the 1990s.* Cambridge: MIT Press, 1990.

Kuttner, Robert. *Revolt of the Haves: Tax Rebellions and Hard Times.* New York: Simon & Schuster, 1980.

Kyvig, David E. *Repealing National Prohibition.* Chicago: University of Chicago Press, 1979.

Lacey, Michael J. and Knud Haakonssen, eds. *A Culture of Rights: The Bill of Rights in Philosophy, Politics, and Law—1791 and 1991.* Cambridge: Cambridge University Press, 1991.

Lash, Joseph P. *Eleanor and Franklin: The Story of Their Relationship, Based on Eleanor Roosevelt's Private Papers.* New York: W. W. Norton, 1971.

Leavitt, Helen. *Superhighway—Superhoax.* Garden City, NY: Doubleday, 1970.

Lerner, Max. *America as a Civilization: Life and Thought in the United States Today.* New York: Simon & Schuster, 1957.

————. *Ideas Are Weapons: The History & Uses of Ideas.* New York: Viking, 1939.

————. *Ideas for the Ice Age: Studies in a Revolutionary Era.* New York: Viking, 1941.

————. *It Is Later Than You Think: The Need for a Militant Democracy.* New York: Viking, 1938.

Levinson, Sanford. *Constitutional Faith.* Princeton: Princeton University Press, 1988.

Linebaugh, Peter. *The London Hanged: Crime and Civil Society in the Eighteenth Century*. Cambridge: Cambridge University Press, 1992.

Lobel, Jules, ed. *A Less Than Perfect Union: Alternative Perspectives on the U.S. Constitution*. New York: Monthly Review Press, 1988.

Lowi, Theodore J. *The End of Liberalism: The Second Republic of the United States*. New York: W. W. Norton, 1979.

————. *The Personal President: Power Invested, Promise Unfulfilled*. Ithaca: Cornell University Press, 1985.

Lynd, Staughton. *Intellectual Origins of American Radicalism*. New York: Pantheon, 1968.

MacDonald, William. *A New Constitution for a New America*. New York: B. W. Huebsch, 1921.

Madison, James. *Notes of Debates in the Federal Convention of 1787 Reported by James Madison*. New York: W. W. Norton, 1966.

Manley, John F. and Kenneth M. Dolbeare, eds. *The Case Against the Constitution: From the Antifederalists to the Present*. Armonk, NY: M. F. Sharpe, 1987.

Mansfield, Harvey C. Jr. *America's Constitutional Soul*. Baltimore: The Johns Hopkins University Press, 1991.

Marshall, Peter and Glyn Williams, eds. *The British Atlantic Empire Before the American Revolution*. London: Frank Cass, 1980.

Martin, William. *Switzerland: From Roman Times to the Present*. London: Elek Books, 1971.

Marx, Karl. *Capital*. 1867. New York: International, 1967.

Mathieson, William L. *British Slave Emancipation 1838–1849*. New York: Octagon Books, 1967.

Matthews, Richard K. *The Radical Politics of Thomas Jefferson: A Revisionist View*. Lawrence, KS: University Press of Kansas, 1984.

McCoy, Drew R. *The Elusive Republic: Political Economy in Jeffersonian America*. New York: W. W. Norton, 1980.

McDonald, Forrest. *E Pluribus Unum: The Formation of the American Republic*. Indianapolis: Liberty Press, 1979.

McIlwain, Charles Howard. *The American Revolution: A Constitutional Interpretation*. Ithaca: Cornell University Press, 1958.

————. *Constitutionalism Ancient & Modern*. Ithaca: Cornell University Press, 1940.

McPherson, James M. *Battle Cry of Freedom: The Civil War Era*. Oxford University Press, 1988.

Mill, John Stuart. *Mill on Bentham and Coleridge*. F. R. Leavis, editor. Cambridge: Cambridge University Press, 1980.

Miller, Arthur Selwyn. *Democratic Dictatorship: The Emergent Constitution of Control*. Westport, CT: Greenwood Press, 1981.

Miller, John C. *The Federalist Era 1789–1801*. New York: Harper & Row, 1960.

Miller, Richard Lawrence. *The Case for Legalizing Drugs.* New York: Praeger, 1990.

Miller, William Lee. *The Business of May Next: James Madison and the Founding.* Charlottesville: University Press of Virginia, 1992.

Milton, John. "Areopagitica." In *Complete Poems and Major Prose,* Merritt Y. Hughes, ed. 1644. Indianapolis: Bobbs-Merrill, 1957.

Morgan, Edmund S. *Inventing the People: The Rise of Popular Sovereignty in England and America.* New York: W. W. Norton, 1988.

Morgan, Kenneth O., ed. *The Oxford History of Britain.* New York: Oxford University Press, 1988.

Morison, Samuel Eliot. *The Oxford History of the American People.* New York: New American Library, 1972.

Murphy, Paul L. *The Constitution in Crisis Times, 1918–1969.* New York: Harper & Row, 1972.

Murray, Robert K. *Red Scare: A Study in National Hysteria, 1919–1920.* Minneapolis: University of Minnesota Press, 1955.

Nairn, Tom. *The Enchanted Glass: Britain and its Monarchy.* London: Hutchinson Radius, 1988.

Narrett, David E. and Joyce S. Goldberg, eds. *Essays on Liberty and Federalism: The Shaping of the U.S. Constitution.* Arlington: Texas A&M University Press, 1988.

Neale, J. E. *Elizabeth I and Her Parliaments: 1559–1581.* London: Jonathan Cape, 1953.

Neely, Mark E. Jr. *The Fate of Liberty: Abraham Lincoln and Civil Liberties.* New York: Oxford University Press, 1991.

Neustadt, Richard E. *Presidential Power and the Modern Presidents: The Politics of Leadership from Roosevelt to Reagan.* New York: Free Press, 1990.

Nore, Ellen. *Charles A. Beard: An Intellectual Biography.* Carbondale: Southern Illinois State University Press, 1983.

Ollman, Bertell and Jonathan Birnbaum. *The United States Constitution: 200 Years of Anti-Federalist, Abolitionist, Feminist, Muckraking, Progressive, and Especially Socialist Criticism.* New York: New York University Press, 1990.

Olson, Mancur. *The Rise and Decline of Nations: Economic Growth, Stagflation, and Social Rigidities.* New Haven: Yale University Press, 1982.

Orfield, Lester B. *The Amending of the Federal Constitution.* New York: Da Capo Press, 1971.

Orwell, George. *The Collected Essays, Journalism, and Letters of George Orwell.* Sonia Orwell and Ian Angus, editors. New York: Harcourt, Brace & World, 1968.

Osborne, David. *Laboratories of Democracy.* Boston: Harvard Business School Press, 1988.

Owen, John B. *The Eighteenth Century 1714–1815.* New York: W. W. Norton, 1974.

Paine, Thomas. *Common Sense*, ed. Isaac Kramnick. London: Penguin, 1986.

————. *The Thomas Paine Reader*. Hammondsworth, Middlesex: Penguin, 1987.

Palmer, R. R. *The Age of the Democratic Revolution: A Political History of Europe and America, 1760–1800*. Princeton: Princeton University Press, 1959–64.

Paludan, Phillip S. *A Covenant with Death: The Constitution, Law, and Equality in the Civil War Era*. Urbana, IL: University of Illinois Press, 1975.

————. *'A People's Contest': The Union and Civil War 1861–1865*. New York: Harper & Row, 1988.

Parekh, Bhikhu, ed. *Jeremy Bentham: Ten Critical Essays*. London: Frank Cass, 1974.

Patterson, Stephen E. *Political Parties in Revolutionary Massachusetts*. Madison: University of Wisconsin Press, 1973.

Perot, H. Ross. *United We Stand: How We Can Take Back Our Country*. New York: Hyperion, 1992.

Perry, Barbara A. and Paul J. Weber. *Unfounded Fears: Myths and Realities of a Constitutional Convention*. New York: Greenwood Press, 1989.

Peterson, Merrill D., ed. *Thomas Jefferson: Writings*. New York: Library of America, 1984.

Phillips, David Graham. *The Treason of the Senate*. Chicago: Quadrangle Books, 1964.

Pocock, J. G. A. *The Ancient Constitution and the Feudal Law: A Study of English Historical Thought in the Seventeenth Century*. Cambridge: Cambridge University Press, 1957.

————. *The Machiavellian Moment: Florentine Political Thought and the Atlantic Republican Tradition*. Princeton: Princeton University Press, 1975.

————. *Virtue, Commerce, and History: Essays on Political Thought and History, Chiefly in the Eighteenth Century*. Cambridge: Cambridge University Press, 1985.

————, ed. *Three British Revolutions: 1641, 1688, 1776*. Princeton: Princeton University Press, 1980.

Polakoff, Keith Ian. *The Politics of Inertia: The Election of 1876 and the End of Reconstruction*. Baton Rouge: Louisiana State University Press, 1973.

Preston, William Jr. *Aliens and Dissenters: Federal Suppression of Radicals 1903–1933*. Cambridge: Harvard University Press, 1963.

Price, Don K. *America's Unwritten Constitution: Science, Religion, and Political Responsibility*. Baton Rouge: Louisiana State University Press, 1983.

Prittie, Terence. *Konrad Adenauer: 1876–1967*. London: Tom Stacey, 1972.

Radosh, Ronald and Joyce Milton. *The Rosenberg File: A Search for the Truth*. New York: Holt, Rinehart and Winston, 1983.

Ravitch, Diane. *The Great School Wars: A History of the New York Public Schools*. New York: Basic Books, 1988.

Reid, John Phillip. *The Concept of Liberty in the Age of the American Revolution.* Chicago: University of Chicago Press, 1988.

Rivlin, Alice M. *Reviving the American Dream: The Economy, the States, and the Federal Government.* Washington, DC: The Brookings Institution, 1992.

Robinson, James W., ed. *Ross Perot Speaks Out: Issue by Issue, What He Says About Our Nation.* Rocklin, CA: Prima Publishing, 1992.

Roe, Gilbert E. *Our Judicial Oligarchy.* New York: B. W. Huebsch, 1912.

Roelofs, H. Mark. *The Poverty of American Politics: A Theoretical Interpretation.* Philadelphia: Temple University Press, 1992.

Rose, Anne C. *Transcendentalism as a Social Movement, 1830–1850.* New Haven: Yale University Press, 1981.

Rossiter, Clinton. *Alexander Hamilton and the Constitution.* New York: Harcourt, Brace & World, 1964.

———, ed. *The Federalist Papers.* New York: Mentor, 1961.

Rowse, A. L. *The England of Elizabeth: The Structure of Society.* London: Macmillan, 1951.

Russell, Bertrand. *A History of Western Philosophy.* New York: Simon & Schuster, 1959.

Ryder, A. J. *Twentieth-Century Germany: From Bismarck to Brandt.* New York: Columbia University Press, 1973.

St. John-Stevas, Norman, ed. *The Collected Works of Walter Bagehot.* Cambridge: Harvard University Press, 1968.

Sandoz, Ellis, ed. *The Roots of Liberty: Magna Carta, Ancient Constitution, and the Anglo-American Tradition of Rule of Law.* Columbia, MO: University of Missouri Press, 1993.

Schlesinger, Arthur M. Jr. *The Age of Roosevelt: The Crisis of the Old Order 1919–1933.* Boston: Houghton Mifflin, 1957.

———. *The Vital Center: The Politics of Freedom.* Cambridge: The Riverside Press, 1949.

Schwartz, Bernard. *From Confederation to Nation: The American Constitution, 1835–1877.* Baltimore: Johns Hopkins University Press, 1973.

Sellers, Charles. *The Market Revolution: Jacksonian America 1815–1846.* New York: Oxford University Press, 1991.

Shannon, Elaine. *Desperados: Latin Drug Lords, U.S. Lawmen, and the War America Can't Win.* New York: Viking, 1988.

Sherrill, Robert. *Why They Call It Politics: A Guide to American Government.* New York: Harcourt Brace Jovanovich, 1972.

Simmons, R. C. *The American Colonies: From Settlement to Independence.* New York: David McKay, 1976.

———, ed. *The United States Constitution: The First 200 Years.* Manchester, UK: Manchester University Press, 1989.

Sinclair, Andrew. *Prohibition: The Era of Excess.* Boston: Little, Brown, 1962.

Smith, Hedrick. *The Power Game: How Washington Works.* New York: Random House, 1988.

Smith, John Edward. *Lucius D. Clay: An American Life.* New York: Henry Hale, 1990.

————, ed. *The Papers of General Lucius D. Clay.* Bloomington: Indiana University Press, 1974.

Spinrad, William. *Civil Liberties.* Chicago: Quadrangle Press, 1970.

Stampp, Kenneth. *The Imperiled Union: Essays on the Background of the Civil War.* New York: Oxford University Press, 1980.

Steintrager, James. *Bentham.* London: George Allen & Unwin, 1977.

Stephen, Leslie. *The English Utilitarians.* New York: Peter Smith, 1950.

Stone, Lawrence. *The Causes of the English Revolution, 1529–1642.* New York: Harper & Row, 1972.

Suber, Peter. *The Paradox of Self-Amendment: A Study of Logic, Law, Omnipotence, and Change.* New York: Peter Lang, 1990.

Szasz, Thomas. *Ceremonial Chemistry: The Ritual Persecution of Drugs, Addicts, Pushers.* Garden City, NY: Anchor Press/Doubleday, 1974.

Teaford, Jon C. *City and Suburbs: The Political Fragmentation of Metropolitan America, 1850–1970.* Baltimore: Johns Hopkins University Press, 1979.

Thompson, E. P. *The Making of the English Working Class.* New York: Random House, 1966.

Thompson, F. M. L., ed. *The Cambridge Society History of Britain 1750–1950: Vol. 3: Social Agencies and Institutions.* Cambridge: Cambridge University Press, 1990.

Tiefer, Charles. *The Semi-Sovereign President: The Bush Administration's Strategy for Governing Without Congress.* Boulder, CO: Westview, 1994.

Tocqueville, Alexis de. *Democracy in America.* 1835. New York: Random House, 1990.

Tovelle, Ellen, ed. *The Political Philosophy of Robert M. La Follette as Revealed in His Speeches and Writings.* Madison, WI: The Robert M. La Follette Co., 1920.

Trefousse, Hans L. *Impeachment of a President: Andrew Jackson, the Blacks, and Reconstruction.* Knoxville: University of Tennessee Press, 1975.

————. *The Radical Republicans: Lincoln's Vanguard for Racial Justice.* New York: Knopf, 1969.

Trevelyan, George Otto. *The Early History of Charles James Fox.* New York: AMS Press, 1971.

Tribe, Laurence. *American Constitutional Law*, 2nd ed. Mineola, NY: Foundation Press, 1988.

Trollope, Frances. *Domestic Manners of the Americans.* (orig. pub. 1832.) Donald Smallen, editor. New York: Vintage, 1960.

Truman, David B., ed. *The Congress and America's Future.* Englewood Cliffs, NJ: Prentice Hall, 1973.

Tucker, Robert W. and David C. Hendrickson. *Empire of Liberty: The Statecraft of Thomas Jefferson.* Cambridge: Oxford University Press, 1990.

Urofsky, Melvin I. *A March of Liberty: A Constitutional History of the United States.* New York: Alfred A. Knopf, 1988.

Utley, Robert L. Jr., ed. *Principles of the Constitutional Order: The Ratification Debate.* Lanham, MD: University Press of America, 1989.

Van Deburg, William L. *Slavery & Race in American Popular Culture.* Madison, WI: University of Wisconsin Press, 1984.

Vile, John R. *The Constitutional Amending Process in American Political Thought.* New York: Praeger, 1992.

————. *Rewriting the Constitution: An Examination of Proposals from Reconstruction to the Present.* New York: Praeger, 1991.

Walker, Samuel. *In Defense of American Liberties: A History of the ACLU.* New York and Oxford: Oxford University Press, 1990.

Walvin, James. *Black Ivory: A History of British Slavery.* London: HarperCollins, 1992.

————. *The Black Presence: A Documentary History of the Negro in England, 1555–1860.* London: Orbach & Chambers, 1971.

Wang, Hao. *Reflections on Kurt Gödel.* Cambridge, MA: MIT Press, 1987.

Waskow, Arthur I. *From Race Riot to Sit-In, 1919 and the 1960s: A Study in the Connection Between Conflict and Violence.* Garden City, NY: Anchor Books, 1967.

West, Corinne Comstock and Janelle Renfrow Greenberg. *Subjects and Sovereigns: The Grand Controversy over Legal Sovereignty in Stuart England.* Cambridge: Cambridge University Press, 1981.

White, Leonard D. *The Jacksonians: A Study in Administrative History, 1829–61.* New York: Macmillan, 1954.

Wiebe, Robert H. *The Segmented Society: An Introduction to the Meaning of America.* New York: Oxford University Press, 1975.

Wiecek, William M. *Constitutional Development in a Modernizing Society: The United States, 1803 to 1917.* Washington, DC: American Historical Association, 1985.

Williams, Penry. *The Tudor Regime.* Oxford: Clarendon Press, 1979.

Williams, T. Harry. *Lincoln and the Radicals.* Madison: University of Wisconsin Press, 1941.

Wills, Garry. *Explaining America: The Federalist.* Garden City, NY: Doubleday, 1981.

Wilson, Woodrow. *Congressional Government: A Study in American Politics.* Boston: Houghton Mifflin, 1925.

————. *Constitutional Government in the United States.* New York: Columbia University Press, 1921.

Wolferen, Karel van. *The Enigma of Japanese Power.* New York: Knopf, 1989.

Wood, Robert C. *Suburbia: Its People and Their Politics.* Boston: Houghton Mifflin, 1959.

———— and Vladimir V. Almendinger. *1400 Governments: The Political Economy of the New York Metropolitan Region.* Cambridge, MA: Harvard University Press, 1961.

Woodward, C. Vann. *Reunion and Reaction: The Compromise of 1877 and the End of Reconstruction.* Boston: Little, Brown, 1951.

Yankelovich, Daniel. *Coming to Public Judgment: Making Democracy Work in a Complex World.* Syracuse: Syracuse University Press, 1991.

Young, Hugo. *The Iron Lady: A Biography of Margaret Thatcher.* New York: Farrar Straus Giroux, 1989.

Zagorin, Perez. *The Court and the Country: The Beginning of the English Revolution.* New York: Atheneum, 1970.

Zangrando, Robert L. *The NAACP Crusade Against Lynching, 1909–1950.* Philadelphia: Temple University Press, 1980.

Zinn, Howard. *A People's History of the United States.* New York: HarperCollins, 1990.

Index